I0815244

SHETLAND FINE LACE KNITTING

Recreating patterns from the past

Carol Christiansen

SHETLAND FINE LACE KNITTING

Recreating patterns from the past

THE CROWOOD PRESS

First published in 2024 by
The Crowood Press Ltd
Ramsbury, Marlborough
Wiltshire SN8 2HR

enquiries@crowood.com
www.crowood.com

© Shetland Amenity Trust 2024

All rights reserved. No part of this publication may be reproduced or transmitted in any form or by any means, electronic or mechanical, including photocopy, recording, or any information storage and retrieval system, without permission in writing from the publishers.

British Library Cataloguing-in-Publication Data
A catalogue record for this book is available from the British Library.

ISBN 978 0 7198 4287 0

Cover design by Sergey Tsvetkov
Front cover image: An exquisitely made large Shetland shawl, border detail. Maker(s) unknown. TEX 8930.

Back cover image: St Edward's Crown knitted sample.

All images Shetland Museum and Archives (www.shetlandmuseumandarchives.org.uk), except: frontispiece, pages 47,136 (Alex Boak); pages 9, 10, 45 (Alexa Fitzgibbon); pages 16, 21, 46, 107, 121, 146, 177 (Didier Piquer); page 28 (Doris Pecka, Pixabay); page 33 (Brian Johnston); page 66 (right) (Carol Christiansen); pages 97, 179 (Susan Williams); page 153 (Alexander Bassano, Public domain, via Wikimedia Commons); page 154 (Firebrace/Wikimedia Commons); pages 196 (right), 197 (left) (with permission of Kate Andrews); page 198 (bottom) (Lowes Cato Dickinson, reproduced by Mary Louisa Bruce, Public domain, via Wikimedia Commons); pages 200 (right), 201 (with permission of Patricia Sangster); page 204 (Vivian Ross-Smith)

Publisher's note
Due to the constraints and limitations of the page size, some of the more detailed patterns may need to be photocopied and enlarged.

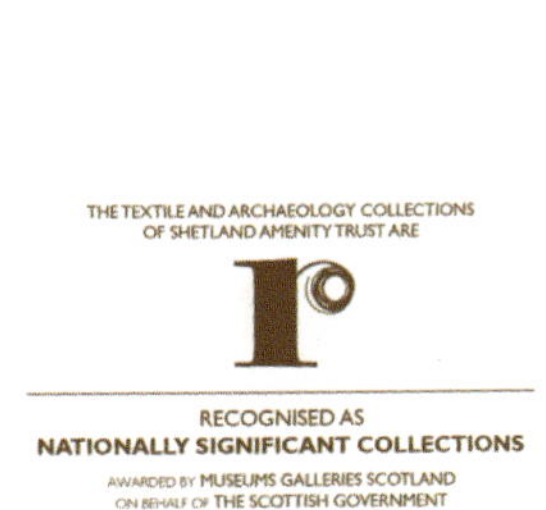

Typeset by Envisage IT
Printed and bound in India by Nutech Print Services - India

CONTENTS

INTRODUCTION

Shetland Museum has over 400 pieces of knitted lace made in the Shetland tradition, the largest collection of this knitting tradition in the world. The majority of the pieces were made on the islands, almost exclusively by women, from the 1830s to the present day. The collection includes shawls, stoles, scarves, fingerless mitts, stockings and socks, women's blouses and children's pullovers, camisoles, headscarves or kerchiefs, collars and veils, tea tray and pillow covers, and a burnous – a mid-nineteenth-century woman's cloak modelled on a garment from North Africa and the Middle East. Like most knitting produced in Shetland, fine lace was not worn by Shetlanders themselves, but produced for export. The composition of the collection therefore is primarily developed from donations from outside Shetland, of pieces returned to the islands by generous donors, one hundred or more years after they were first made in the islands.

The material presented in this book is the result of a two-year project to record Shetland designs and enhance the often insufficient descriptions of lace pieces in the Museum's collection. We hoped to understand the development of the craft, share this knowledge with contemporary makers, and address the renewed interest in Shetland knitted lace. The number of expert lace spinners, designers, knitters and finishers in Shetland has dwindled in the last fifty years and there was an urgency to meet with local lace makers to record information for future generations. The project was generously funded by Museums Galleries Scotland's Development Fund for Recognised Collections.

The Lace Assessment Project team consisted of four people who met several times a month to examine lace pieces, to choose motifs and to record and review progress. Selected motifs were studied closely by two Shetland women, sisters who are lace knitters themselves and come from a family heritage of lace knitting. They charted the motifs using Stitchmastery software and then hand-knitted the charts using two-ply machine-spun Shetland wool.

The motifs were selected from the large number of garments in the Museum's collection, mainly shawls and stoles, but also blouses and other pieces. We first concentrated on unknown or unfamiliar motifs, unique patterns or those with few other examples. An important aim was to analyse and record patterns that possibly had not been seen by anyone other than the original knitter or wearer. These would add to our knowledge of the known and recognised Shetland lace design corpus and help us understand design development. It was an opportunity to bring history forward, to allow makers who practised as many as 170 years ago to share their design and knitting skills with modern makers through their surviving work, creating an intimate conversation between contemporary and historical practitioners through their shared craft.

Common motifs, seen in many pieces in the collection although often in different ways, are also included. Some have been analysed and charted by other authors, but they are important to design development of the craft and form a group of standard patterns that help to define Shetland knitted lace.

Shawl detail, yarn spun by Eliza Sutherland, knitted by her mother Johann Sutherland in 1921. (TEX 2004.303)

Many motifs have variations and some are presented here to show how patterns were altered slightly. It is not possible to know which of the variations is the original. Some variations may suggest design development over time but this is difficult to trace. The variations show how flexible and creative Shetland makers were with knitted lace design and they prove that there were no strict rules in the creation of Shetland lace patterns. Knitters could practise a degree of individuality of their craft, while still remaining true to the Shetland lace tradition.

PATTERN NAMES AND NAMING

Pattern naming of Shetland lace motifs is a complex historical and design conundrum. We found no evidence, as is sometimes thought, that knitting pattern names from Shetland are embedded in folk belief or have strict ownership by one family. Like makers everywhere, Shetland's lace knitters were inspired by the work of others. Their lifelong skills in design and knitting meant that patterns were easily copied or interpreted, which led to the spread of patterns and their variations, sometimes with name differences. Lace patterns commonly shared and recorded tend to have names of natural processes, animals, or features they resemble, such as Da Print o' Da Wave, Peerie Flea (small fly), or Sparl (the lowest part of a sheep's intestine used to make a type of sausage). Such naming conventions indicate that many lace knitters were crofting women and took inspiration for pattern development and naming from their rural surroundings. Naming was done if the pattern needed to be discussed or taught,

Print o' Da Wave centre with Peerie Fleas and Eyelid Waves, Branches and Lace Hole Diamonds in stole border. (TEX 7760)

so some patterns created by an individual and not shared may not have been named. The most common motifs in Shetland lace knitting had names but some names varied across Shetland or in the way the motifs were used. We have adopted the naming conventions used in Unst, the island home of lace knitting, where we had some certainty they were commonly used there and where we could understand a consensus of name form, although name variations exist in Unst as well.

As part of the Lace Project we met with groups of knitters on the Shetland mainland and separately in Unst to have a better understanding of pattern names. It is clear much has been lost, and pattern name recording would benefit greatly from focused research by local lace knitters, historians and dialect specialists. We have tentatively noted other name forms used in Shetland where these could be verified from more than one source and we have used the Shetland convention of naming motifs and their setting where applicable, e.g., 'Diamond of Lace Holes inset with four Ferns'. Other authors have applied their own names to Shetland lace motifs but this obscures and confuses the historical record of names originating in Shetland. We have avoided creating names where possible for this reason. For patterns with no known name we have used a basic descriptor, e.g., 'Crown'. We hope that future research will uncover more names and naming conventions used by Shetland's lace knitters.

YARNS

Hand-spinning for most textiles was practised very late in Shetland compared to elsewhere. Lace knitting was the last commercial textile craft practised in Shetland to be made from machine-made yarns simply because no industrially produced yarn could rival that made by a skilled lace spinner. Even today, with many machine-made yarns available, none

Wool from the lower neck of the Shetland breed was used for the finest lace knitting.

Crofthouse and byre, built c. 1850s.

can compare with the fineness, evenness and strength of the best yarns represented by the Museum's collection.

The majority of the collection is made from hand-spun woollen yarns from the Shetland breed of sheep. Skilled lace spinners chose and processed wool carefully. The yarns were spun smoothly and evenly and were usually made with two threads plied together. The slightest changes in the thickness or evenness of the yarn would be visible in the finished piece, so it was extremely important for the hand-spinner to spin consistently, even allowing for pauses in work. Some original pieces appear to have uneven spinning but this is sometimes the result of use and laundering over many years. We have chosen to record motifs irrespective of their current state or quality. The design of the motif was the most important aspect and the project provided the opportunity to see past the garment's condition and study the patterns for their design characteristics.

The knitted samples made for the project used Jamieson and Smith's 2-ply Supreme Lace Weight in natural white. This yarn is thicker than most lace yarns in our collection but it was not possible to source an evenly fine hand-spun yarn in a large enough quantity for all of the samples. Motifs in original pieces and the samples made of their designs may look different for this reason.

HOW TO USE THIS BOOK

This publication draws solely on historical examples found in Shetland Museum's collection of lace knitted in the Shetland tradition. Each individual motif is presented in an image of the original piece, a knitted sample of the motif and its pattern is shown in in chart and written formats.

The patterns are organised by their role in garment design and then by their appearance, since their shape often dictated how they were used. In Chapter 7, pieces from which a number of patterns were selected for study are discussed and shown in the context of the whole garment design.

WORKING METHODS

Shetland knitters, including those knitting lace, were professionals knitting for accuracy and speed. Some of their working methods make this clear. Every row is knitted rather than purled back, so the fabric has a garter stitch instead of stockinette ground. Most often decreasing was done by k2tog on right and left sides of the pattern, rather than the ssk or s1 k1 psso

Stitch Key

- knit
- purl
- yarn over
- knit 2 together
- knit 3 together
- sl1, k1, pass slipped stitch over
- no stitch
- knit 2
- knit 2 together twice
- knit 1, purl 1 into yarn over of previous row
- yarn over twice
- pattern repeat

and k2tog paired convention as is common today. Similarly, k3tog was used instead of s1 k2 psso. These differences did not detract from the beauty of the design or knitting of each piece. It simply made knitting faster, and easier for Shetland knitters to remember the pattern and stitch sequences, thereby avoiding mistakes. Lace knitters today may use the patterns as presented, substitute their own conventions where they wish, or simply use the patterns as inspiration for their own designs.

FOR COLLECTORS AND COLLECTION MANAGERS

If you own historical knitted lace items that you think may have originated in Shetland or were knitted in the Shetland lace tradition, the images and charts will help you identify and understand what you have. The book contains a mixture of common and unusual designs. If none of the patterns in your garment look like the images in the book, your knitted lace is unlikely to have been created in the Shetland tradition.

ACKNOWLEDGEMENTS

The Shetland Lace Assessment Project could not have been accomplished without the help of a large number of people. It would have been impossible without the knowledge and skills of local lace knitters. In this capacity we called on sisters Anne Eunson and Kathleen Anderson to chart and knit the samples. Their work was integral to understanding and recording the knitted lace pieces in our collection, in addition to recreating them. Tracey Hawkins worked as the project's Collection Assistant, managing the enormous amount of data generated by charting, cataloguing, historical research, pattern name workshops, and photography. As with Anne and Kathleen, her skills and technical knowledge were fundamental to the project's success.

We asked a small team of test knitters to each knit some of the charts, with all volunteering their time. Thank you to Muriel Fox, Angie Knight, James Neilson, Marlene Sim and Jeanette Henry. At the two Lace Pattern Names workshops, we presented patterns to local knitters, some of whom are specialists in lace knitting, to identify pattern names and variations. The information that emerged has helped to confirm that pattern naming has extensive deficiencies in historical recording, along with variations across Shetland and among families of lace knitters.

Thanks are paid to my colleagues Curator Jenny Murray, who has worked patiently through three years with Shetland lace occupying much of the office and work areas, and Victoria Tait, our Publications Officer, for her advice and support. My trusted colleague at the University of Glasgow, Dr Roslyn Chapman, read a draft of the text and, as always, made valuable suggestions. Cathy and Hannah from Stitchmastery software performed much-needed support at times. Finally, I wish to acknowledge my dedicated volunteer Jenny Butler, who has worked tirelessly to carefully prepare new storage mounts and re-roll the Museum's lace collection, after we unrolled hundreds of shawls, stoles and scarves for examination.

CHAPTER 1

THE SHETLAND KNITTED LACE TRADITION

The craft of fine openwork knitting in Shetland is firmly embedded in the Victorian period. Shetland knitted lace was almost exclusively made for export, with few Shetlanders wearing it themselves. It was considered a luxury item because of its fineness, complexity of design, and limited quantities due to the time required to make it.

The craft seems to have emerged on Unst, the northernmost inhabited island in the British Isles. More specifically, it was centred in the southern part of the small island, which is only 20km (12 miles) long and 10km (6 miles) wide. Unst lace makers who moved to other parts of Shetland continued their craft. Many of the finest pieces in Shetland Museum's collection have connections to Unst. The island is still regarded as the home of the Shetland knitted lace tradition and lace knitters on the island continue the craft. The Unst Heritage Centre has an important collection of fine lace pieces from the island.

The earliest evidence of the craft is from the late 1830s, the same time that eighteen-year-old Victoria ascended the British throne. Queen Victoria (1819–1901) was a fashion icon: she championed the craft of Shetland's fine lace makers, acquired lace pieces herself, and influenced others to follow her example. Her influence helped to promote the craft and make it an international trade. The excessive material wealth of segments of Victorian society also boosted fine lace knitting in Shetland.

Victorian fashion changed significantly during Queen Victoria's long reign and many types of garments and accessories were worn. This helped to create a demand for rendering many garments in Shetland knitted lace, from neckerchiefs to opera cloaks. Merchants who received special orders for unusual garments, such as cloaks, or in fibres such as silk or mohair, provided work to specialist makers in the islands.

Makers worked from their cottages and most earned an income or practised a subsistence lifestyle through other types of work (crofting, gutting fish, peat-cutting) besides knitting. They delivered their finished knitwear to local merchants, who mainly provided them goods in exchange, a system known as 'truck'. The system was outlawed in the late 1880s because it was unfair to makers, although it continued at a local level in some areas. Some merchants, especially in Lerwick, began to pay cash for knitted goods as early as the 1870s (Chapman, p.164).

As boat transport and postal services between Shetland and the Scottish mainland improved in the late nineteenth century, some lace makers developed their own customer base. The most accomplished makers took in private commissions and did repairs, cleaning and dressing of the finest garments. A fine, intricate lace shawl could take up to a year to create, even for the most talented makers. Despite the extreme complexity and fineness of many of the garments, it was not a lucrative business for the maker. Most makers were women who had few other employment options.

Shetland lace knitting has been dominated by two garments: shawls and stoles. These flat textiles appear to have been complex in their design from an early period.

A red and white cape, c. 1850, designed in the style of a burnous, a North African garment. (TEX 7780)

A very large stole, 1905, which weighed only 30.7 grams.

As Victorian fashion developed, other garments were made in the technique: scarves, stockings, face and hat veils, fichus, pelerines, clouds, tippets, cloaks, wristlets, and decorative borders and bodices for camisoles and other garments. In the 1920s, as women's fashion changed, blouses and bed jackets gained popularity. Later, slipovers and cardigans were created. They incorporated many of the same motifs used throughout the previous century or more of the craft.

MAKING AND MAKERS

The processes associated with knitted lace making are multi-faceted and demanding. It is a craft that requires attention to detail throughout all phases, from selecting the wool to dressing the finished garment. The very highest quality of fineness, evenness, design balance and accuracy could only be accomplished by the most specialised makers with exceptional skills.

Making a lace garment began with raising sheep for the appropriate fine wool and removing the wool from specific areas of the fleece by plucking or 'rooing'. Some spinners carded the wool but some preferred to spin direct from the wool staple that had been carefully combed but kept intact. Yarns were spun and plied on the Shetland spinnie, a small, upright spinning wheel. Professional lace spinners were specialists, since the craft required an extremely fine but even draw, long enough to make a single shawl. Even a minor change in thickness would be visible in the finished garment but not readily apparent to the knitter as she knitted the piece. Knitters who made the finest shawls worked with spinners whose yarns they trusted to be evenly fine.

We know very little about individual knitters and nothing of design influences and inspiration for their lace pieces in the Museum's collection. Lace garments were usually knitted by one person, although knitters working in pairs are recorded (Chapman, p.92). The knitter was usually the creator of the design. Knitters did not use patterns, where every stitch was written out or charted. Some made notes or knitted small samples to work out a complex design but then memorised the pattern. If notes were required, these consisted of the number of stitches ('loops') to cast on. A knitter's notebook (TEX 76174) in the collection provides an example of a lace shawl 'pattern'. The knitter carried the rest of the design in her head.

White Shawl
Lace 14 scallops
Border 8 shell pieces
Begin with 144 loops to start border

After a fine lace flat garment was knitted it was put through a bleaching process by placing it in the upper level of a barrel, with a piece of sulphur set alight and smoking at the bottom. This allowed the smoke to penetrate the lace and whiten the natural cream colour of the wool. After bleaching it was lightly washed or wetted and dressed on a frame. Each of these processes required certain skills and led some individuals to specialise. The most intricately designed and well-made garments were often the work of several people, as specialist spinners, knitters and finishers each applied their expertise to a single piece. Other makers attempted to carry out the various processes themselves, sometimes with mixed results.

In some cases we know who the maker was, but for specialist work we may have only one name, probably the

Four Unst women unload dried peat from ponies.

knitter, when several specialists may have contributed to making the garment. The skill of the hand-spinner was as important as that of the knitter but the identity of spinners specialising in lace yarns remains largely unknown.

In only a handful of cases do we have multiple examples of one individual's work. We can use these pieces to investigate the favoured motifs of that individual maker or designer, how they used them in different design elements, and how they varied them for a particular customer or design.

The Museum's collection of knitted lace represents a wide variety of skill levels in all processes. Every garment, fragment or sample can hold information about the way Shetland knitted lace was created and adds to our knowledge of design development and the continued use of certain conventions. More importantly, each item is what remains of the skill and knowledge of a maker who is no longer with us. We consider each piece in our collection to be unique and precious, a legacy of the creativity, and the hand and mental agility of its maker or makers. These textiles have much to tell us about the craft, but the complexity of design and execution make their story difficult to decipher.

CHAPTER 2

VERTICAL CENTRE PATTERNS

Shawls have received the greatest study and attention in books and exhibitions about Shetland lace, yet stoles and scarves are more varied in design. They are small enough that knitters could experiment with new patterns and design configurations, having fewer pattern repeats and being much quicker to make than a large shawl. Many stoles and scarves have very complex borders, as will be seen in Chapter 4. Many use vertical patterns in their centres, forming strong visual lines to accentuate the length and narrowness of the garment. These patterns are less commonly found in shawls, since the typical way shawls were worn was folded in half to form a triangle, causing linear patterns to appear on the diagonal.

Vertical patterns also are placed inside knitted shapes such as diamonds and trees, or used to vertically connect two shapes together. Simple vertical patterns may be placed side-by-side, where it is especially effective at the top of a border. Vertical patterns used in these ways are covered in Chapter 4.

Many individual vertical patterns are relatively simple, and therefore are used interchangeably in combination with other vertical patterns to form new pattern pairings or groupings. This gives the designer free rein to create different centre patterns, infills for shapes and other areas where a simple but decorative alternative to plain knitting is desired. Some of the most common vertical patterns are presented here, but shown in the many ways they were used singly or in combination with other patterns.

Fair Isle's North Lighthouse pathway.

STEEKS

Steeks are the most basic linear patterns and a very simple way of introducing vertical openwork in lace knitting. The word steek has two common meanings in the Scots language. As a noun it simply means a stitch in sewing or knitting and as a verb it means to close or fasten. Its meaning as a narrow bridge of stitches when knitting in the round is not known in traditional Shetland knitting. Rather it is the name for the simplest form of lace stitches, a yarn over and one or more decreases, repeated vertically.

Due to their simplicity, steeks are often overlooked but they have been used creatively by Shetland lace knitters to form simple but effective centres for shawls, stoles and scarves. Simple steeks may be combined with other patterns, or themselves repeated to create simple mesh patterns and zigzags. For these uses, see Chapters 3 and 4.

The simplest steek is yo, k2tog, or k2tog, yo, worked vertically every row or every other row. A more complex steek is where k2tog decreases are worked just before and after each yarn over with a knit stitch between (k2tog, yo, k1, yo, k2tog). Working these types of steek patterns gives a slight ridge to the outer side or sides of the yarn over, formed by the decreases. A third steek variation is yo, k3tog, yo.

A simple, flat steek, without the ridges caused by a k2tog, can be achieved by knitting yo, k1, yo. But this steek creates an additional stitch that must be 'removed' with a decrease in another part of the row.

2.1

Steeks and garter stitch

TEX 8933 Scarf

The two most basic and common Shetland lace stitches, Steeks and garter stitches, are positioned in vertical columns.

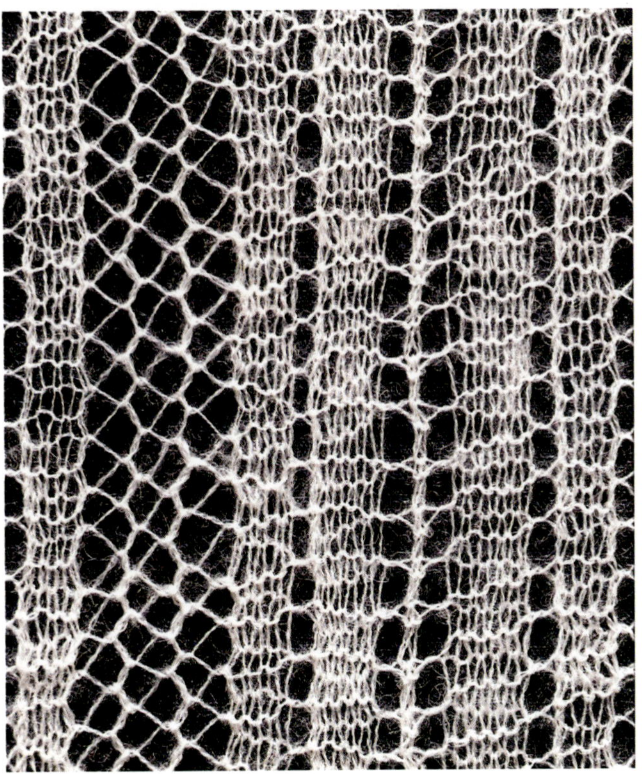

Steeks and garter stitch original pattern.

Here three types of Steeks are used. The first two are a simple yo, k2tog and the more complex yo, k3tog, yo, both worked every other row. The third type is a repositioning of the simple steek combination of yo and k2tog, here worked every row, with the k2tog worked before the yo in one row and after the yo in the alternate row. They are used here with garter stitch in different widths to make a streamlined, simple pattern for the centre of a stole.

Row 1 and all RS rows: K4, yo, k2tog, k4, yo, k3tog, yo, k5, yo, k2tog, k3, (yo, k2tog) x 3.
Row 2 and all WS rows: K1, (yo, k2tog) x 3, k22.

Steeks and garter stitch knitted sample.

	29	28	27	26	25	24	23	22	21	20	19	18	17	16	15	14	13	12	11	10	9	8	7	6	5	4	3	2	1	
14		O	/	O	/	O	/											22												
	/	O	/	O	/	O				/	O			5			O	⋏	O					/	O					13
12		O	/	O	/	O	/											22												
	/	O	/	O	/	O				/	O			5			O	⋏	O					/	O					11
10		O	/	O	/	O	/											22												
	/	O	/	O	/	O				/	O			5			O	⋏	O					/	O					9
8		O	/	O	/	O	/											22												
	/	O	/	O	/	O				/	O			5			O	⋏	O					/	O					7
6		O	/	O	/	O	/											22												
	/	O	/	O	/	O				/	O			5			O	⋏	O					/	O					5
4		O	/	O	/	O	/											22												
	/	O	/	O	/	O				/	O			5			O	⋏	O					/	O					3
2		O	/	O	/	O	/											22												
	/	O	/	O	/	O				/	O			5			O	⋏	O					/	O					1
	29	28	27	26	25	24	23	22	21	20	19	18	17	16	15	14	13	12	11	10	9	8	7	6	5	4	3	2	1	

Steeks and garter stitch chart.

2.2

Steeks and Vees

TEX 1997.91 Shawl

Steeks and Vees original pattern.

Steeks and Vees knitted sample.

Steeks can be used effectively alongside any number of small, discrete individual patterns placed vertically to create an easy, openwork pattern. This shawl centre is made of a column of Vees alternating with three Steeks placed side-by-side, forming a mesh to give a very open effect.

Row 1 (RS): K1, (yo, k2tog) x 3, k8, (yo, k2tog) x 3, k1. (22 sts)

Row 2 and all WS rows: Knit.

Row 3: K1, (yo, k2tog) x 4, k3, k2tog, yo, k1, (yo, k2tog) x 3, k1.

Row 5: K1, (yo, k2tog) x 3, k1, yo, k2tog, k1, k2tog, yo, k2, (yo, k2tog) x 3, k1.

Row 7: K1, (yo, k2tog) x 3, k2, yo, k3tog, yo, k3, (yo, k2tog) x 3, k1.

Row 9: Repeat row 1.

Row 11: Repeat row 3.

Row 13: Repeat row 5.

Row 15: Repeat row 7.

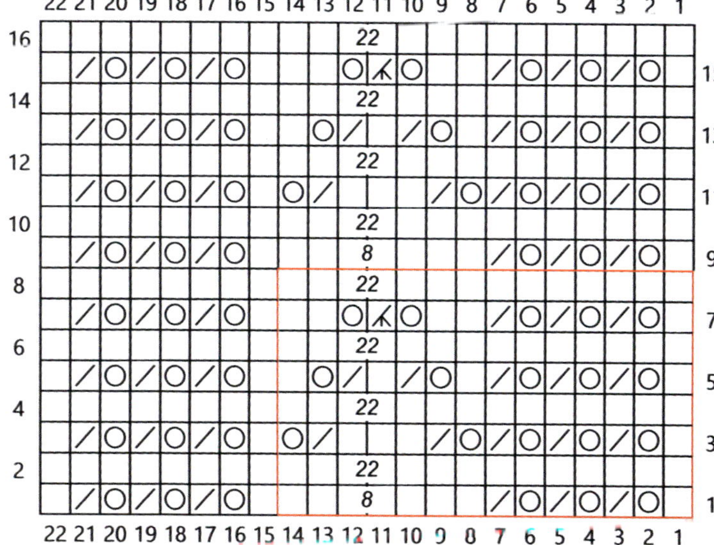

Steeks and Vees stitch chart.

2.3

Vees and Ovals

TEX 2004.331 Stole

Vees and Ovals original pattern.

Vees and Ovals knitted sample.

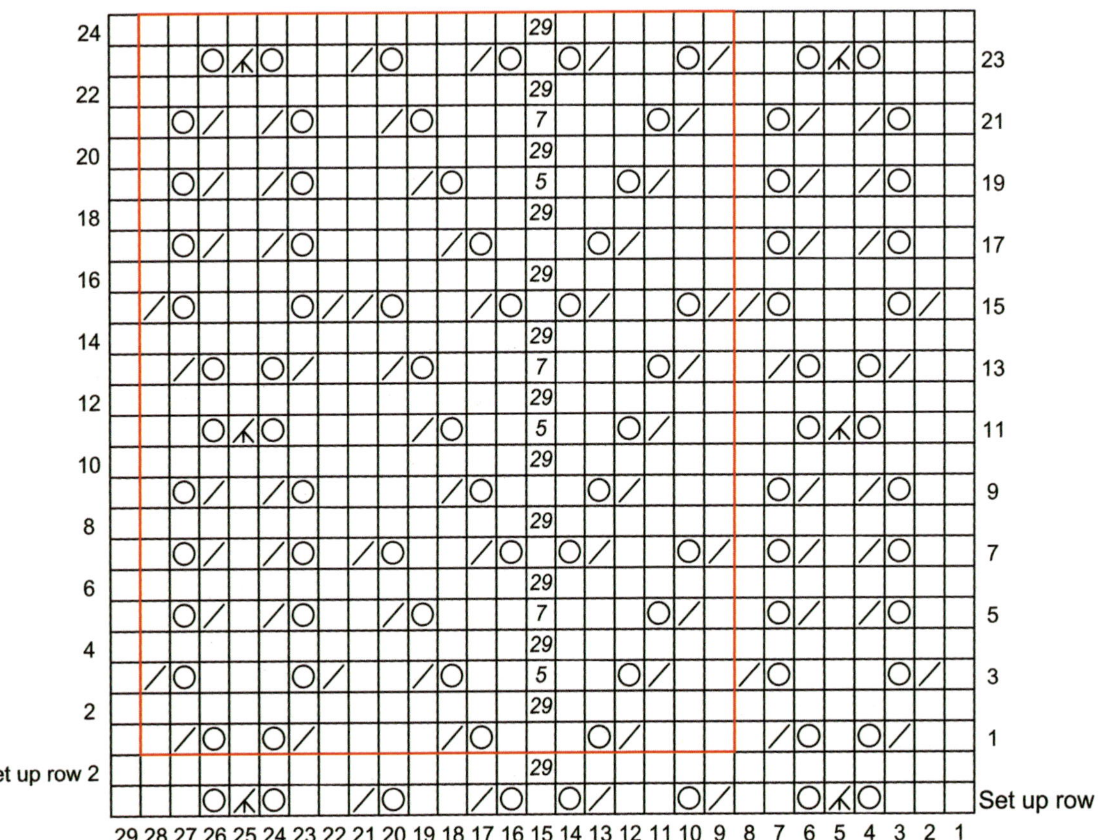

Vees and Ovals chart.

This simple pattern does not contain Steeks but is another vertical combination of Vee-forms, here with Ovals. Both elements were used individually in borders, tucked here and there to add laciness, but here they stand on their own.

Set up row 1 (RS): K3, yo, k3tog, (yo, k2, k2tog) x 2, yo, k1, (yo, k2tog, k2) x 2, yo, k3tog, yo, k3. (29 sts)
Set up row 2 and all WS rows: Knit.
Row 1: K2, k2tog, yo, k1, yo, k2tog, k4, k2tog, yo, k3, yo, k2tog, k4, k2tog, yo, k1, yo, k2tog, k2.
Row 3: K1, k2tog, yo, k3, yo, k2tog, k2, k2tog, yo, k5, yo, k2tog, k2, k2tog, yo, k3, yo, k2tog, k1.
Row 5: K2, yo, k2tog, k1, k2tog, yo, k2, k2tog, yo, k7, yo, k2tog, k2, yo, k2tog, k1, k2tog, yo, k2.
Row 7: K2, yo, k2tog, (k1, k2tog, yo) x 2, k2, k2tog, yo, k1, yo, k2tog, k2, (yo, k2tog, k1) x 2, k2tog, yo, k2.
Row 9: K2, yo, k2tog, k1, k2tog, yo, k4, k2tog, yo, k3, yo, k2tog, k4, yo, k2tog, k1, k2tog, yo, k2.
Row 11: K3, yo, k3tog, yo, k4, k2tog, yo, k5, yo, k2tog, k4, yo, k3tog, yo, k3.
Row 13: K2, k2tog, yo, k1, yo, k2tog, k2, k2tog, yo, k7, yo, k2tog, k2, k2tog, yo, k1, yo, k2tog, k2.
Row 15: K1, k2tog, yo, k3, yo, k2tog x 2, yo, k2, k2tog, yo, k1, yo, k2tog, k2, yo, k2tog x 2, yo, k3, yo, k2tog, k1.
Row 17: Repeat row 9.
Row 19: K2, yo, k2tog, k1, k2tog, yo, k3, k2tog, yo, k5, yo, k2tog, k3, yo, k2tog, k1, k2tog, yo, k2.
Row 21: Repeat row 5.
Row 23: Repeat set up row 1.

ZIGZAG

The Zigzag is one of the most striking and important patterns used in Shetland lace knitting. It forms the basis for many vertical patterns, especially the famous Shetland lace pattern Da Print o' Da Wave. It is used in lace edges and occasionally as infill for large pattern shapes, discussed in Chapters 4 and 6.

A Zigzag's width and frequency of its back-and-forth turns were at the designer's discretion and variations are presented here. Repeated vertical columns of Zigzags usually had their points aiming in the same direction across a row. Where Diamonds or larger eyelet motifs like Cat's Paw were paired with a Zigzag, the points of the Zigzag were set at the narrowest or widest points of these patterns. In some cases the patterns chosen to pair with one or more Zigzags did not share the same divisible row repeat as the Zigzag. With small patterns such as Lace Holes, this was not apparent but with larger patterns the Zigzag repeat became offset with the paired pattern repeat. Lace knitters faced such a problem in different ways, and these are explored more fully later in this chapter (see page 37, 'Working with pattern repeats arranged vertically').

Zigzagging wall.

2.4

Zigzag and garter stitch

TEX 2012.491 Stole

Alternating columns of four-hole Zigzag and Garter stitch is the most basic of Zigzag patterns. Here the two patterns form an elegant centre for a stole.

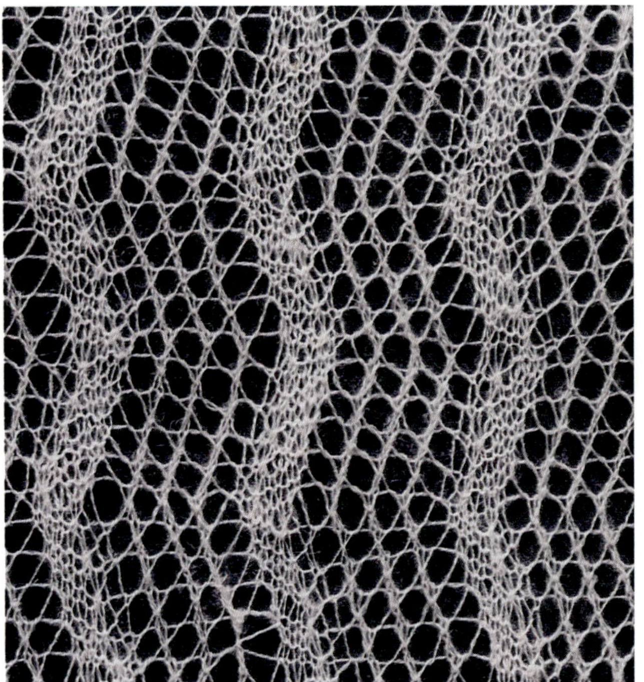

Zigzag and garter stitch original pattern.

Row 1 (RS): K1, ((k2tog, yo) x 4, k4) x 2. (25 sts)
Row 2 (WS): K3, (yo, k2tog) x 4, k4, (yo, k2tog) x 4, k2.
Row 3: K3, (k2tog, yo) x 4, k4, (k2tog, yo) x 4, k2.
Row 4: K1, ((yo, k2tog) x 4, k4) x 2.

Zigzag and garter stitch knitted sample.

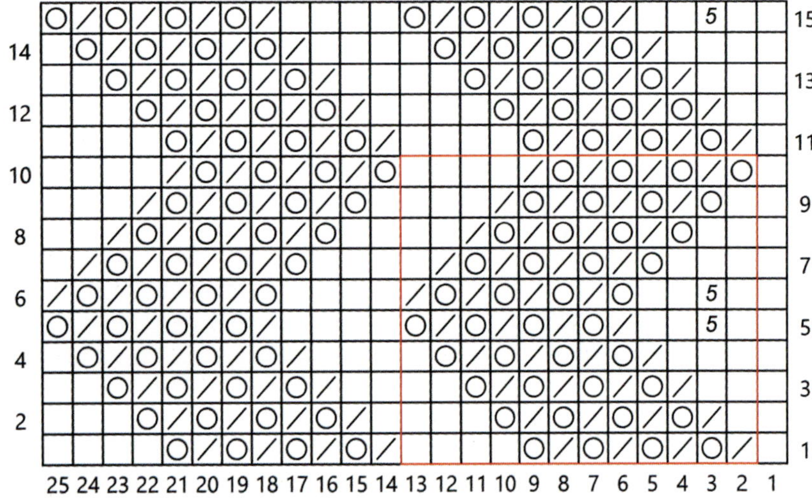

Zigzag and garter stitch chart.

Row 5: K5, (k2tog, yo) x 4, k4, (k2tog, yo) x 4.
Row 6: (K2tog, yo) x 4, k4, (k2tog, yo) x 4, k5.
Row 7: (K4, (yo, k2tog) x 4) x 2, k1.
Row 8: K2, (k2tog, yo) x 4, k4, (k2tog, yo) x 4, k3.
Row 9: K2, (yo, k2tog) x 4, k4, (yo, k2tog) x 4, k3.
Row 10: (K4, (k2tog, yo) x 4) x 2, k1.
Row 11: Repeat row 1.
Row 12: Repeat row 2.
Row 13: Repeat row 3.
Row 14: Repeat row 4.
Row 15: Repeat row 5.

2.5

Zigzag and Lace Holes

TEX 2015.107 Stole

Zigzag and Lace Holes original pattern.

The pairing of four-hole Zigzag with narrow columns of Lace Holes forms the centre of a stole. Repeats of each pattern are outlined separately in the chart because they do not share a divisible row repeat. This is inconspicuous in the finished piece because of the vast difference of the row repeats between the two patterns. The Zigzags have prominence here, but if a more balanced look were desired the Lace Hole columns could be widened.

Row 1 (RS): K2, (yo, k2tog) x 4, k15, k2tog, yo x 2, k2tog x 2, yo x 2, k2tog, k6, (yo, k2tog) x 4, k10. (57 sts)
Row 2 (WS): K9, (k2tog, yo) x 4, k8, p1, k3, p1, k16, (k2tog, yo) x 4, k3.
Row 3: K4, (yo, k2tog) x 4, k15, k2tog, yo x 2, k2tog, k10, (yo, k2tog) x 4, k8.
Row 4: K7, (k2tog, yo) x 4, k12, p1, k16, (k2tog, yo) x 4, k5.
Row 5: K6, (yo, k2tog) x 4, k11, k2tog, yo x 2, k2tog x 2, yo x 2, k2tog, k10, (yo, k2tog) x 4, k6.
Row 6: K5, (k2tog, yo) x 4, k12, p1, k3, p1, k12, (k2tog, yo) x 4, k7.
Row 7: K8, (yo, k2tog) x 4, k11, k2tog, yo x 2, k2tog, k14, (yo, k2tog) x 4, k4.
Row 8: K3, (k2tog, yo) x 4, k16, p1, k12, (k2tog, yo) x 4, k9.
Row 9: K10, (yo, k2tog) x 4, k7, k2tog, yo x 2, k2tog x 2, yo x 2, k2tog, k14, (yo, k2tog) x 4, k2.
Row 10: K1, (k2tog, yo) x 4, k16, p1, k3, p1, k8, (k2tog, yo) x 4, k11.
Row 11: K9, (k2tog, yo) x 4, k10, k2tog, yo x 2, k2tog, k15, (k2tog, yo) x 4, k3.
Row 12: K4, (yo, k2tog) x 4, k15, p1, k13, (yo, k2tog) x 4, k8.
Row 13: K7, (k2tog, yo) x 4, k10, k2tog, yo x 2, k2tog x 2, yo x 2, k2tog, k11, (k2tog, yo) x 4, k5.
Row 14: K6, (yo, k2tog) x 4, k11, p1, k3, p1, k13, (yo, k2tog) x 4, k6.

Zigzag and Lace Holes knitted sample.

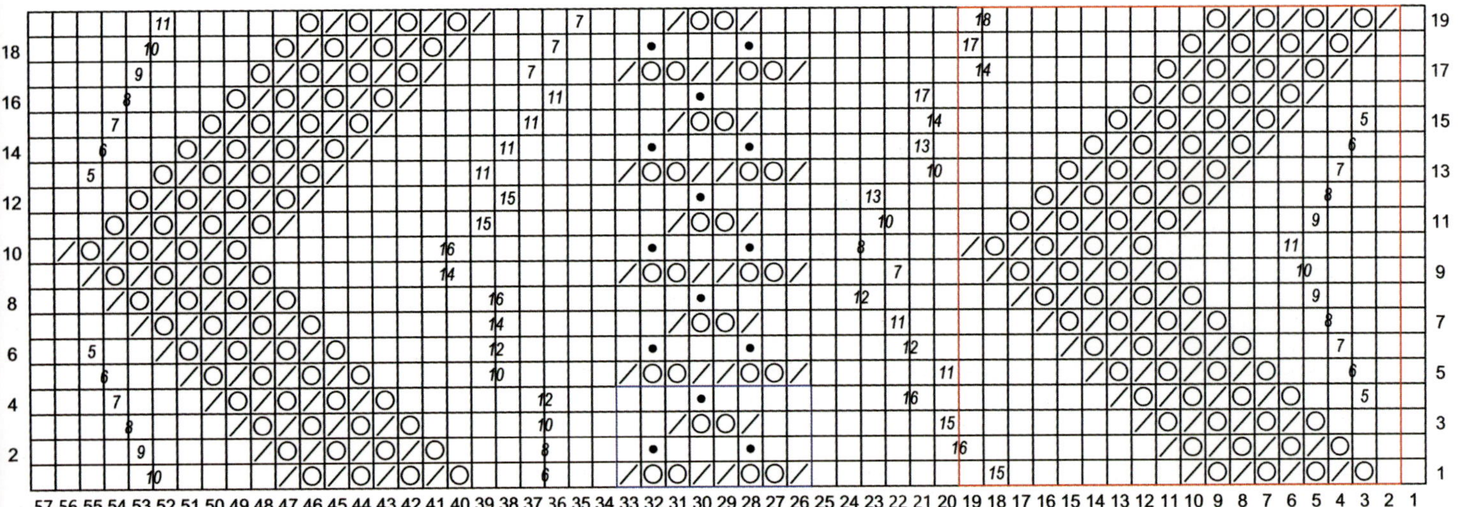

Zigzag and Lace Holes chart.

Row 15: K5, (k2tog, yo) x 4, k14, k2tog, yo x 2, k2tog, k11, (k2tog, yo) x 4, k7.

Row 16: K8, (yo, k2tog) x 4, k11, p1, k17, (yo, k2tog) x 4, k4.

Row 17: K3, (k2tog, yo) x 4, k14, k2tog, yo x 2, k2tog x 2, yo x 2, k2tog, k7, (k2tog, yo) x 4, k9.

Row 18: K10, (yo, k2tog) x 4, k7, p1, k3, p1, k17, (yo, k2tog) x 4, k2.

Row 19: K1, (k2tog, yo) x 4, k18, k2tog, yo x 2, k2tog, k7, (k2tog, yo) x 4, k11.

2.6

Zigzag and Bead mesh

TEX 7784 Scarf

Zigzag and Bead mesh original pattern.

A narrow scarf has a centre pattern made of three columns – two very wide six-hole Zigzags and a centre column of a pretty Bead stitch variation formed into a repeating mesh pattern. Here the two patterns have complementary row repeats.

Row 1 (RS): K6, (k2tog, yo) x 6, k5, (k2tog, yo, k1, yo, k2tog, k1) x 3, k2tog, yo, k1, yo, k2tog, k5. (51 sts)
Row 2 (WS): K4, k2tog, (yo, k3, yo, k3tog) x 3, yo, k3, yo, k2tog, k5, (yo, k2tog) x 6, k5.
Row 3: K4, (k2tog, yo) x 6, k7, (yo, k2tog, k1, k2tog, yo, k1) x 3, yo, k2tog, k1, k2tog, yo, k5.
Row 4: K6, (yo, k3tog, yo, k3) x 3, yo, k3tog, yo, k9, (yo, k2tog) x 6, k3.
Row 5: K2, (k2tog, yo) x 6, k9, (k2tog, yo, k1, yo, k2tog, k1) x 3, k2tog, yo, k1, yo, k2tog, k5.
Row 6: K4, k2tog, (yo, k3, yo, k3tog) x 3, yo, k3, yo, k2tog, k9, (yo, k2tog) x 6, k1.
Row 7: K3, (yo, k2tog) x 6, k8, (yo, k2tog, k1, k2tog, yo, k1) x 3, yo, k2tog, k1, k2tog, yo, k5.
Row 8: K6, (yo, k3tog, yo, k3) x 3, yo, k3tog, yo, k8, (k2tog, yo) x 6, k4.

Zigzag and Bead mesh knitted sample.

Row 9: K5, (yo, k2tog) x 6, k6, (k2tog, yo, k1, yo, k2tog, k1) x 3, k2tog, yo, k1, yo, k2tog, k5.
Row 10: K4, k2tog, (yo, k3, yo, k3tog) x 3, yo, k3, yo, k2tog, k4, (k2tog, yo) x 6, k6.
Row 11: K7, (yo, k2tog) x 6, k4, (yo, k2tog, k1, k2tog, yo, k1) x 3, yo, k2tog, k1, k2tog, yo, k5.
Row 12: K6, (yo, k3tog, yo, k3) x 3, yo, k3tog, yo, k4, (k2tog, yo) x 6, k8.
Row 13: Repeat row 1.
Row 14: Repeat row 2.
Row 15: Repeat row 3.
Row 16: Repeat row 4.
Row 17: Repeat row 5.
Row 18: Repeat row 6.
Row 19: Repeat row 7.
Row 20: Repeat row 8.
Row 21: Repeat row 9.
Row 22: Repeat row 10.
Row 23: Repeat row 11.

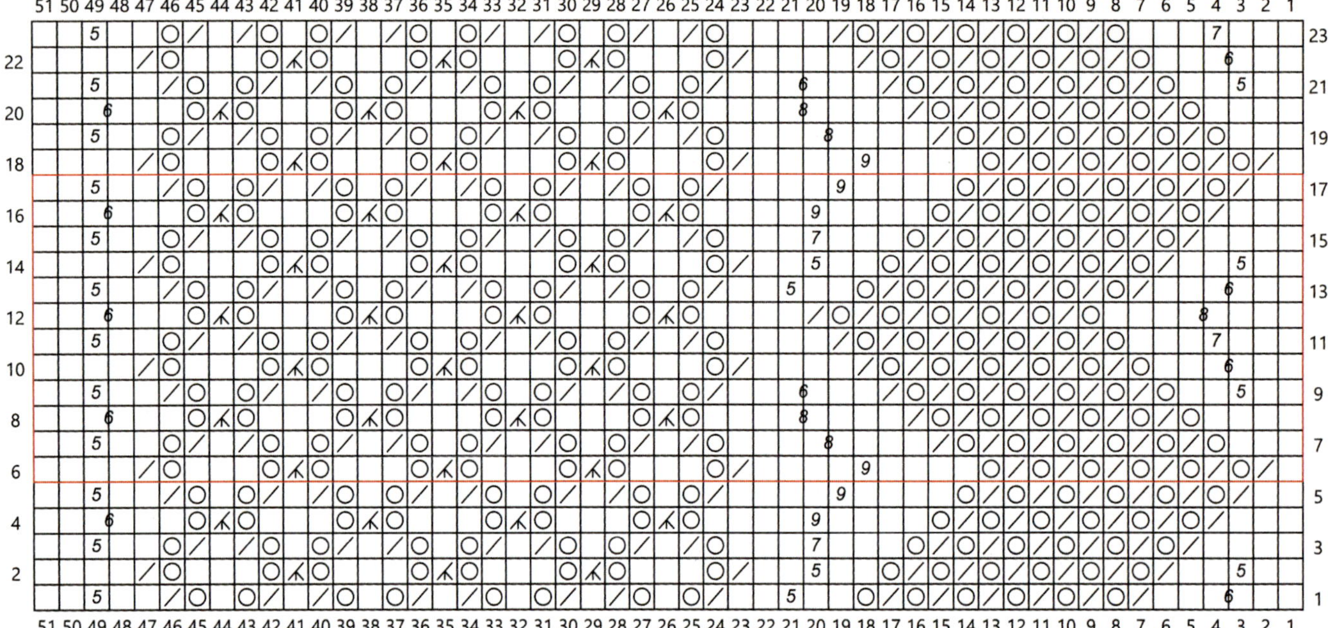

Zigzag and Bead mesh chart.

2.7

Zigzag and mesh stitch

TEX 2004.336 Stole

Zigzag and mesh stitch knitted sample.

Zigzag and mesh stitch original pattern.

Three-hole Zigzags are used alongside an unusual mesh pattern, unknown to the contemporary lace knitters we consulted. It has some similarities to Lace Holes and the Peerie Flea. It is easy to work and creates a delicate and pretty lace mesh pattern. The pattern is presented here as a large section worked, with the repeats of both patterns outlined.

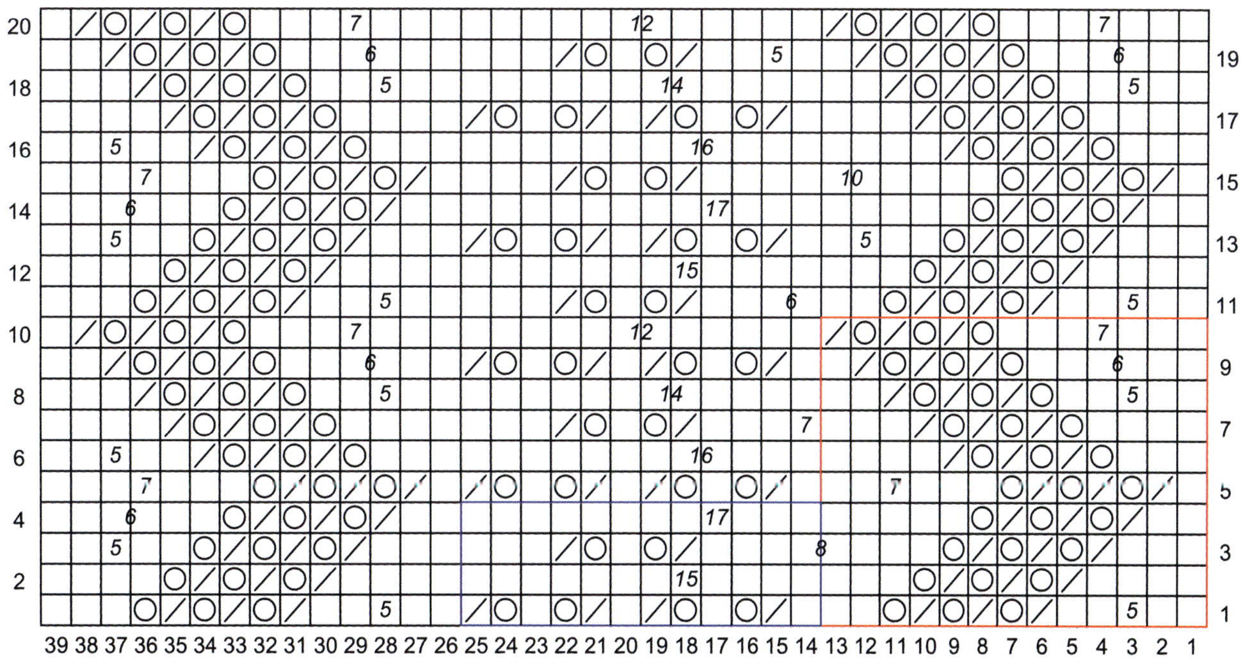

Zigzag and mesh stitch chart.

Shapes in the landscape – Eshaness coastline.

Row 1 (RS): (K5, (k2tog, yo) x 3, k3, k2tog, yo, k1, yo, k2tog, k1, k2tog, yo, k1, yo, k2tog), k5, (k2tog, yo) x 3, k3. (39 sts)
Row 2 (WS): K4, (yo, p2tog) x 3, k4, (k15, (yo, p2tog) x 3, k4).
Row 3: (K3, (k2tog, yo) x 3, k8, k2tog, yo, k1, yo, k2tog, k3), k3, (k2tog, yo) x 3, k5.
Row 4: K6, (yo, p2tog) x 3, k2, (k17, (yo, p2tog) x 3, k2).
Row 5: (K1, (k2tog, yo) x 3, k7, k2tog, yo, k1, yo, k2tog, k1, k2tog, yo, k1, yo, k2tog), k1, (k2tog, yo) x 3, k7.
Row 6: K5, (p2tog, yo) x 3, k3, (k16, (p2tog, yo) x 3, k3).
Row 7: (K4, (yo, k2tog) x 3, k7, k2tog, yo, k1, yo, k2tog, k3), k4, (yo, k2tog) x 3, k4.
Row 8: K3, (p2tog, yo) x 3, k5, (k14, (p2tog, yo) x 3, k5).
Row 9: (K6, (yo, k2tog) x 3, k2, k2tog, yo, k1, yo, k2tog, k1, k2tog, yo, k1, yo, k2tog), k6, (yo, k2tog) x 3, k2.
Row 10: K1, (p2tog, yo) x 3, k7, (k12, (p2tog, yo) x 3, k7).
Row 11: (K5, (k2tog, yo) x 3, k6, k2tog, yo, k1, yo, k2tog, k3), k5, (k2tog, yo) x 3, k3.
Row 12: Repeat row 2.
Row 13: (K3, (k2tog, yo) x 3, k5, k2tog, yo, k1, yo, k2tog, k1, k2tog, yo, k1, yo, k2tog), k3, (k2tog, yo) x 3, k5.
Row 14: Repeat row 4.
Row 15: (K1, (k2tog, yo) x 3, k10, k2tog, yo, k1, yo, k2tog, k3), k1, (k2tog, yo) x 3, k7.
Row 16: Repeat row 6.
Row 17: (K4, (yo, k2tog) x 3, k4, k2tog, yo, k1, yo, k2tog, k1, k2tog, yo, k1, yo, k2tog), k4, (yo, k2tog) x 3, k4.
Row 18: Repeat row 8.
Row 19: (K6, (yo, k2tog) x 3, k5, k2tog, yo, k1, yo, k2tog, k3), k6, (yo, k2tog) x 3, k2.
Row 20: Repeat row 10.

ZIGZAG WITH DIAMONDS

Zigzag stitch is also used as a mesh background within which plain knitted Diamonds are worked. The Diamonds appear to be suspended and the pattern has been referred to in Unst as Diamond Drop. The Diamonds are used singly or in a cluster of four and can 'hang' to the right, left, or both sides of the Zigzag stitch. The Diamonds are given prominence when placed with a narrow, single Zigzag. A double Zigzag provides better pattern balance with a larger cluster of four Diamonds.

2.8

Single Diamond Drop on alternating sides
TEX 2017.94 Shawl

Here the Diamonds alternate to the right and left sides of a single Zigzag mesh background, making a balanced pattern for the centre of a shawl.

Single Diamond Drop on alternating sides original pattern.

Row 1 (RS): (K2tog, yo) x 3, k9, yo, k2tog, yo, k3tog, (yo, k2tog) x 2, yo, k9, (yo, k2tog) x 3. (39 sts)
Row 2 and all WS rows: Knit.
Row 3: K2, (yo, k2tog) x 3, k5, (k2tog, yo) x 3, k1, (yo, k2tog) x 3, k5, (k2tog, yo) x 3, k2.

Single Diamond Drop on alternating sides knitted sample.

Row 5: (K3, (yo, k2tog) x 3, k3, (k2tog, yo) x 3) x 2, k3.
Row 7: K4, (yo, k2tog) x 3, k1, (k2tog, yo) x 3, k5, (yo, k2tog) x 3, k1, (k2tog, yo) x 3, k4.
Row 9: K5, (yo, k2tog) x 2, yo, k3tog, (yo, k2tog) x 2, yo, k7, (yo, k2tog) x 2, yo, k3tog, (yo, k2tog) x 2, yo, k5.
Row 11: K6, (yo, k2tog) x 2, yo, k3tog, yo, k2tog, yo, k9, (yo, k2tog) x 2, yo, k3tog, yo, k2tog, yo, k6.
Row 13: K4, (k2tog, yo) x 3, k1, (yo, k2tog) x 3, k5, (k2tog, yo) x 3, k1, (yo, k2tog) x 3, k4.
Row 15: (K3, (k2tog, yo) x 3, k3, (yo, k2tog) x 3) x 2, k3.
Row 17: K2, (k2tog, yo) x 3, k5, (yo, k2tog) x 3, k1, (k2tog, yo) x 3, k5, (yo, k2tog) x 3, k2.
Row 19: K1, (k2tog, yo) x 3, k7, (yo, k2tog) x 2, yo, k3tog, (yo, k2tog) x 2, yo, k7, (yo, k2tog) x 3, k1.
Row 21: Repeat row 1.
Row 23: Repeat row 3.
Row 25: Repeat row 5.
Row 27: Repeat row 7.
Row 29: Repeat row 9.
Row 31: Repeat row 11.
Row 33: Repeat row 13.
Row 35: Repeat row 15.
Row 37: Repeat row 17.
Row 39: Repeat row 19.

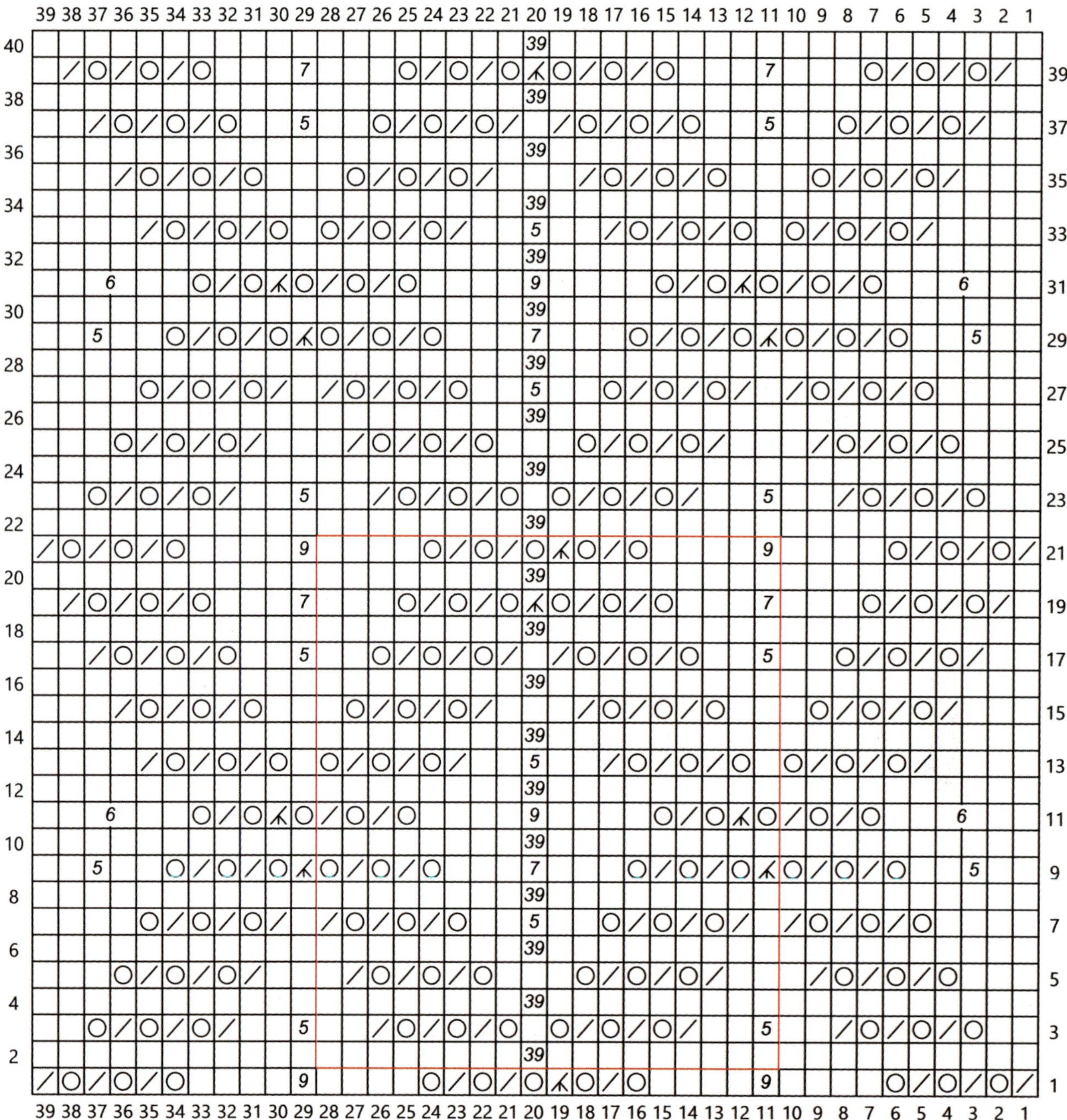

Single Diamond Drop on alternating sides chart.

2.9

Cluster of four Diamond Drop on one side
TEX 7755 Shawl

Cluster of four Diamond Drop on one side original pattern.

A large Diamond shape made from four smaller Diamonds clustered together is set against a double Zigzag mesh for a shawl centre.

Set up row 1 (RS): K1, yo, k3tog, (yo, k2tog) x 2, yo, k7, yo, k2tog, k6, (yo, k2tog) x 3, yo, k3tog, (yo, k2tog) x 2, yo, k7, yo, k2tog, k6, (yo, k2tog) x 2, yo, k3tog, yo, k1. (59 sts)
Set up row 2 and all WS rows: Knit.
Row 3: K2, (yo, k2tog) x 4, k3, k2tog, yo, k1, yo, k2tog, k3, (k2tog, yo) x 4, k1, (yo, k2tog) x 4, k3, k2tog, yo, k1, yo, k2tog, k3, (k2tog, yo) x 4, k2.
Row 5: (K3, (yo, k2tog) x 4, k1, k2tog, yo, k3, yo, k2tog, k1, (k2tog, yo) x 4) x 2, k3.
Row 7: K4, (yo, k2tog) x 3, yo, k3tog, yo, k5, yo, k3tog, (yo, k2tog) x 3, yo, k5, (yo, k2tog) x 3, yo, k3tog, yo, k5, yo, k3tog, (yo, k2tog) x 3, yo, k4.

Cluster of four Diamond Drop on one side knitted sample.

Row 9: K5, (yo, k2tog) x 4, k5, (k2tog, yo) x 4, k7, (yo, k2tog) x 4, k5, (k2tog, yo) x 4, k5.
Row 11: (K3, k2tog, yo, k1, (yo, k2tog) x 4, k3, (k2tog, yo) x 4, k1, yo, k2tog) x 2, k3.
Row 13: K2, k2tog, yo, k3, (yo, k2tog) x 4, k1, (k2tog, yo) x 4, k3, yo, k2tog, k1, k2tog, yo, k3, (yo, k2tog) x 4, k1, (k2tog, yo) x 4, k3, yo, k2tog, k2.
Row 15: K1, k2tog, yo, k5, (yo, k2tog) x 3, yo, k3tog, (yo, k2tog) x 3, yo, k5, yo, k3tog, yo, k5, (yo, k2tog) x 3, yo, k3tog, (yo, k2tog) x 3, yo, k5, yo, k2tog, k1.
Row 17: K1, yo, k2tog, k6, (yo, k2tog) x 3, yo, k3tog, (yo, k2tog) x 2, yo, k7, yo, k2tog, k6, (yo, k2tog) x 3, yo, k3tog, (yo, k2tog) x 2, yo, k6, k2tog, yo, k1.
Row 19: K2, yo, k2tog, k3, (k2tog, yo) x 4, k1, (yo, k2tog) x 4, k3, k2tog, yo, k1, yo, k2tog, k3, (k2tog, yo) x 4, k1, (yo, k2tog) x 4, k3, k2tog, yo, k2.
Row 21: (K3, yo, k2tog, k1, (k2tog, yo) x 4, k3, (yo, k2tog) x 4, k1, k2tog, yo) x 2, k3.
Row 23: K4, yo, k3tog, (yo, k2tog) x 3, yo, k5, (yo, k2tog) x 3, yo, k3tog, yo, k5, yo, k3tog, (yo, k2tog) x 3, yo, k5, (yo, k2tog) x 3, yo, k3tog, yo, k4.
Row 25: K4, (k2tog, yo) x 4, k7, (yo, k2tog) x 4, k5, (k2tog, yo) x 4, k7, (yo, k2tog) x 4, k4.
Row 27: (K3, (k2tog, yo) x 4, k1, yo, k2tog, k3, k2tog, yo, k1, (yo, k2tog) x 4) x 2, k3.
Row 29: K2, (k2tog, yo) x 4, k3, yo, k2tog, k1, k2tog, yo, k3, (yo, k2tog) x 4, k1, (k2tog, yo) x 4, k3, yo, k2tog, k1, k2tog, yo, k3, (yo, k2tog) x 4, k2.
Row 31: K1, (k2tog, yo) x 4, k5, yo, k3tog, yo, k5, (yo, k2tog) x 3, yo, k3tog, (yo, k2tog) x 3, yo, k5, yo, k3tog, yo, k5, (yo, k2tog) x 4, k1.

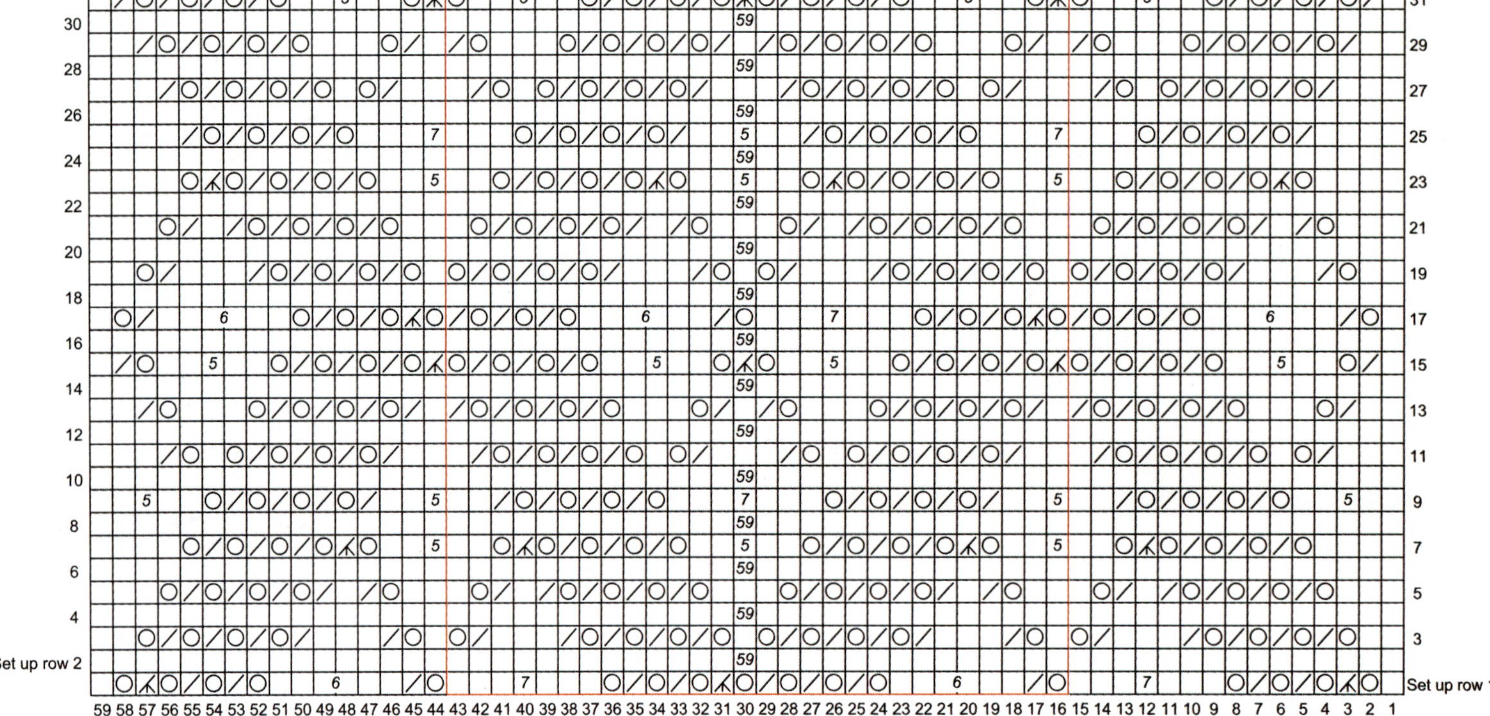

Cluster of four Diamond Drop on one side chart.

DA PRINT O' DA WAVE

The pattern most associated with Shetland fine lace knitting is Da Print o' Da Wave. It is a very old pattern, found in published pattern books as early as 1842 where it is attributed to Shetland (Gaugain, p.46, 105). It also appears in other nineteenth-century lace knitting books and in garments from other areas of Europe, so its origin as exclusively assigned to Shetland is in doubt (Carter, p.64, 170). Da Print o' Da Wave is the name given to it in Shetland, also known as Da Print an' Da Wave. It describes undulating lines found on Shetland's many sandy beaches. This name is not found elsewhere, so although the pattern may have travelled through the export of knitted pieces, its Shetland name did not. It is always worked in garter stitch in Shetland, often in stockinette stitch elsewhere.

As worked, the basic pattern appears as droplet or leaf shapes alternating on either side of a single 'stem'. They are separated by Zigzag stitch, usually of narrow width. This pattern may present an optical illusion – is it the droplets that resemble the waves in sand, or the zigzag lines?

A pattern as old and well-represented as Da Print o' Da Wave has many variations. In very general terms, the droplets tend to be narrower with sharper points the older the design is, and become more full and rounded over the nearly two centuries this pattern has been used. We have presented two patterns in the 'classic' design of droplets alternating back and forth on either side. They look quite different from each other in the way they have been knitted in the original garments. This is partly due to the yarn and subsequent gauge used.

2.10

Da Print o' Da Wave 1

TEX 2004.338 Stole

Da Print o' Da Wave 1 original pattern.

Da Print o' Da Wave 1 knitted sample.

The yarn used for this stole was hand-spun but rather crepey. The droplets are small and very rounded.

Row 1 (RS): K2, (yo, k2tog) x 2, yo, k1, k2tog, k3, k2tog, k1, yo, k1, (yo, k2tog) x 3, k2. (24 sts)

Row 2 and all WS rows: Purl.

Row 3: K3, (yo, k2tog) x 2, yo, (k1, k2tog) x 2, k1, yo, k3, (yo, k2tog) x 3, k1.

Row 5: K4, (yo, k2tog) x 2, yo, k1, k3tog, k1, yo, k5, (yo, k2tog) x 3.

Row 7: K2, (k2tog, yo) x 3, k1, yo, k1, k2tog, k3, k2tog, k1, (yo, k2tog) x 2, yo, k2.

Row 9: K1, (k2tog, yo) x 3, k3, yo, (k1, k2tog) x 2, k1, (yo, k2tog) x 2, yo, k3.

Row 11: (K2tog, yo) x 3, k5, yo, k1, k3tog, k1, (yo, k2tog) x 2, yo, k4.

Wave imprints on sand, Uyea.

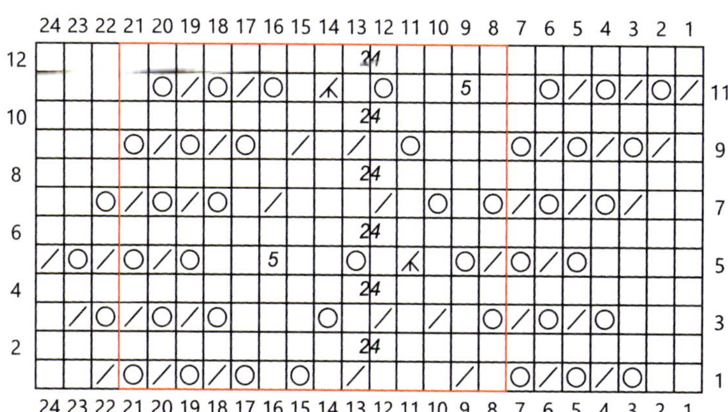

Da Print o' Da Wave 1 chart.

2.11

Da Print o' Da Wave 2

TEX 81467 Scarf

Da Print o' Da Wave 2 original pattern.

Da Print o' Da Wave 2 knitted sample.

We tend to think that all Shetland lace was made from local hand-spun wool but this was not always the case. Lace knitters also worked in silk, cotton and mohair, often for special orders. Here a narrow scarf, probably dating to the 1920s, is worked in fine silk. The droplets are narrow and sharply pointed in this variation.

Row 1 (RS): K2, ((yo, k2tog) x 3, k7, k2tog, yo, k1) x 2, (yo, k2tog) x 3, k3. (43 sts)

Row 2 and all WS rows: Knit.

Row 3: (K3, (yo, k2tog) x 3, k5, k2tog, yo) x 2, k3, (yo, k2tog) x 3, k2.

Row 5: K4, ((yo, k2tog) x 3, k3, k2tog, yo, k5) x 2, (yo, k2tog) x 3, k1.

Row 7: K5, ((yo, k2tog) x 3, k1, k2tog, yo, k7) x 2, (yo, k2tog) x 3.

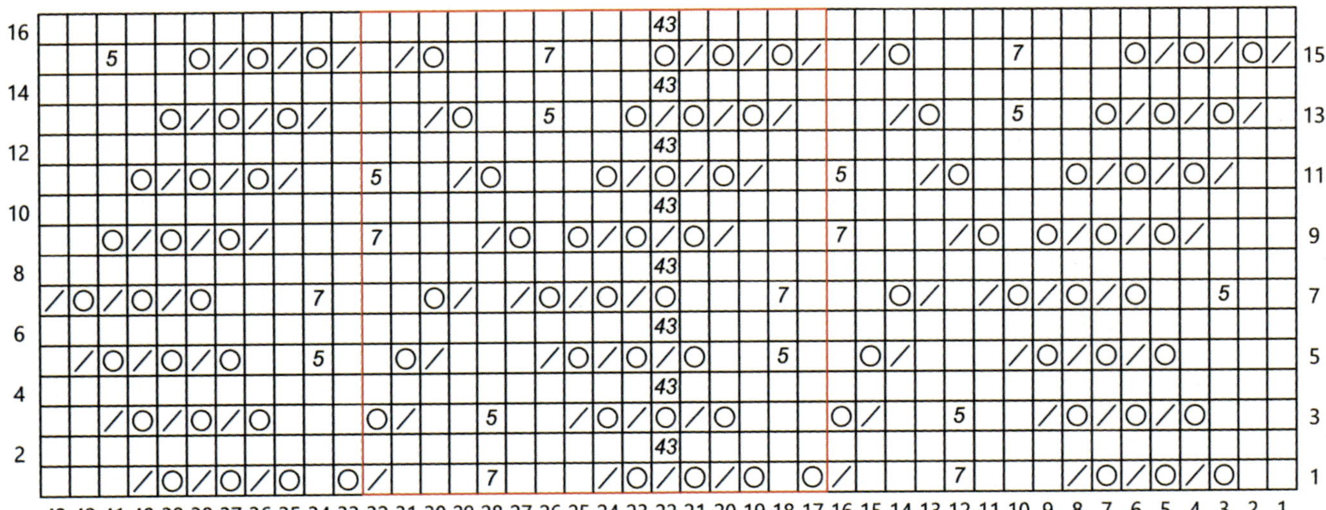

Da Print o' Da Wave 2 chart.

Row 9: K3, ((k2tog, yo) x 3, k1, yo, k2tog, k7) x 2, (k2tog, yo) x 3, k2.
Row 11: K2, ((k2tog, yo) x 3, k3, yo, k2tog, k5) x 2, (k2tog, yo) x 3, k3.
Row 13: K1, ((k2tog, yo) x 3, k5, yo, k2tog, k3) x 2, (k2tog, yo) x 3, k4.
Row 15: ((K2tog, yo) x 3, k7, yo, k2tog, k1) x 2, (k2tog, yo) x 3, k5.

DA PRINT O' DA WAVE VARIATIONS

Patterns similar to Da Print o' Da Wave occur where multiples of droplets alternate either side of a single 'stem'. It can be argued whether these really are examples of the famous pattern. This type has been referred to elsewhere as the 'Elaborated Print of the Wave' (Miller, p.103–104).

2.12

Da Print o' Da Wave 3
TEX 2019.39 Stole

The stole was made in Unst in the second half of the twentieth century for the Tulloch knitwear firm in Lerwick. The yarn is hand-spun with a hard twist, giving the stole a delicate, drapey feel. Here the droplets are small and clustered in twos along a 'stem'.

Da Print o' Da Wave 3 original pattern.

Da Print o' Da Wave 3 knitted sample.

Set up row 1 (RS): K1, (k2tog, yo) x 3, k5, yo, k3tog, (yo, k2tog) x 2, yo, k5, yo, k2tog, k1. (27 sts)
Set up row 2 and all WS rows: Knit.
Row 3: (K2tog, yo, k1, (yo, k2tog) x 3, k3) x 2, k2tog, yo, k1.
Row 5: K4, (yo, k2tog) x 3, k1, k2tog, yo, k3, (yo, k2tog) x 3, k1, k2tog, yo, k2.
Row 7: (K5, (yo, k2tog) x 2, yo, k3tog, yo) x 2, k3.
Row 9: (K3, k2tog, yo, k1, (yo, k2tog) x 3) x 2, k3.
Row 11: K2, k2tog, yo, k3, (yo, k2tog) x 3, k1, k2tog, yo, k3, (yo, k2tog) x 3, k2.
Row 13: K1, k2tog, yo, k5, (yo, k2tog) x 2, yo, k3tog, yo, k5, (yo, k2tog) x 3, k1.
Row 15: (K1, yo, k2tog, k3, (k2tog, yo) x 3) x 2, k3.
Row 17: K2, yo, k2tog, k1, (k2tog, yo) x 3, k3, yo, k2tog, k1, (k2tog, yo) x 3, k4.
Row 19: K3, (yo, k3tog, (yo, k2tog) x 2, yo, k5) x 2.
Row 21: (K3, (k2tog, yo) x 3, k1, yo, k2tog) x 2, k3.
Row 23: K2, (k2tog, yo) x 3, k3, yo, k2tog, k1, (k2tog, yo) x 3, k3, yo, k2tog, k2.
Row 25: Repeat set up row 1.

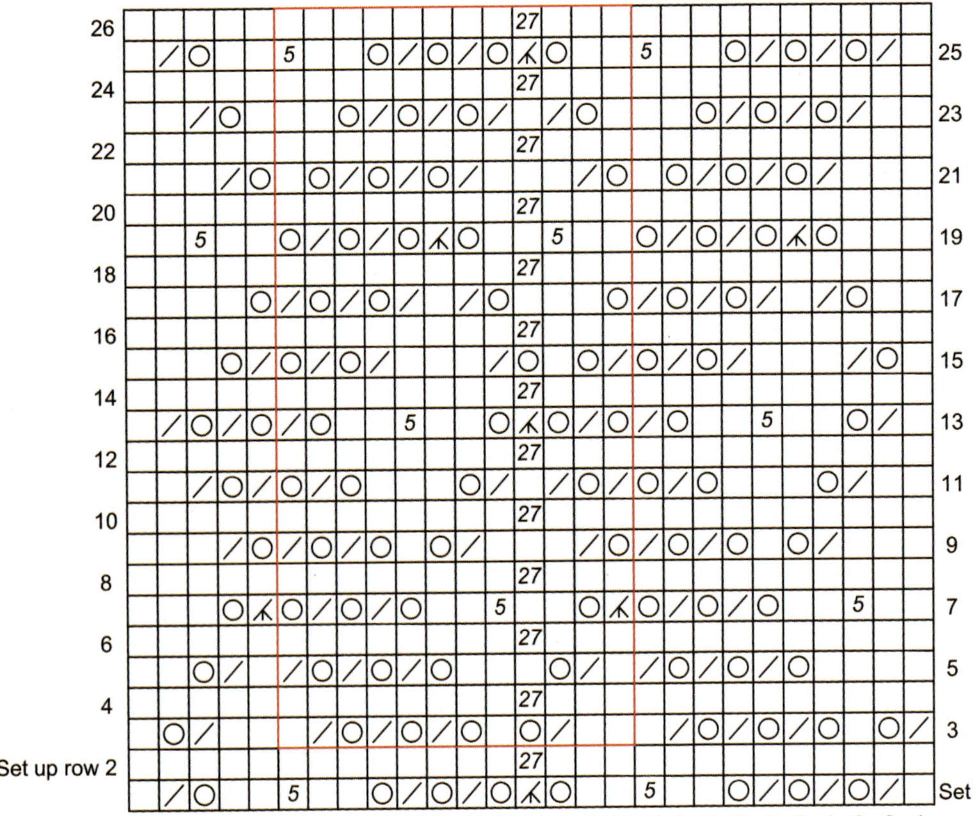

Da Print o' Da Wave 3 chart.

2.13

Da Print o' Da Wave 4

TEX 2017.131 Stole

Da Print o' Da Wave 4 original pattern.

Da Print o' Da Wave 4 knitted sample.

To the eye, this pattern resembles a petite, delicate Da Print o' Da Wave. It has waving 'stems' with three small droplet shapes hanging down from either side, alternating with columns of Zigzag. In reality, this pattern is simply 'pinches' of k3tog between the Zigzag columns. The original stole has an extra yarn over in each Zigzag column, requiring the droplet

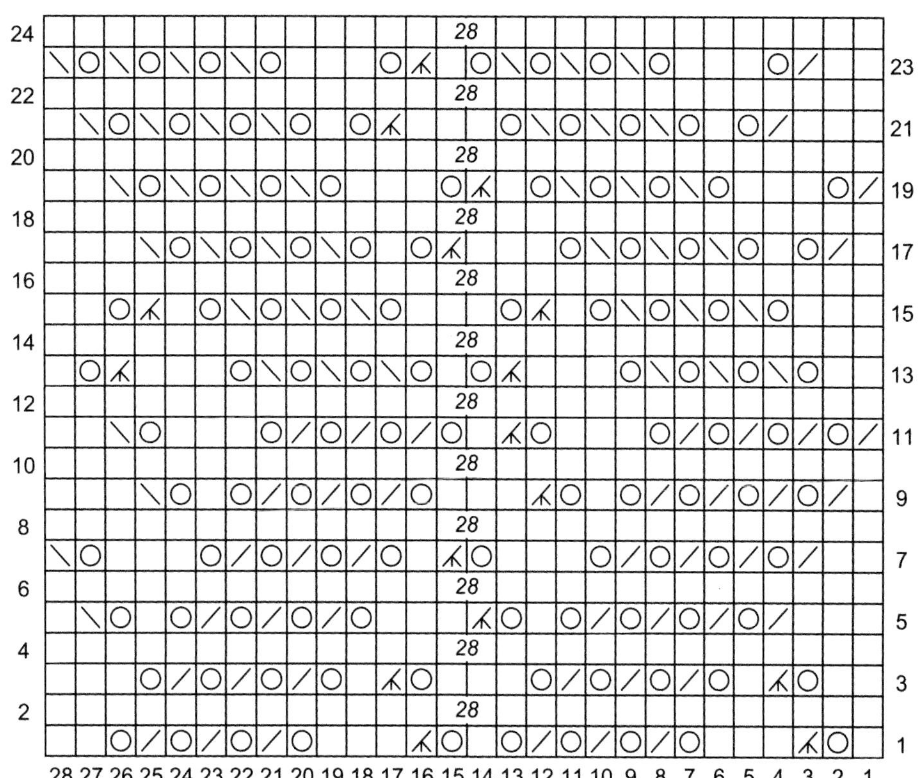

Da Print o' Da Wave 4 chart.

always to be formed by a yarn over paired with a k3tog. This makes for a cumbersome pattern repeat. We have amended the original slightly by adding a k2tog in some Zigzag rows and replacing the yo, k3tog of the droplet with a yo, k2tog in those rows, to allow for a straightforward pattern repeat.

Row 1 (RS): (K1, yo, k3tog, k3, (yo, k2tog) x 3, yo) x 2, k2. (28 sts)
Row 2 and all WS rows: Knit.
Row 3: K2, (yo, k3tog, k1, (yo, k2tog) x 3, yo, k3) x 2.
Row 5: K3, (k2tog, yo) x 4, k1, yo, k3tog, k3, (yo, k2tog) x 3, yo, k1, yo, ssk, k1.
Row 7: K2, (k2tog, yo) x 4, k3, yo, k3tog, k1, (yo, k2tog) x 3, yo, k3, yo, ssk.
Row 9: K1, (k2tog, yo) x 4, k1, yo, k3tog, k3, (yo, k2tog) x 3, yo, k1, yo, ssk, k3.
Row 11: (K2tog, yo) x 4, k3, yo, k3tog, k1, (yo, k2tog) x 3, yo, k3, yo, ssk, k2.
Row 13: K2, ((yo, ssk) x 3, yo, k3, k3tog, yo, k1) x 2.
Row 15: (K3, (yo, ssk) x 3, yo, k1, k3tog, yo) x 2, k2.
Row 17: K1, k2tog, yo, k1, (yo, ssk) x 3, yo, k3, k3tog, yo, k1, (yo, ssk) x 4, k3.
Row 19: K2tog, yo, k3, (yo, ssk) x 3, yo, k1, k3tog, yo, k3, (yo, ssk) x 4, k2.
Row 21: K3, k2tog, yo, k1, (yo, ssk) x 3, yo, k3, k3tog, yo, k1, (yo, ssk) x 4, k1.
Row 23: K2, k2tog, yo, k3, (yo, ssk) x 3, yo, k1, k3tog, yo, k3, (yo, ssk) x 4.

WORKING WITH PATTERN REPEATS ARRANGED VERTICALLY

People sometimes ask if Shetland's lace knitters were always exacting, their designs and workmanship perfect. 'No' is the answer. There was a wide range of skills and abilities among those who knitted Shetland lace in the past. The most photographed and copied traditional Shetland lace is often the highest quality of the craft, but it represents a small proportion of the vast quantity of Shetland lace made in the last two centuries.

Like most Shetland knitting, fine lace was made as efficiently as possible within the demanding design techniques.

Less-skilled lace knitters and those who concentrated their efforts on simpler garments such as veils, traded their knitting to a merchant for food and household goods. Garments that the merchant considered unsellable were rejected and taken back home by the knitter. Some of these pieces undoubtedly found their way into Shetland Museum's collection simply because they never left the islands. They represent varying degrees of spinning, design and knitting skills from which valuable information can be gleaned about the difficulties and pitfalls of designing and making Shetland lace. By studying these pieces, even the less skilled knitters of the past have important things to teach us.

Presented here are a few patterns using Zigzags where design has not been worked in an exacting way and where pattern repeats do not always match up.

2.14

Zigzag, Steeks and Ovals
TEX 8934 Scarf

Zigzag, Steeks and Ovals original pattern.

This scarf illustrates clearly how even an accomplished lace knitter was not always exacting in design creation. The centre of the scarf alternates an Oval pattern with Zigzags, separated by single Steeks. The Oval motif is almost heart-shaped, somewhat similar to Cat's Paw but more elongated. What makes this Oval pattern interesting is how at the narrowest point the k2tog on either side of the yo alternates at every other

Zigzag, Steeks and Ovals knitted sample.

Oval in vertical succession. This gives the pattern a subtle but sophisticated snaking effect that complements the back and forth movement of the two Zigzags with which it alternates.

The Zigzags are not the same, however. One has a 10-row repeat, the other a 14-row repeat, whereas the Oval pattern has a 22-row repeat, or 11 rows high at each narrow point. Does it matter? This piece is still interesting, beautiful and well-knitted. If it were to be corrected so that the two patterns had the same row repeat, the Zigzags would have to be 22 rows high, which would give them so much prominence it would create a visual imbalance to the centre of this small scarf. Here the Oval pattern and 10-row Zigzag repeat charts are presented for those who wish to try the 'mistake' pattern or consider ways this pattern combination can be worked to an exacting visual standard, perhaps using a different gauge yarn or garment type.

Row 1 (RS): K17, (k2tog, yo) x 3, k5. (28 sts)
Row 2 (WS): K6, (yo, k2tog) x 3, k1, k2tog, yo, k5, yo, k2tog, k3, k2tog, yo, k1.
Row 3: K18, (yo, k2tog) x 3, k4.
Row 4: K3, (k2tog, yo) x 3, k4, k2tog, yo, k3, k2tog, yo, k1, yo, k2tog, k2, k2tog, yo, k1.
Row 5: K20, (yo, k2tog) x 3, k2.
Row 6: K1, (k2tog, yo) x 3, k6, k2tog, yo, k2, k2tog, yo, k3, yo, k2tog, k1, k2tog, yo, k1.
Row 7: K22, (yo, k2tog) x 3.
Row 8: K2, (yo, k2tog) x 3, k5, k2tog, yo, k1, k2tog, yo, k5, yo, k2tog x 2, yo, k1.
Row 9: K19, (k2tog, yo) x 3, k3.
Row 10: K4, (yo, k2tog) x 3, k3, k2tog, yo, k3, yo, k1, k3tog, k1, yo, k2, k2tog, yo, k1.
Row 11: K6, yo, k3tog, yo, k8, (k2tog, yo) x 3, k5.

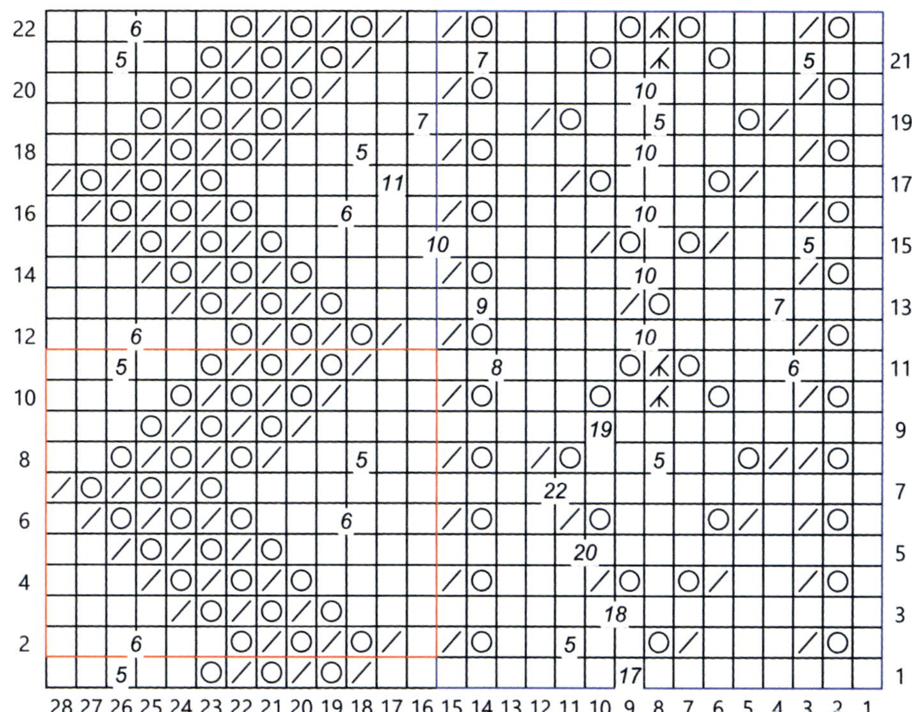

Zigzag, Steeks and Ovals chart.

Row 12: K6, (yo, k2tog) x 3, k1, k2tog, yo, k10, k2tog, yo, k1.

Row 13: K7, yo, k2tog, k9, (yo, k2tog) x 3, k4.

Row 14: K3, (k2tog, yo) x 3, k4, k2tog, yo, k10, k2tog, yo, k1.

Row 15: K5, k2tog, yo, k1, yo, k2tog, k10, (yo, k2tog) x 3, k2.

Row 16: K1, (k2tog, yo) x 3, k6, k2tog, yo, k10, k2tog, yo, k1.

Row 17: K4, k2tog, yo, k3, yo, k2tog, k11, (yo, k2tog) x 3.

Row 18: K2, (yo, k2tog) x 3, k5, k2tog, yo, k10, k2tog, yo, k1.

Row 19: K3, k2tog, yo, k5, yo, k2tog, k7, (k2tog, yo) x 3, k3.

Row 20: K4, (yo, k2tog) x 3, k3, k2tog, yo, k10, k2tog, yo, k1.

Row 21: K5, yo, k1, k3tog, k1, yo, k7, (k2tog, yo) x 3, k5.

Row 22: K6, (yo, k2tog) x 3, k1, k2tog, yo, k4, yo, k3tog, yo, k3, k2tog, yo, k1.

2.15

Zigzag with four Diamonds, Print o' Da Wave variation and Lattice of Peerie Fleas

TEX 2012.428b Stole

This unusual stole is probably very early, possibly dating to the mid-nineteenth century. It combines a five-hole wide Zigzag, Diamonds with four different infills repeated vertically, a narrow three-hole Zigzag with branching points in the form of a half Da Print o' Da Wave pattern, and a pretty diamond lattice of Peerie Fleas in the centre.

We studied this piece because of its unusual use and placement of classic Shetland lace patterns, but this design is not without its problems. Like the example above, the five-hole Zigzag on the outside edges of the centre panel has row repeats that are not the same as the Diamond row repeat with which it is paired. The Zigzag turns direction every ninth row, or an 18-row repeat, whereas the individual Diamonds are worked in a 16-row repeat. Because of this, the points of the Zigzag do not consistently meet the Diamonds in the same place.

Although the knitter began with the points of the Zigzag centred at the indents of the Diamonds, this arrangement gradually collapsed. By the seventh Diamond in the column, the points of the Diamonds and Zigzags are facing each other. By the twelfth Diamond, the Zigzag placement fits nicely again with the Diamonds.

Zigzag with four Diamonds, Print o' Da Wave variation and lattice of Peerie Fleas original pattern.

We have corrected this pattern by reducing the Zigzag repeat by two rows. Here we have presented the pattern with the points of the Zigzag meeting the points of the Diamonds. This can be altered so that the points of the Zigzag tuck into the narrow area where the Diamonds meet. In addition, we have included a separate chart of the of the unusual Print o' Da Wave variation used in this scarf and the pretty lattice diamond formed from the classic Shetland pattern, Da Peerie Flea.

2.15a

Zigzag with four Diamonds section
TEX 2012.428b Stole

Row 1 (RS): K1, (k2tog, yo) x 5, k30. (41 sts)
Row 2 (WS): K8, k2tog, yo, k1, yo, k2tog, k15, (k2tog, yo) x 5, k3.
Row 3: K4, (yo, k2tog) x 5, k13, k2tog, yo, k3, yo, k2tog, k7.
Row 4: K6, k2tog, yo, k5, yo, k2tog, k11, (k2tog, yo) x 5, k5.
Row 5: K6, (yo, k2tog) x 5, k9, (k2tog, yo, k1) x 2, yo, k2tog, k1, yo, k2tog, k5.
Row 6: K4, k2tog, yo, k1, k2tog, yo, k3, yo, k2tog, k1, yo, k2tog, k7, (k2tog, yo) x 5, k7.
Row 7: K8, (yo, k2tog) x 5, k5, k2tog, yo, k1, k2tog, yo, k5, yo, k2tog, k1, yo, k2tog, k3.
Row 8: K2, k2tog, yo, k1, k2tog, yo, k7, yo, k2tog, k1, yo, k2tog, k3, (k2tog, yo) x 5, k9.
Row 9: K10, (yo, k2tog) x 5, (k1, k2tog, yo) x 2, k9, (yo, k2tog, k1) x 2.
Row 10: K3, yo, k2tog, k1, yo, k2tog, k5, k2tog, yo, k1, k2tog, yo, k5, (yo, k2tog) x 5, k8.
Row 11: K7, (k2tog, yo) x 5, k7, yo, k2tog, k1, yo, k2tog, k3, k2tog, yo, k1, k2tog, yo, k4.
Row 12: K5, (yo, k2tog, k1) x 2, k2tog, yo, k1, k2tog, yo, k9, (yo, k2tog) x 5, k6.
Row 13: K5, (k2tog, yo) x 5, k11, yo, k2tog, k1, yo, k3tog, yo, k1, k2tog, yo, k6.
Row 14: K7, yo, k2tog, k3, k2tog, yo, k13, (yo, k2tog) x 5, k4.
Row 15: K3, (k2tog, yo) x 5, k15, yo, k2tog, k1, k2tog, yo, k8.
Row 16: K9, yo, p3tog, yo, k17, (yo, k2tog) x 5, k2.
Row 17: Repeat row 1.
Row 18: Repeat row 2.
Row 19: Repeat row 3.
Row 20: Repeat row 4.
Row 21: K6, (yo, k2tog) x 5, k9, k2tog, yo, k7, yo, k2tog, k5.
Row 22: K4, k2tog, yo, k9, yo, k2tog, k7, (k2tog, yo) x 5, k7.
Row 23: K8, (yo, k2tog) x 5, k5, k2tog, yo, k11, yo, k2tog, k3.
Row 24: K2, k2tog, yo, k13, yo, k2tog, k3, (k2tog, yo) x 5, k9.
Row 25: K10, (yo, k2tog) x 5, k1, k2tog, yo, k15, yo, k2tog, k1.
Row 26: K3, yo, k2tog, k11, k2tog, yo, k5, (yo, k2tog) x 5, k8.
Row 27: K7, (k2tog, yo) x 5, k7, yo, k2tog, k9, k2tog, yo, k4.
Row 28: K5, yo, k2tog, k7, k2tog, yo, k9, (yo, k2tog) x 5, k6.
Row 29: K5, (k2tog, yo) x 5, k11, yo, k2tog, k5, k2tog, yo, k6.

Zigzag with four Diamonds section original pattern.

Row 30: Repeat row 14.
Row 31: Repeat row 15.
Row 32: Repeat row 16.
Row 33: Repeat row 1.
Row 34: Repeat row 2.
Row 35: Repeat row 3.
Row 36: Repeat row 4.
Row 37: K6, (yo, k2tog) x 5, k9, k2tog, yo, k2, k2tog, yo twice, k2tog, k2, yo, k2tog, k5. (42 sts)
Row 38: K4, k2tog, yo, k4, knit, purl into yarnovers, k4, yo, k2tog, k7, (k2tog, yo) x 5, k7.
Row 39: K8, (yo, k2tog) x 5, k5, k2tog, yo, k2, k2tog, yo x 2, k2tog twice, yo x 2, k2tog, k2, yo, k2tog, k3.
Row 40: K2, k2tog, yo, k4, p1, k1, knit 2, p1, k5, yo, k2tog, k3, (k2tog, yo) x 5, k9.
Row 41: K10, (yo, k2tog) x 5, k1, k2tog, yo, k2, k2tog, yo x 2, k2tog x 2, yo twice, k2tog x 2, yo x 2, k2tog, k2, yo, k2tog, k1.

Zigzag with four Diamonds section knitted sample.

Row 42: K3, yo, k2tog, k1, p1, k3, knit, purl into yarnovers, k2, p1, k2, k2tog, yo, k5, (yo, k2tog) x 5, k8.
Row 43: K7, (k2tog, yo) x 5, k7, yo, k2tog, k1, k2tog, yo x 2, k2tog twice, yo x 2, k2tog, k1, k2tog, yo, k4.
Row 44: K5, yo, k2tog, k1, p1, k1, knit 2, p1, k2, k2tog, yo, k9, (yo, k2tog) x 5, k6.
Row 45: K5, (k2tog, yo) x 5, k11, yo, k2tog, k1, k2tog, yo twice, k2tog, k1, k2tog, yo, k6.
Row 46: K7, yo, k2tog, k1, knit, purl into yarnovers, k1, k2tog, yo, k13, (yo, k2tog) x 5, k4.
Row 47: K3, (k2tog, yo) x 5, k15, yo, k2tog x 3, yo, k8. (41 sts)
Row 48: Repeat row 16.
Row 49: Repeat row 1.
Row 50: Repeat row 2.
Row 51: Repeat row 3.
Row 52: Repeat row 4.
Row 53: Repeat row 5.
Row 54: K4, k2tog, yo, k2, k2tog, yo, k1, yo, k2tog, k2, yo, k2tog, k7, (k2tog, yo) x 5, k7.
Row 55: K8, (yo, k2tog) x 5, k5, k2tog, yo, k3, k2tog, yo, k1, (yo, k2tog, k3) x 2.

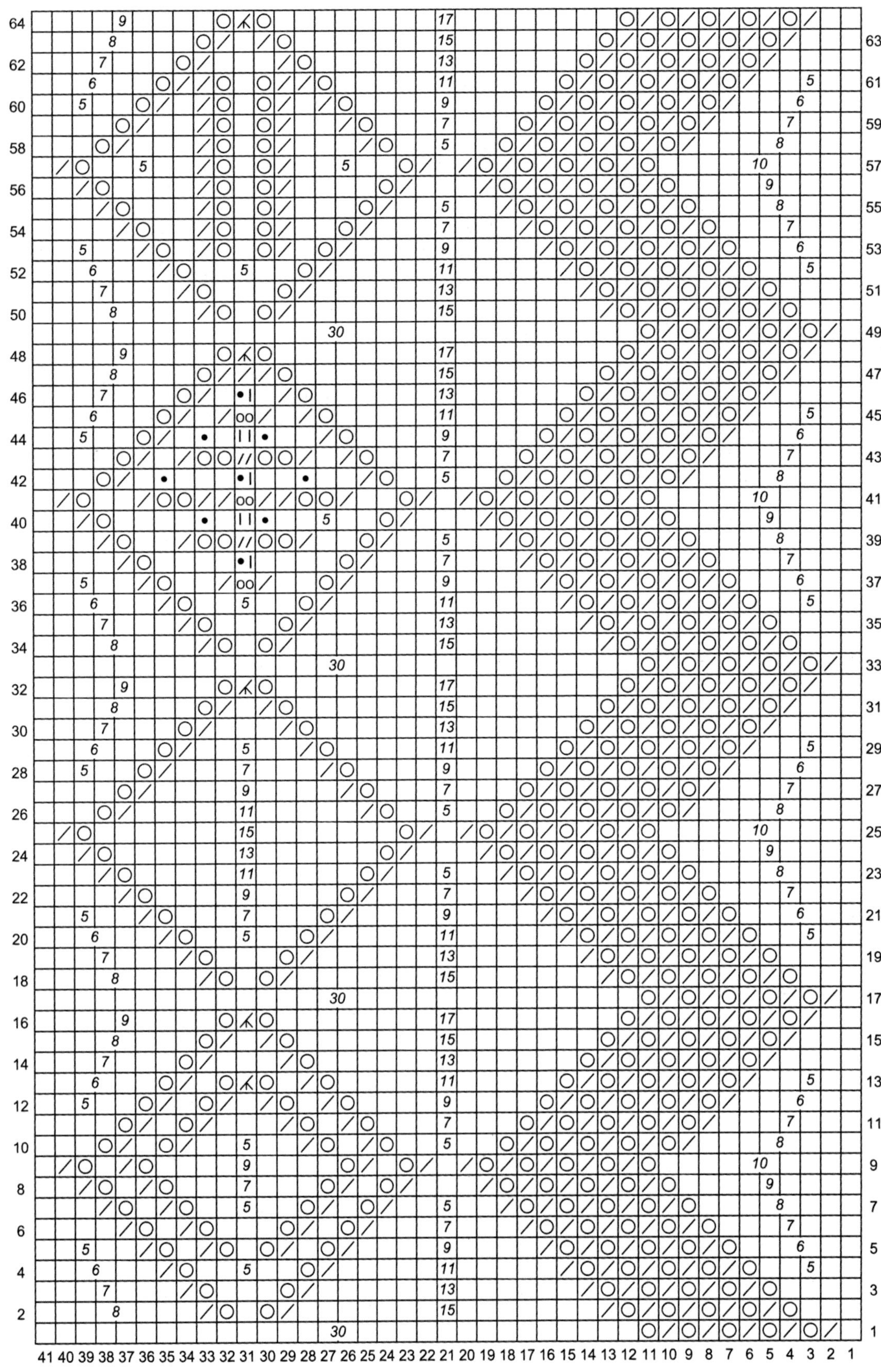

Zigzag with four Diamonds section chart.

Row 56: K2, k2tog, yo, k4, k2tog, yo, k1, yo, k2tog, k4, yo, k2tog, k3, (k2tog, yo) x 5, k9.
Row 57: K10, (yo, k2tog) x 5, k1, k2tog, yo, k5, k2tog, yo, k1, yo, k2tog, k5, yo, k2tog, k1.
Row 58: K3, yo, k2tog, k3, k2tog, yo, k1, yo, k2tog, k3, k2tog, yo, k5, (yo, k2tog) x 5, k8.
Row 59: K7, (k2tog, yo) x 5, k7, yo, k2tog, k2, k2tog, yo, k1, yo, k2tog, k2, k2tog, yo, k4.
Row 60: K5, yo, k2tog, k1, k2tog, yo, k1, yo, k2tog, k1, k2tog, yo, k9, (yo, k2tog) x 5, k6.
Row 61: K5, (k2tog, yo) x 5, k11, yo, k2tog x 2, yo, k1, yo, k2tog x 2, yo, k6.
Row 62: Repeat row 14.
Row 63: Repeat row 15.
Row 64: Repeat row 16.

2.15b

Print o' Da Wave variation and Lattice of Peerie Fleas
TEX 2012.428b

Print o' Da Wave variation and lattice of Peerie Fleas original pattern.

Row 1 (RS): K7, k2tog, k1, (yo, k2tog) x 2, yo, k3, yo, k1, k2tog, k17, k2tog, yo, k1, yo, k2tog, k17, k2tog, k1, yo, k3, (yo, k2tog) x 2, yo, k1, k2tog, k7. (79 sts)
Row 2 (WS): K36, k2tog, yo, k3, yo, k2tog, k36.
Row 3: K6, k2tog, k1, (yo, k2tog) x 2, yo, k5, yo, k1, k2tog, k17, yo, k3tog, yo, k17, k2tog, k1, yo, k5, (yo, k2tog) x 2, yo, k1, k2tog, k6.
Row 4: Knit.
Row 5: K5, k2tog, k1, (yo, k2tog) x 2, (yo, k1) x 2, k2tog, k16, k2tog, yo, k1, yo, k2tog, k5, k2tog, yo, k1, yo, k2tog, k16, k2tog, (k1, yo) x 2, (k2tog, yo) x 2, k1, k2tog, k5.
Row 6: K31, k2tog, yo, k3, yo, k2tog, k3, k2tog, yo, k3, yo, k2tog, k31.
Row 7: K4, k2tog, k1, (yo, k2tog) x 2, yo, k3, yo, k1, k2tog, k16, yo, k3tog, yo, k7, yo, k3tog, yo, k16, k2tog, k1, yo, k3, (yo, k2tog) x 2, yo, k1, k2tog, k4.
Row 8: Knit.
Row 9: K3, k2tog, k1, (yo, k2tog) x 2, yo, k5, yo, k1, k2tog, k9, k2tog, yo, k1, yo, k2tog, k15, k2tog, yo, k1, yo, k2tog, k9, k2tog, k1, yo, k5, (yo, k2tog) x 2, yo, k1, k2tog, k3.
Row 10: K26, k2tog, yo, k3, yo, k2tog, k13, k2tog, yo, k3, yo, k2tog, k26.
Row 11: K2, k2tog, (k1, yo) x 2, (k2tog, yo) x 2, k1, k2tog, k15, yo, k3tog, yo, k17, yo, k3tog, yo, k15, k2tog, k1, (yo, k2tog) x 2, (yo, k1) x 2, k2tog, k2.
Row 12: Knit.
Row 13: K1, k2tog, k1, yo, k3, (yo, k2tog) x 2, yo, k1, k2tog, k8, k2tog, yo, k1, yo, k2tog, k25, k2tog, yo, k1, yo, k2tog, k8, k2tog, k1, (yo, k2tog) x 2, yo, k3, yo, k1, k2tog, k1.
Row 14: K21, k2tog, yo, k3, yo, k2tog, k23, k2tog, yo, k3, yo, k2tog, k21.
Row 15: K2tog, k1, yo, k5, (yo, k2tog) x 2, yo, k1, k2tog, k8, yo, k3tog, yo, k27, yo, k3tog, yo, k8, k2tog, k1, (yo, k2tog) x 2, yo, k5, yo, k1, k2tog.
Row 16: Knit.
Row 17: K5, k2tog, (k1, yo) x 2, (k2tog, yo) x 2, k1, k2tog, k11, k2tog, yo, k1, yo, k2tog, k15, k2tog, yo, k1, yo, k2tog, k11, k2tog, k1, (yo, k2tog) x 2, (yo, k1) x 2, k2tog, k5.
Row 18: Repeat row 10.
Row 19: K4, k2tog, k1, yo, k3, (yo, k2tog) x 2, yo, k1, k2tog, k11, yo, k3tog, yo, k17, yo, k3tog, yo, k11, k2tog, k1, (yo, k2tog) x 2, yo, k3, yo, k1, k2tog, k4.
Row 20: Knit.
Row 21: K3, k2tog, k1, yo, k5, (yo, k2tog) x 2, yo, k1, k2tog, k14, k2tog, yo, k1, yo, k2tog, k5, k2tog, yo, k1, yo, k2tog, k14, k2tog, k1, (yo, k2tog) x 2, yo, k5, yo, k1, k2tog, k3.
Row 22: Repeat row 6.

Print o' Da Wave variation and lattice of Peerie Fleas knitted sample.

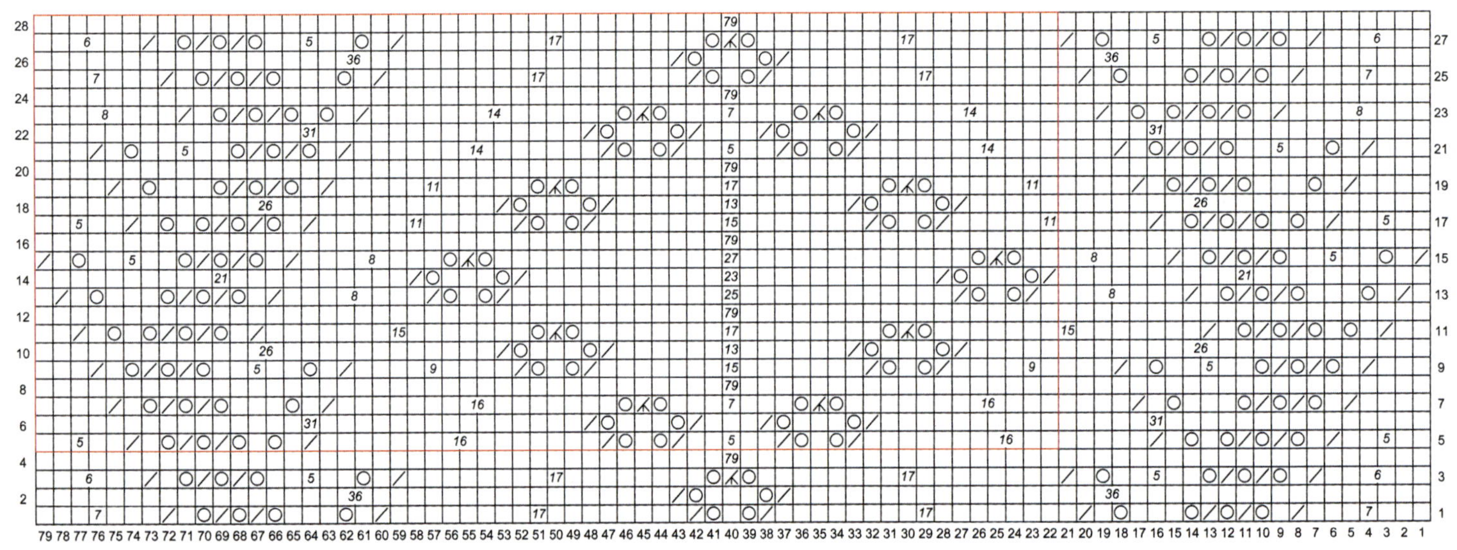

Print o' Da Wave variation and lattice of Peerie Fleas chart.

Row 23: K8, k2tog, k1, (yo, k2tog) x 2, (yo, k1) x 2, k2tog, k14, yo, k3tog, yo, k7, yo, k3tog, yo, k14, k2tog, (k1, yo) x 2, (k2tog, yo) x 2, k1, k2tog, k8.

Row 24: Knit.

Row 25: Repeat row 1.

Row 26: Repeat row 2.

Row 27: Repeat row 3.

Row 28: Knit.

Spindrift on the tops of waves.

CHAPTER 3

COMPLEX CENTRE PATTERNS

While vertical centre patterns usually have a few patterns repeated over and again, they can often be identified individually. In complex centre patterns, there can be many patterns placed in ways so they flow in and out of each other. In some cases they are placed so closely together that they appear as a new, single pattern. It can be difficult for the eye to identify the limits of each individual motif, as the motifs are 'blended' and 'tucked' together by the knitter. They form intricate and delicate fabrics that are used as centres or as individual motifs in borders.

One type of complex centre pattern is known as the Puzzle. There are many variations of the Puzzle and some discussion across Shetland of what individual patterns are included in a Puzzle pattern. It usually contains Trees and Branches, sometimes placed end-to-end to form a Spider Web pattern, but often separated with other patterns such as a Hexagon. These are combined with other patterns such as small Diamonds of different patterns, Plain, Lace Hole, and so on. Patterns 3.6 and 3.7 in this chapter are two examples of Puzzle variations. The Puzzle is always a centre pattern, primarily found in shawls, and was worked by the more skilled lace knitter.

Patterns at low tide.

Stacked lobster pots.

3.1

Hexagons and Diamonds of Lace Holes
TEX 2013.39 Shawl

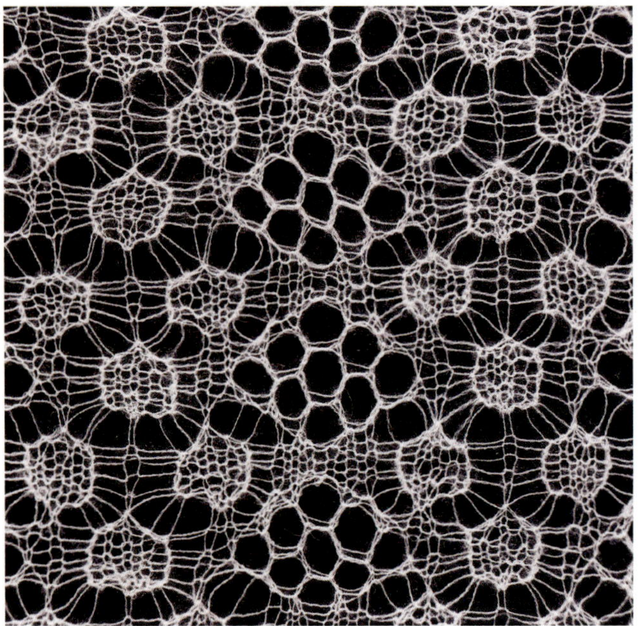

Hexagons and Diamonds of Lace Holes original pattern.

This is the centre pattern of Jeannie Mann's 'Wedding Ring' shawl (*see* Pattern 7.9). It is really a vertical centre pattern but is included here because of the way she juxtaposed the patterns to create an overall fabric design that does not appear vertical. The Hexagons in this pattern look like squares and the openwork around them accentuates this look. They are broken up by Lace Hole Diamonds, giving this shawl centre a geometric look, which is unusual in Shetland lace.

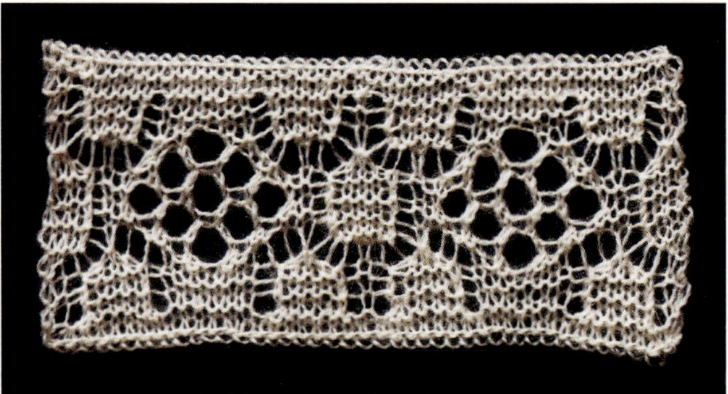

Hexagons and Diamonds of Lace Holes knitted sample.

Rows 1–4: (K1, yo, k2tog, k3, k2tog, yo, k6, yo, k2tog, k3, k2tog, yo) x 2, k1. (43 sts)
Row 5: K2, yo, k2tog, k1, k2tog, yo, k2, k2tog, yo x 2, k2tog, k2, yo, k2tog, k1, k2tog, yo, k3, yo, k2tog, k1, k2tog, yo, k2, k2tog, yo x 2, k2tog, k2, yo, k2tog, k1, k2tog, yo, k2.
Row 6: K3, yo, p3tog, yo, k4, p1, (k5, yo, p3tog, yo) x 2, k4, p1, k5, yo, p3tog, yo, k3.
Row 7: K2, k2tog, yo, k3, k2tog, yo x 2, k2tog x 2, yo x 2, k2tog, k3, yo, k2tog, k3, k2tog, yo, k3, k2tog, yo x 2, k2tog x 2, yo x 2, k2tog, k3, yo, k2tog, k2.
Row 8: K2, k2tog, yo, k4, p1, k3, p1, k5, yo, k2tog, k3, k2tog, yo, k4, p1, k3, p1, k5, yo, k2tog, k2.

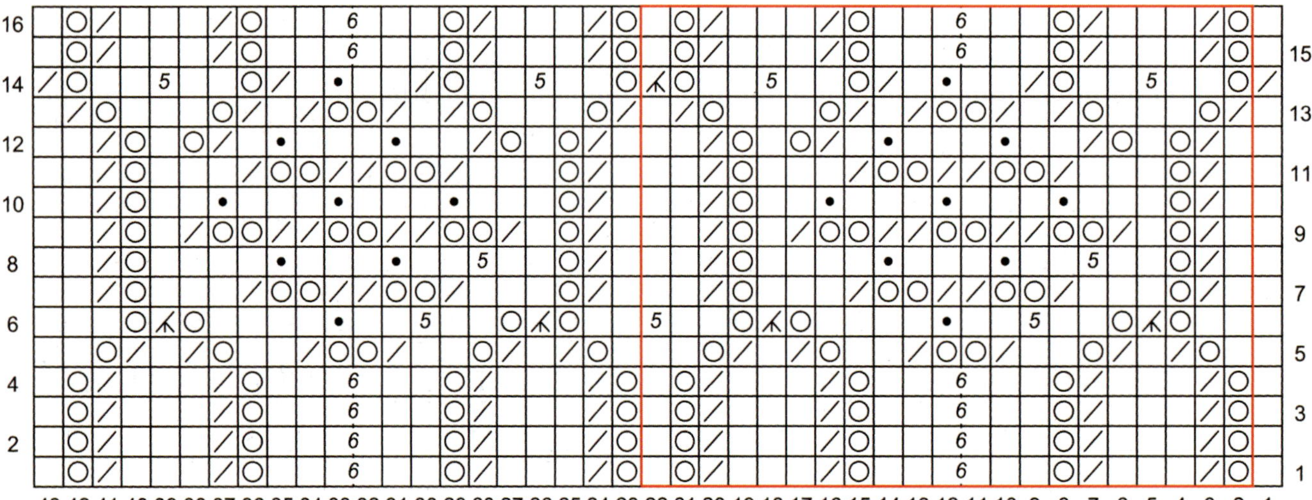

Hexagons and Diamonds of Lace Holes chart.

Row 9: K2, k2tog, yo, k1, k2tog, (yo x 2, k2tog x 2) x 2, yo x 2, k2tog, k1, yo, k2tog, k3, k2tog, yo, k1, k2tog, (yo x 2, k2tog x 2) x 2, yo x 2, k2tog, k1, yo, k2tog, k2.
Row 10: K2, k2tog, yo, k2, (p1, k3) x 3, yo, k2tog, k3, k2tog, yo, k2, (p1, k3) x 3, yo, k2tog, k2.
Row 11: Repeat row 7.
Row 12: K2, k2tog, yo, k1, yo, k2tog, k1, p1, k3, p1, k2, k2tog, yo, k1, yo, k2tog, k3, k2tog, yo, k1, yo, k2tog, k1, p1, k3, p1, k2, k2tog, yo, k1, yo, k2tog, k2.
Row 13: (K1, k2tog, yo, k3, yo, k2tog, k1, k2tog, yo x 2, k2tog, k1, k2tog, yo, k3, yo, k2tog) x 2, k1.
Row 14: K2tog, yo, k5, yo, k2tog, k1, p1, k2, k2tog, yo, k5, yo, p3tog, yo, k5, yo, k2tog, k1, p1, k2, k2tog, yo, k5, yo, k2tog.
Rows 15–16: (K1, yo, k2tog, k3, k2tog, yo, k6, yo, k2tog, k3, k2tog, yo) x 2, k1.

3.2

Branches, Bead and Plain Diamonds

TEX 2004.364 Shawl

Branches, Bead and Plain Diamonds original pattern.

A quite simple pattern of three different motifs that when placed together look complex.

Row 1 (RS): (K1, yo, k2tog, k7, k2tog, yo) x 2, k1. (25 sts)
Row 2 (WS): K2, yo, k2tog, k5, k2tog, yo, k3, yo, k2tog, k5, k2tog, yo, k2.
Row 3: K3, yo, k2tog, k3, k2tog, yo, k5, yo, k2tog, k3, k2tog, yo, k3.
Row 4: K4, yo, k2tog, k1, k2tog, yo, k7, yo, k2tog, k1, k2tog, yo, k4.
Row 5: K5, yo, k3tog, yo, k9, yo, k3tog, yo, k5.

Branches, Bead and Plain Diamonds knitted sample.

Rows 6–7: Knit.
Row 8: K2tog, yo, k9, k2tog, yo, k10, k2tog, yo.
Row 9: Knit.
Row 10: K2tog, yo, k9, yo, p3tog, yo, k9, yo, k2tog.
Row 11: (K1, k2tog, yo, k7, yo, k2tog) x 2, k1.
Row 12: (K2tog, yo) x 2, k5, yo, k2tog, yo, p3tog, yo, k2tog, yo, k5, (yo, k2tog) x 2.
Row 13: (K1, (k2tog, yo) x 2, k3, (yo, k2tog) x 2) x 2, k1.
Row 14: Repeat row 12.
Row 15: Repeat row 11.
Row 16: Repeat row 10.
Rows 17–18: Knit.
Row 19: K4, k2tog, yo, k1, yo, k2tog, k7, k2tog, yo, k1, yo, k2tog, k4.

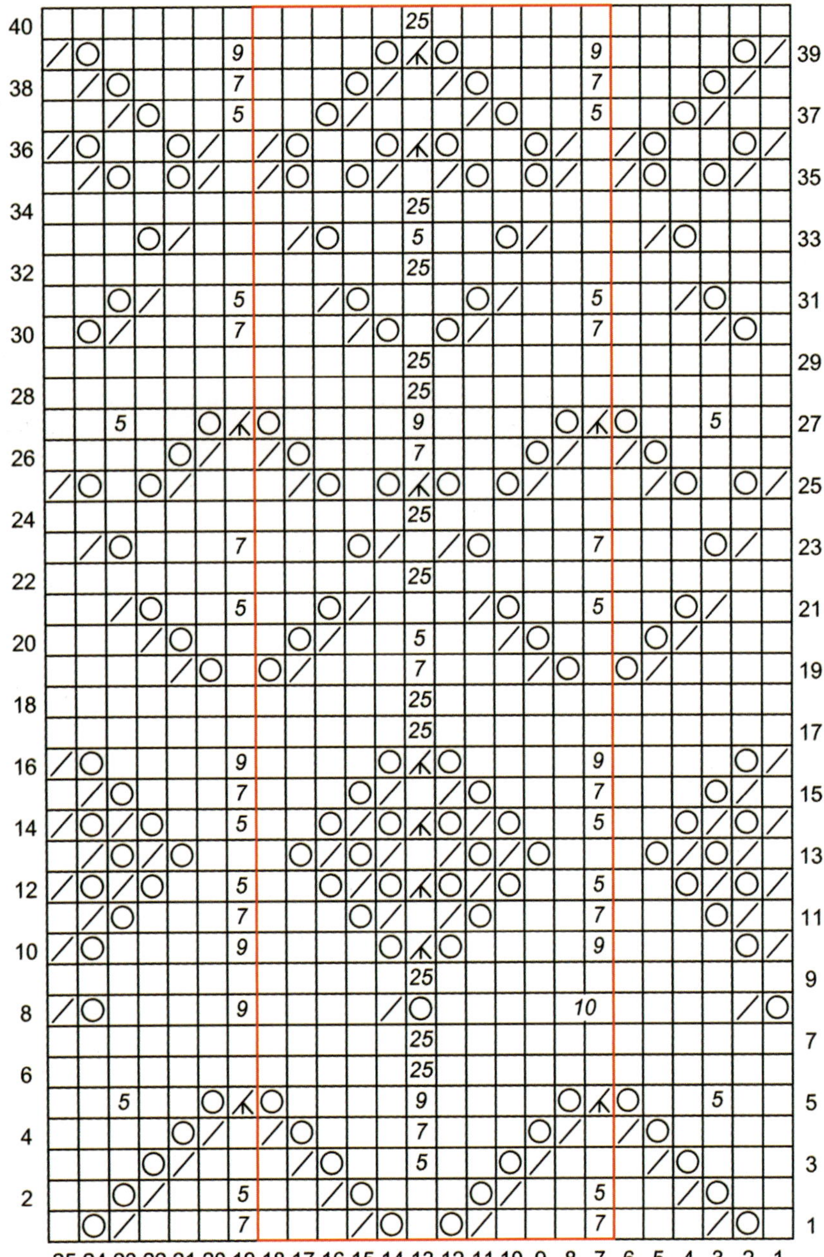

Branches, Bead and Plain Diamonds chart.

Row 20: K3, k2tog, yo, k3, yo, k2tog, k5, k2tog, yo, k3, yo, k2tog, k3.

Row 21: K2, k2tog, yo, k5, yo, k2tog, k3, k2tog, yo, k5, yo, k2tog, k2.

Row 22: Knit.

Row 23: Repeat row 11.

Row 24: Knit.

Row 25: K2tog, yo, k1, yo, k2tog, k3, k2tog, yo, k1, yo, k3tog, yo, k1, yo, k2tog, k3, k2tog, yo, k1, yo, k2tog.

Row 26: Repeat row 4.

Row 27: Repeat row 5.

Rows 28–29: Knit.

Row 30: Repeat row 1.
Row 31: Repeat row 2.
Row 32: Knit.
Row 33: Repeat row 3.
Row 34: Knit.
Row 35: (K1, k2tog, yo, k1, yo, k2tog) x 4, k1.
Row 36: K2tog, yo, k2, yo, k2tog, k1, k2tog, yo, k2, yo, p3tog, yo, k2, yo, k2tog, k1, k2tog, yo, k2, yo, k2tog.
Row 37: Repeat row 21.
Row 38: Repeat row 11.
Row 39: K2tog, yo, k9, yo, k3tog, yo, k9, yo, k2tog.
Row 40: Knit.

3.3

Lace Hole, Plain and Bead Diamonds, with Branch
TEX 2014.25 Shawl

Lace hole, Plain and Bead Diamonds, with Branch original pattern.

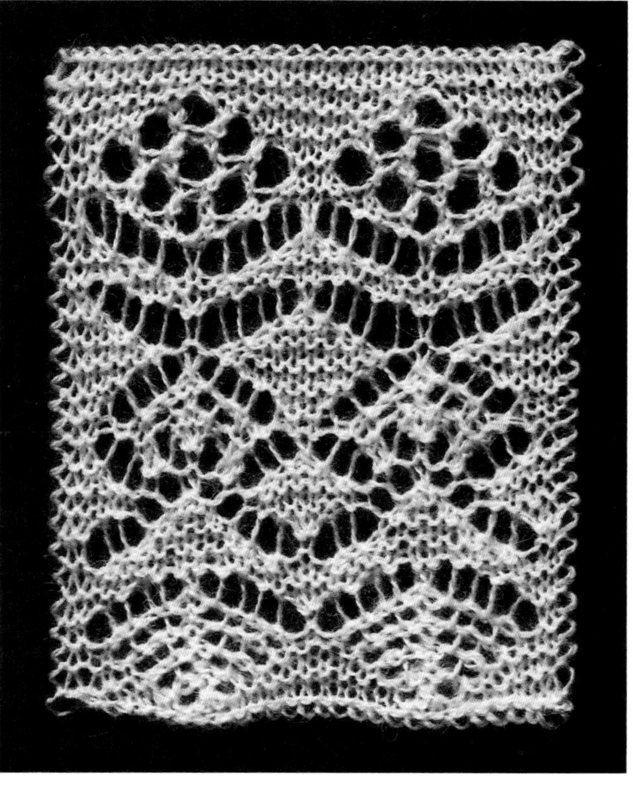

Lace hole, Plain and Bead Diamonds, with Branch knitted sample.

The Diamonds of Lace Holes are set in two broken Waves and resemble a small posy of flowers. Below them are Bead and plain Diamonds and Branches. This pattern has similar elements to Pattern 3.2 above, but presents a different look.

Row 1 (RS): K5, k2tog, yo, k10, k2tog, yo, k6. (25 sts)
Row 2 (WS): K5, yo, p3tog, yo, k9, yo, p3tog, yo, k5.
Row 3: K4, yo, k2tog, k1, k2tog, yo, k7, yo, k2tog, k1, k2tog, yo, k4.
Row 4: K3, yo, k2tog, yo, p3tog, yo, k2tog, yo, k5, yo, k2tog, yo, p3tog, yo, k2tog, yo, k3.
Row 5: K2, (yo, k2tog) x 2, k1, (k2tog, yo) x 2, k3, (yo, k2tog) x 2, k1, (k2tog, yo) x 2, k2.
Row 6: (K1, (yo, k2tog) x 2, yo, p3tog, (yo, k2tog) x 2, yo) x 2, k1.
Row 7: Repeat row 5.
Row 8: Repeat row 4.
Row 9: Repeat row 3.
Row 10: Repeat row 2.
Row 11: Knit.
Row 12: (K1, yo, k2tog, k7, k2tog, yo) x 2, k1.
Row 13: K2, yo, k2tog, k5, k2tog, yo, k3, yo, k2tog, k5, k2tog, yo, k2.
Row 14: K3, yo, k2tog, k3, k2tog, yo, k5, yo, k2tog, k3, k2tog, yo, k3.
Row 15: Knit.
Row 16: Repeat row 3.
Row 17: Knit.

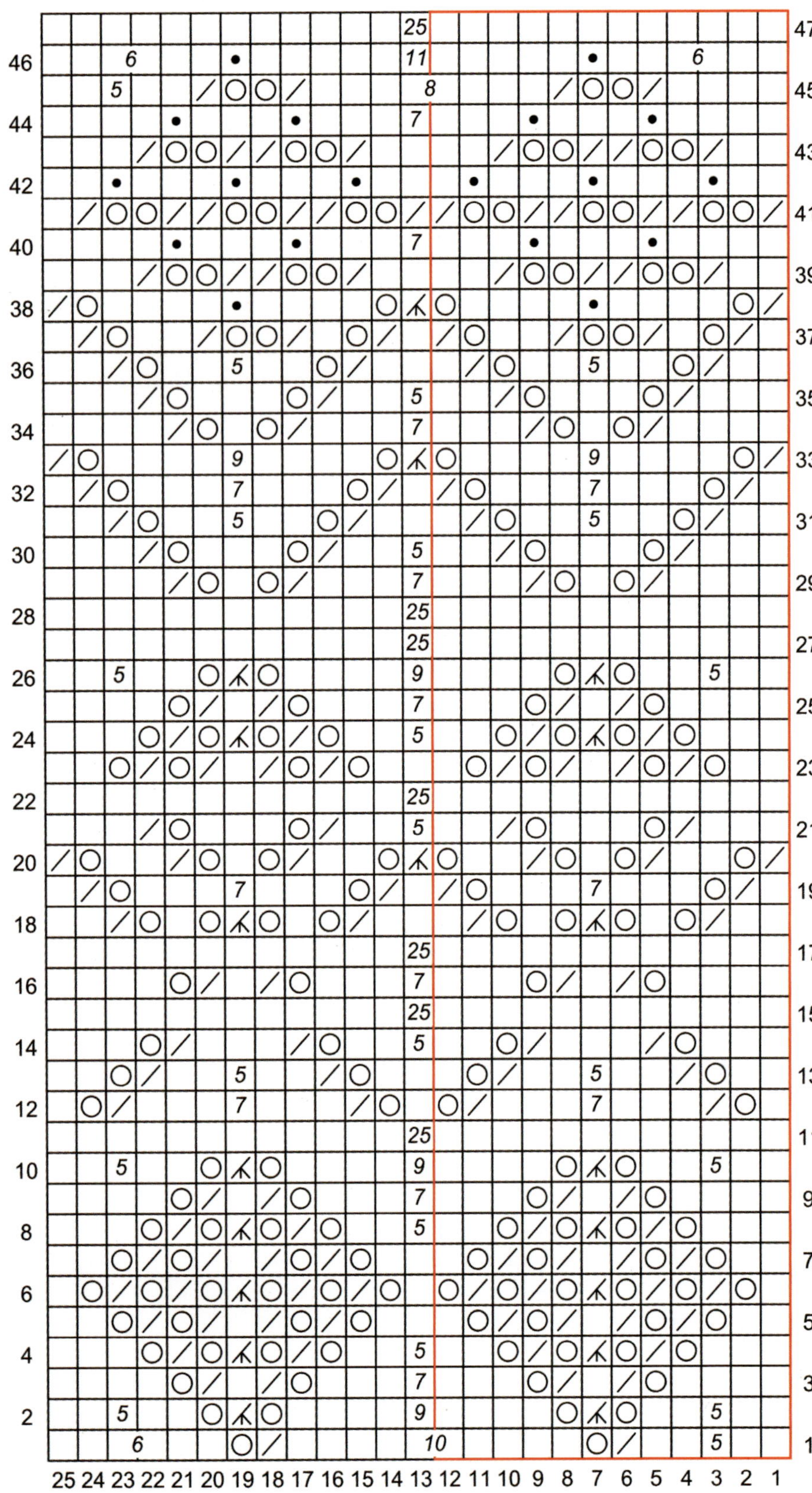

Lace hole, Plain and Bead Diamonds, with Branch chart.

Row 18: K2, k2tog, yo, k1, yo, p3tog, yo, k1, yo, k2tog, k3, k2tog, yo, k1, yo, p3tog, yo, k1, yo, k2tog, k2.
Row 19: (K1, k2tog, yo, k7, yo, k2tog) x 2, k1.
Row 20: K2tog, yo, k2, k2tog, yo, k1, yo, k2tog, k2, yo, p3tog, yo, k2, k2tog, yo, k1, yo, k2tog, k2, yo, k2tog.
Row 21: K3, k2tog, yo, k3, yo, k2tog, k5, k2tog, yo, k3, yo, k2tog, k3.
Row 22: Knit.
Row 23: Repeat row 5.
Row 24: Repeat row 4.
Row 25: Repeat row 3.
Row 26: Repeat row 2.
Rows 27–28: Knit.
Row 29: K4, k2tog, yo, k1, yo, k2tog, k7, k2tog, yo, k1, yo, k2tog, k4.
Row 30: Repeat row 21.
Row 31: K2, k2tog, yo, k5, yo, k2tog, k3, k2tog, yo, k5, yo, k2tog, k2.
Row 32: Repeat row 19.
Row 33: K2tog, yo, k9, yo, k3tog, yo, k9, yo, k2tog.
Row 34: Repeat row 29.
Row 35: Repeat row 21.
Row 36: Repeat row 31.
Row 37: (K1, k2tog, yo, k1, k2tog, yo x 2, k2tog, k2, yo, k2tog) x 2, k1.
Row 38: K2tog, yo, k4, p1, k4, yo, p3tog, yo, k4, p1, k4, yo, k2tog.
Row 39: K2, k2tog, yo x 2, k2tog x 2, yo x 2, k2tog, k4, k2tog, yo x 2, k2tog x 2, yo x 2, k2tog, k3.
Row 40: K4, p1, k3, p1, k7, p1, k3, p1, k4.
Row 41: K2tog, (yo x 2, k2tog x 2) x 5, yo x 2, k2tog, k1.
Row 42: K2, (p1, k3) x 5, p1, k2.
Row 43: Repeat row 39.
Row 44: Repeat row 40.
Row 45: K4, k2tog, yo x 2, k2tog, k8, k2tog, yo x 2, k2tog, k5.
Row 46: K6, p1, k11, p1, k6.
Row 47: Knit.

3.4

Plain Diamonds, Branches and Trees
TEX 8927 Shawl

Plain Diamonds, Branches and Trees original pattern.

Plain Diamonds, Branches and Trees knitted sample.

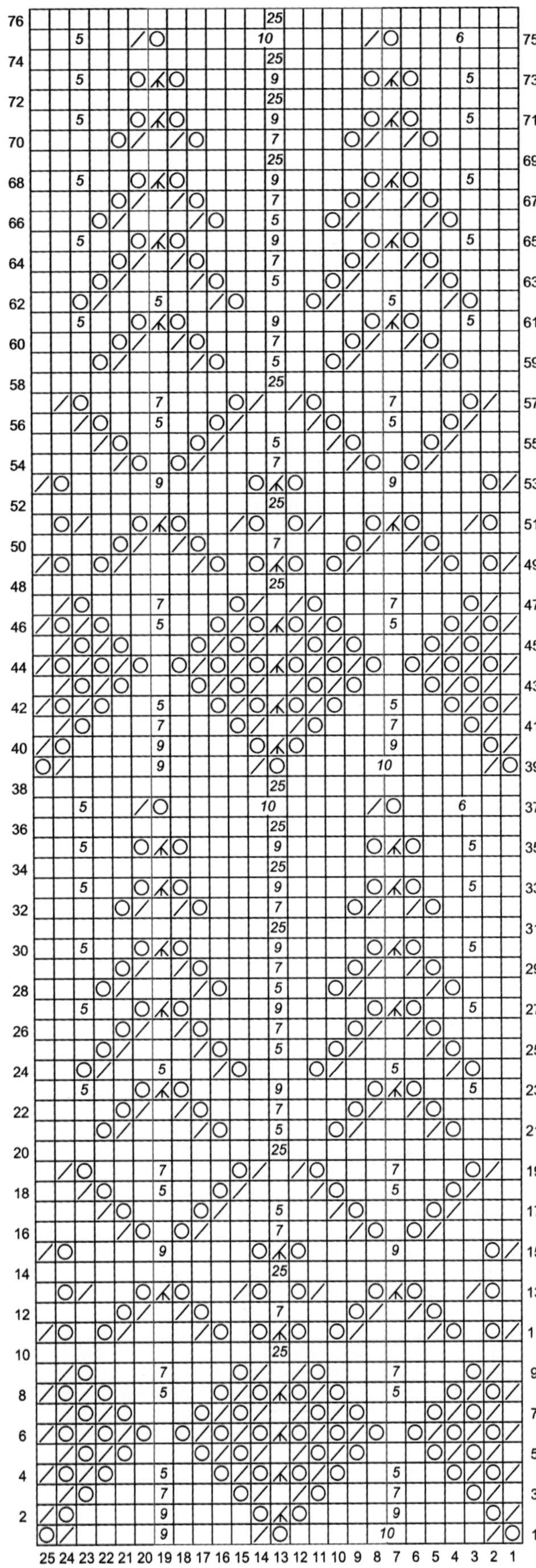

Plain Diamonds, Branches and Tree chart.

This unusual shawl was made about 1855 or 1857 as a christening shawl (*see* Chapter 7, Sutherland Christening Shawl). It is triangular in shape, as many early christening shawls were. But it is unusual in having a hood with drawstring to fit around the infant's head, rather than a raised, rounded peak, which draped to the forehead. The centre pattern has a striking vertical appearance and is also used for the hood, which is a separate piece joined to the top of the centre.

Row 1 (RS): Yo, k2tog, k10, yo, k2tog, k9, k2tog, yo. (25 sts)
Row 2 (WS): K2tog, yo, k9, yo, p3tog, yo, k9, yo, k2tog.
Row 3: (K1, k2tog, yo, k7, yo, k2tog) x 2, k1.
Row 4: (K2tog, yo) x 2, k5, yo, k2tog, yo, p3tog, yo, k2tog, yo, k5, (yo, k2tog) x 2.
Row 5: (K1, (k2tog, yo) x 2, k3, (yo, k2tog) x 2) x 2, k1.
Row 6: (K2tog, yo) x 3, k1, (yo, k2tog) x 2, yo, p3tog, (yo, k2tog) x 2, yo, k1, (yo, k2tog) x 3.
Row 7: Repeat row 5.
Row 8: Repeat row 4.
Row 9: Repeat row 3.
Row 10: Knit.
Row 11: K2tog, yo, k1, yo, k2tog, k3, k2tog, yo, k1, yo, k3tog, yo, k1, yo, k2tog, k3, k2tog, yo, k1, yo, k2tog.
Row 12: K4, yo, k2tog, k1, k2tog, yo, k7, yo, k2tog, k1, k2tog, yo, k4.
Row 13: (K1, yo, k2tog, k2, yo, k3tog, yo, k2, k2tog, yo) x 2, k1.
Row 14: Knit.
Row 15: K2tog, yo, k9, yo, k3tog, yo, k9, yo, k2tog.
Row 16: K4, k2tog, yo, k1, yo, k2tog, k7, k2tog, yo, k1, yo, k2tog, k4.
Row 17: K3, k2tog, yo, k3, yo, k2tog, k5, k2tog, yo, k3, yo, k2tog, k3.
Row 18: K2, k2tog, yo, k5, yo, k2tog, k3, k2tog, yo, k5, yo, k2tog, k2.
Row 19: Repeat row 3.
Row 20: Knit.
Row 21: K3, yo, k2tog, k3, k2tog, yo, k5, yo, k2tog, k3, k2tog, yo, k3.
Row 22: Repeat row 12.
Row 23: K5, yo, k3tog, yo, k9, yo, k3tog, yo, k5.
Row 24: K2, yo, k2tog, k5, k2tog, yo, k3, yo, k2tog, k5, k2tog, yo, k2.
Row 25: Repeat row 21.
Row 26: Repeat row 12.
Row 27: Repeat row 23.
Row 28: Repeat row 21.
Row 29: Repeat row 12.
Row 30: K5, yo, p3tog, yo, k9, yo, p3tog, yo, k5.
Row 31: Knit.
Row 32: Repeat row 12.
Row 33: Repeat row 23.
Row 34: Knit.
Row 35: Repeat row 23.
Row 36: Knit.
Row 37: K6, yo, k2tog, k10, yo, k2tog, k5.
Row 38: Knit.
Rows 39–76: Repeat rows 1–38.

3.5

Branches, Columns of Beads, Plain and Lace Hole Diamonds
TEX 2004.371 Shawl

Branches, Columns of Beads, Plain and Lace Hole Diamonds original pattern.

This is a complex centre with many elements. The pattern grouping alternates its position horizontally, so there appears to be continual variation in the vertical line. This is a clever way to introduce more complexity into a centre pattern.

Row 1 (RS): K6, yo, k2tog, k10, yo, k2tog, k5. (25 sts)
Row 2 (WS): Knit.
Row 3: K5, yo, k3tog, yo, k9, yo, k3tog, yo, k5.
Row 4: K4, yo, k2tog, k1, k2tog, yo, k7, yo, k2tog, k1, k2tog, yo, k4.
Row 5: K3, yo, k2tog, yo, k3tog, yo, k2tog, yo, k5, yo, k2tog, yo, k3tog, yo, k2tog, yo, k3.
Row 6: K2, (yo, k2tog) x 2, k1, (k2tog, yo) x 2, k3, (yo, k2tog) x 2, k1, (k2tog, yo) x 2, k2.

Branches, Columns of Beads, Plain and Lace Hole Diamonds knitted sample.

Row 7: (K1, (yo, k2tog) x 2, yo, k3tog, (yo, k2tog) x 2, yo) x 2, k1.
Row 8: Repeat row 6.
Row 9: Repeat row 5.

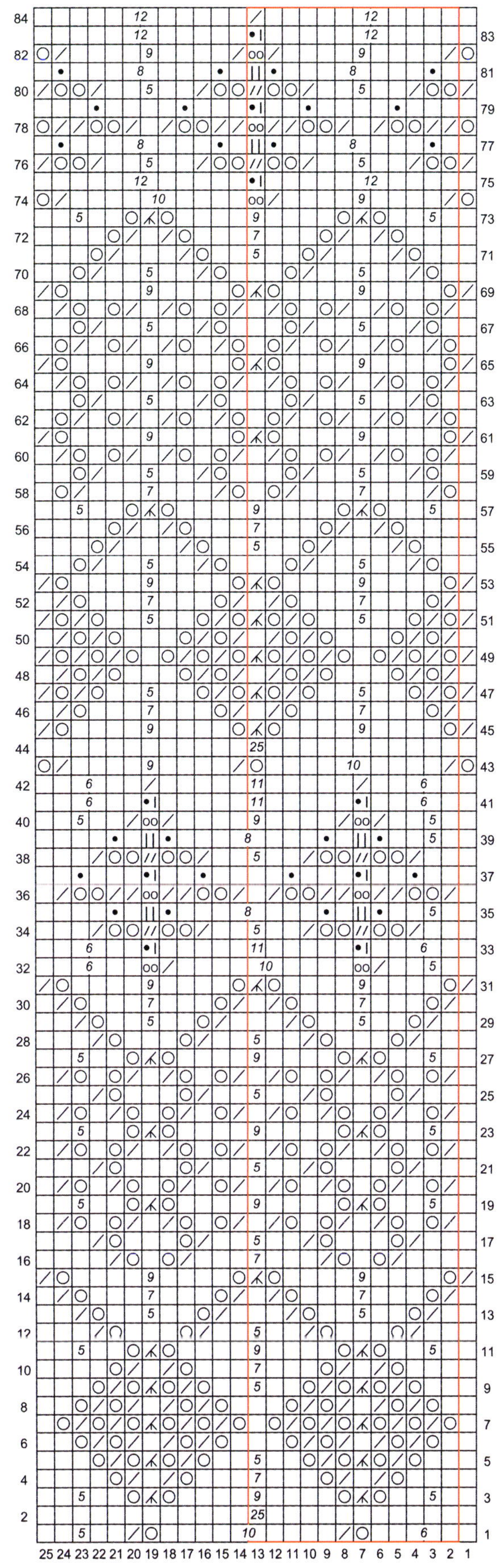

Branches, Columns of Beads, Plain and Lace Hole Diamonds chart.

Row 10: Repeat row 4.
Row 11: Repeat row 3.
Row 12: K3, k2tog, yo, k3, yo, k2tog, k5, k2tog, yo, k3, yo, k2tog, k3.
Row 13: K2, k2tog, yo, k5, yo, k2tog, k3, k2tog, yo, k5, yo, k2tog, k2.
Row 14: (K1, k2tog, yo, k7, yo, k2tog) x 2, k1.
Row 15: K2tog, yo, k9, yo, k3tog, yo, k9, yo, k2tog.
Row 16: K4, k2tog, yo, k1, yo, k2tog, k7, k2tog, yo, k1, yo, k2tog, k4.
Row 17: Repeat row 12.
Row 18: (K1, k2tog, yo, k1, yo, k2tog) x 4, k1.
Row 19: Repeat row 3.
Row 20: ((K1, k2tog, yo) x 2, (k1, yo, k2tog) x 2) x 2, k1.
Row 21: Repeat row 12.
Rows 22–25: Repeat rows 18–21.
Row 26: Repeat row 18.
Row 27: Repeat row 3.
Row 28: Repeat row 12.
Row 29: Repeat row 13.
Row 30: Repeat row 14.
Row 31: Repeat row 15.
Row 32: K6, yo twice, k2tog, k10, yo twice, k2tog, k5. (27 sts)
Row 33: K6, knit, purl into yarnovers, k11, knit, purl into yarnovers, k6.
Row 34: K3, k2tog, yo x 2, k2tog twice, yo x 2, k2tog, k5, k2tog, yo x 2, k2tog twice, yo x 2, k2tog, k3.
Row 35: K5, p1, k2, k1, p1, k8, p1, k2, k1, p1, k4.
Row 36: (K1, k2tog, yo x 2, k2tog x 2, yo twice, k2tog x 2, yo x 2, k2tog) x 2, k1.
Row 37: K3, p1, k2, knit, purl into yarnovers, k3, p1, k4, p1, k2, knit, purl into yarnovers, k3, p1, k2.
Row 38: Repeat row 34.
Row 39: Repeat row 35.
Row 40: K5, k2tog, yo twice, k2tog, k9, k2tog, yo twice, k2tog, k5.
Row 41: Repeat row 33.
Row 42: K6, k2tog, k11, k2tog, k6. (25 sts)
Row 43: Yo, k2tog, k10, yo, k2tog, k9, k2tog, yo.
Row 44: Knit.
Row 45: Repeat row 15.
Row 46: Repeat row 14.
Row 47: (K2tog, yo) x 2, k5, yo, k2tog, yo, k3tog, yo, k2tog, yo, k5, (yo, k2tog) x 2.
Row 48: (K1, (k2tog, yo) x 2, k3, (yo, k2tog) x 2) x 2, k1.
Row 49: (K2tog, yo) x 3, k1, (yo, k2tog) x 2, yo, k3tog, (yo, k2tog) x 2, yo, k1, (yo, k2tog) x 3.
Row 50: Repeat row 48.
Row 51: Repeat row 47.
Row 52: Repeat row 14.
Row 53: Repeat row 15.
Row 54: K2, yo, k2tog, k5, k2tog, yo, k3, yo, k2tog, k5, k2tog, yo, k2.
Row 55: K3, yo, k2tog, k3, k2tog, yo, k5, yo, k2tog, k3, k2tog, yo, k3.
Row 56: Repeat row 4.
Row 57: Repeat row 3.
Row 58: (K1, yo, k2tog, k7, k2tog, yo) x 2, k1.
Row 59: Repeat row 54.
Row 60: Repeat row 18.
Row 61: Repeat row 15.
Row 62: ((K1, yo, k2tog) x 2, (k1, k2tog, yo) x 2) x 2, k1.
Row 63: Repeat row 54.
Rows 64–67: Repeat rows 60–63.
Row 68: Repeat row 18.
Row 69: Repeat row 15.
Row 70: Repeat row 54.
Row 71: Repeat row 55.
Row 72: Repeat row 4.
Row 73: Repeat row 3.
Row 74: Yo, k2tog, k10, yo twice, k2tog, k9, k2tog, yo. (26 sts)
Row 75: K12, knit, purl into yarnovers, k12.
Row 76: K2tog, yo x 2, k2tog, k5, k2tog, yo x 2, k2tog twice, yo x 2, k2tog, k5, k2tog, yo x 2, k2tog.
Row 77: K2, p1, k8, p1, k2, k1, p1, k8, p1, k1.
Row 78: Yo, k2tog x 2, yo x 2, k2tog, k1, k2tog, yo x 2, k2tog x 2, yo twice, k2tog x 2, yo x 2, k2tog, k1, k2tog, yo x 2, k2tog x 2, yo.
Row 79: (K4, p1) x 2, k2, knit, purl into yarnovers, k3, p1, k4, p1, k3.
Row 80: Repeat row 76.
Row 81: Repeat row 77.
Row 82: Yo, k2tog, k9, k2tog, yo twice, k2tog, k9, k2tog, yo.
Row 83: Repeat row 75.
Row 84: K12, k2tog, k12. (25 sts).

3.6

Hexagon, Plain Diamond, Trees and Branches

TEX 2004.367 Shawl

Hexagon, Plain Diamond, Trees and Branches original pattern.

Hexagon, Plain Diamond, Trees and Branches knitted sample.

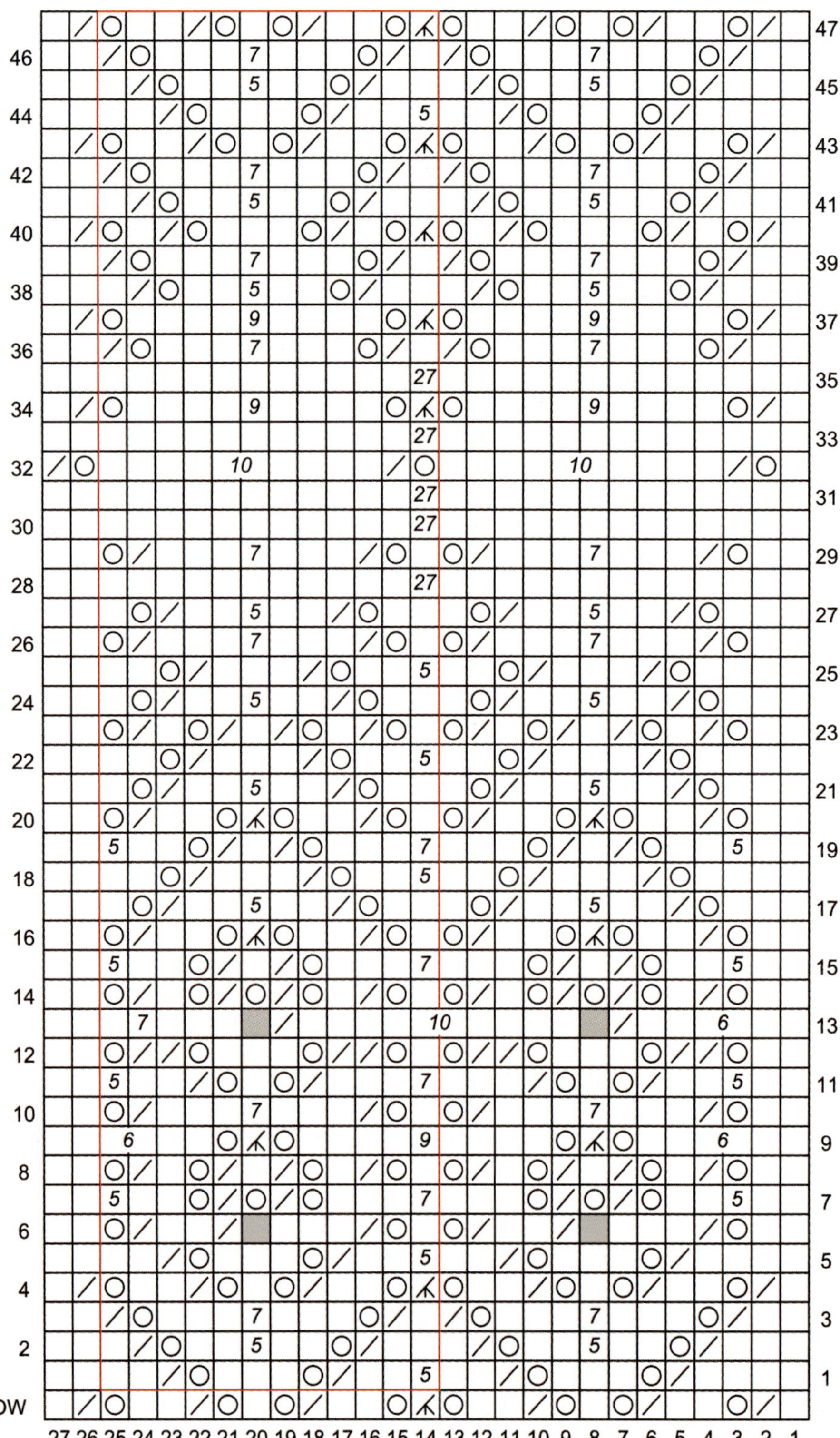

Hexagon, Plain Diamond, Trees and Branches chart.

The centre pattern for a shawl is a Puzzle variation. Here the Trees and Branches are positioned point-to-point, creating an open appearance next to the density of the plain Diamonds.

Set up row (WS): K1, k2tog, yo, k2, k2tog, yo, k1, yo, k2tog, k2, yo, k3tog, yo, k2, k2tog, yo, k1, yo, k2tog, k2, yo, k2tog, k1. (27 sts)
Row 1: K4, k2tog, yo, k3, yo, k2tog, k5, k2tog, yo, k3, yo, k2tog, k4.
Row 2: (K3, k2tog, yo, k5, yo, k2tog) x 2, k3.
Row 3: K2, k2tog, yo, k7, yo, k2tog, k1, k2tog, yo, k7, yo, k2tog, k2.
Row 4: Repeat set up row.
Row 5: Repeat row 1.
Row 6: K2, yo, k2tog, k2, k2tog, k3, k2tog, yo, k1, yo, k2tog, k2, k2tog, k3, k2tog, yo, k2. (25 sts)
Row 7: K5, (yo, k2tog) x 2, yo, k7, (yo, k2tog) x 2, yo, k5. (27 sts)
Row 8: K2, (yo, k2tog, k1) x 2, (k2tog, yo, k1) x 2, (yo, k2tog, k1) x 2, k2tog, yo, k1, k2tog, yo, k2.
Row 9: K6, yo, k3tog, yo, k9, yo, k3tog, yo, k6.
Row 10: K2, yo, k2tog, k7, k2tog, yo, k1, yo, k2tog, k7, k2tog, yo, k2.
Row 11: K5, k2tog, yo, k1, yo, k2tog, k7, k2tog, yo, k1, yo, k2tog, k5.
Row 12: K2, yo, k2tog x 2, yo, k3, yo, k2tog x 2, yo, k1, yo, k2tog x 2, yo, k3, yo, k2tog x 2, yo, k2.
Row 13: K6, k2tog, k10, k2tog, k7. (25 sts)
Row 14: K2, yo, k2tog, k1, yo, k2tog, yo, (k2tog, yo, k1) x 2, yo, k2tog, k1, (yo, k2tog) x 2, yo, k1, k2tog, yo, k2. (27 sts)
Row 15: K5, yo, k2tog, k1, k2tog, yo, k7, yo, k2tog, k1, k2tog, yo, k5.
Row 16: K2, yo, k2tog, k2, yo, k3tog, yo, k2, k2tog, yo, k1, yo, k2tog, k2, yo, k3tog, yo, k2, k2tog, yo, k2.
Row 17: (K3, yo, k2tog, k5, k2tog, yo) x 2, k3.
Row 18: K4, yo, k2tog, k3, k2tog, yo, k5, yo, k2tog, k3, k2tog, yo, k4.
Rows 19–22: Repeat rows 15–18.
Row 23: Repeat row 8.
Row 24: Repeat row 17.
Row 25: Repeat row 18.
Row 26: Repeat row 10.
Row 27: Repeat row 17.
Row 28: Knit.
Row 29: Repeat row 10.
Rows 30–31: Knit.
Row 32: (K2tog, yo, k10) x 2, k2tog, yo, k1.
Row 33: Knit.
Row 34: K1, k2tog, yo, k9, yo, k3tog, yo, k9, yo, k2tog, k1.
Row 35: Knit.
Row 36: Repeat row 3.
Row 37: Repeat row 34.
Row 38: Repeat row 2.
Row 39: Repeat row 3.
Row 40: (K1, k2tog, yo) x 2, k3, yo, k2tog, k1, yo, k3tog, yo, k1, k2tog, yo, k3, (yo, k2tog, k1) x 2.
Row 41: Repeat row 2.
Row 42: Repeat row 3.
Row 43: Repeat set up row.
Row 44: Repeat row 1.
Row 45: Repeat row 2.
Row 46: Repeat row 3.
Row 47: Repeat set up row.

3.7

Hexagon, Plain and Lace Hole Diamonds, Trees and Branches
TEX 2012.428a Stole

This pattern is another Puzzle variation. It has elements similar to Pattern 3.6 but they are combined in a different way. Unusually it is the centre of a stole, rather than a shawl.

Row 1 (RS): K7, yo, k2tog, k12, yo, k2tog, k7. (30 sts)
Row 2 (WS): Knit.
Row 3: K6, yo, k3tog, yo, k11, yo, k3tog, yo, k7.
Row 4: Knit.
Row 5: K5, yo, k2tog, k1, k2tog, yo, k9, yo, k2tog, k1, k2tog, yo, k6.
Row 6: K7, yo, k3tog, yo, k11, yo, k3tog, yo, k6.
Row 7: K4, yo, k2tog, k3, k2tog, yo, k7, yo, k2tog, k3, k2tog, yo, k5.
Row 8: K6, yo, k2tog, k1, k2tog, yo, k9, yo, k2tog, k1, k2tog, yo, k5.
Row 9: K3, yo, k2tog, k1, yo, k3tog, yo, k1, k2tog, yo, k5, yo, k2tog, k1, yo, k3tog, yo, k1, k2tog, yo, k4.
Row 10: K5, yo, k2tog, k3, k2tog, yo, k7, yo, k2tog, k3, k2tog, yo, k4.

Hexagon, Plain and Lace Hole Diamonds, Trees and Branches original pattern.

Row 11: K2, ((yo, k2tog, k1) x 2, k2tog, yo, k1, k2tog, yo, k3) x 2.
Row 12: K4, yo, k2tog, k1, yo, k3tog, yo, k1, k2tog, yo, k5, yo, k2tog, k1, yo, k3tog, yo, k1, k2tog, yo, k3.
Row 13: ((K1, yo, k2tog) x 2, k3, k2tog, yo, k1, k2tog, yo) x 2, k2.
Row 14: (K3, (yo, k2tog, k1) x 2, k2tog, yo, k1, k2tog, yo) x 2, k2.
Row 15: Repeat row 9.
Row 16: Repeat row 10.
Row 17: Repeat row 5.
Row 18: Repeat row 6.
Row 19: Knit.
Row 20: K6, k2tog, yo, k1, yo, k2tog, k9, k2tog, yo, k1, yo, k2tog, k5.

Hexagon, Plain and Lace Hole Diamonds, Trees and Branches knitted sample.

Row 21: K4, k2tog, yo, k3, yo, k2tog, k7, k2tog, yo, k3, yo, k2tog, k5.
Row 22: K4, k2tog, yo, k5, yo, k2tog, k5, k2tog, yo, k5, yo, k2tog, k3.
Row 23: K2, (k2tog, yo, k7, yo, k2tog, k3) x 2.
Row 24: K2, (k2tog, yo, k2, k2tog, yo, k1, yo, k2tog, k2, yo, k2tog, k1) x 2.
Row 25: K2tog, yo, k2, k2tog, yo, k3, yo, k2tog, k2, yo, k3tog, yo, k2, k2tog, yo, k3, yo, k2tog, k2, yo, k2tog, k1.
Row 26: Knit.
Row 27: (K1, yo, k2tog, k2, yo, k2tog, yo, k3tog, yo, k2, k2tog, yo) x 2, k2.
Row 28: Repeat row 8.
Row 29: (K1, yo, k2tog, k3, yo, k3tog, yo, k3, k2tog, yo) x 2, k2.
Row 30: Knit.
Row 31: (K1, yo, k2tog, k2, k2tog, yo) x 4, k2.
Row 32: K5, k2tog, yo, k3, yo, k2tog, k7, k2tog, yo, k3, yo, k2tog, k4.
Row 33: (K1, yo, k2tog, k9, k2tog, yo) x 2, k2.
Row 34: K6, yo, k3tog, yo, k2tog, yo, k9, yo, k3tog, yo, k2tog, yo, k5.
Row 35: (K1, yo, k2tog, k2, yo, k2tog, k1, k2tog, yo, k2, k2tog, yo) x 2, k2.

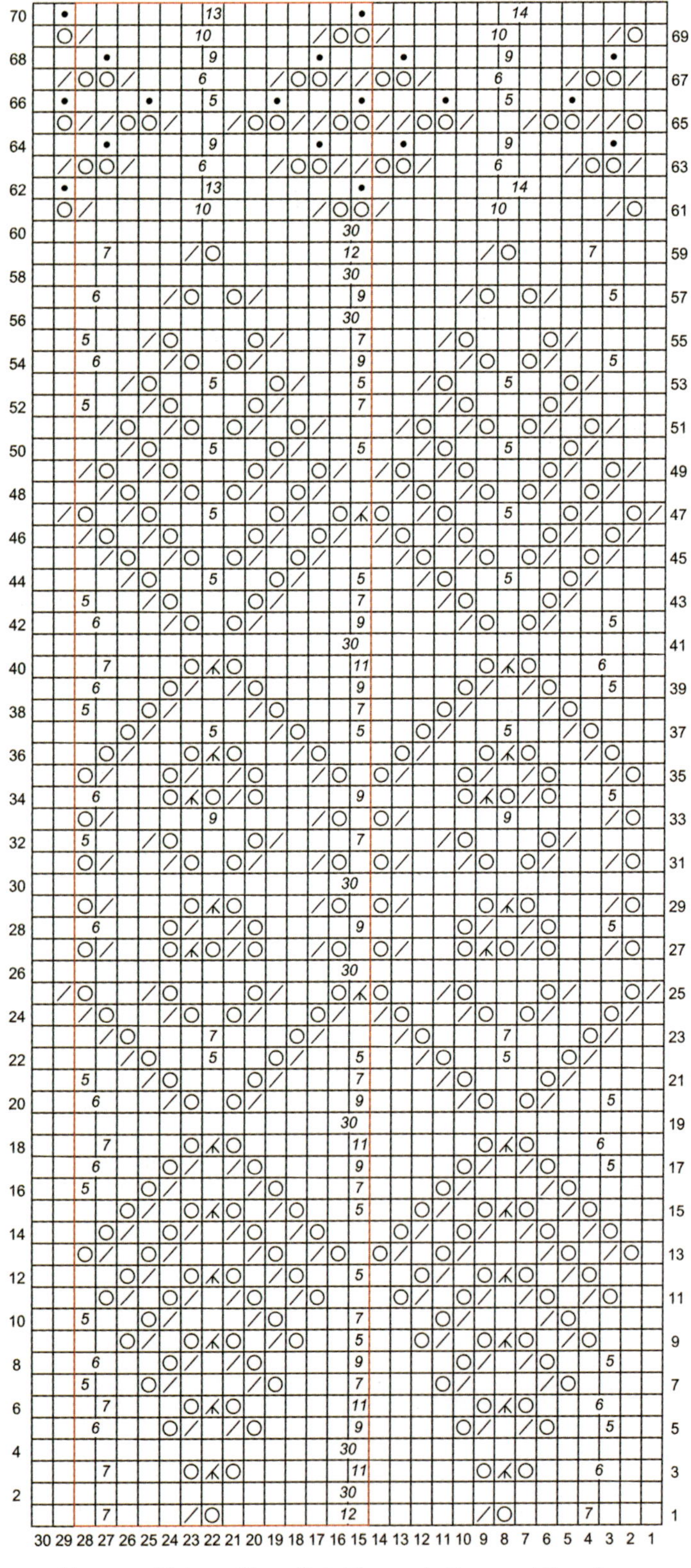

Hexagon, Plain and Lace Hole Diamonds, Trees and Branches chart.

Row 36: (K3, yo, k2tog, k2, yo, k3tog, yo, k2, k2tog, yo) x 2, k2.
Row 37: K3, yo, k2tog, k5, k2tog, yo, k5, yo, k2tog, k5, k2tog, yo, k4.
Row 38: Repeat row 10.
Row 39: Repeat row 5.
Row 40: Repeat row 6.
Row 41: Knit.
Row 42: Repeat row 20.
Row 43: Repeat row 21.
Row 44: Repeat row 22.
Row 45: K2, ((k2tog, yo, k1) x 2, yo, k2tog, k1, yo, k2tog, k3) x 2.
Row 46: K2, (k2tog, yo, k1, k2tog, yo, k3, (yo, k2tog, k1) x 2) x 2.
Row 47: K2tog, yo, k1, k2tog, yo, k5, yo, k2tog, k1, yo, k3tog, yo, k1, k2tog, yo, k5, (yo, k2tog, k1) x 2.
Row 48: (K3, (k2tog, yo, k1) x 2, yo, k2tog, k1, yo, k2tog) x 2, k2.
Row 49: ((K1, k2tog, yo) x 2, k3, yo, k2tog, k1, yo, k2tog) x 2, k2.
Row 50: Repeat row 22.
Row 51: Repeat row 45.
Row 52: Repeat row 32.
Row 53: K3, k2tog, yo, k5, yo, k2tog, k5, k2tog, yo, k5, yo, k2tog, k4.
Row 54: Repeat row 20.
Row 55: Repeat row 21.
Row 56: Knit.
Row 57: K5, k2tog, yo, k1, yo, k2tog, k9, k2tog, yo, k1, yo, k2tog, k6.
Row 58: Knit.
Row 59: Repeat row 1.
Row 60: Knit.
Row 61: K1, yo, k2tog, k10, k2tog, yo x 2, k2tog, k10, k2tog, yo, k1.
Row 62: K1, p1, k13, p1, k14.
Row 63: K1, k2tog, yo x 2, k2tog, k6, k2tog, yo x 2, k2tog x 2, yo x 2, k2tog, k6, k2tog, yo x 2, k2tog, k1.
Row 64: (K3, p1, k9, p1) x 2, k2.
Row 65: K1, yo, k2tog x 2, yo x 2, k2tog, k2, k2tog, (yo x 2, k2tog x 2) x 2, yo x 2, k2tog, k2, k2tog, yo x 2, k2tog x 2, yo, k1.
Row 66: K1, p1, k3, p1, k5, (p1, k3) x 2, p1, k5, p1, k4.
Row 67: Repeat row 63.
Row 68: Repeat row 64.
Row 69: Repeat row 61.
Row 70: Repeat row 62.

CHAPTER 4

SINGLE PATTERNS IN BORDERS

What marks Shetland lace apart from most other knitted lace traditions is the complexity of design in borders. Typically the borders hold the largest number of patterns in the garment, more so than the centre. Pattern number and placement have much to do with design success, how pleasing the border is to the eye and whether certain patterns are given prominence over others. Some knitters endeavoured to create a design relationship between the border and centre, with certain shapes or infill patterns used in both. The repetition of pattern in border and centre was best achieved when not overdone, as the border was meant to stand out as the boldest or most intricate part of the garment's design. Traditional design is firmly rooted in the period in which it reached its peak of success in fashion, and borders became the main area of design focus because they were the most visible part of the lace garment when worn.

Large square shawls were the product of the early Victorian period, beginning in the 1840s. They continued to be appropriate and elegant accessories into the 1920s for elderly matrons still wearing late-Victorian and Edwardian fashions. Classic Shetland lace shawl design became established between the 1850s and 1870s, when women's dress style and body shaping was popularised by the sloped shoulder, a waist severely narrowed by corsetry, and exceptionally wide skirts suspended and expanded by crinolines. By the 1860s skirts became more oval in form, with an expanse at the back. The skirt's shape, whether round or oval, formed the perfect backdrop to show off one's fine shawl.

The shawl was folded into a triangle, but not quite in half, allowing it to drape at the back in two tiers. Worn over the shoulders, the shawl's smaller tier was on top, its corner point at the centre back ending at or just below the waist. The larger tier hung below the smaller tier, also with its corner forming a line from the centre back. The full skirt provided a wide, sloping stage on which both tiers of the border were exhibited. They fanned out in a dramatic V-shape from the centre of the lower tier, with the intricate patterns of the border in full view. As the wearer moved, her crinoline kept the skirt aloft and with little disturbance to the shawl upon it.

Stoles and scarves were draped and bunched around the neck or over the shoulders, allowing the borders to spread and lie flat against the upper chest. Very long scarves could be wound around the neck with the border ends at the upper torso, remaining the most visible part of the garment.

Most shawl borders have patterns throughout, with very few areas of plain knitting between patterns. This is especially the case with very early shawls dating to the 1850s, where patterns are intermingled and intertwined. As time went on, shawl borders continued to have many patterns in their design but the motifs gradually became more horizontal in placement, evenly spaced and well-balanced. Stoles and

Thirteen different patterns, placed within or adjacent to one another, decorate the border of a stole with simple centre. (TEX 2004.334)

scarves also have very many patterns arranged in a complex fashion, but occasionally they are given a simple, bold border, with a few eye-catching motifs, whereas this is not the case for shawls.

BORDER MOTIFS

The individual patterns in borders are many and are used repeatedly or with slight alterations to allow them to fit into the overall design. The patterns range from Balanced Diamonds with very simple infills, to complex patterns formed from the conjoining of other patterns. When five, ten or fifteen of these patterns are used together, a border can become very dense and multifaceted. It is this complexity that marks Shetland lace knitting above other traditions in lace knitting.

Conversely, large patterns are sometimes used singly as a statement motif for a border, with smaller, decorative designs framing it. There is no formula for borders in Shetland lace knitting; they can include few or many patterns, placed as the knitter wishes.

Presented here are some of the most common patterns, with additional interesting and unusual ones. They are grouped by shape, and within their group, from simple to more complicated in design.

Some knitters chose a large, single pattern to dominate the design and create a bold statement in the border. (TEX 2010.340)

Elongated Diamonds, Balanced Diamonds and Ferns

Diamonds are the most common outline form used in border patterns. They may be elongated and shaped like the outline of a coniferous tree, or can be a Balanced Diamond in which all four sides are the same length.

Ferns are also diamond-shaped but do not have an edge defining them. They appear upside-down because the top

Rounded Diamonds in fishing net.

always has an arch of openwork, below which various patterns are placed. Ferns are often referred to as Madeiras, but this term was not historically used in Unst.

As a basic form, Diamonds contain a wide variety of infills. Some infill patterns (Steeks, Zigzag) are presented in other chapters, which points to the versatility of simple patterns and the many ways they can be used.

Elongated Diamonds

Diamond shapes are easily made elongated by spacing the upper part with a yarn over/decrease combination every other row, instead of every row as with the lower half.

4.1

Elongated Diamond inset with Steek variation 1

TEX 1990.306 Veil

The Steek running vertically in the centre of this Elongated Diamond is a simple k2tog, yo, k1, yo, k2tog form. The k2tog stitches on either side cause the Steek's outer edges to have little bumps but the infill garter stitches lie horizontally and the look is clean. It is used in a black stole, adding drama to this simple motif.

Row 1 (RS): K8, k2tog, yo, k1, yo, k2tog, k8. (21 sts)
Row 2 (WS): K7, k2tog, yo, k3, yo, k2tog, k7.
Row 3: K6, k2tog, yo, k5, yo, k2tog, k6.
Row 4: K5, k2tog, yo, k7, yo, k2tog, k5.

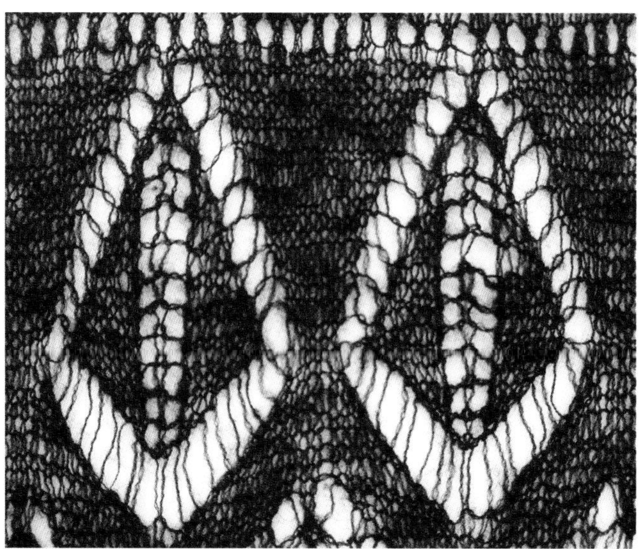

Elongated Diamond inset with Steek variation 1 original pattern.

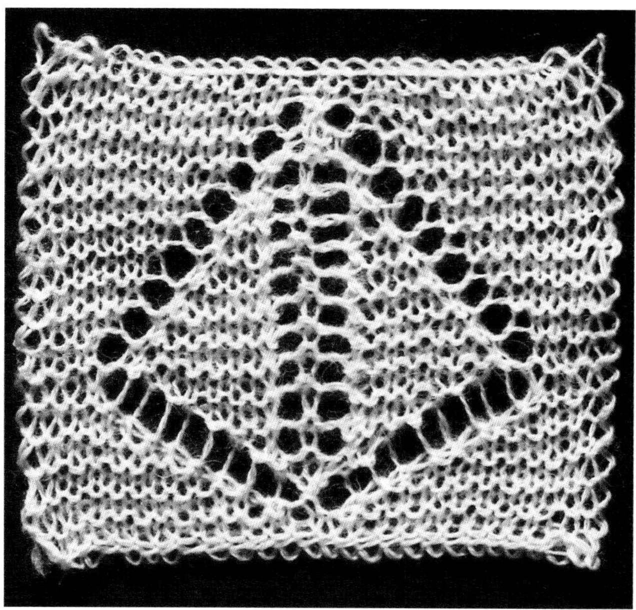

Elongated Diamond inset with Steek variation 1 knitted sample.

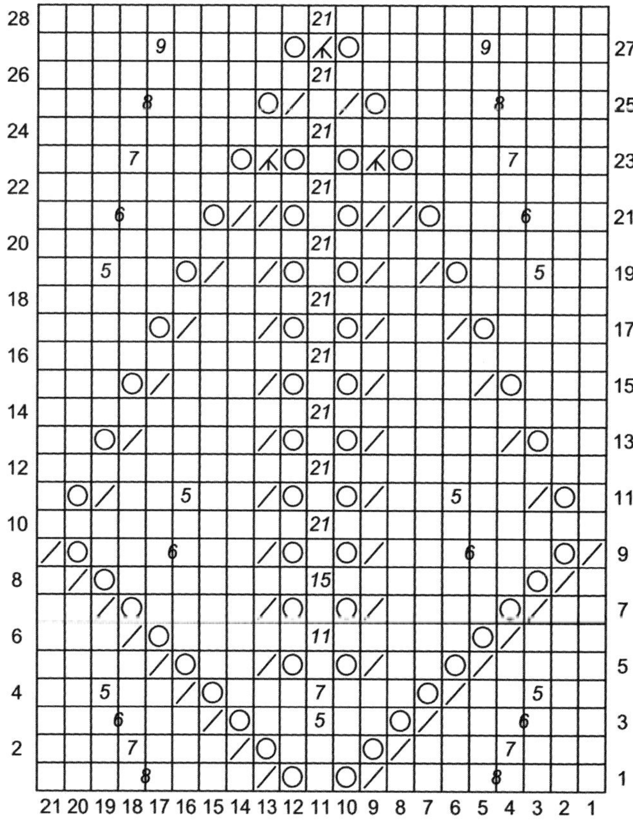

Elongated Diamond inset with Steek variation 1 chart.

Row 5: K4, k2tog, yo, k2, k2tog, yo, k1, yo, k2tog, k2, yo, k2tog, k4.
Row 6: K3, k2tog, yo, k11, yo, k2tog, k3.
Row 7: K2, k2tog, yo, k4, k2tog, yo, k1, yo, k2tog, k4, yo, k2tog, k2.
Row 8: K1, k2tog, yo, k15, yo, k2tog, k1.
Row 9: K2tog, yo, k6, k2tog, yo, k1, yo, k2tog, k6, yo, k2tog.
Row 10: Knit.
Row 11: (K1, yo, k2tog, k5, k2tog, yo) x 2, k1.
Row 12: Knit.
Row 13: K2, yo, k2tog, k4, k2tog, yo, k1, yo, k2tog, k4, k2tog, yo, k2.
Row 14: Knit.
Row 15: K3, yo, k2tog, k3, k2tog, yo, k1, yo, k2tog, k3, k2tog, yo, k3.
Row 16: Knit.
Row 17: K4, yo, k2tog, k2, k2tog, yo, k1, yo, k2tog, k2, k2tog, yo, k4.
Row 18: Knit.
Row 19: K5, yo, k2tog, k1, k2tog, yo, k1, yo, k2tog, k1, k2tog, yo, k5.
Row 20: Knit.
Row 21: K6, yo, k2tog x 2, yo, k1, yo, k2tog x 2, yo, k6.
Row 22: Knit.
Row 23: K7, yo, k3tog, yo, k1, yo, k3tog, yo, k7.
Row 24: Knit.
Row 25: K8, yo, k2tog, k1, k2tog, yo, k8.
Row 26: Knit.
Row 27: K9, yo, k3tog, yo, k9.
Row 28: Knit.

4.2

Elongated Diamond inset with Steek variation 2
TEX 7772 Shawl

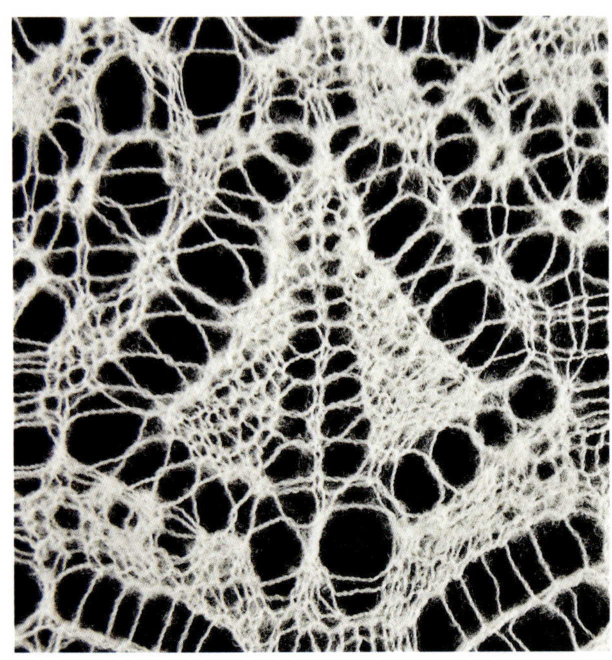

Elongated Diamond inset with Steek variation 2 original pattern.

This Elongated Diamond is unusual in that it is formed with the yarn over/decrease combination every other row, instead of every row in its lower section. Here the centre vertical Steek is formed by yo, k1, yo, and the stitch increases caused by the two yarn overs are balanced by pairing k3tog with the yarn overs that form the outline of the Elongated Diamond. The Steek itself lies flatter than in the previous pattern, but the garter stitch infill lies at a downward slant.

Elongated Diamond inset with Steek variation 2 knitted sample.

Row 1 (RS): K10, yo, k3tog, yo, k10. (23 sts)
Row 2 and all WS rows: Knit.
Row 3: K8, k2tog, yo, k3, yo, k2tog, k8.
Row 5: K6, k3tog, yo, k2, yo, k1, yo, k2, yo, k3tog, k6.
Row 7: K4, k3tog, yo, k4, yo, k1, yo, k4, yo, k3tog, k4.
Row 9: K2, k3tog, yo, k6, yo, k1, yo, k6, yo, k3tog, k2.

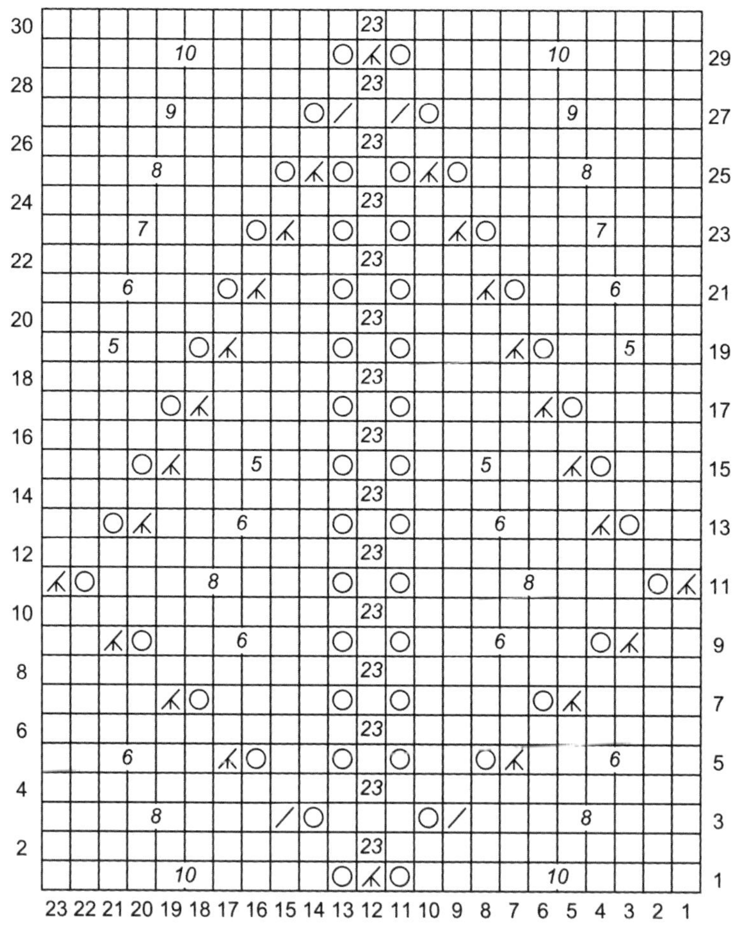

Elongated Diamond inset with Steek variation 2 chart.

Row 11: K3tog, yo, k8, yo, k1, yo, k8, yo, k3tog.
Row 13: K2, yo, k3tog, k6, yo, k1, yo, k6, k3tog, yo, k2.
Row 15: K3, yo, k3tog, k5, yo, k1, yo, k5, k3tog, yo, k3.
Row 17: K4, yo, k3tog, k4, yo, k1, yo, k4, k3tog, yo, k4.
Row 19: K5, yo, k3tog, k3, yo, k1, yo, k3, k3tog, yo, k5.
Row 21: K6, yo, k3tog, k2, yo, k1, yo, k2, k3tog, yo, k6.
Row 23: K7, yo, k3tog, (k1, yo) x 2, k1, k3tog, yo, k7.
Row 25: K8, yo, k3tog, yo, k1, yo, k3tog, yo, k8.
Row 27: K9, yo, k2tog, k1, k2tog, yo, k9.
Row 29: Repeat row 1.

4.3

Elongated Diamond inset with Tree
TEX 8929 Shawl

A Tree shape is made from a central Steek and then 'branches' are added to both sides. It has been placed within an Elongated Diamond with a double outline.

Row 1 (RS): K13, yo, k3tog, yo, k13. (29 sts)
Row 2 and all WS rows: Knit.
Row 3: K10, k3tog, (yo, k1) x 3, yo, k3tog, k10.
Row 5: K8, k3tog, yo, k2tog, (yo, k1) x 3, yo, k2tog, yo, k3tog, k8.
Row 7: K6, k3tog, yo, k2tog, yo, k3, yo, k1, yo, k3, yo, k2tog, yo, k3tog, k6.
Row 9: K4, k3tog, yo, k2tog, yo, k2, k2tog, (yo, k1) x 3, yo, k2tog, k2, yo, k2tog, yo, k3tog, k4.

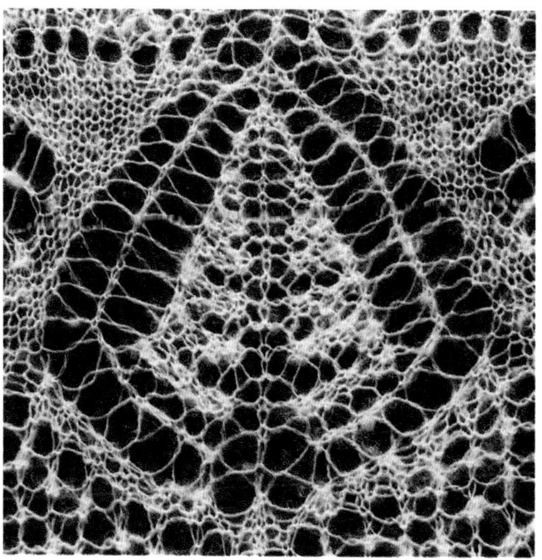

Elongated Diamond inset with Tree original pattern.

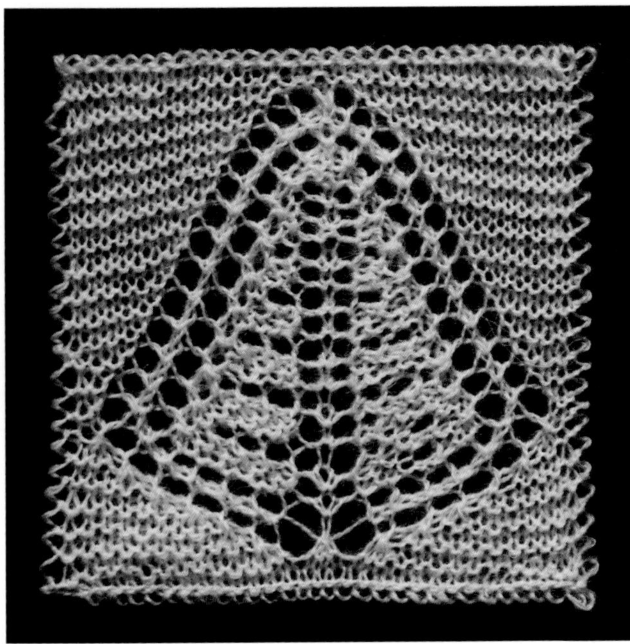

Elongated Diamond inset with Tree knitted sample.

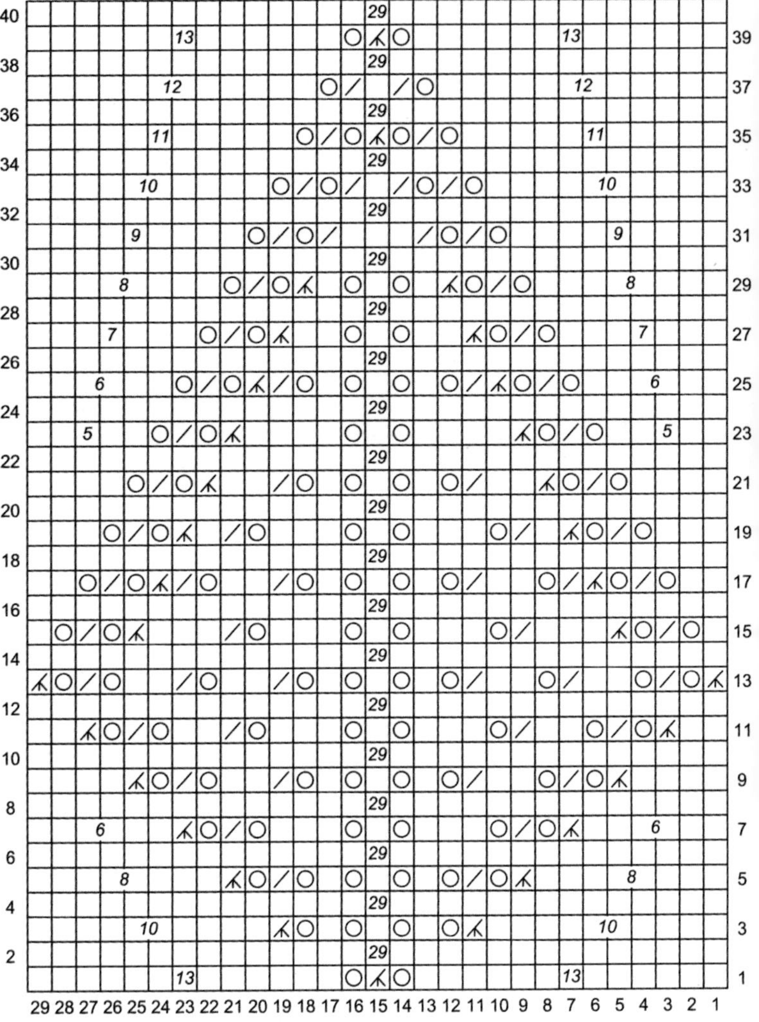

Elongated Diamond inset with Tree chart.

Row 11: K2, k3tog, yo, k2tog, yo, k2, k2tog, yo, k3, yo, k1, yo, k3, yo, k2tog, k2, yo, k2tog, yo, k3tog, k2.

Row 13: K3tog, yo, (k2tog, yo, k2) x 2, k2tog, (yo, k1) x 3, (yo, k2tog, k2) x 2, yo, k2tog, yo, k3tog.

Row 15: K1, yo, k2tog, yo, k3tog, k3, k2tog, yo, k3, yo, k1, yo, k3, yo, k2tog, k3, k3tog, yo, k2tog, yo, k1.

Row 17: K2, yo, k2tog, yo, k3tog, k2tog, yo, k2, k2tog, (yo, k1) x 3, yo, k2tog, k2, yo, k2tog, k3tog, yo, k2tog, yo, k2.

Row 19: K3, yo, k2tog, yo, k3tog, k1, k2tog, yo, k3, yo, k1, yo, k3, yo, k2tog, k1, k3tog, yo, k2tog, yo, k3.

Row 21: K4, yo, k2tog, yo, k3tog, k2, k2tog, (yo, k1) x 3, yo, k2tog, k2, k3tog, yo, k2tog, yo, k4.

Row 23: K5, yo, k2tog, yo, k3tog, k4, yo, k1, yo, k4, k3tog, yo, k2tog, yo, k5.

Row 25: K6, yo, k2tog, yo, k3tog, k2tog, (yo, k1) x 3, yo, k2tog, k3tog, yo, k2tog, yo, k6.

Row 27: K7, yo, k2tog, yo, k3tog, k2, yo, k1, yo, k2, k3tog, yo, k2tog, yo, k7.

Row 29: K8, yo, k2tog, yo, k3tog, (k1, yo) x 2, k1, k3tog, yo, k2tog, yo, k8.

Row 31: K9, (yo, k2tog) x 2, k3, (k2tog, yo) x 2, k9.

Row 33: K10, (yo, k2tog) x 2, k1, (k2tog, yo) x 2, k10.

Row 35: K11, yo, k2tog, yo, k3tog, yo, k2tog, yo, k11.

Row 37: K12, yo, k2tog, k1, k2tog, yo, k12.

Row 39: Repeat row 1.

4.4

Elongated Diamond inset with Peerie Fleas

TEX 2015.148 Scarf

Elongated Diamond inset with Peerie Fleas original pattern.

Elongated Diamond inset with Peerie Fleas knitted sample.

The Peerie Flea (small fly) is a traditional pattern used here to form a dainty mesh inside an Elongated Diamond. The lower edge of the Diamond is made more open by a knit stitch between the decrease and the yarn over.

Row 1 (RS): Knit. (37 sts)
Row 2 (WS): K15, k2tog, (k1, yo) x 2, k1, k2tog, k15.
Row 3: K14, k2tog, k1, yo, k3, yo, k1, k2tog, k14.
Row 4: K13, k2tog, k1, yo, k5, yo, k1, k2tog, k13.
Row 5: K12, k2tog, k1, yo, k7, yo, k1, k2tog, k12.
Row 6: K11, k2tog, k1, yo, k9, yo, k1, k2tog, k11.
Row 7: K10, k2tog, k1, yo, k11, yo, k1, k2tog, k10.
Row 8: K9, k2tog, k1, yo, k13, yo, k1, k2tog, k9.
Row 9: K8, k2tog, k1, yo, k5, k2tog, yo, k1, yo, k2tog, k5, yo, k1, k2tog, k8.
Row 10: K7, k2tog, k1, yo, k5, k2tog, yo, k3, yo, k2tog, k5, yo, k1, k2tog, k7.
Row 11: K6, k2tog, k1, yo, k8, yo, k3tog, yo, k8, yo, k1, k2tog, k6.
Row 12: K5, k2tog, k1, yo, k21, yo, k1, k2tog, k5.
Row 13: K4, k2tog, k1, yo, k5, k2tog, yo, k1, yo, k2tog, k3, k2tog, yo, k1, yo, k2tog, k5, yo, k1, k2tog, k4.
Row 14: K3, k2tog, k1, yo, k5, k2tog, yo, k3, yo, k2tog, k1, k2tog, yo, k3, yo, k2tog, k5, yo, k1, k2tog, k3.
Row 15: K2, k2tog, k1, yo, k8, yo, k3tog, yo, k5, yo, k3tog, yo, k8, yo, k1, k2tog, k2.
Row 16: K1, k2tog, k1, yo, k29, yo, k1, k2tog, k1.
Row 17: K2tog, k1, yo, k5, (k2tog, yo, k1, yo, k2tog, k3) x 2, k2tog, yo, k1, yo, k2tog, k5, yo, k1, k2tog.
Row 18: K7, (k2tog, yo, k3, yo, k2tog, k1) x 2, k2tog, yo, k3, yo, k2tog, k7.
Row 19: K3, yo, k2tog, k4, (yo, k3tog, yo, k5) x 2, yo, k3tog, yo, k4, k2tog, yo, k3
Row 20: Knit.
Row 21: K4, yo, k2tog, k6, k2tog, yo, k1, yo, k2tog, k3, k2tog, yo, k1, yo, k2tog, k6, k2tog, yo, k4.
Row 22: K11, k2tog, yo, k3, yo, k2tog, k1, k2tog, yo, k3, yo, k2tog, k11.
Row 23: K5, yo, k2tog, k6, yo, k3tog, yo, k5, yo, k3tog, yo, k6, k2tog, yo, k5.

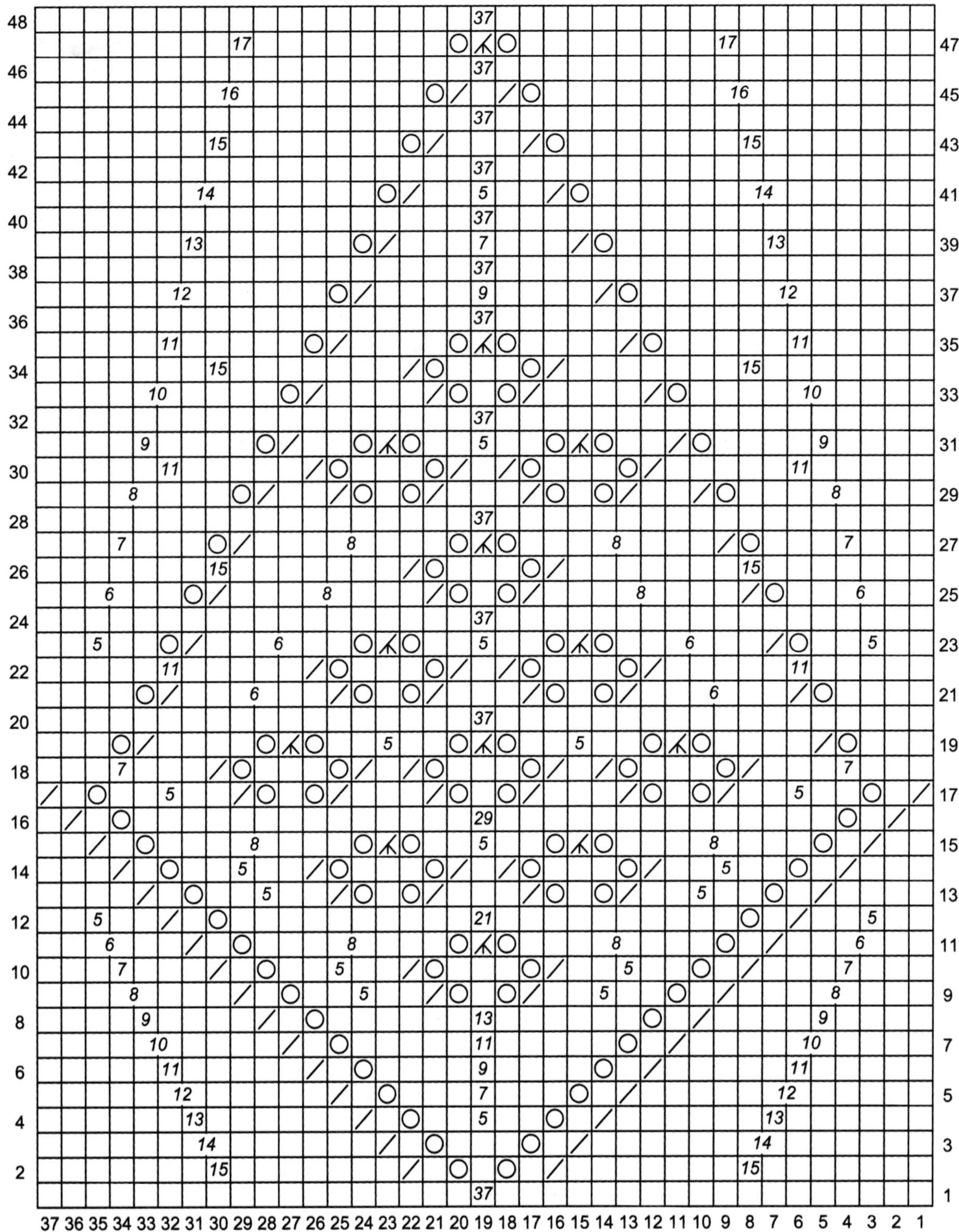

Elongated Diamond inset with Peerie Fleas chart.

Row 24: Knit.
Row 25: K6, yo, k2tog, k8, k2tog, yo, k1, yo, k2tog, k8, k2tog, yo, k6.
Row 26: K15, k2tog, yo, k3, yo, k2tog, k15.
Row 27: K7, yo, k2tog, k8, yo, k3tog, yo, k8, k2tog, yo, k7.
Row 28: Knit.
Row 29: K8, yo, k2tog, k2, k2tog, yo, k1, yo, k2tog, k3, k2tog, yo, k1, yo, k2tog, k2, k2tog, yo, k8.
Row 30: Repeat row 22.
Row 31: K9, yo, k2tog, k2, yo, k3tog, yo, k5, yo, k3tog, yo, k2, k2tog, yo, k9.
Row 32: Knit.
Row 33: K10, yo, k2tog, k4, k2tog, yo, k1, yo, k2tog, k4, k2tog, yo, k10.
Row 34: Repeat row 26.
Row 35: K11, yo, k2tog, k4, yo, k3tog, yo, k4, k2tog, yo, k11.
Row 36: Knit.
Row 37: K12, yo, k2tog, k9, k2tog, yo, k12.
Row 38: Knit.
Row 39: K13, yo, k2tog, k7, k2tog, yo, k13.
Row 40: Knit.
Row 41: K14, yo, k2tog, k5, k2tog, yo, k14.
Row 42: Knit.
Row 43: K15, yo, k2tog, k3, k2tog, yo, k15.
Row 44: Knit.
Row 45: K16, yo, k2tog, k1, k2tog, yo, k16.
Row 46: Knit.
Row 47: K17, yo, k3tog, yo, k17.
Row 48: Knit.

4.5

Elongated Diamond inset with Bead mesh variation 1
TEX 2019.43 Shawl

Elongated Diamond inset with Bead mesh variation 1 original pattern.

Elongated Diamond inset with Bead mesh variation 1 knitted sample.

The pattern in the middle of this Elongated Diamond is essentially the Bead stitches stacked and joined on top of each other, with additional lace stitches to both sides, forming a mesh.

Row 1 (RS): K16, yo, k3tog, yo, k16. (35 sts)
Row 2 (WS): K13, k2tog, k1, yo, k3, yo, k1, k2tog, k13.
Row 3: K12, k2tog, k1, yo, k5, yo, k1, k2tog, k12.
Row 4: K11, k2tog, k1, yo, k7, yo, k1, k2tog, k11.
Row 5: K10, k2tog, k1, yo, k9, yo, k1, k2tog, k10.
Row 6: K9, k2tog, k1, yo, k11, yo, k1, k2tog, k9.
Row 7: K8, k2tog, k1, yo, k4, k2tog, yo, k1, yo, k2tog, k4, yo, k1, k2tog, k8.
Row 8: K7, k2tog, k1, yo, k4, k2tog, yo, k3, yo, k2tog, k4, yo, k1, k2tog, k7.

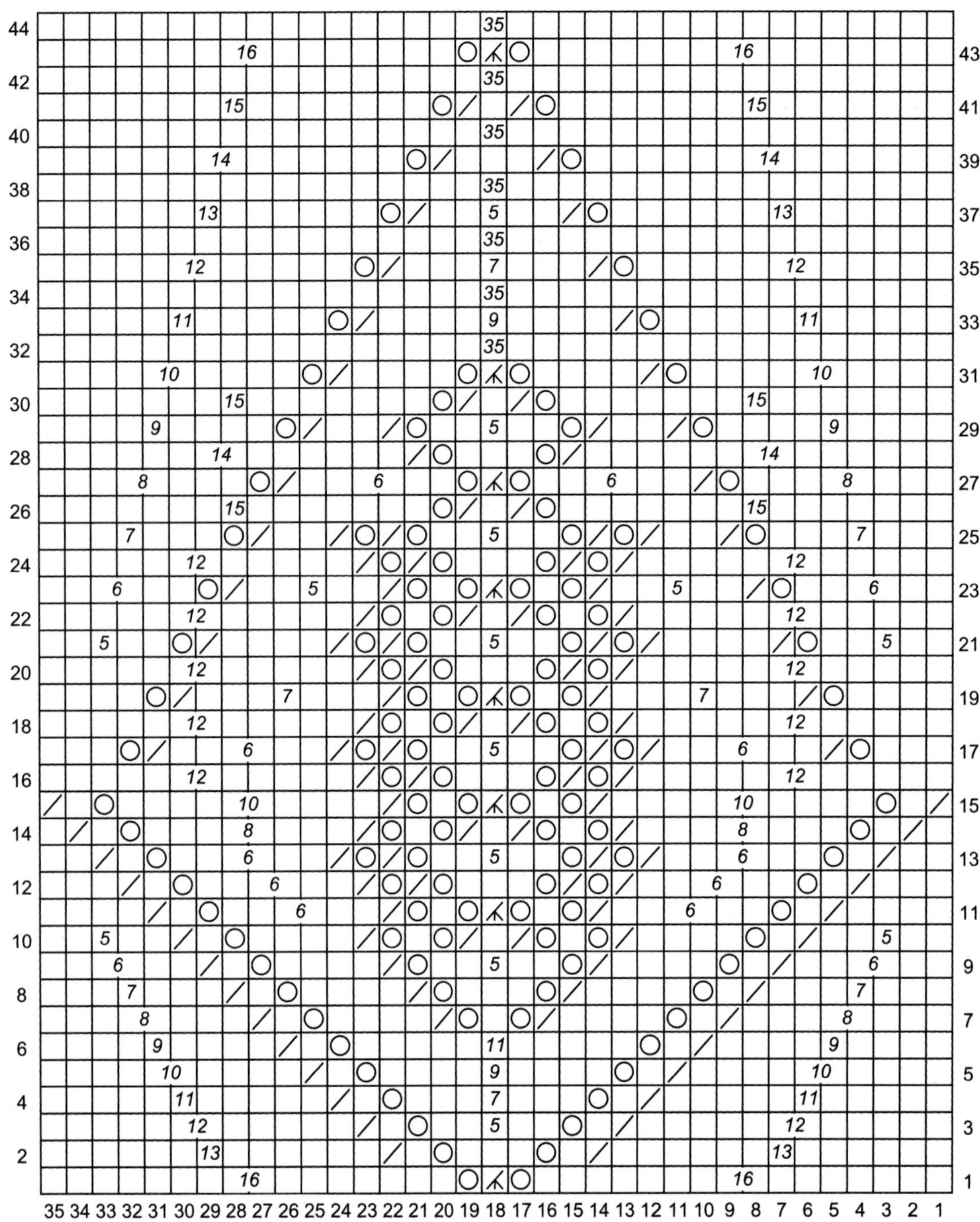

Elongated Diamond inset with Bead mesh variation 1 chart.

Row 9: K6, k2tog, k1, yo, k4, k2tog, yo, k5, yo, k2tog, k4, yo, k1, k2tog, k6.
Row 10: K5, k2tog, k1, yo, k4, k2tog, yo, k1, yo, k2tog, k1, k2tog, yo, k1, yo, k2tog, k4, yo, k1, k2tog, k5.
Row 11: K4, k2tog, k1, yo, k6, k2tog, yo, k1, yo, k3tog, yo, k1, yo, k2tog, k6, yo, k1, k2tog, k4.
Row 12: K3, k2tog, k1, yo, k6, (k2tog, yo) x 2, k3, (yo, k2tog) x 2, k6, yo, k1, k2tog, k3.
Row 13: K2, k2tog, k1, yo, k6, (k2tog, yo) x 2, k5, (yo, k2tog) x 2, k6, yo, k1, k2tog, k2.
Row 14: K1, k2tog, k1, yo, k8, k2tog, yo, k1, yo, k2tog, k1, k2tog, yo, k1, yo, k2tog, k8, yo, k1, k2tog, k1.

Row 15: K2tog, k1, yo, k10, k2tog, yo, k1, yo, k3tog, yo, k1, yo, k2tog, k10, yo, k1, k2tog.
Row 16: K12, (k2tog, yo) x 2, k3, (yo, k2tog) x 2, k12.
Row 17: K3, yo, k2tog, k6, (k2tog, yo) x 2, k5, (yo, k2tog) x 2, k6, k2tog, yo, k3.
Row 18: K12, k2tog, yo, k1, yo, k2tog, k1, k2tog, yo, k1, yo, k2tog, k12.
Row 19: K4, yo, k2tog, k7, k2tog, yo, k1, yo, k3tog, yo, k1, yo, k2tog, k7, k2tog, yo, k4.
Row 20: Repeat row 16.
Row 21: K5, yo, k2tog, k4, (k2tog, yo) x 2, k5, (yo, k2tog) x 2, k4, k2tog, yo, k5.
Row 22: Repeat row 18.
Row 23: K6, yo, k2tog, k5, k2tog, yo, k1, yo, k3tog, yo, k1, yo, k2tog, k5, k2tog, yo, k6.
Row 24: Repeat row 16.
Row 25: K7, yo, k2tog, k2, (k2tog, yo) x 2, k5, (yo, k2tog) x 2, k2, k2tog, yo, k7.
Row 26: K15, yo, k2tog, k1, k2tog, yo, k15.
Row 27: K8, yo, k2tog, k6, yo, k3tog, yo, k6, k2tog, yo, k8.
Row 28: K14, k2tog, yo, k3, yo, k2tog, k14.
Row 29: K9, yo, k2tog, k2, k2tog, yo, k5, yo, k2tog, k2, k2tog, yo, k9.
Row 30: Repeat row 26.
Row 31: K10, yo, k2tog, k4, yo, k3tog, yo, k4, k2tog, yo, k10.
Row 32: Knit.
Row 33: K11, yo, k2tog, k9, k2tog, yo, k11.
Row 34: Knit.
Row 35: K12, yo, k2tog, k7, k2tog, yo, k12.
Row 36: Knit.
Row 37: K13, yo, k2tog, k5, k2tog, yo, k13.
Row 38: Knit.
Row 39: K14, yo, k2tog, k3, k2tog, yo, k14.
Row 40: Knit.
Row 41: Repeat row 26.
Row 42: Knit.
Row 43: Repeat row 1.
Row 44: Knit.

4.6

Elongated Diamond inset with Bead mesh variation 2
TEX 1997.86 Shawl

Once again the Bead stitch is at the centre of this infill but the mesh surrounding it is more extended and complex.

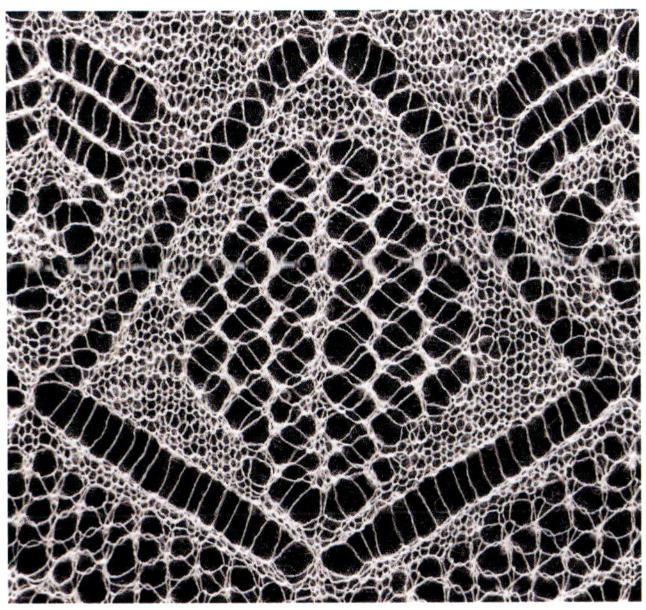

Elongated Diamond inset with Bead mesh variation 2 original pattern.

Elongated Diamond inset with Bead mesh variation 2 knitted sample.

Although worked very similarly to the previous pattern, it has a different look.

Row 1 (RS): K18, k2tog, yo, k1, yo, k2tog, k18. (41 sts)
Row 2 (WS): K17, k2tog, yo, k3, yo, k2tog, k17.

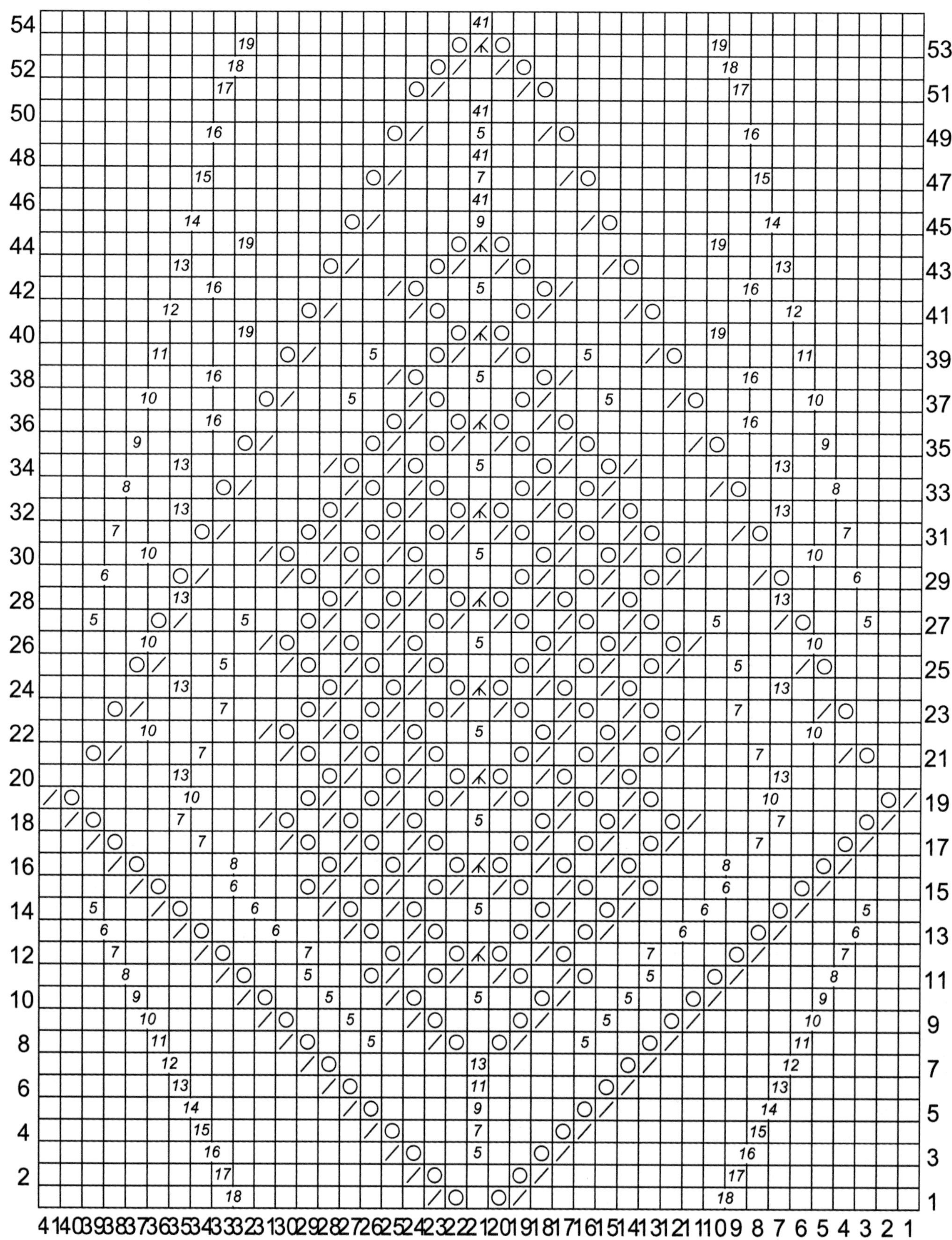

Elongated Diamond inset with Bead mesh variation 2 chart.

Row 3: K16, k2tog, yo, k5, yo, k2tog, k16.
Row 4: K15, k2tog, yo, k7, yo, k2tog, k15.
Row 5: K14, k2tog, yo, k9, yo, k2tog, k14.
Row 6: K13, k2tog, yo, k11, yo, k2tog, k13.
Row 7: K12, k2tog, yo, k13, yo, k2tog, k12.
Row 8: K11, k2tog, yo, k5, k2tog, yo, k1, yo, k2tog, k5, yo, k2tog, k11.
Row 9: K10, k2tog, yo, k5, k2tog, yo, k3, yo, k2tog, k5, yo, k2tog, k10.
Row 10: K9, (k2tog, yo, k5) x 2, yo, k2tog, k5, yo, k2tog, k9.
Row 11: K8, k2tog, yo, k5, (yo, k2tog, k1) x 2, k2tog, yo, k1, k2tog, yo, k5, yo, k2tog, k8.
Row 12: K7, k2tog, yo, k7, yo, k2tog, k1, yo, k3tog, yo, k1, k2tog, yo, k7, yo, k2tog, k7.
Row 13: (K6, k2tog, yo) x 2, k1, k2tog, yo, k3, yo, k2tog, k1, (yo, k2tog, k6) x 2.
Row 14: K5, k2tog, yo, k6, k2tog, yo, k1, k2tog, yo, k5, yo, k2tog, k1, yo, k2tog, k6, yo, k2tog, k5.
Row 15: K4, k2tog, yo, k6, (yo, k2tog, k1) x 3, (k2tog, yo, k1) x 2, k2tog, yo, k6, yo, k2tog, k4.
Row 16: K3, k2tog, yo, k8, (yo, k2tog, k1) x 2, yo, k3tog, (yo, k1, k2tog) x 2, yo, k8, yo, k2tog, k3.
Row 17: K2, k2tog, yo, k7, (k2tog, yo, k1) x 2, k2tog, yo, k3, (yo, k2tog, k1) x 2, yo, k2tog, k7, yo, k2tog, k2.
Row 18: K1, k2tog, yo, k7, (k2tog, yo, k1) x 2, k2tog, yo, k5, (yo, k2tog, k1) x 2, yo, k2tog, k7, yo, k2tog, k1.
Row 19: K2tog, yo, k10, (yo, k2tog, k1) x 3, (k2tog, yo, k1) x 2, k2tog, yo, k10, yo, k2tog.
Row 20: K13, (yo, k2tog, k1) x 2, yo, k3tog, (yo, k1, k2tog) x 2, yo, k13.
Row 21: K2, yo, k2tog, k7, (k2tog, yo, k1) x 2, k2tog, yo, k3, (yo, k2tog, k1) x 2, yo, k2tog, k7, k2tog, yo, k2.
Row 22: K10, (k2tog, yo, k1) x 2, k2tog, yo, k5, (yo, k2tog, k1) x 2, yo, k2tog, k10.
Row 23: K3, yo, k2tog, k7, (yo, k2tog, k1) x 3, (k2tog, yo, k1) x 2, k2tog, yo, k7, k2tog, yo, k3.
Row 24: Repeat row 20.
Row 25: K4, yo, k2tog, k5, (k2tog, yo, k1) x 2, k2tog, yo, k3, (yo, k2tog, k1) x 2, yo, k2tog, k5, k2tog, yo, k4.
Row 26: Repeat row 22.
Row 27: K5, yo, k2tog, k5, (yo, k2tog, k1) x 3, (k2tog, yo, k1) x 2, (k2tog, yo, k5) x 2.
Row 28: Repeat row 20.
Row 29: K6, yo, k2tog, k3, (k2tog, yo, k1) x 2, k2tog, yo, k3, (yo, k2tog, k1) x 2, yo, k2tog, k3, k2tog, yo, k6.
Row 30: Repeat row 22.
Row 31: K7, yo, k2tog, k3, (yo, k2tog, k1) x 3, (k2tog, yo, k1) x 2, k2tog, yo, k3, k2tog, yo, k7.
Row 32: Repeat row 20.
Row 33: K8, yo, k2tog, k4, k2tog, yo, k1, k2tog, yo, k3, yo, k2tog, k1, yo, k2tog, k4, k2tog, yo, k8.
Row 34: K13, k2tog, yo, k1, k2tog, yo, k5, yo, k2tog, k1, yo, k2tog, k13.
Row 35: K9, yo, k2tog, k4, (yo, k2tog, k1) x 2, k2tog, yo, k1, k2tog, yo, k4, k2tog, yo, k9.
Row 36: K16, yo, k2tog, k1, yo, k3tog, yo, k1, k2tog, yo, k16.
Row 37: K10, yo, k2tog, k5, k2tog, yo, k3, yo, k2tog, k5, k2tog, yo, k10.
Row 38: Repeat row 3.
Row 39: K11, yo, k2tog, k5, yo, k2tog, k1, k2tog, yo, k5, k2tog, yo, k11.
Row 40: K19, yo, k3tog, yo, k19.
Row 41: K12, yo, k2tog, k3, k2tog, yo, k3, yo, k2tog, k3, k2tog, yo, k12.
Row 42: Repeat row 3.
Row 43: K13, yo, k2tog, k3, yo, k2tog, k1, k2tog, yo, k3, k2tog, yo, k13.
Row 44: Repeat row 40.
Row 45: K14, yo, k2tog, k9, k2tog, yo, k14.
Row 46: Knit.
Row 47: K15, yo, k2tog, k7, k2tog, yo, k15.
Row 48: Knit.
Row 49: K16, yo, k2tog, k5, k2tog, yo, k16.
Row 50: Knit.
Row 51: K17, yo, k2tog, k3, k2tog, yo, k17.
Row 52: K18, yo, k2tog, k1, k2tog, yo, k18.
Row 53: Repeat row 40.
Row 54: Knit.

4.7

Elongated Diamond inset with centre Fancy stitch and Zigzag

TEX 2014.25 Shawl

This beautiful pattern has an unusual centre stitch flanked on either side by four-hole Zigzags. The top of the Elongated Diamond is made with two edges. It is not clear why this was done in the original piece. We have included the second outer edge to remain true to the original but it can be omitted.

Elongated Diamond inset with centre Fancy stitch and Zigzag original pattern.

Elongated Diamond inset with centre Fancy stitch and Zigzag knitted sample.

Row 1 (RS): K21, k2tog, yo, k1, yo, k2tog, k21. (47 sts)
Row 2 (WS): K20, k2tog, yo, k3, yo, k2tog, k20.
Row 3: K19, k2tog, yo, k5, yo, k2tog, k19.
Row 4: K18, k2tog, yo, k7, yo, k2tog, k18.
Row 5: K17, k2tog, yo, k9, yo, k2tog, k17.
Row 6: K16, k2tog, yo, k11, yo, k2tog, k16.
Row 7: K15, k2tog, yo, k13, yo, k2tog, k15.
Row 8: K14, k2tog, yo, k15, yo, k2tog, k14.
Row 9: K13, (k2tog, yo) x 5, k1, (yo, k2tog) x 5, k13.
Row 10: K12, (k2tog, yo) x 5, k3, (yo, k2tog) x 5, k12.
Row 11: K11, (k2tog, yo) x 5, k5, (yo, k2tog) x 5, k11.
Row 12: K10, (k2tog, yo) x 5, k7, (yo, k2tog) x 5, k10.
Row 13: K9, (k2tog, yo) x 5, k9, (yo, k2tog) x 5, k9.
Row 14: K8, (k2tog, yo) x 5, k11, (yo, k2tog) x 5, k8.
Row 15: K7, (k2tog, yo) x 5, k13, (yo, k2tog) x 5, k7.
Row 16: K6, k2tog, yo, k3, (yo, k2tog) x 4, k3, k2tog x 2, k4, (yo, k2tog) x 3, yo, k3, yo, k2tog, k6. (46 sts)
Row 17: K5, k2tog, yo, k5, (yo, k2tog) x 3, yo, k3, k2tog x 2, k3, (yo, k2tog) x 3, yo, k5, yo, k2tog, k5.
Row 18: K4, k2tog, yo, k7, (yo, k2tog) x 3, yo, k2, k2tog x 2, k2, (yo, k2tog) x 3, yo, k7, yo, k2tog, k4.
Row 19: K3, k2tog, yo, k9, (yo, k2tog) x 3, yo, k1, k2tog x 2, k1, (yo, k2tog) x 3, yo, k9, yo, k2tog, k3.
Row 20: K2, k2tog, yo, k11, (yo, k2tog) x 3, yo, k2tog x 2, (yo, k2tog) x 3, yo, k11, yo, k2tog, k2.
Row 21: K1, k2tog, yo, k10, (k2tog, yo) x 4, k1, 1/1 RC, k1, (yo, k2tog) x 4, k10, yo, k2tog, k1.
Row 22: K2tog, yo, k10, (k2tog, yo) x 4, k6, (yo, k2tog) x 4, k10, yo, k2tog.
Row 23: K11, (k2tog, yo) x 4, k8, (yo, k2tog) x 4, k11.
Row 24: K2, yo, k2tog, k6, (k2tog, yo) x 4, k10, (yo, k2tog) x 4, k6, k2tog, yo, k2.
Row 25: K9, (k2tog, yo) x 4, k12, (yo, k2tog) x 4, k9.
Row 26: K3, yo, k2tog, k6, (yo, k2tog) x 3, yo, k4, k2tog x 2, k4, (yo, k2tog) x 3, yo, k6, k2tog, yo, k3.
Row 27: K12, (yo, k2tog) x 3, yo, k3, k2tog x 2, k3, (yo, k2tog) x 3, yo, k12.
Row 28: K2tog, yo, k2, yo, k2tog, k7, (yo, k2tog) x 3, yo, k2, k2tog x 2, k2, (yo, k2tog) x 3, yo, k7, k2tog, yo, k2, yo, k2tog.
Row 29: K14, (yo, k2tog) x 3, yo, k1, k2tog x 2, k1, (yo, k2tog) x 3, yo, k14.
Row 30: K2, yo, k2tog, k1, yo, k2tog, k8, (yo, k2tog) x 3, yo, k2tog x 2, (yo, k2tog) x 3, yo, k8, k2tog, yo, k1, k2tog, yo, k2.

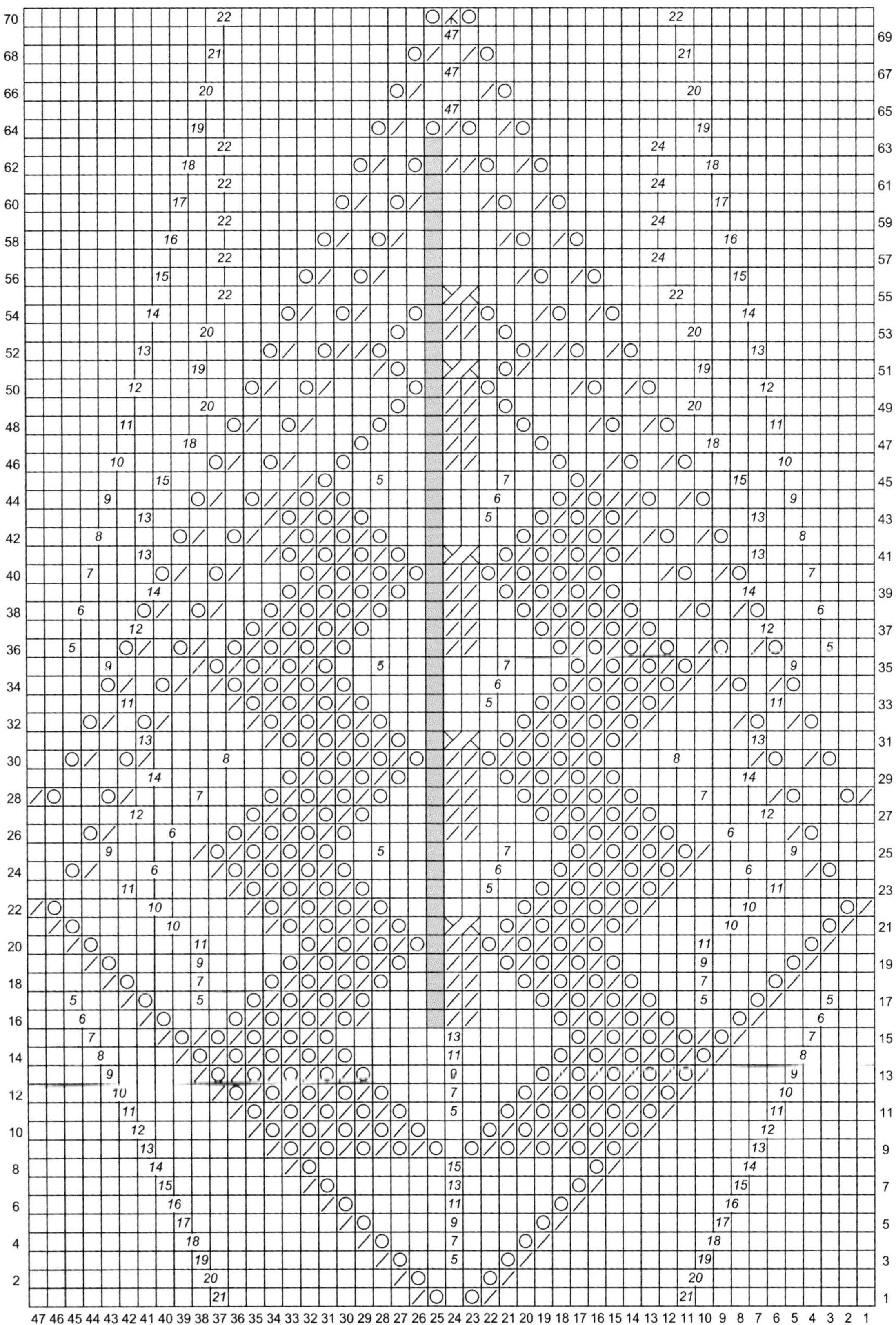

Elongated Diamond inset with centre Fancy stitch and Zigzag chart.

Row 31: K13, (k2tog, yo) x 4, k1, 1/1 RC, k1, (yo, k2tog) x 4, k13.
Row 32: K3, yo, k2tog, k1, yo, k2tog, k4, (k2tog, yo) x 4, k6, (yo, k2tog) x 4, k4, k2tog, yo, k1, k2tog, yo, k3.
Row 33: Repeat row 23.
Row 34: K4, (yo, k2tog, k1) x 2, (k2tog, yo) x 4, k10, (yo, k2tog) x 4, (k1, k2tog, yo) x 2, k4.
Row 35: Repeat row 25.
Row 36: K5, (yo, k2tog, k1) x 2, (yo, k2tog) x 3, yo, k4, k2tog x 2, k4, (yo, k2tog) x 3, (yo, k1, k2tog) x 2, yo, k5.
Row 37: Repeat row 27.
Row 38: K6, yo, k2tog, k1, yo, k2tog, k2, (yo, k2tog) x 3, yo, k2, k2tog x 2, k2, (yo, k2tog) x 3, yo, k2, k2tog, yo, k1, k2tog, yo, k6.
Row 39: Repeat row 29.
Row 40: K7, yo, k2tog, k1, yo, k2tog, k3, (yo, k2tog) x 3, yo, k2tog x 2, (yo, k2tog) x 3, yo, k3, k2tog, yo, k1, k2tog, yo, k7.
Row 41: Repeat row 31.
Row 42: K8, (yo, k2tog, k1) x 2, (k2tog, yo) x 3, k6, (yo, k2tog) x 3, (k1, k2tog, yo) x 2, k8.
Row 43: K13, (k2tog, yo) x 3, k8, (yo, k2tog) x 3, k13.
Row 44: K9, yo, k2tog, k1, yo, k2tog x 2, yo, k2tog, yo, k10, yo, k2tog, yo, k2tog x 2, yo, k1, k2tog, yo, k9.
Row 45: K15, k2tog, yo, k12, yo, k2tog, k15.
Row 46: K10, yo, k2tog, k1, yo, k2tog, k2, yo, k4, k2tog x 2, k4, yo, k2, k2tog, yo, k1, k2tog, yo, k10.
Row 47: K18, yo, k3, k2tog x 2, k3, yo, k18.
Row 48: K11, yo, k2tog, k1, yo, k2tog, k3, yo, k2, k2tog x 2, k2, yo, k3, k2tog, yo, k1, k2tog, yo, k11.
Row 49: K20, yo, k1, k2tog x 2, k1, yo, k20.
Row 50: K12, yo, k2tog, k1, yo, k2tog, k4, yo, k2tog x 2, yo, k4, k2tog, yo, k1, k2tog, yo, k12.
Row 51: K19, k2tog, yo, k1, 1/1 RC, k1, yo, k2tog, k19.
Row 52: K13, yo, k2tog, k1, yo, k2tog x 2, yo, k6, yo, k2tog x 2, yo, k1, k2tog, yo, k13.
Row 53: Repeat row 49.
Row 54: K14, yo, k2tog, k1, yo, k2tog, k2, yo, k2tog x 2, yo, k2, k2tog, yo, k1, k2tog, yo, k14.
Row 55: K22, 1/1 RC, k22.
Row 56: K15, yo, k2tog, k1, yo, k2tog, k6, k2tog, yo, k1, k2tog, yo, k15.
Row 57: Knit.
Row 58: K16, yo, k2tog, k1, yo, k2tog, k4, k2tog, yo, k1, k2tog, yo, k16.
Row 59: Knit.
Row 60: K17, yo, k2tog, k1, yo, k2tog, k2, k2tog, yo, k1, k2tog, yo, k17.
Row 61: Knit.
Row 62: K18, yo, k2tog, k1, yo, k2tog x 2, yo, k1, k2tog, yo, k18.
Row 63: Knit.
Row 64: K19, yo, k2tog, k1, yo, k2tog, yo, k1, k2tog, yo, k19. (47 sts)
Row 65: Knit.
Row 66: K20, yo, k2tog, k3, k2tog, yo, k20.
Row 67: Knit.
Row 68: K21, yo, k2tog, k1, k2tog, yo, k21.
Row 69: Knit.
Row 70: K22, yo, p3tog, yo, k22.

Sprootin' Seed, Da Auld Wife or Paisley

There are two forms of Elongated Diamonds that have a 'hook' at the top. The hook can be worked either to the right or left but usually it is found to the left. An Elongated Diamond with a small hook has been named as Sprootin' Seed, and another source has it named Da Auld Wife (The Old Woman). Sometimes the pattern is called Paisley by those outwith Shetland because the shape is similar to the *boteh* form found in Paisley shawls from the nineteenth century. The larger hook has been named Paisley here because the known Sprootin' Seed/Auld Wife patterns all have a small hook. Like other Elongated Diamonds, this form can be infilled with different patterns.

4.8

Sprootin' Seed with Sparl infill
TEX 2004.349 Shawl

Patterns are sometimes named after natural features they resemble. A Sparl is the lower intestine of an animal. The pattern is a simple alternative to a Steek infill.

Row 1 (RS): Knit. (23 sts)
Row 2 (WS): K9, (k2tog, yo) x 2, k10.
Row 3: K8, k2tog, yo, k3, yo, k2tog, k8.
Row 4: K7, k2tog, yo, k5, yo, k2tog, k7.
Row 5: K6, k2tog, yo, k7, yo, k2tog, k6.
Row 6: K5, k2tog, yo, k9, yo, k2tog, k5.

Sprootin' Seed with Sparl infill original pattern.

Sprootin' Seed with Sparl infill knitted sample.

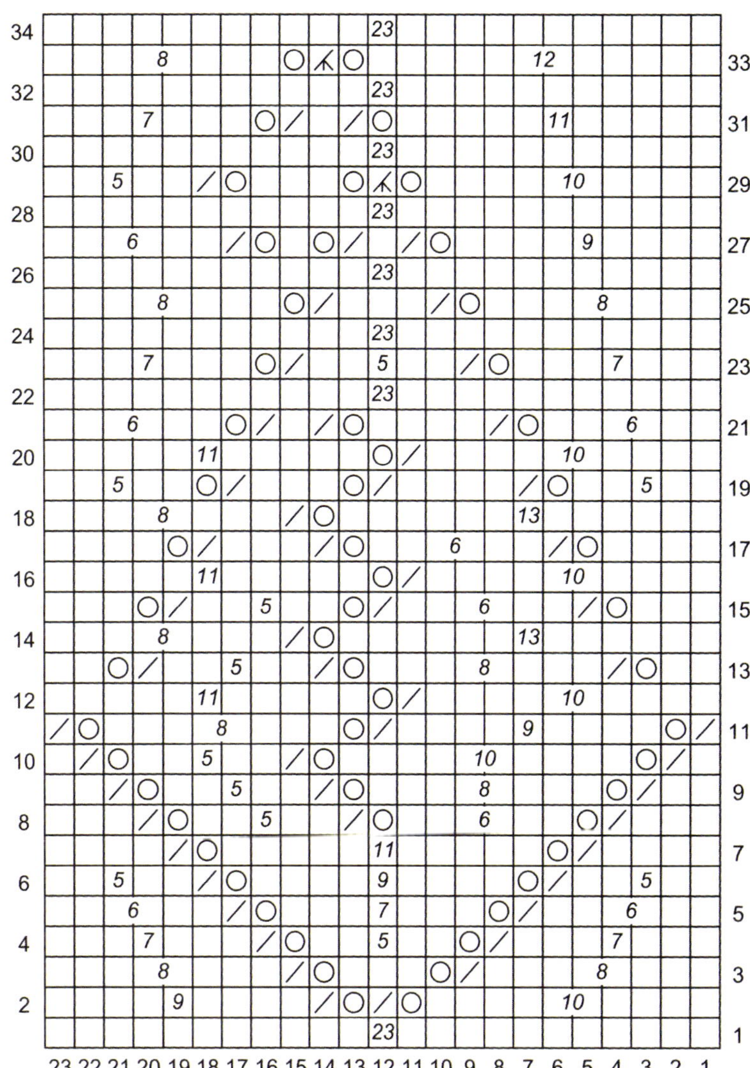

Sprootin' Seed with Sparl infill chart.

Row 7: K4, k2tog, yo, k11, yo, k2tog, k4.
Row 8: K3, k2tog, yo, k5, k2tog, yo, k6, yo, k2tog, k3.
Row 9: K2, k2tog, yo, k8, yo, k2tog, k5, yo, k2tog, k2.
Row 10: K1, k2tog, yo, k5, k2tog, yo, k10, yo, k2tog, k1.
Row 11: K2tog, yo, k9, k2tog, yo, k8, yo, k2tog.
Row 12: K11, yo, k2tog, k10.
Row 13: K2, yo, k2tog, k8, yo, k2tog, k5, k2tog, yo, k2.
Row 14: K8, k2tog, yo, k13.
Row 15: K3, yo, k2tog, k6, k2tog, yo, k5, k2tog, yo, k3.
Row 16: Repeat row 12.
Row 17: K4, yo, k2tog, k6, yo, k2tog, k3, k2tog, yo, k4.
Row 18: Repeat row 14.
Row 19: K5, yo, k2tog, k4, k2tog, yo, k3, k2tog, yo, k5.
Row 20: Repeat row 12.
Row 21: K6, yo, k2tog, k4, yo, k2tog, k1, k2tog, yo, k6.
Row 22: Knit.
Row 23: K7, yo, k2tog, k5, k2tog, yo, k7.
Row 24: Knit.
Row 25: K8, yo, k2tog, k3, k2tog, yo, k8.
Row 26: Knit.
Row 27: K9, yo, k2tog, k1, k2tog, yo, k1, yo, k2tog, k6.
Row 28: Knit.
Row 29: K10, yo, k3tog, yo, k3, yo, k2tog, k5.
Row 30: Knit.
Row 31: K11, yo, k2tog, k1, k2tog, yo, k7.
Row 32: Knit.
Row 33: K12, yo, k3tog, yo, k8.
Row 34: Knit.

4.9

Paisley with Bead columns and Zigzag infill

TEX 7754 Shawl

The bold centre Zigzag is flanked by the Bead stitch. The knitter wished to fill as much of the Paisley pattern as possible, placing the Bead stitch alternately on either side of the Zigzag.

Row 1 (RS): Knit. (39 sts)
Row 2 (WS): K17, k2tog, yo, k1, yo, k2tog, k17.
Row 3: K16, k2tog, yo, k3, yo, k2tog, k16.
Row 4: K15, k2tog, yo, k5, yo, k2tog, k15.
Row 5: K14, k2tog, yo, k7, yo, k2tog, k14.
Row 6: K13, k2tog, yo, k9, yo, k2tog, k13.
Row 7: K12, k2tog, yo, k11, yo, k2tog, k12.
Row 8: K11, k2tog, yo, k13, yo, k2tog, k11.
Row 9: K10, k2tog, yo, k15, yo, k2tog, k10.
Row 10: K9, k2tog, yo, k17, yo, k2tog, k9.
Row 11: K8, k2tog, yo, k4, (yo, k2tog) x 6, k3, yo, k2tog, k8.
Row 12: K7, k2tog, yo, k3, k2tog, yo, k1, (yo, k2tog) x 6, k3, yo, k2tog, k7.
Row 13: K6, k2tog, yo, k3, (k2tog, yo) x 6, (k3, yo, k2tog) x 2, k6.
Row 14: K5, k2tog, yo, k3, k2tog, yo, k5, (yo, k2tog) x 6, k3, yo, k2tog, k5.
Row 15: K4, k2tog, yo, k3, k2tog, yo, k1, (yo, k2tog) x 6, k1, k2tog, yo, k6, yo, k2tog, k4.
Row 16: K3, k2tog, yo, k8, yo, p3tog, (yo, k2tog) x 5, yo, (k3, yo, k2tog) x 2, k3.
Row 17: K2, k2tog, yo, k3, k2tog, yo, k5, (yo, k2tog) x 6, k9, yo, k2tog, k2.
Row 18: K1, k2tog, yo, k9, k2tog, yo, k1, (yo, k2tog) x 6, k1, k2tog, yo, k6, yo, k2tog, k1.
Row 19: K2tog, yo, k8, yo, k3tog, (yo, k2tog) x 5, yo, k3, yo, k2tog, k9, yo, k2tog.
Row 20: K10, k2tog, yo, k5, (yo, k2tog) x 6, k10.
Row 21: K2, yo, k2tog, k5, k2tog, yo, k1, (yo, k2tog) x 6, k1, k2tog, yo, k8, k2tog, yo, k2.
Row 22: K13, yo, p3tog, (yo, k2tog) x 5, yo, k3, yo, k2tog, k8.
Row 23: K3, yo, k2tog, k2, k2tog, yo, k5, (yo, k2tog) x 6, k8, k2tog, yo, k3.
Row 24: K12, k2tog, yo, k1, (yo, k2tog) x 6, k1, k2tog, yo, k9.
Row 25: K4, yo, k2tog, k4, yo, k3tog, (yo, k2tog) x 5, yo, k3, yo, k2tog, k5, k2tog, yo, k4.
Row 26: Repeat row 20.
Row 27: K5, yo, k2tog, k2, k2tog, yo, k1, (yo, k2tog) x 6, k1, (k2tog, yo, k5) x 2.

Paisley with Bead columns and Zigzag infill original pattern.

Paisley with Bead columns and Zigzag infill knitted sample.

Row 28: Repeat row 22.
Row 29: K6, yo, k2tog, k6, (yo, k2tog) x 6, k5, k2tog, yo, k6.
Row 30: Repeat row 24.
Row 31: K7, yo, k2tog, k1, yo, k3tog, (yo, k2tog) x 5, yo, k3, yo, k2tog, k2, k2tog, yo, k7.
Row 32: Repeat row 20.
Row 33: K8, yo, k2tog, k2, (yo, k2tog) x 6, k1, k2tog, yo, k2, k2tog, yo, k8.
Row 34: K13, yo, p3tog, (yo, k2tog) x 5, yo, k13.
Row 35: K9, yo, k2tog, k3, (yo, k2tog) x 6, k2, k2tog, yo, k9.
Row 36: K12, k2tog, yo, k1, (yo, k2tog) x 6, k12.

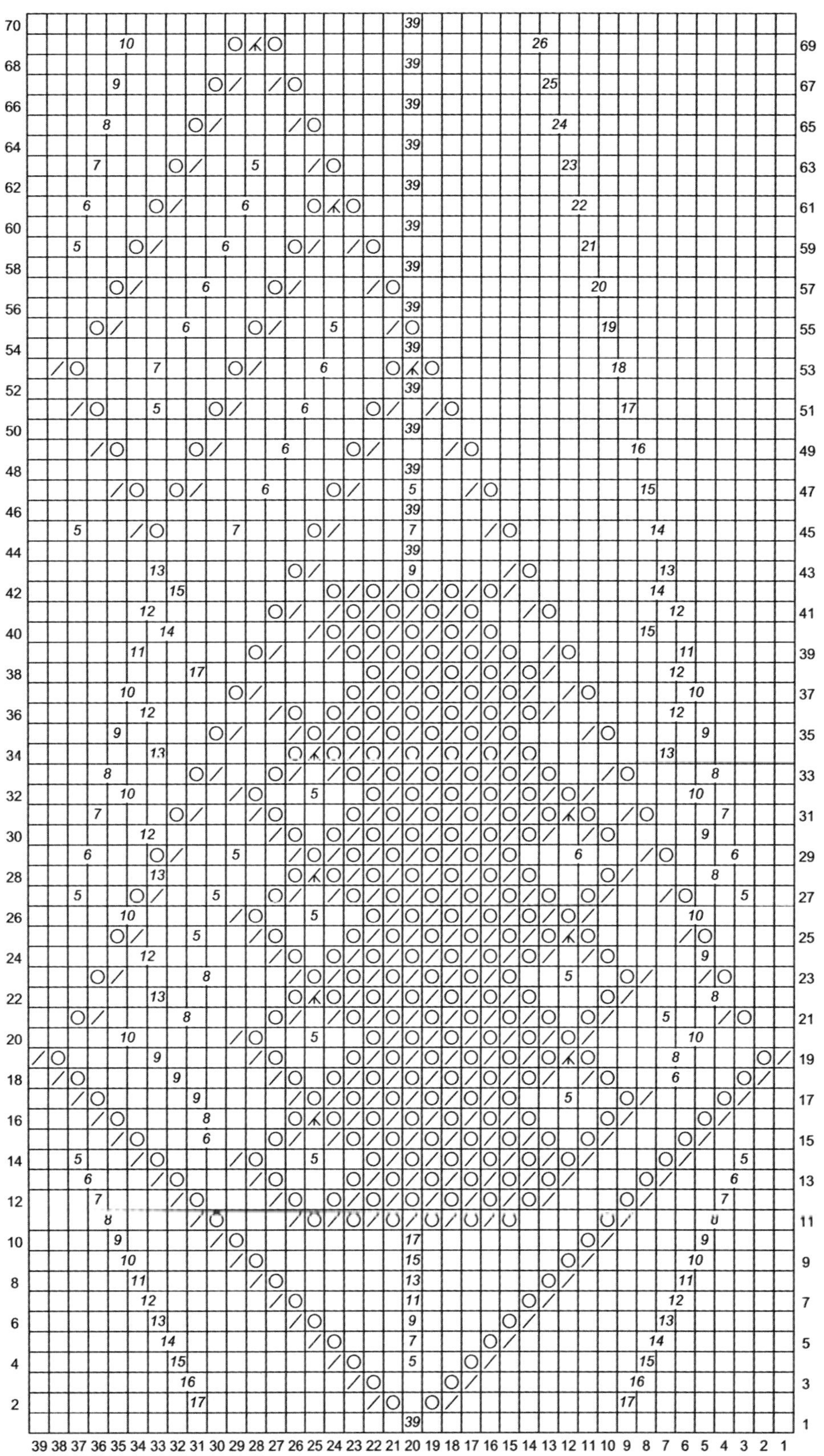

Paisley with Bead columns and Zigzag infill chart.

Row 37: K10, yo, k2tog, k1, (k2tog, yo) x 5, k4, k2tog, yo, k10.
Row 38: K17, (yo, k2tog) x 5, k12.
Row 39: K11, yo, k2tog, k1, (yo, k2tog) x 5, k2, k2tog, yo, k11.
Row 40: K14, (k2tog, yo) x 5, k15.
Row 41: K12, yo, k2tog, k2, (yo, k2tog) x 4, k1, k2tog, yo, k12.
Row 42: K15, (yo, k2tog) x 5, k14.
Row 43: K13, yo, k2tog, k9, k2tog, yo, k13.
Row 44: Knit.
Row 45: K14, yo, k2tog, k7, k2tog, yo, k7, yo, k2tog, k5.
Row 46: Knit.
Row 47: K15, yo, k2tog, k5, k2tog, yo, k6, k2tog, yo, k1, yo, k2tog, k4.
Row 48: Knit.
Row 49: K16, yo, k2tog, k3, k2tog, yo, k6, k2tog, yo, k3, yo, k2tog, k3.
Row 50: Knit.
Row 51: K17, yo, k2tog, k1, k2tog, yo, k6, k2tog, yo, k5, yo, k2tog, k2.
Row 52: Knit.
Row 53: K18, yo, k3tog, yo, k6, k2tog, yo, k7, yo, k2tog, k1.
Row 54: Knit.
Row 55: K19, yo, k2tog, k5, k2tog, yo, k6, k2tog, yo, k3.
Row 56: Knit.
Row 57: K20, yo, k2tog, k3, k2tog, yo, k6, k2tog, yo, k4.
Row 58: Knit.
Row 59: K21, yo, k2tog, k1, k2tog, yo, k6, k2tog, yo, k5.
Row 60: Knit.
Row 61: K22, yo, k3tog, yo, k6, k2tog, yo, k6.
Row 62: Knit.
Row 63: K23, yo, k2tog, k5, k2tog, yo, k7.
Row 64: Knit.
Row 65: K24, yo, k2tog, k3, k2tog, yo, k8.
Row 66: Knit.
Row 67: K25, yo, k2tog, k1, k2tog, yo, k9.
Row 68: Knit.
Row 69: K26, yo, k3tog, yo, k10.
Row 70: Knit.

Balanced Diamonds

Balanced Diamonds are those in which all four sides of the diamond are of equal length, differing from Elongated Diamonds. Some borders are made of nothing but Balanced Diamonds, all with different infills. Balanced Diamonds may or may not have a defined edge, some may simply be formed by other patterns, such as the Bead stitch, placed in a diamond formation. We have also added two complex forms in which the Balanced Diamond is edged with additional outlines to make the motif stand out in the border.

4.10

Balanced Diamond with Eyelid column
TEX 7760 Stole

Balanced Diamond with Eyelid column original pattern.

There are many variations on a small circular pattern with a centre hole. Eyelid is a common motif from Unst.

Row 1 (RS): K12, k2tog, yo, k1, yo, k2tog, k12. (29 sts)
Row 2 (WS): K11, k2tog, yo, k3, yo, k2tog, k11.
Row 3: K10, k2tog, yo, k5, yo, k2tog, k10.
Row 4: K9, k2tog, yo, k7, yo, k2tog, k9.
Row 5: K8, k2tog, yo, k9, yo, k2tog, k8.
Row 6: K7, k2tog, yo, k3, k2tog, yo, k1, yo, k2tog, k3, yo, k2tog, k7.
Row 7: K6, (k2tog, yo, k3) x 2, yo, k2tog, k3, yo, k2tog, k6.
Row 8: K5, k2tog, yo, k15, yo, k2tog, k5.
Row 9: K4, k2tog, yo, k6, yo, k2tog, yo, k3tog, yo, k6, yo, k2tog, k4.

Balanced Diamond with Eyelid column knitted sample.

Row 10: K3, k2tog, yo, k8, yo, k3tog, yo, k8, yo, k2tog, k3.

Row 11: K2, k2tog, yo, k21, yo, k2tog, k2.

Row 12: K1, k2tog, yo, k9, k2tog, yo, k1, yo, k2tog, k9, yo, k2tog, k1.

Row 13: K2tog, yo, k9, k2tog, yo, k3, yo, k2tog, k9, yo, k2tog.

Row 14: Knit.

Row 15: K1, yo, k2tog, k9, yo, k2tog, yo, k3tog, yo, k9, k2tog, yo, k1.

Row 16: K2, yo, k2tog, k9, yo, k3tog, yo, k9, k2tog, yo, k2.

Row 17: K3, yo, k2tog, k19, k2tog, yo, k3.

Row 18: K4, yo, k2tog, k6, k2tog, yo, k1, yo, k2tog, k6, k2tog, yo, k4.

Row 19: K5, yo, k2tog, k4, k2tog, yo, k3, yo, k2tog, k4, k2tog, yo, k5.

Row 20: K6, yo, k2tog, k13, k2tog, yo, k6.

Row 21: K7, yo, k2tog, k3, yo, k2tog, yo, k3tog, yo, k3, k2tog, yo, k7.

Row 22: K8, yo, k2tog, k3, yo, k3tog, yo, k3, k2tog, yo, k8.

Row 23: K9, yo, k2tog, k7, k2tog, yo, k9.

Row 24: K10, yo, k2tog, k5, k2tog, yo, k10.

Row 25: K11, yo, k2tog, k3, k2tog, yo, k11.

Row 26: K12, yo, k2tog, k1, k2tog, yo, k12.

Row 27: K13, yo, k3tog, yo, k13.

Balanced Diamond with Eyelid column chart.

4.11

Balanced Diamond with Peerie Flea column variation and Lace Holes
TEX 1997.86 Shawl

Balanced Diamond with Peerie Flea column variation and Lace Holes original pattern.

Balanced Diamond with Peerie Flea column variation and Lace Holes knitted sample.

A column of Peerie Flea stitches alternates with mirrored openwork stitches to give this Balanced Diamond a solid centre infill. It is flanked in the side corners by Lace Holes.

Row 1 (RS): K18, k2tog, yo, k1, yo, k2tog, k18. (41 sts)
Row 2 (WS): K17, k2tog, yo, k3, yo, k2tog, k17.
Row 3: K16, k2tog, yo, k5, yo, k2tog, k16.
Row 4: K15, k2tog, yo, k7, yo, k2tog, k15.
Row 5: K14, k2tog, yo, k9, yo, k2tog, k14.
Row 6: K13, k2tog, yo, k11, yo, k2tog, k13.
Row 7: K12, k2tog, yo, k4, k2tog, yo, k1, yo, k2tog, k4, yo, k2tog, k12.
Row 8: K11, k2tog, yo, k4, k2tog, yo, k3, yo, k2tog, k4, yo, k2tog, k11.
Row 9: K10, k2tog, yo, k7, yo, k3tog, yo, k7, yo, k2tog, k10.
Row 10: K9, k2tog, yo, k19, yo, k2tog, k9.
Row 11: K8, k2tog, yo, k7, yo, k2tog, k3, k2tog, yo, k7, yo, k2tog, k8.
Row 12: K7, k2tog, yo, k9, yo, k2tog, k1, k2tog, yo, k9, yo, k2tog, k7.
Row 13: K6, k2tog, yo, k8, k2tog, yo, k5, yo, k2tog, k8, yo, k2tog, k6.
Row 14: K5, k2tog, yo, k27, yo, k2tog, k5.
Row 15: K4, k2tog, yo, k12, k2tog, yo, k1, yo, k2tog, k12, yo, k2tog, k4.
Row 16: K3, k2tog, yo, k12, k2tog, yo, k3, yo, k2tog, k12, yo, k2tog, k3.
Row 17: K2, k2tog, yo, k15, yo, k3tog, yo, k15, yo, k2tog, k2.
Row 18: K1, k2tog, yo, k4, k2tog, yo x 2, k2tog, k19, k2tog, yo x 2, k2tog, k4, yo, k2tog, k1.
Row 19: K2tog, yo, k7, p1, k7, yo, k2tog, k3, k2tog, yo, k8, p1, k6, yo, k2tog.
Row 20: K5, k2tog, yo x 2, k2tog x 2, yo x 2, k2tog, k5, yo, k2tog, k1, k2tog, yo, k5, k2tog, yo x 2, k2tog x 2, yo x 2, k2tog, k5.
Row 21: K7, p1, k3, p1, k4, k2tog, yo, k5, yo, k2tog, k5, p1, k3, p1, k6.
Row 22: K2tog, yo, k5, k2tog, yo x 2, k2tog, k19, k2tog, yo x 2, k2tog, k5, yo, k2tog.
Row 23: K2, yo, k2tog, k5, p1, k8, k2tog, yo, k1, yo, k2tog, k9, p1, k4, k2tog, yo, k2.
Row 24: (K3, yo, k2tog, k12, k2tog, yo) x 2, k3.
Row 25: K4, yo, k2tog, k13, yo, k3tog, yo, k13, k2tog, yo, k4.
Row 26: K5, yo, k2tog, k27, k2tog, yo, k5.
Row 27: K6, yo, k2tog, k9, yo, k2tog, k3, k2tog, yo, k9, k2tog, yo, k6.
Row 28: K7, yo, k2tog, k9, yo, k2tog, k1, k2tog, yo, k9, k2tog, yo, k7.
Row 29: K8, yo, k2tog, k6, k2tog, yo, k5, yo, k2tog, k6, k2tog, yo, k8.
Row 30: K9, yo, k2tog, k19, k2tog, yo, k9.

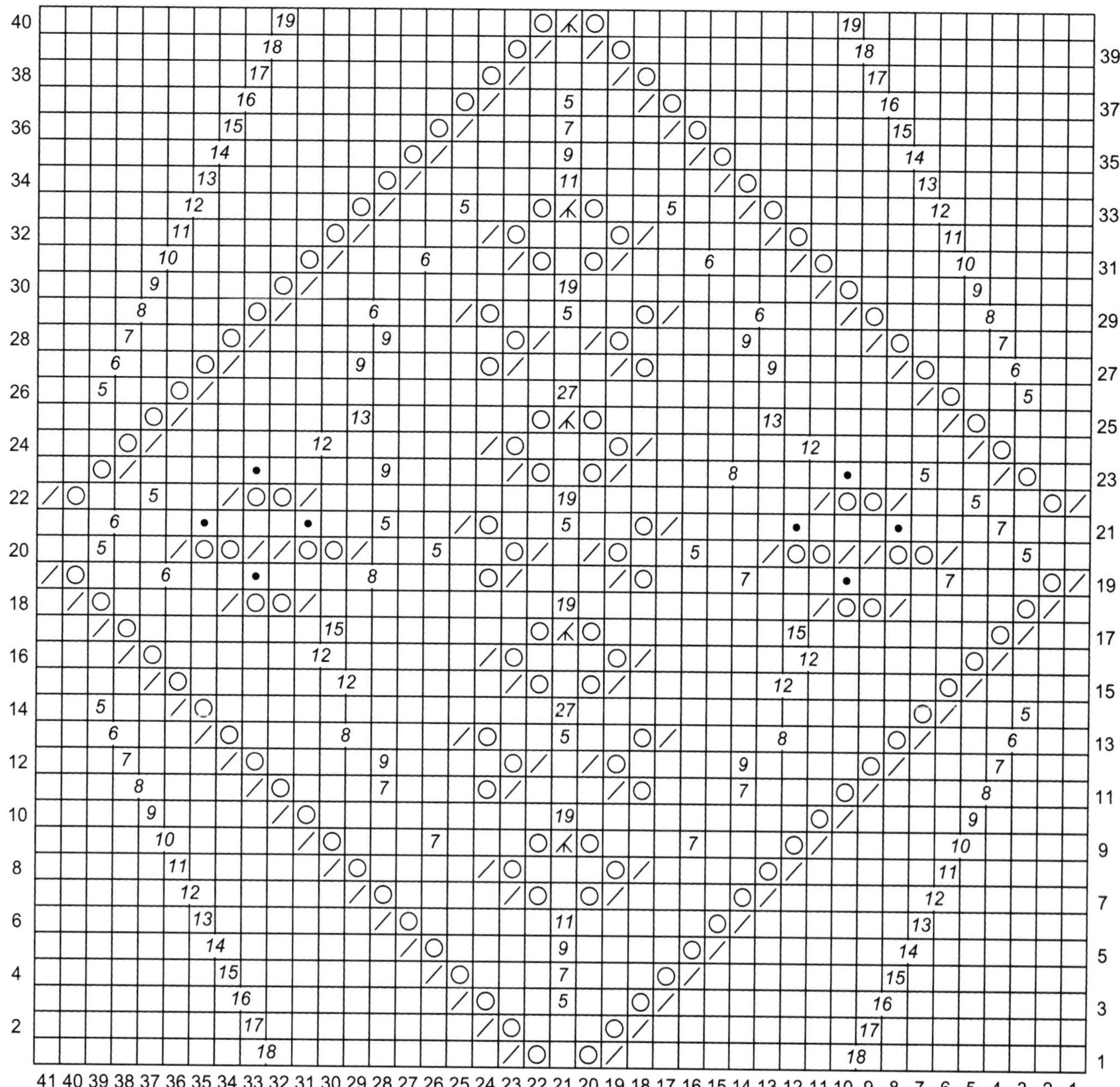

Balanced Diamond with Peerie Flea column variation and Lace Holes chart.

Row 31: K10, yo, k2tog, k6, k2tog, yo, k1, yo, k2tog, k6, k2tog, yo, k10.

Row 32: K11, yo, k2tog, k4, k2tog, yo, k3, yo, k2tog, k4, k2tog, yo, k11.

Row 33: K12, yo, k2tog, k5, yo, k3tog, yo, k5, k2tog, yo, k12.

Row 34: K13, yo, k2tog, k11, k2tog, yo, k13.

Row 35: K14, yo, k2tog, k9, k2tog, yo, k14.

Row 36: K15, yo, k2tog, k7, k2tog, yo, k15.

Row 37: K16, yo, k2tog, k5, k2tog, yo, k16.

Row 38: K17, yo, k2tog, k3, k2tog, yo, k17.

Row 39: K18, yo, k2tog, k1, k2tog, yo, k18.

Row 40: K19, yo, k3tog, yo, k19.

4.12

Balanced Diamond inset with four Diamonds of Lace Holes
TEX 2004.171 Shawl

Balanced Diamond inset with four Diamonds of Lace Holes original pattern.

Balanced Diamond inset with four Diamonds of Lace Holes knitted sample.

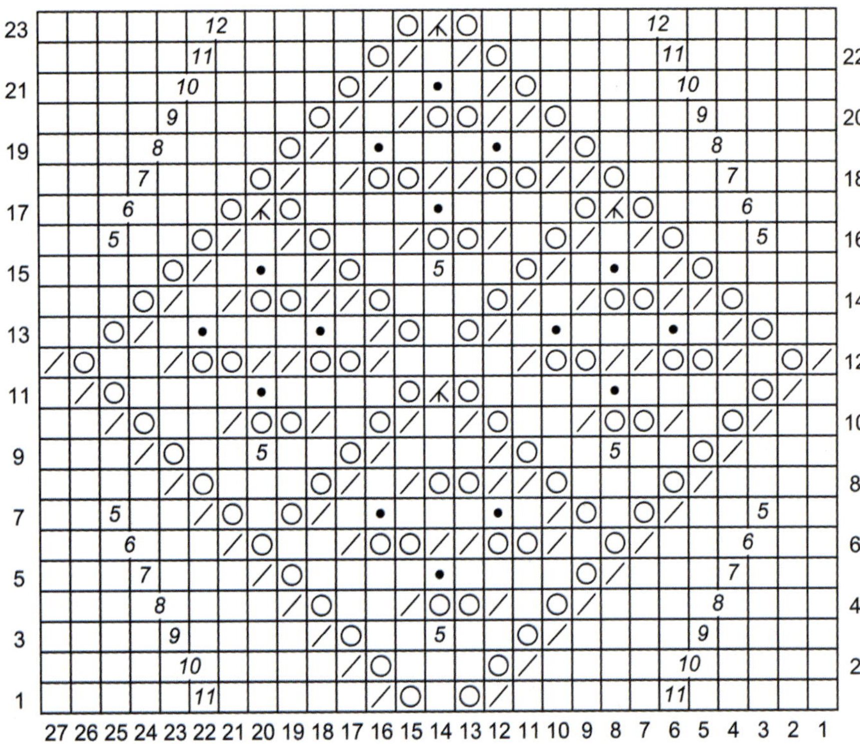

Balanced Diamond inset with four Diamonds of Lace Holes chart.

A Balanced Diamond is inset with four small Diamonds, each filled with four Lace Holes. The motif fills in a space between the lace edge and the first Wave pattern, where otherwise there would be plain knitting, to give this border added complexity from the start.

Row 1 (WS): K11, k2tog, yo, k1, yo, k2tog, k11. (27 sts)
Row 2 (RS): K10, k2tog, yo, k3, yo, k2tog, k10.
Row 3: K9, k2tog, yo, k5, yo, k2tog, k9.
Row 4: K8, k2tog, yo, k1, k2tog, yo x 2, k2tog, k2, yo, k2tog, k8.

Row 5: K7, k2tog, yo, k4, p1, k4, yo, k2tog, k7.
Row 6: K6, k2tog, yo, k1, k2tog, yo x 2, k2tog x 2, yo x 2, k2tog, k2, yo, k2tog, k6.
Row 7: K5, k2tog, yo, k1, yo, k2tog, k1, p1, k3, p1, k1, k2tog, yo, k1, yo, k2tog, k5.
Row 8: K4, k2tog, yo, k3, yo, k2tog x 2, yo x 2, k2tog, k1, k2tog, yo, k3, yo, k2tog, k4.
Row 9: (K3, k2tog, yo, k5, yo, k2tog) x 2, k3.
Row 10: K2, k2tog, yo, k1, k2tog, yo x 2, k2tog, k2, yo, k2tog, k1, k2tog, yo, k1, k2tog, yo x 2, k2tog, k2, yo, k2tog, k2.
Row 11: K1, k2tog, yo, k4, p1, k4, yo, k3tog, yo, k4, p1, k4, yo, k2tog, k1.
Row 12: K2tog, yo, k1, k2tog, yo x 2, k2tog x 2, yo x 2, k2tog, k4, k2tog, yo x 2, k2tog x 2, yo x 2, k2tog, k2, yo, k2tog.
Row 13: K2, yo, k2tog, k1, p1, k3, p1, k1, k2tog, yo, k1, yo, k2tog, k1, p1, k3, p1, k1, k2tog, yo, k2.
Row 14: (K3, yo, k2tog x 2, yo x 2, k2tog, k1, k2tog, yo) x 2, k3.
Row 15: K4, yo, k2tog, k1, p1, k1, k2tog, yo, k5, yo, k2tog, k1, p1, k1, k2tog, yo, k4.
Row 16: K5, yo, k2tog, k1, k2tog, yo, k1, k2tog, yo x 2, k2tog, k2, yo, k2tog, k1, k2tog, yo, k5.
Row 17: K6, yo, k3tog, yo, k4, p1, k4, yo, k3tog, yo, k6.
Row 18: K7, yo, (k2tog x 2, yo x 2) x 2, k2tog, k1, k2tog, yo, k7.
Row 19: K8, yo, k2tog, k1, p1, k3, p1, k1, k2tog, yo, k8.
Row 20: K9, yo, k2tog x 2, yo x 2, k2tog, k1, k2tog, yo, k9.
Row 21: K10, yo, k2tog, k1, p1, k1, k2tog, yo, k10.
Row 22: K11, yo, k2tog, k1, k2tog, yo, k11.
Row 23: K12, yo, k3tog, yo, k12.

4.13

Balanced Diamond of Beads

TEX 2014.25 Shawl

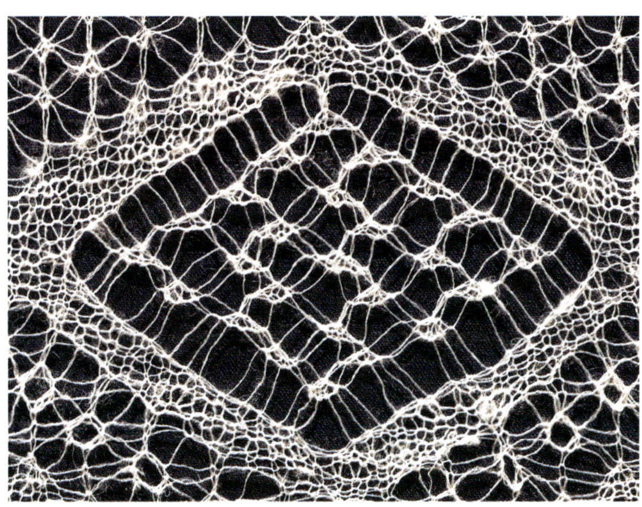

Balanced Diamond of Beads original pattern.

Balanced Diamond of Beads knitted sample.

Bead stitch is comfortably placed within a Balanced Diamond for an overall pattern effect. This motif is common in Shetland lace borders.

Row 1 (RS): K15, k2tog, yo, k16. (33 sts)
Row 2 (WS): K14, k2tog, yo, k1, yo, k2tog, k14.
Row 3: K13, k2tog, yo, k3, yo, k2tog, k13.
Row 4: K12, k2tog, yo, k5, yo, k2tog, k12.
Row 5: K11, k2tog, yo, k1, yo, k2tog, k1, k2tog, yo, k1, yo, k2tog, k11.
Row 6: K10, k2tog, yo, k3, yo, p3tog, yo, k3, yo, k2tog, k10.
Row 7: K9, k2tog, yo, k4, k2tog, yo, k5, yo, k2tog, k9.
Row 8: K8, (k2tog, yo, k1, yo, k2tog, k1) x 2, k2tog, yo, k1, yo, k2tog, k8.
Row 9: K7, k2tog, (yo, k3, yo, k3tog) x 2, yo, k3, yo, k2tog, k7.
Row 10: K6, (k2tog, yo, k4) x 2, k2tog, yo, k5, yo, k2tog, k6.
Row 11: K5, (k2tog, yo, k1, yo, k2tog, k1) x 3, k2tog, yo, k1, yo, k2tog, k5.

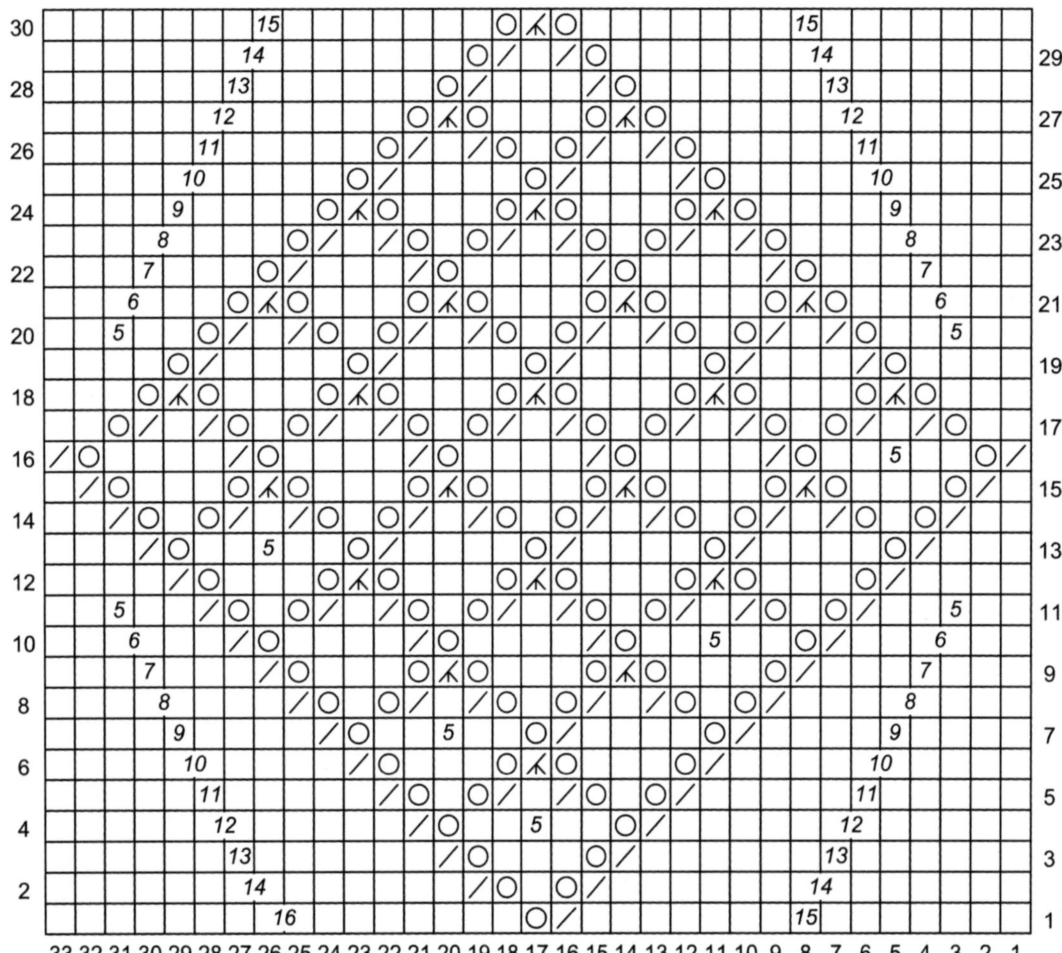

Balanced Diamond of Beads chart.

Row 12: K4, k2tog, (yo, k3, yo, p3tog) x 3, yo, k3, yo, k2tog, k4.

Row 13: K3, (k2tog, yo, k4) x 3, k2tog, yo, k5, yo, k2tog, k3.

Row 14: K2, (k2tog, yo, k1, yo, k2tog, k1) x 4, k2tog, yo, k1, yo, k2tog, k2.

Row 15: K1, k2tog, (yo, k3, yo, k3tog) x 4, yo, k3, yo, k2tog, k1.

Row 16: (K2tog, yo, k4) x 4, k2tog, yo, k5, yo, k2tog.

Row 17: K2, (yo, k2tog, k1, k2tog, yo, k1) x 4, yo, k2tog, k1, k2tog, yo, k2.

Row 18: (K3, yo, p3tog, yo) x 5, k3.

Row 19: K4, yo, k2tog, k3, (k2tog, yo, k4) x 4.

Row 20: K5, (yo, k2tog, k1, k2tog, yo, k1) x 3, yo, k2tog, k1, k2tog, yo, k5.

Row 21: K6, (yo, k3tog, yo, k3) x 3, yo, k3tog, yo, k6.

Row 22: K7, yo, k2tog, k3, (k2tog, yo, k4) x 2, k2tog, yo, k7.

Row 23: K8, (yo, k2tog, k1, k2tog, yo, k1) x 2, yo, k2tog, k1, k2tog, yo, k8.

Row 24: K9, (yo, p3tog, yo, k3) x 2, yo, p3tog, yo, k9.

Row 25: K10, yo, k2tog, k3, k2tog, yo, k4, k2tog, yo, k10.

Row 26: K11, yo, k2tog, k1, k2tog, yo, k1, yo, k2tog, k1, k2tog, yo, k11.

Row 27: K12, yo, k3tog, yo, k3, yo, k3tog, yo, k12.

Row 28: K13, yo, k2tog, k3, k2tog, yo, k13.

Row 29: K14, yo, k2tog, k1, k2tog, yo, k14.

Row 30: K15, yo, p3tog, yo, k15.

4.14

Balanced Diamond of Peerie Fleas

TEX 2015.148 Stole

Balanced Diamond of Peerie Fleas original pattern.

Balanced Diamond of Peerie Fleas knitted sample.

Here the Peerie Flea pattern is repeated and spaced evenly to create a Balanced Diamond shape without a defined edge.

Row 1 (RS): K13, k2tog, yo, k1, yo, k2tog, k13. (31 sts)
Row 2 (WS): K12, k2tog, yo, k3, yo, k2tog, k12.
Row 3: K14, yo, k3tog, yo, k14.
Row 4: Knit.

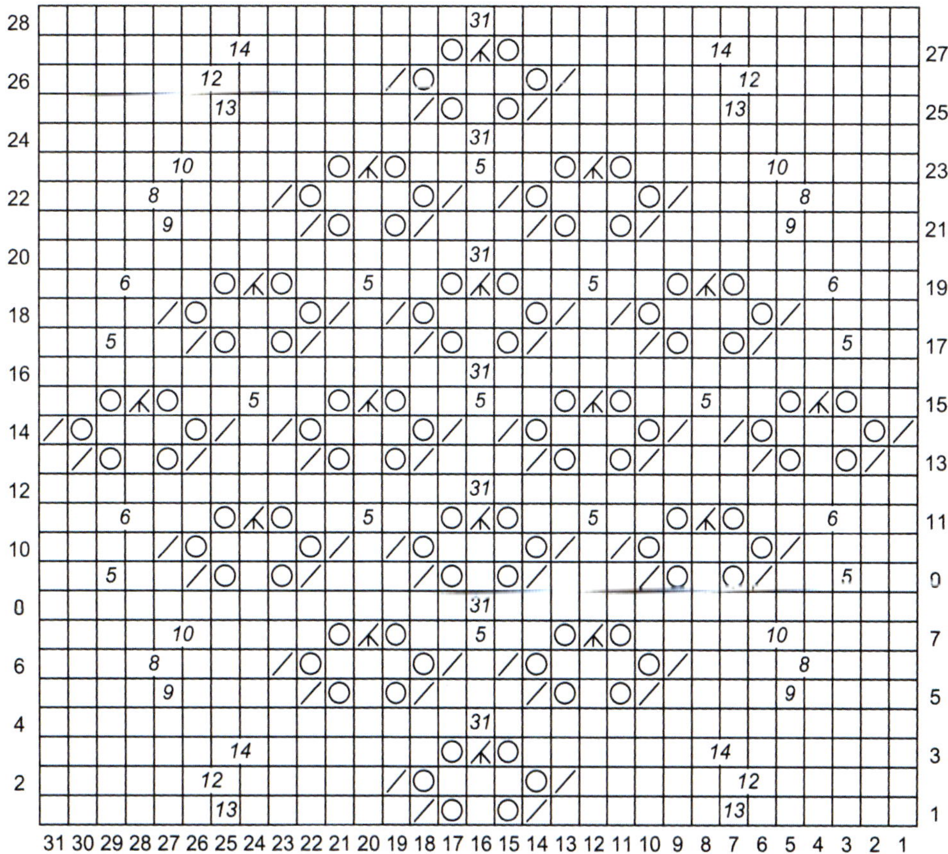

Balanced Diamond of Peerie Fleas chart.

Row 5: K9, k2tog, yo, k1, yo, k2tog, k3, k2tog, yo, k1, yo, k2tog, k9.
Row 6: K8, k2tog, yo, k3, yo, k2tog, k1, k2tog, yo, k3, yo, k2tog, k8.
Row 7: K10, yo, k3tog, yo, k5, yo, k3tog, yo, k10.
Row 8: Knit.
Row 9: K5, (k2tog, yo, k1, yo, k2tog, k3) x 2, k2tog, yo, k1, yo, k2tog, k5.
Row 10: K4, (k2tog, yo, k3, yo, k2tog, k1) x 2, k2tog, yo, k3, yo, k2tog, k4.
Row 11: K6, (yo, k3tog, yo, k5) x 2, yo, k3tog, yo, k6.
Row 12: Knit.
Row 13: K1, (k2tog, yo, k1, yo, k2tog, k3) x 3, k2tog, yo, k1, yo, k2tog, k1.
Row 14: (K2tog, yo, k3, yo, k2tog, k1) x 3, k2tog, yo, k3, yo, k2tog.
Row 15: K2, (yo, k3tog, yo, k5) x 3, yo, k3tog, yo, k2.
Row 16: Knit.
Row 17: Repeat row 9.
Row 18: Repeat row 10.
Row 19: Repeat row 11.
Row 20: Knit.
Row 21: Repeat row 5.
Row 22: Repeat row 6.
Row 23: Repeat row 7.
Row 24: Knit.
Row 25: Repeat row 1.
Row 26: Repeat row 2.
Row 27: Repeat row 3.
Row 28: Knit.

4.15

Balanced Diamond with complex centre
TEX 1997.86 Shawl

Balanced Diamond with complex centre original pattern.

Balanced Diamond with complex centre knitted sample.

Shetland lace knitters were masters at combining patterns to make new, complex forms. Here a Balanced Diamond is infilled with a central Lozenge, which itself is filled with two Peerie Fleas. It is flanked on either side by pairs of Beads, which are connected by Steeks formed from the sides of the Lozenge. Above and below, and to the outer sides, are mesh forms, the lower one forming a Fern motif.

Row 1 (RS): K19, yo, k3tog, yo, k19. (41 sts)
Row 2 (WS): K17, k2tog, yo, k3, yo, k2tog, k17.
Row 3: K16, k2tog, yo, k5, yo, k2tog, k16.
Row 4: K15, k2tog, yo, k7, yo, k2tog, k15.
Row 5: K14, k2tog, yo, k9, yo, k2tog, k14.
Row 6: K13, k2tog, yo, k5, yo, k2tog, k4, yo, k2tog, k13.
Row 7: K12, k2tog, yo, k13, yo, k2tog, k12.
Row 8: K11, k2tog, yo, k6, yo, k3tog, yo, k6, yo, k2tog, k11.
Row 9: K10, k2tog, yo, k6, yo, k2tog, k1, k2tog, yo, k6, yo, k2tog, k10.
Row 10: K9, k2tog, yo, k6, yo, k2tog, yo, k3tog, yo, k2tog, yo, k6, yo, k2tog, k9.
Row 11: K8, k2tog, yo, k3, k2tog, yo, k1, (yo, k2tog) x 2, k1, (k2tog, yo) x 2, k1, yo, k2tog, k3, yo, k2tog, k8.

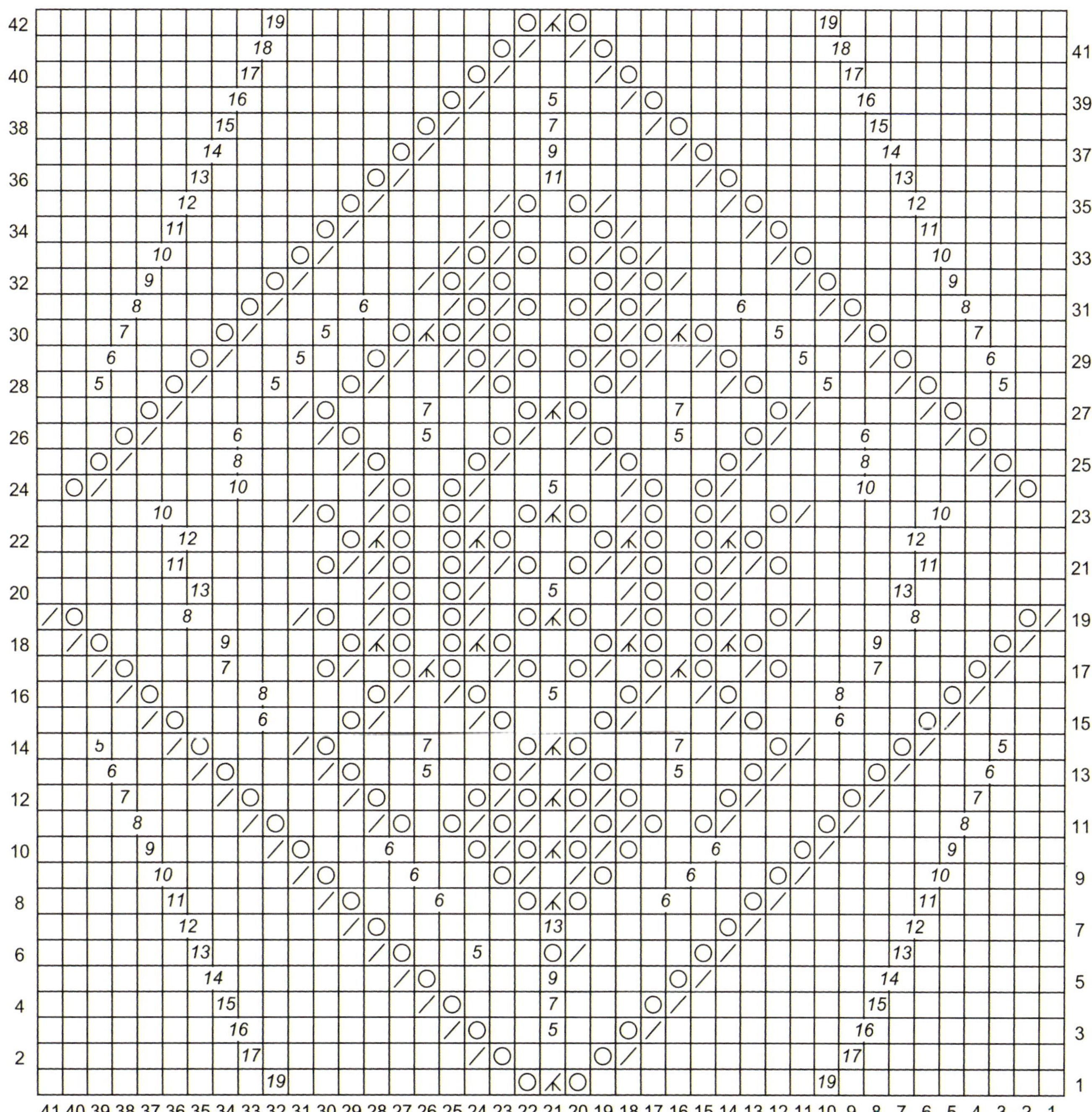

Balanced Diamond with complex centre chart.

Row 12: K7, (k2tog, yo, k3) x 2, yo, k2tog, yo, k3tog, yo, k2tog, yo, (k3, yo, k2tog) x 2, k7.

Row 13: K6, k2tog, yo, k3, k2tog, yo, k5, yo, k2tog, k1, k2tog, yo, k5, yo, k2tog, k3, yo, k2tog, k6.

Row 14: K5, k2tog, yo, k3, k2tog, yo, k7, yo, k3tog, yo, k7, yo, k2tog, k3, yo, k2tog, k5.

Row 15: K4, k2tog, yo, k6, yo, k2tog, k3, k2tog, yo, k3, yo, k2tog, k3, k2tog, yo, k6, yo, k2tog, k4.

Row 16: K3, k2tog, yo, k8, yo, k2tog, k1, k2tog, yo, k5, yo, k2tog, k1, k2tog, yo, k8, yo, k2tog, k3.
Row 17: K2, k2tog, yo, k7, yo, k2tog, k1, yo, k3tog, yo, k1, k2tog, yo, k1, yo, k2tog, k1, yo, k3tog, yo, k1, k2tog, yo, k7, yo, k2tog, k2.
Row 18: K1, k2tog, yo, k9, yo, k3tog, yo, k1, yo, k3tog, yo, k3, yo, k3tog, yo, k1, yo, k3tog, yo, k9, yo, k2tog, k1.
Row 19: K2tog, yo, k8, (k2tog, yo, k1) x 2, yo, k2tog, k1, yo, k3tog, yo, k1, k2tog, yo, (k1, yo, k2tog) x 2, k8, yo, k2tog.
Row 20: K13, k2tog, yo, k1, yo, k2tog, k5, k2tog, yo, k1, yo, k2tog, k13.
Row 21: K11, (yo, k2tog x 2, yo, k1) x 3, yo, k2tog x 2, yo, k11.
Row 22: K12, yo, k3tog, yo, k1, yo, k3tog, yo, k3, yo, k3tog, yo, k1, yo, k3tog, yo, k12.
Row 23: K10, (k2tog, yo, k1) x 2, yo, k2tog, k1, yo, k3tog, yo, k1, k2tog, yo, (k1, yo, k2tog) x 2, k10.
Row 24: K1, yo, k2tog, k10, k2tog, yo, k1, yo, k2tog, k5, k2tog, yo, k1, yo, k2tog, k10, k2tog, yo, k1.
Row 25: K2, yo, k2tog, k8, k2tog, yo, k3, yo, k2tog, k3, k2tog, yo, k3, yo, k2tog, k8, k2tog, yo, k2.
Row 26: K3, yo, k2tog, k6, k2tog, yo, k5, yo, k2tog, k1, k2tog, yo, k5, yo, k2tog, k6, k2tog, yo, k3.
Row 27: K4, yo, k2tog, k4, k2tog, yo, k7, yo, k3tog, yo, k7, yo, k2tog, k4, k2tog, yo, k4.
Row 28: (K5, yo, k2tog) x 2, k3, k2tog, yo, k3, yo, k2tog, k3, (k2tog, yo, k5) x 2.
Row 29: K6, yo, k2tog, k5, yo, k2tog, k1, (k2tog, yo) x 2, k1, (yo, k2tog) x 2, k1, k2tog, yo, k5, k2tog, yo, k6.
Row 30: K7, yo, k2tog, k5, yo, k3tog, yo, k2tog, yo, k3, yo, k2tog, yo, k3tog, yo, k5, k2tog, yo, k7.
Row 31: K8, yo, k2tog, k6, (k2tog, yo) x 2, k1, (yo, k2tog) x 2, k6, k2tog, yo, k8.
Row 32: K9, yo, k2tog, k4, (k2tog, yo) x 2, k3, (yo, k2tog) x 2, k4, k2tog, yo, k9.
Row 33: K10, yo, k2tog, k4, (k2tog, yo) x 2, k1, (yo, k2tog) x 2, k4, k2tog, yo, k10.
Row 34: K11, yo, k2tog, k4, k2tog, yo, k3, yo, k2tog, k4, k2tog, yo, k11.
Row 35: K12, yo, k2tog, k4, k2tog, yo, k1, yo, k2tog, k4, k2tog, yo, k12.
Row 36: K13, yo, k2tog, k11, k2tog, yo, k13.
Row 37: K14, yo, k2tog, k9, k2tog, yo, k14.
Row 38: K15, yo, k2tog, k7, k2tog, yo, k15.
Row 39: K16, yo, k2tog, k5, k2tog, yo, k16.
Row 40: K17, yo, k2tog, k3, k2tog, yo, k17.
Row 41: K18, yo, k2tog, k1, k2tog, yo, k18.
Row 42: Repeat row 1.

4.16

Balanced Diamond of Eyelid inset with Branch
TEX 2012.428a Stole

A Diamond is formed out of a pattern known in Unst as Eyelid, but due to the Diamond shape, the pattern is offset and does not form a true Eyelid. Nevertheless, it is very pretty when formed this way and beautifully shapes a Branch.

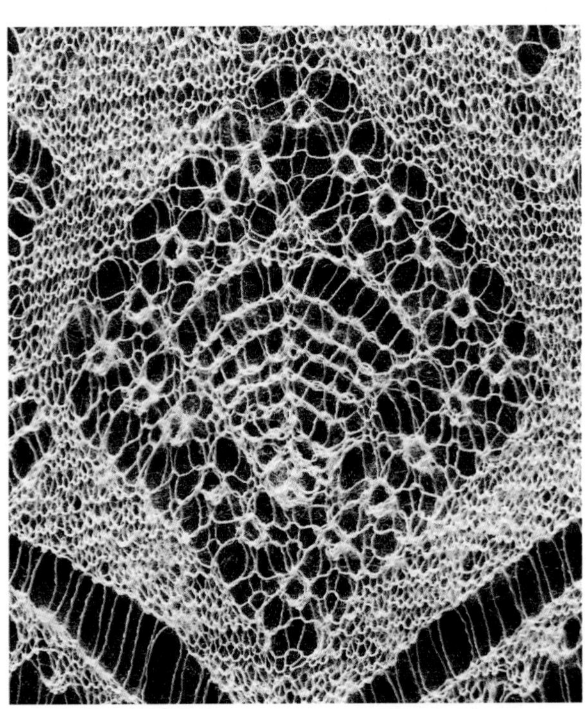

Balanced Diamond of Eyelid inset with Branch original pattern.

Row 1 (RS): K17, k2tog, yo, k18. (37 sts)
Row 2 (WS): Knit.
Row 3: K16, k2tog, yo, k1, yo, k2tog, k16.
Row 4: Knit.
Row 5: K15, k2tog, yo, k3, yo, k2tog, k15.
Row 6: Knit.
Row 7: K13, k2tog, yo, k1, yo, k2tog, yo, k3tog, yo, k1, yo, k2tog, k13.
Row 8: Knit.
Row 9: K12, k2tog, yo, k3, yo, k3tog, yo, k3, yo, k2tog, k12.
Row 10: Knit.
Row 11: K10, k2tog, (yo, k1, yo, k2tog, yo, k3tog) x 2, yo, k1, yo, k2tog, k10.

Balanced Diamond of Eyelid inset with Branch knitted sample.

Row 12: Knit.
Row 13: K9, k2tog, (yo, k3, yo, k3tog) x 2, yo, k3, yo, k2tog, k9.
Row 14: Knit.
Row 15: K7, k2tog, yo, k1, yo, k2tog, yo, k3tog, yo, k7, yo, k2tog, yo, k3tog, yo, k1, yo, k2tog, k7.
Row 16: K18, yo, k2tog, k17.
Row 17: K6, k2tog, yo, k3, yo, k3tog, yo, k9, yo, k3tog, yo, k3, yo, k2tog, k6.
Row 18: K17, yo, p3tog, yo, k17.
Row 19: K4, k2tog, yo, k1, yo, k2tog, yo, k3tog, yo, k13, yo, k2tog, yo, k3tog, yo, k1, yo, k2tog, k4.
Row 20: K16, yo, k2tog, k1, k2tog, yo, k16.
Row 21: K3, k2tog, yo, k3, yo, k3tog, yo, k15, yo, k3tog, yo, k3, yo, k2tog, k3.
Row 22: K15, yo, k2tog, yo, p3tog, yo, k2tog, yo, k15.
Row 23: K1, k2tog, yo, k1, yo, k2tog, yo, k3tog, yo, k5, (yo, k2tog) x 2, k1, (k2tog, yo) x 2, k5, yo, k2tog, yo, k3tog, yo, k1, yo, k2tog, k1.
Row 24: K13, (yo, k2tog) x 2, yo, p3tog, (yo, k2tog) x 2, yo, k13.
Row 25: K2tog, yo, k3, yo, k3tog, yo, k4, (yo, k2tog) x 3, k1, (k2tog, yo) x 3, k4, yo, k3tog, yo, k3, yo, k2tog.
Row 26: K11, (yo, k2tog) x 3, yo, p3tog, (yo, k2tog) x 3, yo, k11.
Row 27: K1, yo, k2tog, yo, k3tog, yo, k1, yo, k2tog, k1, (yo, k2tog) x 4, k1, (k2tog, yo) x 4, k1, k2tog, yo, k1, yo, k2tog, yo, k3tog, yo, k1.
Row 28: Repeat row 26.
Row 29: K2, yo, k3tog, yo, k3, yo, k2tog, k2, (yo, k2tog) x 3, k1, (k2tog, yo) x 3, k2, k2tog, yo, k3, yo, k3tog, yo, k2.
Row 30: Repeat row 24.
Row 31: K4, yo, k2tog, yo, k3tog, yo, k1, yo, k2tog, k2, (yo, k2tog) x 2, k1, (k2tog, yo) x 2, k2, k2tog, yo, k1, yo, k2tog, yo, k3tog, yo, k4.
Row 32: Repeat row 22.
Row 33: K5, yo, k3tog, yo, (k3, yo, k2tog) x 2, k1, (k2tog, yo, k3) x 2, yo, k3tog, yo, k5.
Row 34: Repeat row 18.
Row 35: K7, yo, k2tog, yo, k3tog, yo, k1, yo, k2tog, k7, k2tog, yo, k1, yo, k2tog, yo, k3tog, yo, k7.
Row 36: Knit.
Row 37: K8, yo, k3tog, yo, k3, yo, k2tog, k5, k2tog, yo, k3, yo, k3tog, yo, k8.
Row 38: Knit.
Row 39: K10, yo, k2tog, yo, k3tog, yo, k1, yo, k2tog, k1, k2tog, yo, k1, yo, k2tog, yo, k3tog, yo, k10.
Row 40: Knit.
Row 41: K11, (yo, k3tog, yo, k3) x 2, yo, k3tog, yo, k11.
Row 42: Knit.
Row 43: K13, yo, k2tog, yo, k3tog, yo, k1, yo, k2tog, yo, k3tog, yo, k13.
Row 44: Knit.
Row 45: K14, yo, k3tog, yo, k3, yo, k3tog, yo, k14.
Row 46: Knit.
Row 47: K16, yo, k2tog, yo, k3tog, yo, k16.
Row 48: Knit.
Row 49: K17, yo, k3tog, yo, k17.
Row 50: Knit.

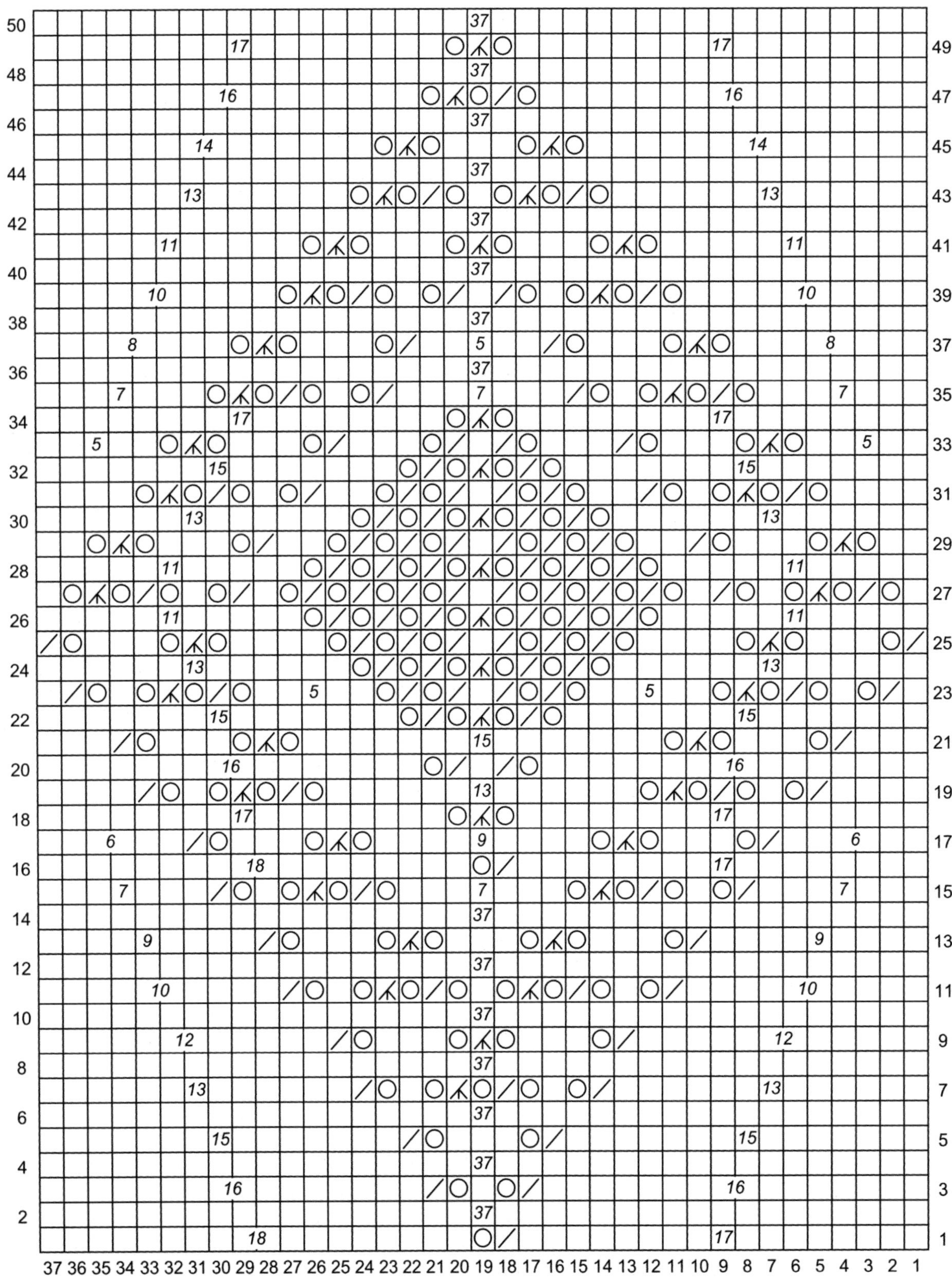

Balanced Diamond of Eyelid inset with Branch chart.

Ferns and Branches

Ferns and Branches are similar in shape to Balanced Diamonds but without an edge all the way round. Branch is the name used in Unst for a form that resembles a simple Tree, and it can appear right side up, as a conifer tree, or upside-down. In this section only patterns incorporating upside-down Branches are presented, as they hang similarly to Ferns, which are more varied.

Both Ferns and upside-down Branches appear to hang like a swag, with Ferns having a range of designs that are more delicate, feminine and pretty than an upside-down Branch. Ferns have a top edge, an inverted 'V' that arches over the pattern below. A Branch may also form part of a Fern, as in Pattern 4.22. Ferns have been designed in a wide variety of patterns over the years, and both motifs are used singly or in clusters. Several common patterns are presented here with a few unusual ones to show how these basic 'swag' forms have been used creatively by Shetland knitters.

Detailed and delicate frond.

4.17

Fern with Steek

TEX 2004.172 Shawl

It is debatable whether this can be considered a true Fern but it is a Fern-like form with a simple Steek centre and a delicate lower edge. It was used to fill a small space above a Wave and immediately below the top of the border.

Row 1 (RS): K13, yo, k2tog, k12. (27 sts)
Row 2 (WS): Knit.
Row 3: K11, k2tog, yo, k1, yo, k2tog, k11.
Row 4: Knit.
Row 5: K9, k2tog, yo, k5, yo, k2tog, k9.
Row 6: Knit.
Row 7: K8, k2tog, yo, k1, yo, k2tog, k1, k2tog, yo, k1, yo, k2tog, k8.
Row 8: Knit.
Row 9: K6, k2tog, yo, k3, k2tog, yo, k1, yo, k2tog, k3, yo, k2tog, k6.
Row 10: Knit.
Row 11: K5, (k2tog, yo, k1, yo, k2tog, k1) x 2, k2tog, yo, k1, yo, k2tog, k5.
Row 12: Knit.

Fern with Steek original pattern.

Row 13: K3, k2tog, yo, k6, k2tog, yo, k1, yo, k2tog, k6, yo, k2tog, k3.
Row 14: Knit.
Row 15: K2, (k2tog, yo, k1, yo, k2tog, k4) x 2, k2tog, yo, k1, yo, k2tog, k2.
Row 16: Knit.

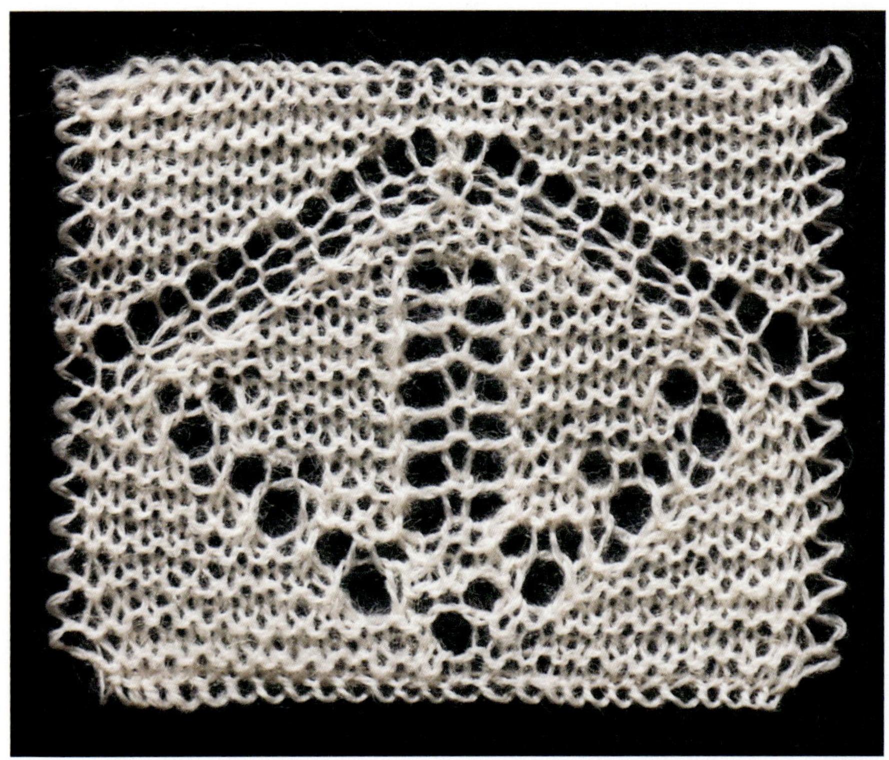

Fern with Steek knitted sample.

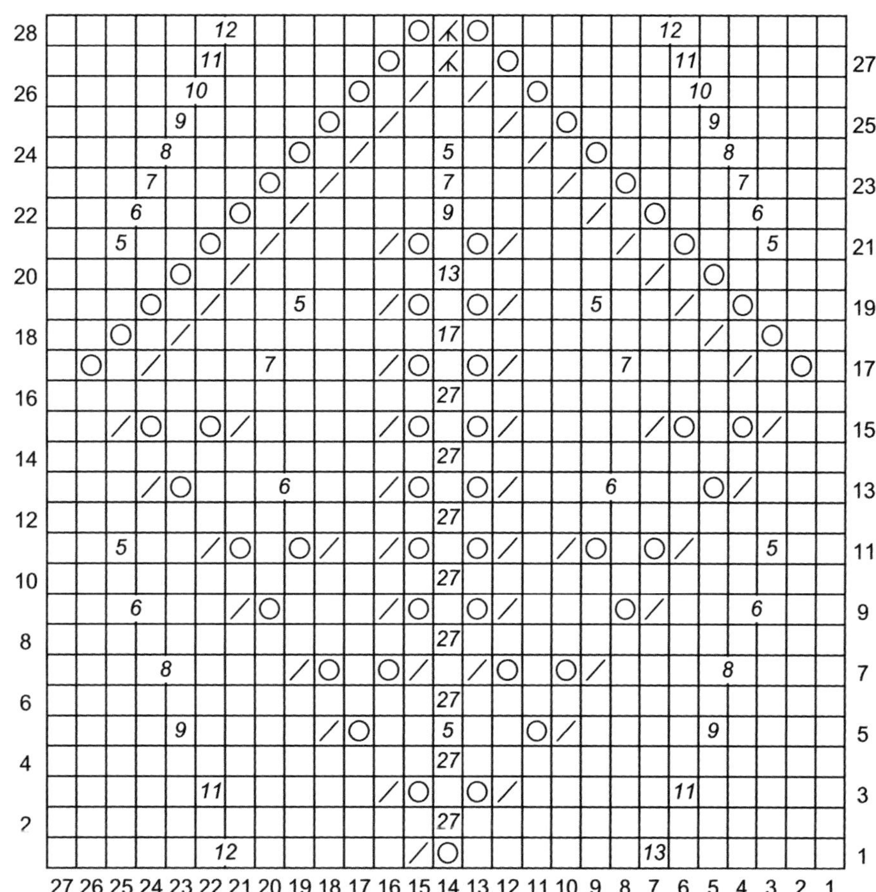

Fern with Steek chart.

Row 17: K1, yo, k1, k2tog, k7, k2tog, yo, k1, yo, k2tog, k7, k2tog, k1, yo, k1.

Row 18: K2, yo, k1, k2tog, k17, k2tog, k1, yo, k2.

Row 19: K3, yo, k1, k2tog, k5, k2tog, yo, k1, yo, k2tog, k5, k2tog, k1, yo, k3.

Row 20: K4, yo, k1, k2tog, k13, k2tog, k1, yo, k4.

Row 21: K5, yo, k1, k2tog, k3, k2tog, yo, k1, yo, k2tog, k3, k2tog, k1, yo, k5.

Row 22: K6, yo, k1, k2tog, k9, k2tog, k1, yo, k6.

Row 23: K7, yo, k1, k2tog, k7, k2tog, k1, yo, k7.

Row 24: K8, yo, k1, k2tog, k5, k2tog, k1, yo, k8.

Row 25: K9, yo, k1, k2tog, k3, k2tog, k1, yo, k9.

Row 26: K10, yo, (k1, k2tog) x 2, k1, yo, k10.

Row 27: K11, yo, k1, k3tog, k1, yo, k11.

Row 28: K12, yo, k3tog, yo, k12.

4.18

Fern with Flooers

TEX 2015.107 Scarf

Fern with Flooers knitted sample.

Fern with Flooers original pattern.

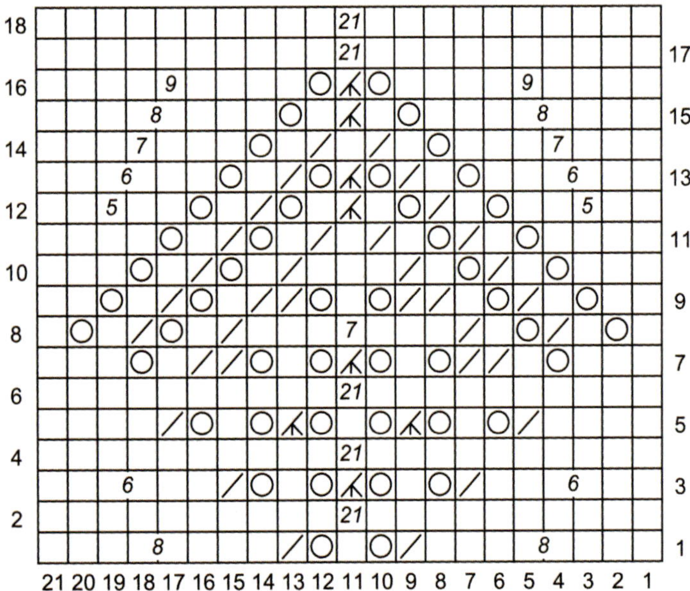

Fern with Flooers chart.

This pretty Fern is somewhat similar to an upside-down Basket o' Flooers. It was used distinctly on its own, at the top of a border.

Row 1 (RS): K8, k2tog, yo, k1, yo, k2tog, k8. (21 sts)
Row 2 (WS): Knit.
Row 3: K6, k2tog, yo, k1, yo, k3tog, yo, k1, yo, k2tog, k6.
Row 4: Knit.
Row 5: K4, k2tog, (yo, k1, yo, k3tog) x 2, yo, k1, yo, k2tog, k4.
Row 6: Knit.
Row 7: K3, yo, k1, k2tog x 2, yo, k1, yo, k3tog, yo, k1, yo, k2tog x 2, k1, yo, k3.
Row 8: K1, (yo, k1, k2tog) x 2, k7, (k2tog, k1, yo) x 2, k1.
Row 9: K2, yo, k1, k2tog, yo, k1, k2tog x 2, yo, k1, yo, k2tog x 2, k1, yo, k2tog, k1, yo, k2.
Row 10: K3, (yo, k1, k2tog) x 2, k3, (k2tog, k1, yo) x 2, k3.
Row 11: K4, (yo, k1, k2tog) x 2, k1, (k2tog, k1, yo) x 2, k4.
Row 12: K5, yo, k1, k2tog, yo, k1, p3tog, k1, yo, k2tog, k1, yo, k5.
Row 13: K6, yo, k1, k2tog, yo, k3tog, yo, k2tog, k1, yo, k6.
Row 14: K7, yo, (k1, k2tog) x 2, k1, yo, k7.
Row 15: K8, yo, k1, k3tog, k1, yo, k8.
Row 16: K9, yo, p3tog, yo, k9.
Rows 17–18: Knit.

4.19

Fern variation 1

TEX 2004.338 Stole

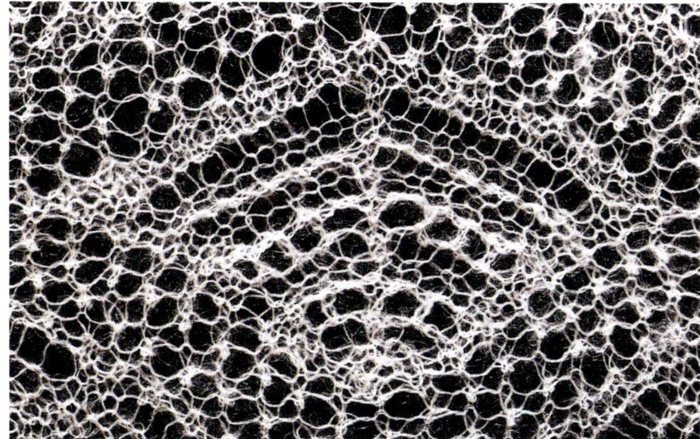

Fern variation 1 original pattern.

Fern variation 1 knitted sample.

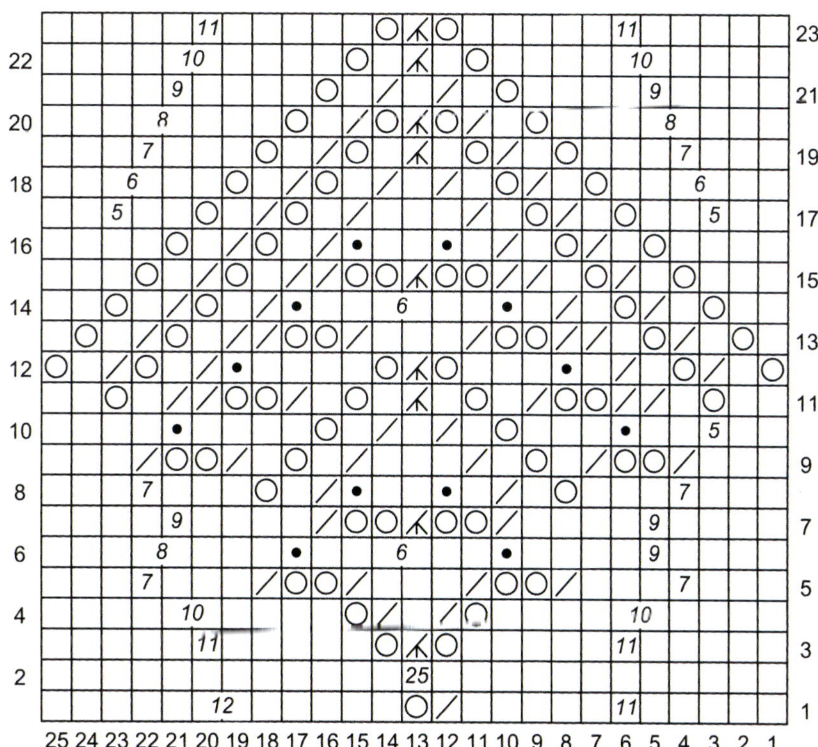

Fern variation 1 chart.

This is a classic Fern form, with softly arching top line and decorative openwork ending at a point below. The original was set between two Waves of Fancy Net.

Row 1 (RS): K11, k2tog, yo, k12. (25 sts)
Row 2 (WS): Knit.
Row 3: K11, yo, k3tog, yo, k11.
Row 4: K10, yo, k2tog, k1, k2tog, yo, k10.
Row 5: K7, k2tog, yo x 2, k2tog, k3, k2tog, yo x 2, k2tog, k7.
Row 6: K8, p1, k6, p1, k9.
Row 7: K9, k2tog, yo x 2, k3tog, yo x 2, k2tog, k9.

Row 8: K7, yo, k1, k2tog, p1, k2, p1, k1, k2tog, k1, yo, k7.
Row 9: K3, k2tog, yo x 2, k2tog, k1, yo, k1, k2tog, k3, k2tog, k1, yo, k1, k2tog, yo x 2, k2tog, k3.
Row 10: K4, p1, k4, yo, (k1, k2tog) x 2, k1, yo, k3, p1, k5.
Row 11: K2, yo, k1, k2tog x 2, yo x 2, k2tog, k1, yo, k1, k3tog, k1, yo, k1, k2tog, yo x 2, k2tog x 2, k1, yo, k2.
Row 12: (Yo, k1, k2tog) x 2, p1, k4, yo, p3tog, yo, k3, p1, k1, (k2tog, k1, yo) x 2.
Row 13: K1, yo, k1, k2tog, yo, k1, k2tog x 2, yo x 2, k2tog, k3, k2tog, yo x 2, k2tog x 2, k1, yo, k2tog, k1, yo, k1.
Row 14: K2, (yo, k1, k2tog) x 2, p1, k6, p1, k1, (k2tog, k1, yo) x 2, k2.
Row 15: K3, yo, k1, k2tog, yo, k1, k2tog x 2, yo x 2, k3tog, yo x 2, k2tog x 2, k1, yo, k2tog, k1, yo, k3.
Row 16: K4, (yo, k1, k2tog) x 2, p1, k2, p1, k1, (k2tog, k1, yo) x 2, k4.
Row 17: K5, (yo, k1, k2tog) x 2, k3, (k2tog, k1, yo) x 2, k5.
Row 18: K6, (yo, k1, k2tog) x 2, k1, (k2tog, k1, yo) x 2, k6.
Row 19: K7, yo, k1, k2tog, yo, k1, k3tog, k1, yo, k2tog, k1, yo, k7.
Row 20: K8, yo, k1, k2tog, yo, p3tog, yo, k2tog, k1, yo, k8.
Row 21: K9, yo, (k1, k2tog) x 2, k1, yo, k9.
Row 22: K10, yo, k1, p3tog, k1, yo, k10.
Row 23: Repeat row 3.

4.20

Fern variation 2

TEX 2015.148 Scarf

A variation of the classic Fern form ends in a single Cat's Paw.

Row 1 (RS): K12, k2tog, yo, k13. (27 sts)
Row 2 (WS): Knit.
Row 3: K11, k2tog, yo, k1, yo, k2tog, k11.
Row 4: Knit.
Row 5: K10, k2tog, yo, k3, yo, k2tog, k10.
Row 6: Knit.
Row 7: K12, yo, k3tog, yo, k12.
Row 8: Knit.
Row 9: K7, yo, k1, k2tog, k7, k2tog, k1, yo, k7.

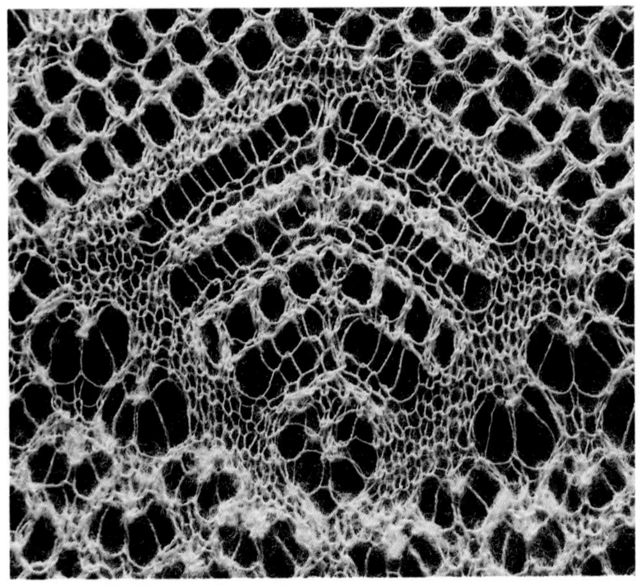

Fern variation 2 original pattern.

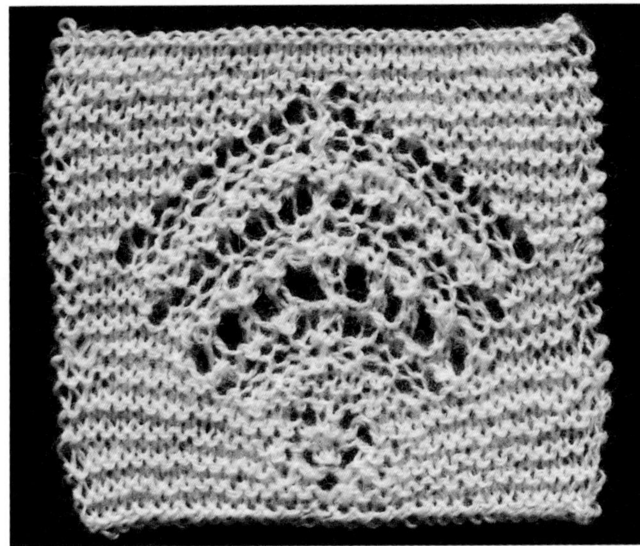

Fern variation 2 knitted sample.

Row 10: K8, yo, k1, k2tog, k5, k2tog, k1, yo, k8.
Row 11: K4, k2tog, yo x 2, k2tog, k1, yo, k1, k2tog, k3, k2tog, k1, yo, k1, k2tog, yo x 2, k2tog, k4.
Row 12: K6, p1, k3, yo, (k1, k2tog) x 2, k1, yo, k3, p1, k6.
Row 13: K3, yo, k1, k2tog x 2, yo x 2, k2tog, k1, yo, k1, k3tog, k1, yo, k1, k2tog, yo x 2, k2tog x 2, k1, yo, k3.
Row 14: K4, yo, k1, k2tog, k1, p1, k3, yo, p3tog, yo, k3, p1, k1, k2tog, k1, yo, k4.
Row 15: K5, yo, k1, k2tog x 2, yo x 2, k2tog, k3, k2tog, yo x 2, k2tog x 2, k1, yo, k5.
Row 16: K6, yo, k1, k2tog, k1, p1, k5, p1, k1, k2tog, k1, yo, k6.
Row 17: K1, yo, k1, k2tog, k3, yo, k1, k2tog x 2, yo x 2, k3tog, yo x 2, k2tog x 2, k1, yo, k3, k2tog, k1, yo, k1.
Row 18: K2, yo, k1, k2tog, k3, yo, k1, k2tog, (k1, p1) x 2, k1, k2tog, k1, yo, k3, k2tog, k1, yo, k2.

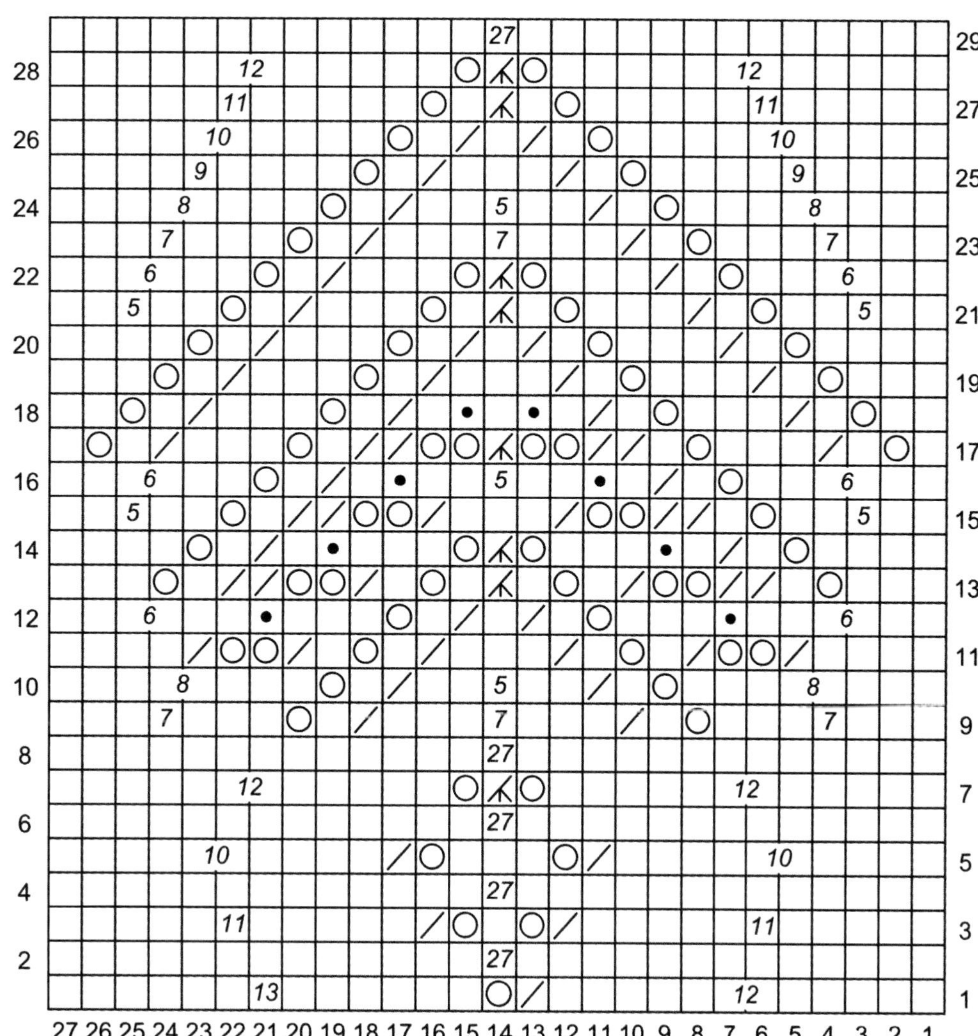

Fern variation 2 chart.

Row 19: (K3, yo, k1, k2tog) x 2, (k3, k2tog, k1, yo) x 2, k3.

Row 20: K4, yo, k1, k2tog, k3, yo, (k1, k2tog) x 2, k1, yo, k3, k2tog, k1, yo, k4.

Row 21: K5, yo, k1, k2tog, k3, yo, k1, k3tog, k1, yo, k3, k2tog, k1, yo, k5.

Row 22: K6, yo, k1, k2tog, k3, yo, p3tog, yo, k3, k2tog, k1, yo, k6.

Row 23: Repeat row 9.

Row 24: Repeat row 10.

Row 25: K9, yo, k1, k2tog, k3, k2tog, k1, yo, k9.

Row 26: K10, yo, (k1, k2tog) x 2, k1, yo, k10.

Row 27: K11, yo, k1, k3tog, k1, yo, k11.

Row 28: K12, yo, p3tog, yo, k12.

Row 29: Knit.

4.21

Fern variation 3

TEX 2019.42 Shawl

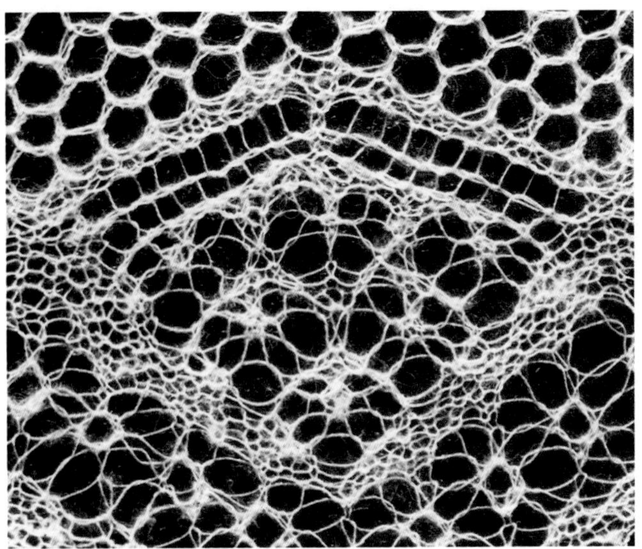

Fern variation 3 original pattern.

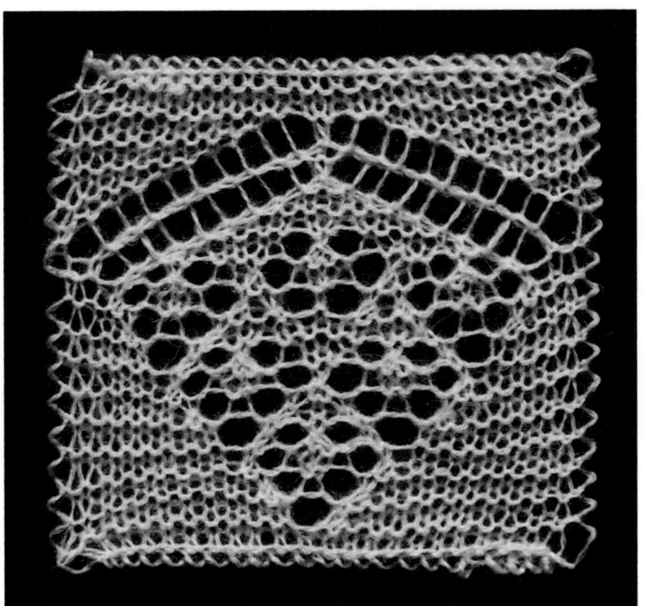

Fern variation 3 knitted sample.

Simple openwork patterns are suspended below the classic Fern arch to form a delicate rendition of this motif.

Row 1 (RS): K10, k2tog, yo, k11. (23 sts)
Row 2 (WS): Knit.
Row 3: K9, k2tog, yo, k1, yo, k2tog, k9.
Row 4: Knit.
Row 5: K8, k2tog, yo, k3, yo, k2tog, k8.
Row 6: Knit.
Row 7: K8, yo, k2tog, yo, k3tog, yo, k2tog, yo, k8.
Row 8: Knit.
Row 9: K6, k2tog, yo, k1, yo, k2tog, k1, k2tog, yo, k1, yo, k2tog, k6.
Row 10: Knit.
Row 11: K5, k2tog, yo, k3, yo, k3tog, yo, k3, yo, k2tog, k5.
Row 12: Knit.
Row 13: K5, yo, k2tog, yo, k3tog, yo, k3, yo, k3tog, yo, k2tog, yo, k5.
Row 14: Knit.
Row 15: K3, k2tog, yo, k1, yo, k2tog, k7, k2tog, yo, k1, yo, k2tog, k3.
Row 16: Knit.

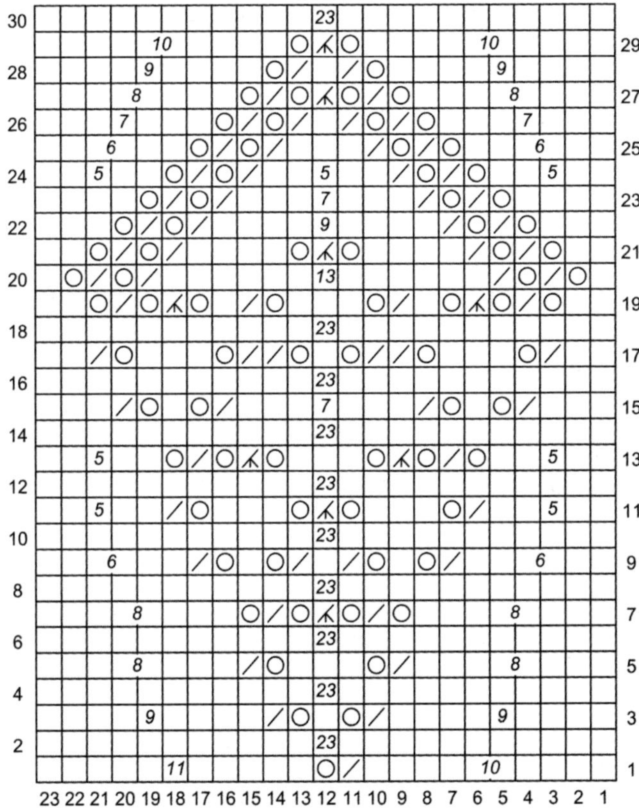

Fern variation 3 chart.

Row 17: K2, k2tog, yo, k3, yo, k2tog x 2, yo, k1, yo, k2tog x 2, yo, k3, yo, k2tog, k2.
Row 18: Knit.
Row 19: K2, yo, k2tog, yo, k3tog, yo, k1, k2tog, yo, k3, yo, k2tog, k1, yo, k3tog, yo, k2tog, yo, k2.
Row 20: K1, (yo, k2tog) x 2, k13, (k2tog, yo) x 2, k1.
Row 21: K2, (yo, k2tog) x 2, k4, yo, k3tog, yo, k4, (k2tog, yo) x 2, k2.
Row 22: K3, (yo, k2tog) x 2, k9, (k2tog, yo) x 2, k3.
Row 23: K4, (yo, k2tog) x 2, k7, (k2tog, yo) x 2, k4.
Row 24: K5, (yo, k2tog) x 2, k5, (k2tog, yo) x 2, k5.
Row 25: K6, (yo, k2tog) x 2, k3, (k2tog, yo) x 2, k6.
Row 26: K7, (yo, k2tog) x 2, k1, (k2tog, yo) x 2, k7.
Row 27: Repeat row 7.
Row 28: K9, yo, k2tog, k1, k2tog, yo, k9.
Row 29: K10, yo, k3tog, yo, k10.
Row 30: Knit.

4.22

Fern inset with three plain Diamonds and a Branch
TEX 2004.172 Shawl

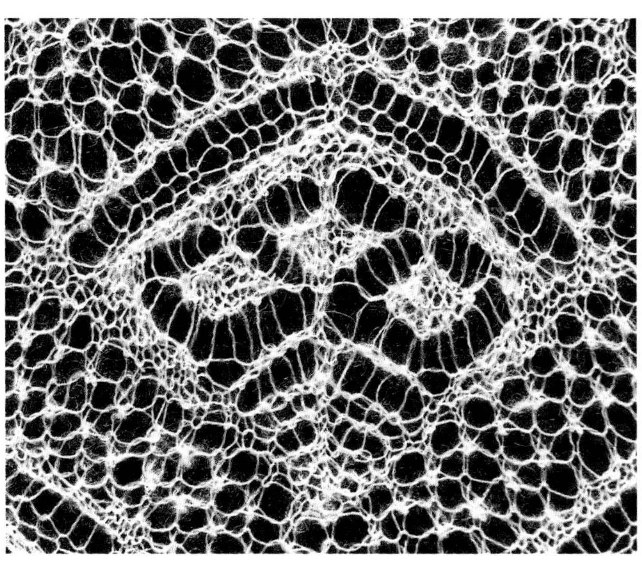

Fern inset with three plain Diamonds and a Branch original pattern.

Fern inset with three plain Diamonds and a Branch knitted sample.

The arching framework of the basic Fern form can have any number of motifs suspended below it, as illustrated in this pattern. A Branch hangs below three plain Diamonds that frame it from above.

Row 1 (RS): K16, yo, k2tog, k15. (33 sts)
Row 2 (WS): K15, yo, k3tog, yo, k15.
Row 3: K14, yo, k2tog, k1, k2tog, yo, k14.
Row 4: K13, yo, k2tog, yo, k3tog, yo, k2tog, yo, k13.
Row 5: K12, (yo, k2tog) x 2, k1, (k2tog, yo) x 2, k12.
Row 6: K11, (yo, k2tog) x 2, yo, k3tog, (yo, k2tog) x 2, yo, k11.
Row 7: K10, (yo, k2tog) x 3, k1, (k2tog, yo) x 3, k10.
Row 8: Repeat row 4.
Row 9: K8, k2tog, yo, (k1, yo, k2tog) x 2, (k1, k2tog, yo) x 2, k1, yo, k2tog, k8.
Row 10: K7, k2tog, yo, k3, yo, k2tog, k1, yo, k3tog, yo, k1, k2tog, yo, k3, yo, k2tog, k7.
Row 11: K6, k2tog, yo, k5, yo, k2tog, k3, k2tog, yo, k5, yo, k2tog, k6.
Row 12: K5, k2tog, yo, k7, yo, k2tog, k1, k2tog, yo, k7, yo, k2tog, k5.
Row 13: K4, k2tog, yo, k9, yo, k3tog, yo, k9, yo, k2tog, k4.
Row 14: Knit.
Row 15: K6, yo, k2tog, k5, k2tog, yo, k3, yo, k2tog, k5, k2tog, yo, k6.
Row 16: K7, yo, k2tog, k3, k2tog, yo, k5, yo, k2tog, k3, k2tog, yo, k7.
Row 17: K1, yo, k1, k2tog, k4, yo, k2tog, k1, k2tog, yo, k7, yo, k2tog, k1, k2tog, yo, k4, k2tog, k1, yo, k1.
Row 18: K2, yo, k1, k2tog, k4, yo, k3tog, yo, k9, yo, k3tog, yo, k4, k2tog, k1, yo, k2.
Row 19: K3, yo, k1, k2tog, k21, k2tog, k1, yo, k3.

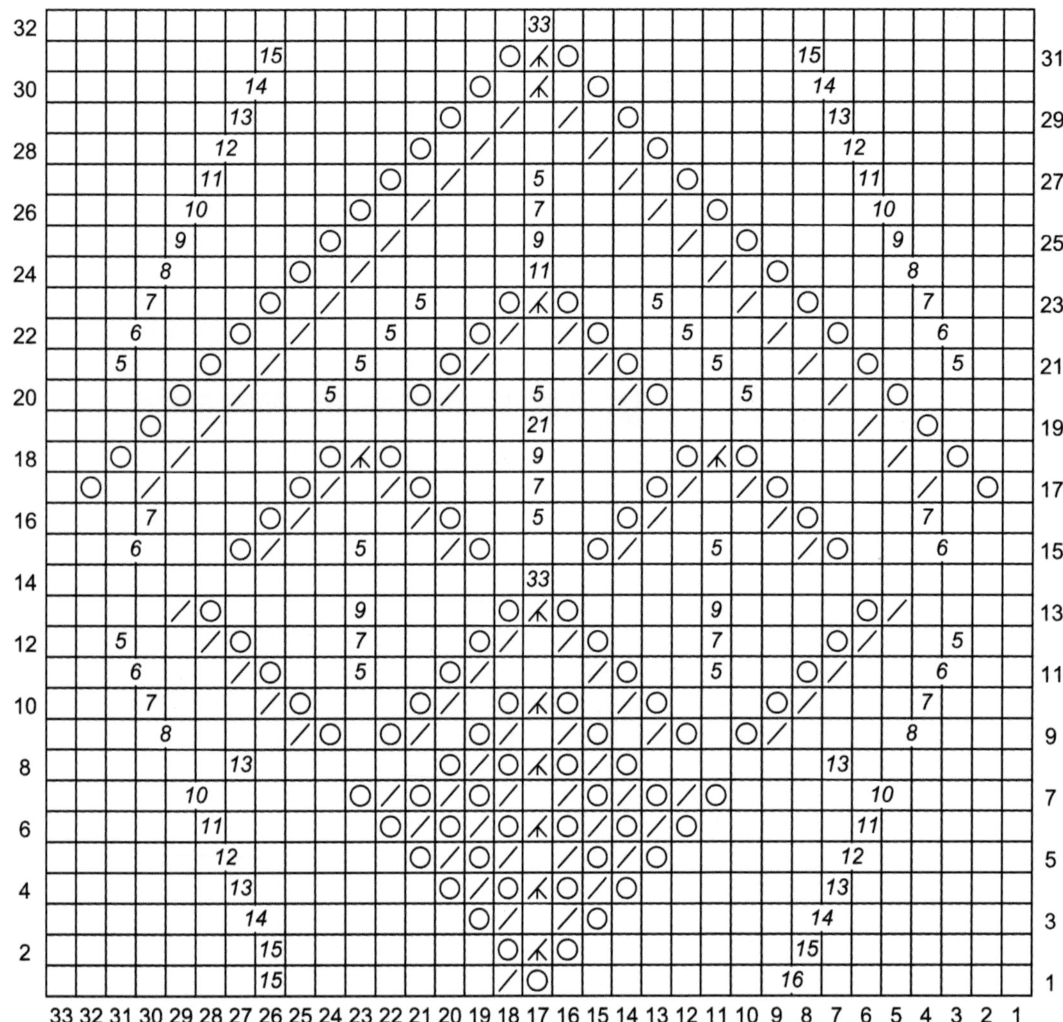

Fern inset with three plain Diamonds and a Branch chart.

Row 20: K4, yo, k1, k2tog, k5, yo, k2tog, k5, k2tog, yo, k5, k2tog, k1, yo, k4.

Row 21: K5, yo, k1, k2tog, k5, yo, k2tog, k3, k2tog, yo, k5, k2tog, k1, yo, k5.

Row 22: K6, yo, k1, k2tog, k5, yo, k2tog, k1, k2tog, yo, k5, k2tog, k1, yo, k6.

Row 23: K7, yo, k1, k2tog, k5, yo, k3tog, yo, k5, k2tog, k1, yo, k7.

Row 24: K8, yo, k1, k2tog, k11, k2tog, k1, yo, k8.

Row 25: K9, yo, k1, k2tog, k9, k2tog, k1, yo, k9.

Row 26: K10, yo, k1, k2tog, k7, k2tog, k1, yo, k10.

Row 27: K11, yo, k1, k2tog, k5, k2tog, k1, yo, k11.

Row 28: K12, yo, k1, k2tog, k3, k2tog, k1, yo, k12.

Row 29: K13, yo, (k1, k2tog) x 2, k1, yo, k13.

Row 30: K14, yo, k1, k3tog, k1, yo, k14.

Row 31: Repeat row 2.

Row 32: Knit.

WAVES AND PATTERNS WITHIN WAVES

Waves are horizontal zigzagging lines of pattern. They are used almost exclusively in borders, either singly or in groups. When used multiple times in a border, each Wave is usually made of a different pattern or alternating patterns. Fancy Net and Lace Holes are common small patterns used to make Waves. Plain Waves (k2tog, yo) are made fancier by knitting short lines of three or four k2tog, yo combinations placed at right angles to the plain Wave to form small 'hooks' along its edge. Such Waves are known as Knotty Waves.

The Wave repertoire is further enhanced by changing the heights of Waves by repeating several rows of the pattern or by alternating different patterns of Waves. Waves are often placed

Storm force waves creating the jagged Shetland coastline.

one on top of the other, to form a deep expanse of pattern. Sometimes they are placed with their points facing or meeting each other. This layout creates diamond shapes that can be filled with many different patterns. Ferns, Trees, and Branches are favourite patterns to use between Waves because there is a wide variety of infills to use with most of these shapes.

The stark zigzag nature of a Wave makes it a focal point of the border. When shawls with Waves in the border were worn against the voluminous skirts of the mid-nineteenth century, the Waves created sharp, dramatic lines from the corner of the shawl outward and upward, accentuating the width of the skirt and drawing the eye to the rest of the shawl and the wearer's feminine figure above.

4.23

Wave of Fancy Net

TEX 2004.336 Scarf

One of the most common Waves uses the Fancy Net pattern. It adds delicateness to a group of Waves and further complexity to any border design.

Row 1 (RS): (K1, yo, k2tog, k19, k2tog, yo) x 2. (48 sts)
Row 2 and all WS rows: Knit.
Row 3: K2tog, yo, k1, yo, k2tog, k15, k2tog, yo, k1, yo, k3tog, yo, k1, yo, k2tog, k15, k2tog, yo, k1, yo.
Row 5: (K1, yo, k3tog, yo, k1, yo, k2tog, k11, k2tog, yo, k1, yo, k3tog, yo) x 2.

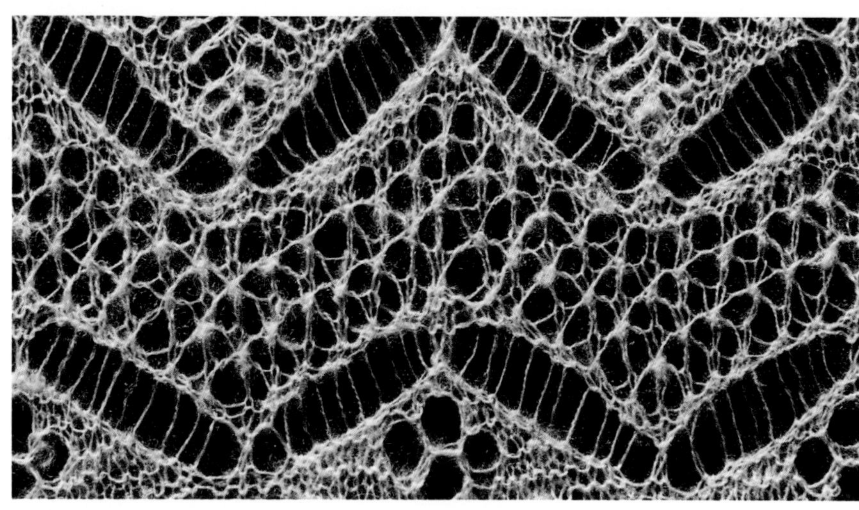

Wave of Fancy Net original pattern.

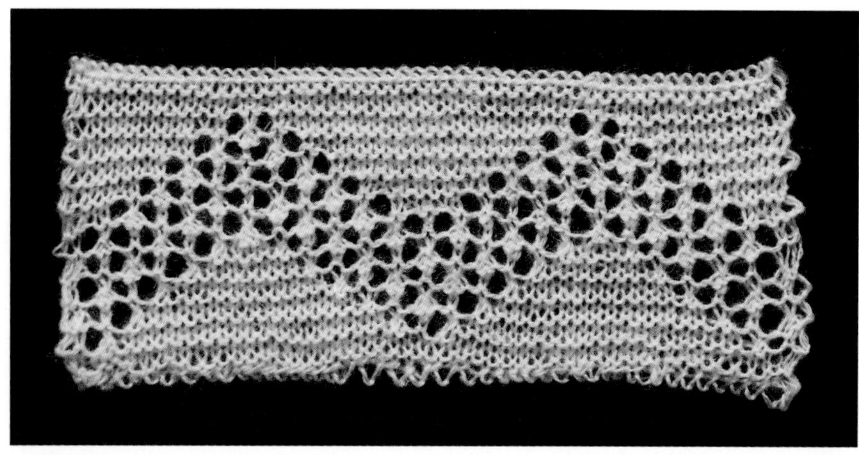

Wave of Fancy Net knitted sample.

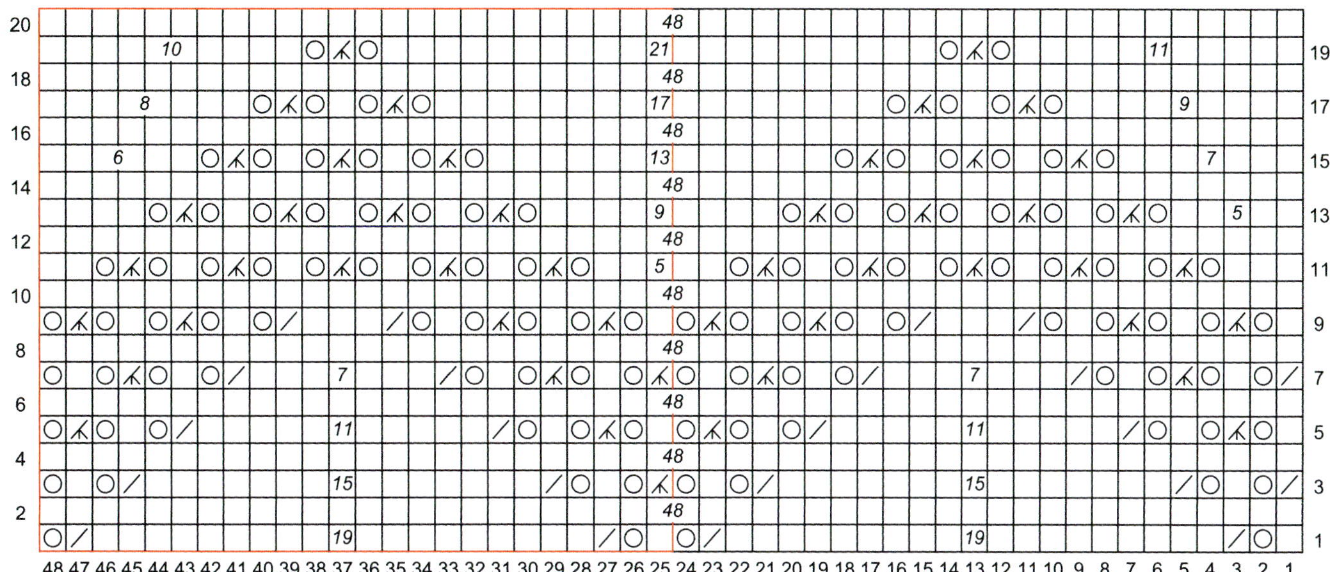
Wave of Fancy Net chart.

Row 7: K2tog, yo, k1, yo, k3tog, yo, k1, yo, k2tog, k7, k2tog, (yo, k1, yo, k3tog) x 2, yo, k1, yo, k3tog, yo, k1, yo, k2tog, k7, k2tog, yo, k1, yo, k3tog, yo, k1, yo.

Row 9: ((K1, yo, k3tog, yo) x 2, k1, yo, k2tog, k3, k2tog, (yo, k1, yo, k3tog) x 2, yo) x 2.

Row 11: K3, (yo, k3tog, yo, k1) x 4, yo, k3tog, yo, k5, (yo, k3tog, yo, k1) x 4, yo, k3tog, yo, k2.

Row 13: K5, (yo, k3tog, yo, k1) x 3, yo, k3tog, yo, k9, (yo, k3tog, yo, k1) x 3, yo, k3tog, yo, k4.

Row 15: K7, (yo, k3tog, yo, k1) x 2, yo, k3tog, yo, k13, (yo, k3tog, yo, k1) x 2, yo, k3tog, yo, k6.

Row 17: K9, yo, k3tog, yo, k1, yo, k3tog, yo, k17, yo, k3tog, yo, k1, yo, k3tog, yo, k8.

Row 19: K11, yo, k3tog, yo, k21, yo, k3tog, yo, k10.

4.24

Branch set in Waves of Fancy Net

TEX 8933 Scarf

A simple Branch is framed by sharp Waves in Fancy Net stitch. The Waves are unusual here in that their sharp points do not meet.

Row 1 (RS): Knit. (32 sts)

Row 2 (WS): K14, k2tog, yo, k1, yo, k2tog, k13.

Row 3: Knit.

Row 4: K12, k2tog, yo, k1, yo, p3tog, yo, k1, yo, k2tog, k11.

Row 5: Knit.

Row 6: K10, k2tog, (yo, k1, yo, p3tog) x 2, yo, k1, yo, k2tog, k9.

Row 7: Knit.

Row 8: K8, k2tog, yo, k1, yo, p3tog, yo, k5, yo, p3tog, yo, k1, yo, k2tog, k7.

Row 9: Knit.

Row 10: K6, k2tog, yo, k1, yo, p3tog, yo, k9, yo, p3tog, yo, k1, yo, k2tog, k5.

Row 11: Knit.

Branch set in Waves of Fancy Net original pattern.

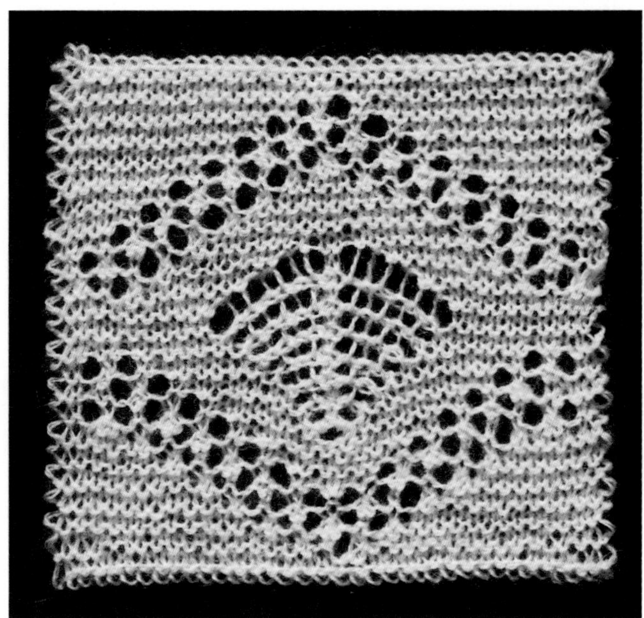

Branch set in Waves of Fancy Net knitted sample.

Row 12: K4, k2tog, yo, k1, yo, p3tog, yo, k13, yo, p3tog, yo, k1, yo, k2tog, k3.
Row 13: Knit.
Row 14: (K1, yo, p3tog, yo) x 2, k8, yo, k2tog, k7, yo, p3tog, yo, k1, yo, p3tog, yo.
Row 15: Knit.
Row 16: K3, (yo, p3tog, yo, k9) x 2, yo, p3tog, yo, k2.
Row 17: K13, yo, k2tog, k1, k2tog, yo, k14.
Row 18: K1, yo, p3tog, yo, k9, yo, k2tog, yo, p3tog, yo, k2tog, yo, k9, yo, p3tog, yo.
Row 19: K11, (yo, k2tog) x 2, k1, (k2tog, yo) x 2, k12.
Row 20: K11, (yo, k2tog) x 2, yo, p3tog, (yo, k2tog) x 2, yo, k10.
Row 21: K9, (yo, k2tog) x 3, k1, (k2tog, yo) x 3, k10.
Row 22: K9, (yo, k2tog) x 3, yo, p3tog, (yo, k2tog) x 3, yo, k8.
Row 23: Repeat row 21.
Row 24: Repeat row 20.
Row 25: Repeat row 19.
Row 26: K2tog, yo, k1, yo, k2tog, k8, yo, k2tog, yo, p3tog, yo, k2tog, yo, k8, k2tog, yo, k1, yo.
Row 27: Repeat row 17.
Row 28: K1, yo, p3tog, yo, k1, yo, k2tog, k8, yo, p3tog, yo, k8, k2tog, yo, k1, yo, p3tog, yo.
Row 29: Knit.
Row 30: K3, yo, p3tog, yo, k1, yo, k2tog, k15, k2tog, yo, k1, yo, p3tog, yo, k2.
Row 31: Knit.
Row 32: K5, yo, p3tog, yo, k1, yo, k2tog, k11, k2tog, yo, k1, yo, p3tog, yo, k4.
Row 33: Knit.
Row 34: K7, yo, p3tog, yo, k1, yo, k2tog, k7, k2tog, yo, k1, yo, p3tog, yo, k6.
Row 35: Knit.
Row 36: K9, yo, p3tog, yo, k1, yo, k2tog, k3, k2tog, yo, k1, yo, p3tog, yo, k8.
Row 37: Knit.
Row 38: K11, (yo, p3tog, yo, k1) x 2, yo, p3tog, yo, k10.
Row 39: Knit.
Row 40: K13, yo, p3tog, yo, k1, yo, p3tog, yo, k12.
Row 41: Knit.
Row 42: K15, yo, p3tog, yo, k14.
Row 43: Knit.

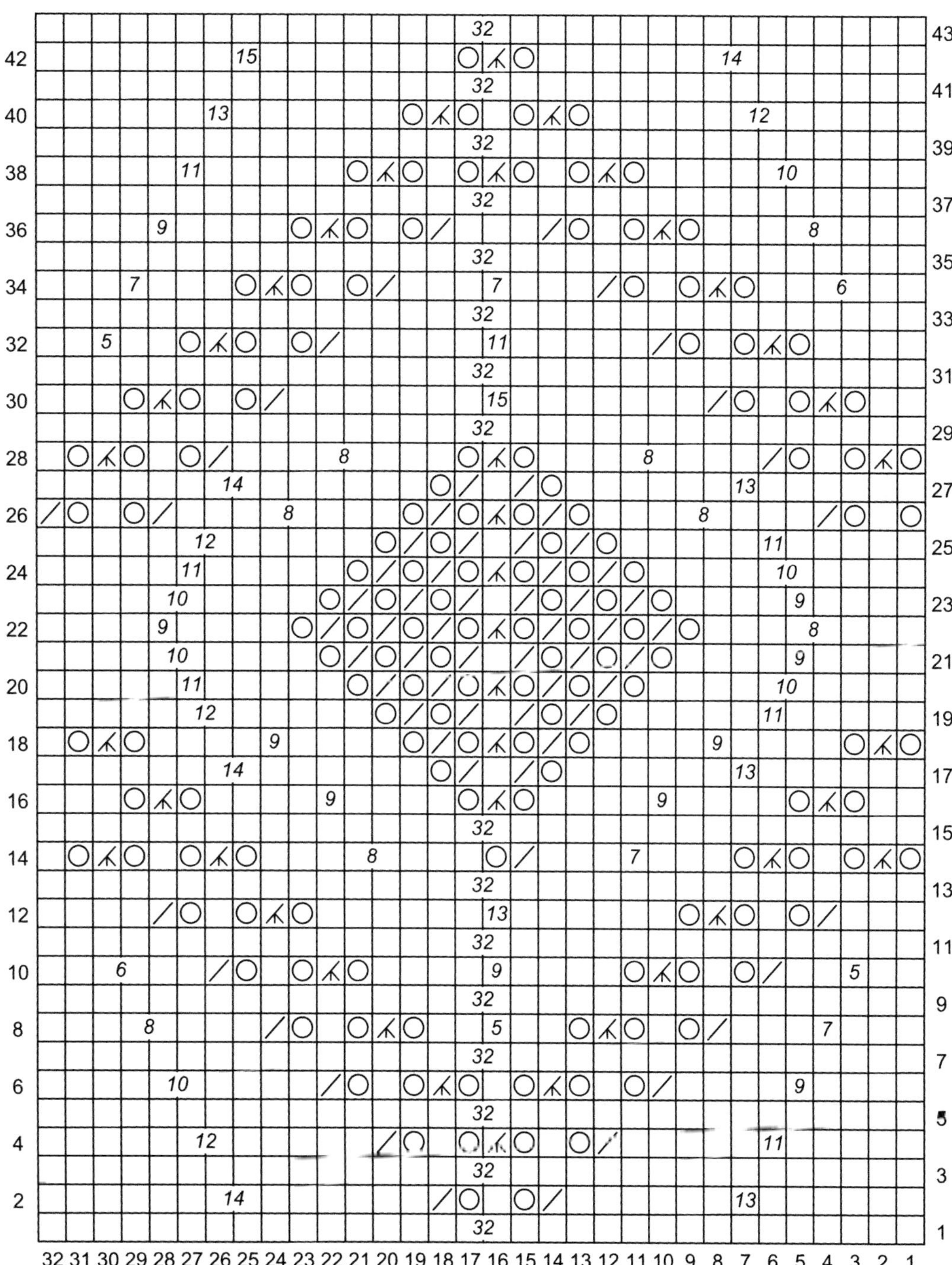

Branch set in Waves of Fancy Net chart.

4.25

Wave of Branches

TEX 76147 Shawl

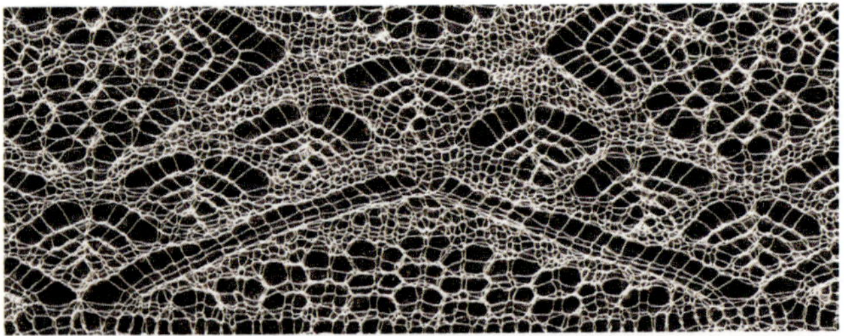

Wave of Branches original pattern.

Wave of Branches knitted sample.

Most Waves are made of very small patterns but occasionally knitters used larger motifs and applied them singly in a zigzag formation. Branches are a good choice because their diamond shape lends itself well to the sharp zigzag line of Waves. When more circular motifs are used such as the Peerie Flea or Eyelid, the effect is less zigzag-like and has more of a resemblance to a gently rounded garland.

Row 1 (RS): Yo, k2tog, k25, k2tog, yo, k26, k2tog, yo. (57 sts)
Row 2 (WS): Knit.
Row 3: K2tog, yo, k25, yo, k3tog, yo, k25, yo, ssk.
Row 4: (K1, ssk, yo, k23, yo, k2tog) x 2, k1.
Row 5: (K2tog, yo) x 2, k2, k2tog, yo, k12, k2tog, yo, k3, yo, ssk, yo, k3tog, yo, k2tog, yo, k2, k2tog, yo, k12, k2tog, yo, k3, (yo, ssk) x 2.
Row 6: (K1, (ssk, yo) x 2, k19, (yo, k2tog) x 2) x 2, k1.
Row 7: (K2tog, yo) x 2, k2, yo, k3tog, yo, k11, yo, k3tog, yo, k2, yo, ssk, yo, k3tog, yo, k2tog, yo, k2, yo, k3tog, yo, k11, yo, k3tog, yo, k2, (yo, ssk) x 2.
Row 8: (K1, ssk, yo, k2, yo, k2tog, k1, ssk, yo, k9, yo, k2tog, k1, ssk, yo, k2, yo, k2tog) x 2, k1.
Row 9: K2tog, yo, k2, yo, ssk, yo, k3tog, yo, k2tog, yo, k2, k2tog, yo, k3, yo, ssk, yo, k3tog, yo, k2tog, yo, k2, yo, k3tog, yo, k2, yo, ssk, yo, k3tog, yo, k2tog, yo, k2, k2tog, yo, k3, yo, ssk, yo, k3tog, yo, k2tog, yo, k2, yo, ssk.
Row 10: K3, ((yo, k2tog) x 2, k1, (ssk, yo) x 2, k5) x 3, (yo, k2tog) x 2, k1, (ssk, yo) x 2, k3.
Row 11: K4, yo, ssk, yo, k3tog, yo, k2tog, yo, k2, yo, k3tog, yo, k2, yo, ssk, yo, k3tog, yo, k2tog, yo, k7, yo, ssk, yo, k3tog, yo, k2tog, yo, k2, yo, k3tog, yo, k2, yo, ssk, yo, k3tog, yo, k2tog, yo, k4.
Row 12: K5, (yo, k2tog, k1, ssk, yo, k2) x 2, yo, k2tog, k1, ssk, yo, k9, (yo, k2tog, k1, ssk, yo, k2) x 2, yo, k2tog, k1, ssk, yo, k5.
Row 13: K6, yo, k3tog, yo, k2, yo, ssk, yo, k3tog, yo, k2tog, yo, k2, yo, k3tog, yo, k11, yo, k3tog, yo, k2, yo, ssk, yo, k3tog, yo, k2tog, yo, k2, yo, k3tog, yo, k6.
Row 14: K10, (yo, k2tog) x 2, k1, (ssk, yo) x 2, k19, (yo, k2tog) x 2, k1, (ssk, yo) x 2, k10.
Row 15: K11, yo, ssk, yo, k3tog, yo, k2tog, yo, k21, yo, ssk, yo, k3tog, yo, k2tog, yo, k11.
Row 16: K12, yo, k2tog, k1, ssk, yo, k23, yo, k2tog, k1, ssk, yo, k12.
Row 17: K13, yo, k3tog, yo, k25, yo, k3tog, yo, k13.
Row 18: Knit.

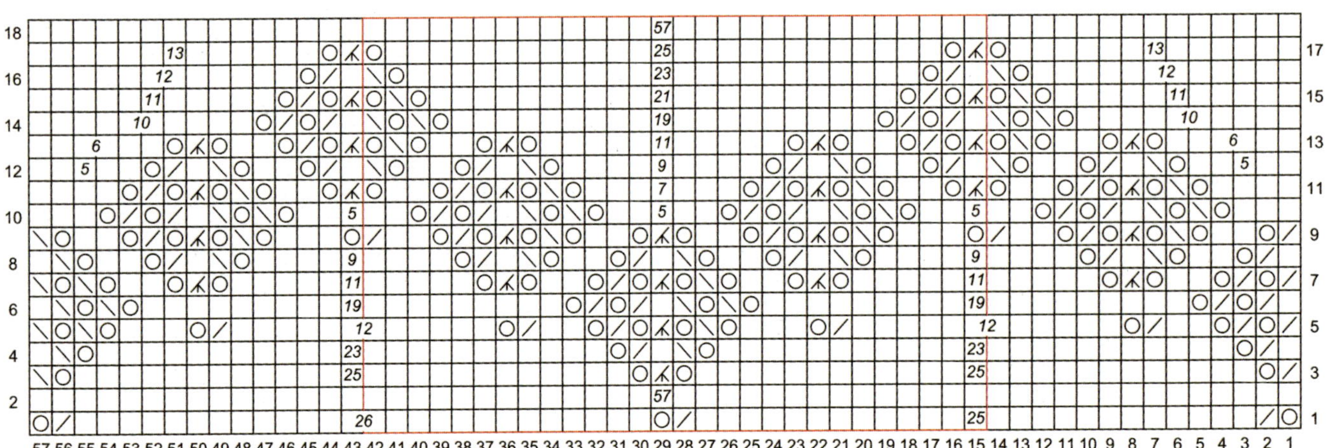

Wave of Branches chart.

4.26

Four Ferns set in Eyelid Waves

TEX 2014.25 Shawl

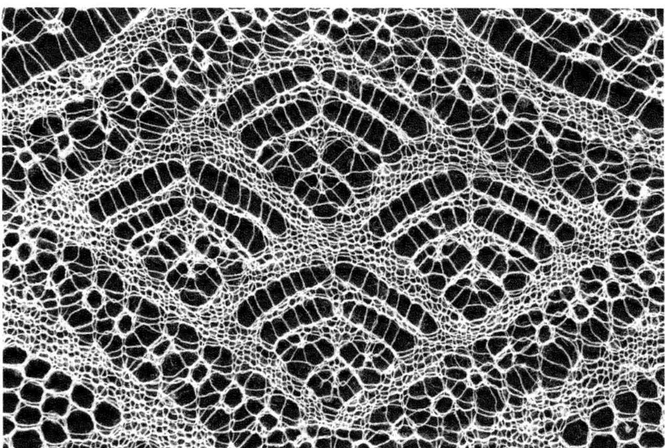

Four Ferns set in Eyelid Waves original pattern.

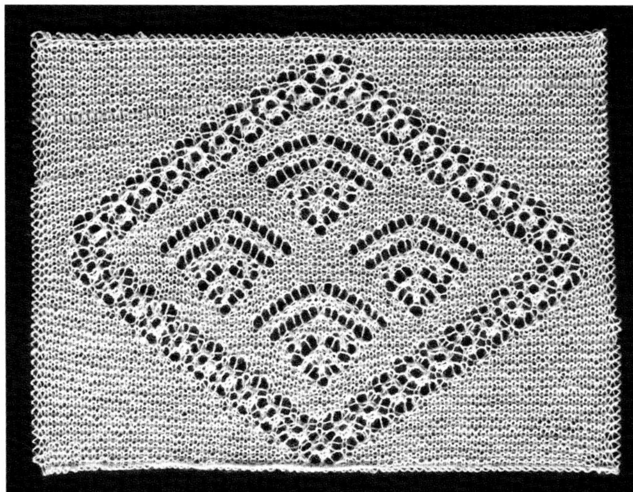

Four Ferns set in Eyelid Waves knitted sample.

This is a beautiful pattern using four small Ferns arranged in a diamond form and surrounded by Waves of Eyelids. It has been slightly altered from the original to allow better spacing of the Ferns on all sides.

Row 1: K32, k2tog, yo, k1, yo, ssk, k32. (69 sts)
Row 2: K31, k2tog, yo, k3, yo, ssk, k31.
Row 3: Knit.
Row 4: K32, yo, ssk, yo, k3tog, yo, k32.
Row 5: K29, k2tog, yo, k1, yo, ssk, k1, k2tog, yo, k1, yo, ssk, k29.
Row 6: K28, k2tog, yo, k3, yo, k3tog, yo, k3, yo, ssk, k28.
Row 7: Knit.
Row 8: K29, yo, ssk, yo, k3tog, yo, k1, yo, ssk, yo, k3tog, yo, k29.
Row 9: K26, (k2tog, yo, k1, yo, ssk, k1) x 2, k2tog, yo, k1, yo, ssk, k26.
Row 10: K25, k2tog, (yo, k3, yo, k3tog) x 2, yo, k3, yo, ssk, k25.
Row 11: Knit.
Row 12: K26, yo, ssk, yo, k3tog, yo, k7, yo, ssk, yo, k3tog, yo, k26.
Row 13: K23, k2tog, yo, k1, yo, ssk, k1, k2tog, yo, k7, yo, ssk, k1, k2tog, yo, k1, yo, ssk, k23.
Row 14: K22, k2tog, yo, k3, yo, k3tog, yo, k9, yo, k3tog, yo, k3, yo, ssk, k22.
Row 15: Knit.
Row 16: K23, yo, ssk, yo, k3tog, yo, k13, yo, ssk, yo, k3tog, yo, k23.
Row 17: K20, k2tog, yo, k1, yo, ssk, k1, k2tog, yo, k5, k2tog, yo, k6, yo, ssk, k1, k2tog, yo, k1, yo, ssk, k20.
Row 18: K19, k2tog, yo, k3, yo, k3tog, yo, k15, yo, k3tog, yo, k3, yo, ssk, k19.
Row 19: Repeat row 1.
Row 20: K20, yo, ssk, yo, k3tog, yo, k6, k2tog, yo, k3, yo, ssk, k6, yo, ssk, yo, k3tog, yo, k20.
Row 21: K17, k2tog, yo, k1, yo, ssk, k1, k2tog, yo, k8, yo, k3tog, yo, k8, yo, ssk, k1, k2tog, yo, k1, yo, ssk, k17.
Row 22: K16, k2tog, yo, k3, yo, k3tog, yo, k7, yo, ssk, k3, k2tog, yo, k7, yo, k3tog, yo, k3, yo, ssk, k16.
Row 23: Knit.
Row 24: K17, yo, ssk, yo, k3tog, yo, k7, k2tog, yo, k1, yo, ssk, k1, k2tog, yo, k1, yo, ssk, k7, yo, ssk, yo, k3tog, yo, k17.
Row 25: K14, k2tog, yo, k1, yo, ssk, k1, k2tog, yo, k11, yo, k3tog, yo, k11, yo, ssk, k1, k2tog, yo, k1, yo, ssk, k14.
Row 26: K13, k2tog, yo, k3, yo, k3tog, yo, k7, yo, ssk, yo, k3tog, yo, k3, yo, k3tog, yo, k2tog, yo, k7, yo, k3tog, yo, k3, yo, ssk, k13.
Row 27: K29, yo, ssk, k7, k2tog, yo, k29.
Row 28: K14, yo, ssk, yo, k3tog, yo, k11, yo, ssk, k5, k2tog, yo, k11, yo, ssk, yo, k3tog, yo, k14.
Row 29: K11, k2tog, yo, k1, yo, ssk, k1, k2tog, yo, k7, (yo, ssk, k3) x 2, k2tog, yo, k3, k2tog, yo, k7, yo, ssk, k1, k2tog, yo, k1, yo, ssk, k11.
Row 30: K10, k2tog, yo, k3, yo, k3tog, yo, k9, yo, ssk, k3, yo, ssk, k1, k2tog, yo, k3, k2tog, yo, k9, yo, k3tog, yo, k3, yo, ssk, k10.
Row 31: K28, yo, ssk, k3, yo, k3tog, yo, k3, k2tog, yo, k28.

Four Ferns set in Eyelid Waves chart.

Row 32: K11, yo, ssk, yo, k3tog, yo, k13, yo, ssk, k7, k2tog, yo, k13, yo, ssk, yo, k3tog, yo, k11.

Row 33: K8, k2tog, yo, k1, yo, ssk, k1, (k2tog, yo, k6) x 2, yo, ssk, (k5, k2tog, yo) x 2, k7, yo, ssk, k1, k2tog, yo, k1, yo, ssk, k8.

Row 34: K7, k2tog, yo, k3, yo, k3tog, yo, k16, yo, ssk, k3, k2tog, yo, k16, yo, k3tog, yo, k3, yo, ssk, k7.

Row 35: K21, k2tog, yo, k1, yo, ssk, k6, yo, ssk, k1, k2tog, yo, k6, k2tog, yo, k1, yo, ssk, k21.

Row 36: K8, yo, ssk, yo, k3tog, yo, k7, k2tog, yo, k3, yo, ssk, k6, yo, k3tog, yo, k6, k2tog, yo, k3, yo, ssk, k7, yo, ssk, yo, k3tog, yo, k8.

Row 37: K5, k2tog, yo, k1, yo, ssk, k1, k2tog, yo, k9, yo, k3tog, yo, k19, yo, k3tog, yo, k9, yo, ssk, k1, k2tog, yo, k1, yo, ssk, k5.

Row 38: K4, k2tog, yo, k3, yo, k3tog, yo, k8, yo, ssk, k3, k2tog, yo, k15, yo, ssk, k3, k2tog, yo, k8, yo, k3tog, yo, k3, yo, ssk, k4.

Row 39: Knit.

Row 40: K5, yo, ssk, yo, k3tog, yo, k8, k2tog, yo, k1, yo, ssk, k1, k2tog, yo, k1, yo, ssk, k11, k2tog, yo, k1, yo, ssk, k1, k2tog, yo, k1, yo, ssk, k8, yo, ssk, yo, k3tog, yo, k5.

Row 41: K2, k2tog, yo, k1, yo, ssk, k1, k2tog, yo, k12, yo, k3tog, yo, k19, yo, k3tog, yo, k12, yo, ssk, k1, k2tog, yo, k1, yo, ssk, k2.

Row 42: K1, k2tog, yo, k3, yo, k3tog, yo, k8, yo, ssk, yo, k3tog, yo, k3, yo, k3tog, yo, k2tog, yo, k9, yo, ssk, yo, k3tog, yo, k3, yo, k3tog, yo, k2tog, yo, k8, yo, k3tog, yo, k3, yo, ssk, k1.

Row 43: K18, yo, ssk, k7, k2tog, yo, k11, yo, ssk, k7, k2tog, yo, k18.

Row 44: K2, yo, ssk, yo, k3tog, yo, k12, yo, ssk, k5, k2tog, yo, k13, yo, ssk, k5, k2tog, yo, k12, yo, ssk, yo, k3tog, yo, k2.

Row 45: K2, yo, ssk, k1, k2tog, yo, k1, yo, ssk, (k5, (yo, ssk, k3) x 2, k2tog, yo, k3, k2tog, yo) x 2, k5, k2tog, yo, k1, yo, ssk, k1, k2tog, yo, k2.

Row 46: K3, yo, k3tog, yo, k3, yo, ssk, k5, yo, ssk, k3, yo, ssk, k1, k2tog, yo, k3, k2tog, yo, k7, yo, ssk, k3, yo, ssk, k1, k2tog, yo, k3, k2tog, yo, k5, k2tog, yo, k3, yo, k3tog, yo, k3.

Row 47: K17, yo, ssk, k3, yo, k3tog, yo, k3, k2tog, yo, k9, yo, ssk, k3, yo, k3tog, yo, k3, k2tog, yo, k17.

Row 48: K5, yo, ssk, yo, k3tog, yo, k8, yo, ssk, k7, k2tog, yo, k11, yo, ssk, k7, k2tog, yo, k8, yo, ssk, yo, k3tog, yo, k5.

Row 49: K5, yo, ssk, k1, k2tog, yo, k1, yo, ssk, k6, yo, ssk, (k5, k2tog, yo) x 2, k6, yo, ssk, k5, k2tog, yo, k6, k2tog, yo, k1, yo, ssk, k1, k2tog, yo, k5.

Row 50: K6, yo, k3tog, yo, k3, yo, ssk, k6, yo, ssk, k3, k2tog, yo, k15, yo, ssk, k3, k2tog, yo, k6, k2tog, yo, k3, yo, k3tog, yo, k6.

Row 51: K21, yo, ssk, k1, k2tog, yo, k6, k2tog, yo, k1, yo, ssk, k6, yo, ssk, k1, k2tog, yo, k21.

Row 52: K8, yo, ssk, yo, k3tog, yo, k9, yo, k3tog, yo, k6, k2tog, yo, k3, yo, ssk, k6, yo, k3tog, yo, k9, yo, ssk, yo, k3tog, yo, k8.

Row 53: K8, yo, ssk, k1, k2tog, yo, k1, yo, ssk, k17, yo, k3tog, yo, k17, k2tog, yo, k1, yo, ssk, k1, k2tog, yo, k8.

Row 54: K9, yo, k3tog, yo, k3, yo, ssk, k14, yo, ssk, k3, k2tog, yo, k14, k2tog, yo, k3, yo, k3tog, yo, k9.

Row 55: Knit.

Row 56: K11, yo, ssk, yo, k3tog, yo, k13, k2tog, yo, k1, yo, ssk, k1, k2tog, yo, k1, yo, ssk, k13, yo, ssk, yo, k3tog, yo, k11.

Row 57: K11, yo, ssk, k1, k2tog, yo, k1, yo, ssk, k14, yo, k3tog, yo, k14, k2tog, yo, k1, yo, ssk, k1, k2tog, yo, k11.

Row 58: K12, yo, k3tog, yo, k3, yo, ssk, k8, yo, ssk, yo, k3tog, yo, k3, yo, k3tog, yo, k2tog, yo, k8, k2tog, yo, k3, yo, k3tog, yo, k12.

Row 59: Repeat row 27.

Row 60: Repeat row 28.

Row 61: K14, yo, ssk, k1, k2tog, yo, k1, yo, ssk, k4, (yo, ssk, k3) x 2, k2tog, yo, k3, k2tog, yo, k4, k2tog, yo, k1, yo, ssk, k1, k2tog, yo, k14.

Row 62: K15, yo, k3tog, yo, k3, yo, ssk, k4, yo, ssk, k3, yo, ssk, k1, k2tog, yo, k3, k2tog, yo, k4, k2tog, yo, k3, yo, k3tog, yo, k15.

Row 63: Repeat row 31.

Row 64: K17, yo, ssk, yo, k3tog, yo, k7, yo, ssk, k7, k2tog, yo, k7, yo, ssk, yo, k3tog, yo, k17.

Row 65: K17, yo, ssk, k1, k2tog, yo, k1, (yo, ssk, k5) x 2, k2tog, yo, k5, k2tog, yo, k1, yo, ssk, k1, k2tog, yo, k17.

Row 66: K18, yo, k3tog, yo, k3, yo, ssk, k5, yo, ssk, k3, k2tog, yo, k5, k2tog, yo, k3, yo, k3tog, yo, k18.

Row 67: K32, yo, ssk, k1, k2tog, yo, k32.

Row 68: K20, yo, ssk, (yo, k3tog, yo, k8) x 2, yo, ssk, yo, k3tog, yo, k20.

Row 69: K20, yo, ssk, k1, k2tog, yo, k1, yo, ssk, k13, k2tog, yo, k1, yo, ssk, k1, k2tog, yo, k20.

Row 70: K21, yo, k3tog, yo, k3, yo, ssk, k11, k2tog, yo, k3, yo, k3tog, yo, k21.

Row 71: Knit.

Row 72: Repeat row 16.
Row 73: K23, yo, ssk, k1, k2tog, yo, k1, yo, ssk, k7, k2tog, yo, k1, yo, ssk, k1, k2tog, yo, k23.
Row 74: K24, yo, k3tog, yo, k3, yo, ssk, k5, k2tog, yo, k3, yo, k3tog, yo, k24.
Row 75: Knit.
Row 76: Repeat row 12.
Row 77: K26, (yo, ssk, k1, k2tog, yo, k1) x 2, yo, ssk, k1, k2tog, yo, k26.
Row 78: K27, (yo, k3tog, yo, k3) x 2, yo, k3tog, yo, k27.
Row 79: Knit.
Row 80: Repeat row 8.
Row 81: K29, yo, ssk, k1, k2tog, yo, k1, yo, ssk, k1, k2tog, yo, k29.
Row 82: K30, yo, k3tog, yo, k3, yo, k3tog, yo, k30.
Row 83: Knit.
Row 84: Repeat row 4.
Row 85: Repeat row 67.
Row 86: K33, yo, k3tog, yo, k33.
Row 87: Knit.

4.27

Balanced Diamond inset with nine Diamonds set in Knotty Waves
TEX 81467 Scarf

Balanced Diamond inset with nine Diamonds set in Knotty Waves original pattern.

A Knotty Wave is formed by adding a series of little Diamonds along the edge of a Wave, which makes the Wave appear to have little knots or hooks. Their form is sharper and more defined if knitted with very fine, smooth, and even yarn. They are used extensively to add more complexity than a simple Wave. This is a narrow scarf, with a span to accommodate only two Waves. It is made from very fine artificial silk with much drape and was probably extremely difficult to knit.

Row 1 (RS): K16, k2tog, yo, k1, yo, k2tog, k16. (37 sts)
Row 2 (WS): K15, k2tog, yo, k3, yo, k2tog, k15.
Row 3: K14, k2tog, yo, k5, yo, k2tog, k14.
Row 4: K13, k2tog, yo, k7, yo, k2tog, k13.

Balanced Diamond inset with nine Diamonds set in Knotty Waves knitted sample.

Row 5: K12, k2tog, yo, k9, yo, k2tog, k12.
Row 6: K11, k2tog, yo, k1, yo, k2tog, k5, k2tog, yo, k1, yo, k2tog, k11.
Row 7: K10, k2tog, yo, k3, yo, k2tog, k3, k2tog, yo, k3, yo, k2tog, k10.
Row 8: K9, k2tog, yo, k5, yo, k2tog, k1, k2tog, yo, k5, yo, k2tog, k9.
Row 9: K8, k2tog, yo, k1, yo, k2tog, k4, yo, k3tog, yo, k4, k2tog, yo, k1, yo, k2tog, k8.
Row 10: K7, (k2tog, yo, k3, yo, k2tog, k1) x 2, k2tog, yo, k3, yo, k2tog, k7.

Row 11: K6, k2tog, (yo, k5, yo, k3tog) x 2, yo, k5, yo, k2tog, k6.
Row 12: K5, k2tog, yo, k1, yo, k2tog, k3, k2tog, yo, k7, yo, k2tog, k3, k2tog, yo, k1, yo, k2tog, k5.
Row 13: K4, k2tog, yo, k3, yo, k2tog, k1, k2tog, yo, k9, yo, k2tog, k1, k2tog, yo, k3, yo, k2tog, k4.
Row 14: K3, k2tog, yo, k5, yo, p3tog, yo, k11, yo, p3tog, yo, k5, yo, k2tog, k3.
Row 15: K2, k2tog, yo, k1, yo, k2tog, k3, k2tog, yo, k13, yo, k2tog, k3, k2tog, yo, k1, yo, k2tog, k2.
Row 16: K1, k2tog, yo, k3, yo, k2tog, k1, k2tog, yo, k15, yo, k2tog, k1, k2tog, yo, k3, yo, k2tog, k1.
Row 17: K2tog, yo, k5, yo, k3tog, yo, k7, k2tog, yo, k8, yo, k3tog, yo, k5, yo, k2tog.
Row 18: K2, yo, k2tog, k3, k2tog, yo, k7, k2tog, yo, k1, yo, k2tog, k7, yo, k2tog, k3, k2tog, yo, k2.
Row 19: K3, yo, k2tog, k1, k2tog, yo, k7, k2tog, yo, k3, yo, k2tog, k7, yo, k2tog, k1, k2tog, yo, k3.
Row 20: K4, yo, p3tog, yo, k7, k2tog, yo, k5, yo, k2tog, k7, yo, p3tog, yo, k4.
Row 21: K4, k2tog, yo, k7, k2tog, yo, k1, yo, k2tog, k1, k2tog, yo, k1, yo, k2tog, k7, yo, k2tog, k4.
Row 22: K3, k2tog, yo, k7, k2tog, yo, k3, yo, p3tog, yo, k3, yo, k2tog, k7, yo, k2tog, k3.
Row 23: K2, k2tog, yo, k7, k2tog, yo, k5, yo, k2tog, k4, yo, k2tog, k7, yo, k2tog, k2.
Row 24: K1, k2tog, yo, k7, (k2tog, yo, k1, yo, k2tog, k1) x 2, k2tog, yo, k1, yo, k2tog, k7, yo, k2tog, k1.
Row 25: K2tog, yo, k7, k2tog, (yo, k3, yo, k3tog) x 2, yo, k3, yo, k2tog, k7, yo, k2tog.
Row 26: K8, (k2tog, yo, k4) x 2, k2tog, yo, k5, yo, k2tog, k8.
Row 27: K1, yo, k2tog, k7, (yo, k2tog, k1, k2tog, yo, k1) x 2, yo, k2tog, k1, k2tog, yo, k7, k2tog, yo, k1.
Row 28: K2, yo, k2tog, k7, (yo, p3tog, yo, k3) x 2, yo, p3tog, yo, k7, k2tog, yo, k2.
Row 29: K3, yo, k2tog, k7, yo, k2tog, k4, yo, k2tog, k3, k2tog, yo, k7, k2tog, yo, k3.
Row 30: K4, yo, k2tog, k7, yo, k2tog, k1, k2tog, yo, k1, yo, k2tog, k1, k2tog, yo, k7, k2tog, yo, k4.
Row 31: K5, yo, k2tog, k7, yo, k3tog, yo, k3, yo, k3tog, yo, k7, k2tog, yo, k5.
Row 32: K3, k2tog, yo, k1, yo, k2tog, k7, yo, k2tog, k3, k2tog, yo, k7, k2tog, yo, k1, yo, k2tog, k3.
Row 33: K2, k2tog, yo, k3, yo, k2tog, k7, yo, k2tog, k1, k2tog, yo, k7, k2tog, yo, k3, yo, k2tog, k2.
Row 34: K1, k2tog, yo, k5, yo, k2tog, k7, yo, p3tog, yo, k7, k2tog, yo, k5, yo, k2tog, k1.
Row 35: K2tog, yo, k4, k2tog, yo, k1, yo, k2tog, k15, k2tog, yo, k1, yo, k2tog, k4, yo, k2tog.
Row 36: K2, yo, k2tog, k1, k2tog, yo, k3, yo, k2tog, k13, k2tog, yo, k3, yo, k2tog, k1, k2tog, yo, k2.
Row 37: K3, yo, k3tog, yo, k5, yo, k2tog, k11, k2tog, yo, k5, yo, k3tog, yo, k3.
Row 38: K4, yo, k2tog, k3, k2tog, yo, k1, yo, k2tog, k9, k2tog, yo, k1, yo, k2tog, k3, k2tog, yo, k4.
Row 39: K5, yo, k2tog, k1, k2tog, yo, k3, yo, k2tog, k7, k2tog, yo, k3, yo, k2tog, k1, k2tog, yo, k5.
Row 40: K6, yo, p3tog, yo, k5, yo, k2tog, k5, k2tog, yo, k5, yo, p3tog, yo, k6.
Row 41: K7, (yo, k2tog, k3, k2tog, yo, k1) x 2, yo, k2tog, k3, k2tog, yo, k7.
Row 42: K8, (yo, k2tog, k1, k2tog, yo, k3) x 2, yo, k2tog, k1, k2tog, yo, k8.
Row 43: K9, (yo, k3tog, yo, k5) x 2, yo, k3tog, yo, k9.
Row 44: K10, yo, k2tog, k3, k2tog, yo, k3, yo, k2tog, k3, k2tog, yo, k10.
Row 45: K11, yo, k2tog, k1, k2tog, yo, k5, yo, k2tog, k1, k2tog, yo, k11.
Row 46: K12, yo, p3tog, yo, k7, yo, p3tog, yo, k12.
Row 47: K13, yo, k2tog, k7, k2tog, yo, k13.
Row 48: K14, yo, k2tog, k5, k2tog, yo, k14.
Row 49: K15, yo, k2tog, k3, k2tog, yo, k15.
Row 50: K16, yo, k2tog, k1, k2tog, yo, k16.
Row 51: K17, yo, k3tog, yo, k17.

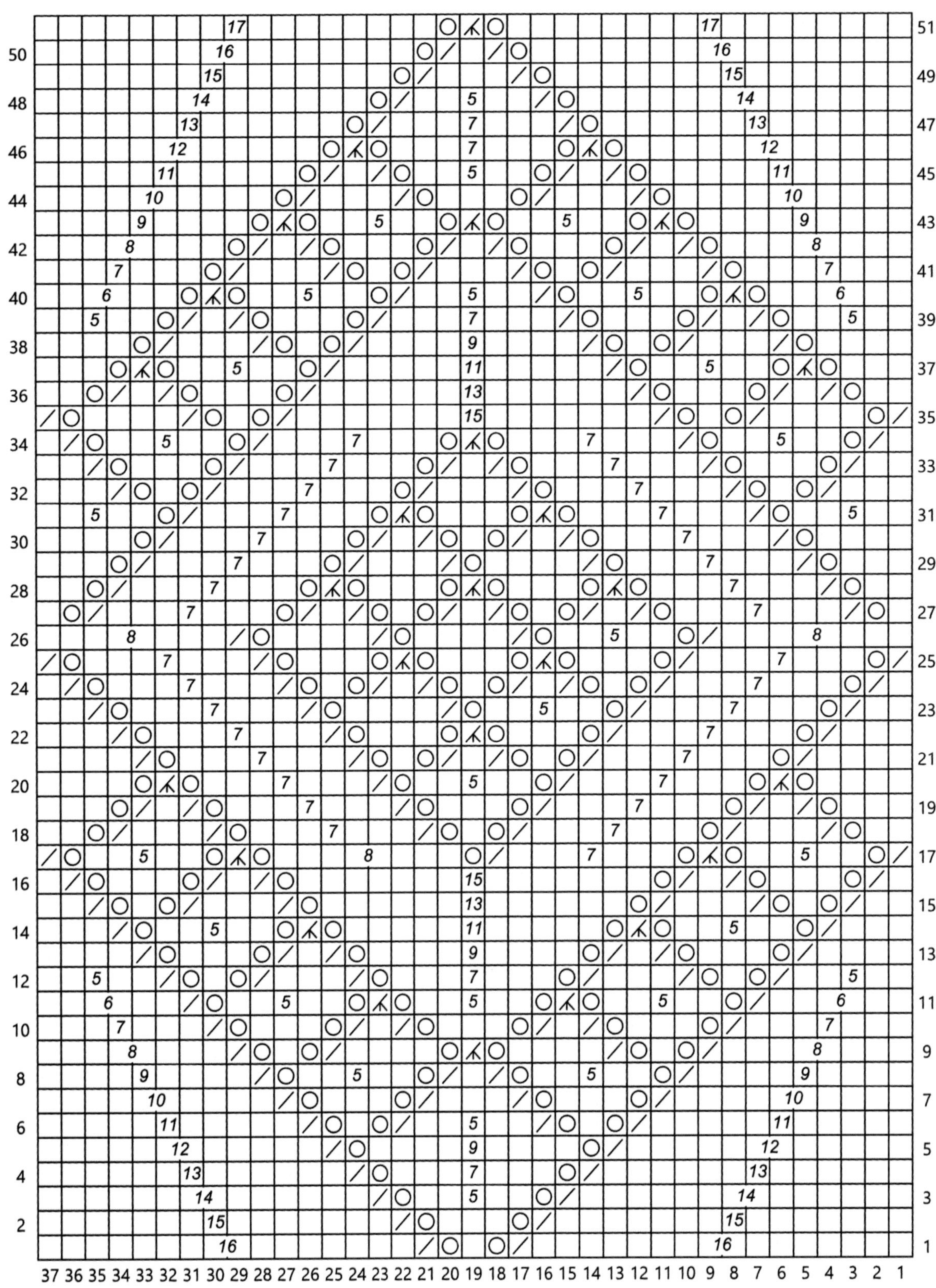

Balanced Diamond inset with nine Diamonds set in Knotty Waves chart.

4.28

Balanced Diamond with complex centre set in broken and continuous simple Waves

TEX 2012.494 Stole

Balanced Diamond with complex centre set in broken and continuous simple Waves original pattern.

Balanced Diamond with complex centre set in broken and continuous simple Waves knitted sample.

This unusual pattern includes six small openwork Diamonds in a cluster, forming the lower half of a Balanced Diamond. The upper part of the pattern is a series of plain Waves, some of which are not continuous but which add height to the overall pattern.

Row 1 (WS): K11, k2tog, yo, k1, yo, k2tog, k14. (33 sts)
Row 2 (RS): K13, k2tog, yo, k3, yo, k2tog, k13.
Row 3: K12, k2tog, yo, k5, yo, k2tog, k12.
Row 4: K11, k2tog, yo, k7, yo, k2tog, k11.
Row 5: K10, k2tog, yo, k9, yo, k2tog, k10.
Row 6: K9, k2tog, yo, k11, yo, k2tog, k9.
Row 7: K8, k2tog, yo, k5, k2tog, yo, k6, yo, k2tog, k8.
Row 8: K7, k2tog, yo, k5, k2tog, yo, k1, yo, k2tog, k5, yo, k2tog, k7.
Row 9: K6, k2tog, yo, k5, k2tog, yo, k3, yo, k2tog, k5, yo, k2tog, k6.
Row 10: (K5, k2tog, yo) x 2, (k5, yo, k2tog) x 2, k5.
Row 11: K4, k2tog, yo, k5, yo, k2tog, k1, k2tog, yo, k1, yo, k2tog, k1, k2tog, yo, k5, yo, k2tog, k4.
Row 12: K3, k2tog, yo, k23, yo, k2tog, k3.
Row 13: K2, k2tog, yo, (k5, k2tog, yo, k1, yo, k2tog) x 2, k5, yo, k2tog, k2.
Row 14: K1, k2tog, yo, k5, k2tog, yo, k3, yo, k2tog, k3, k2tog, yo, k3, yo, k2tog, k5, yo, k2tog, k1.
Row 15: (K2tog, yo, k5) x 2, yo, k2tog, k1, k2tog, yo, (k5, yo, k2tog) x 2.
Row 16: K6, yo, k2tog, k1, k2tog, yo, k1, yo, k2tog, k2, yo, k2tog, k1, k2tog, yo, k1, yo, k2tog, k1, k2tog, yo, k6.
Row 17: Knit.
Row 18: K4, (k2tog, yo, k1, yo, k2tog, k5) x 2, k2tog, yo, k1, yo, k2tog, k4.
Row 19: (K3, k2tog, yo, k3, yo, k2tog) x 3, k3
Row 20: K2, (k2tog, yo, k5, yo, k2tog, k1) x 2, k2tog, yo, k5, yo, k2tog, k2.
Row 21: K1, yo, k2tog, k1, (k2tog, yo, k1, yo, k2tog, k1, k2tog, yo, k2) x 2, k2tog, yo, k1, yo, k2tog, k1, k2tog, yo, k1.
Row 22: Knit.

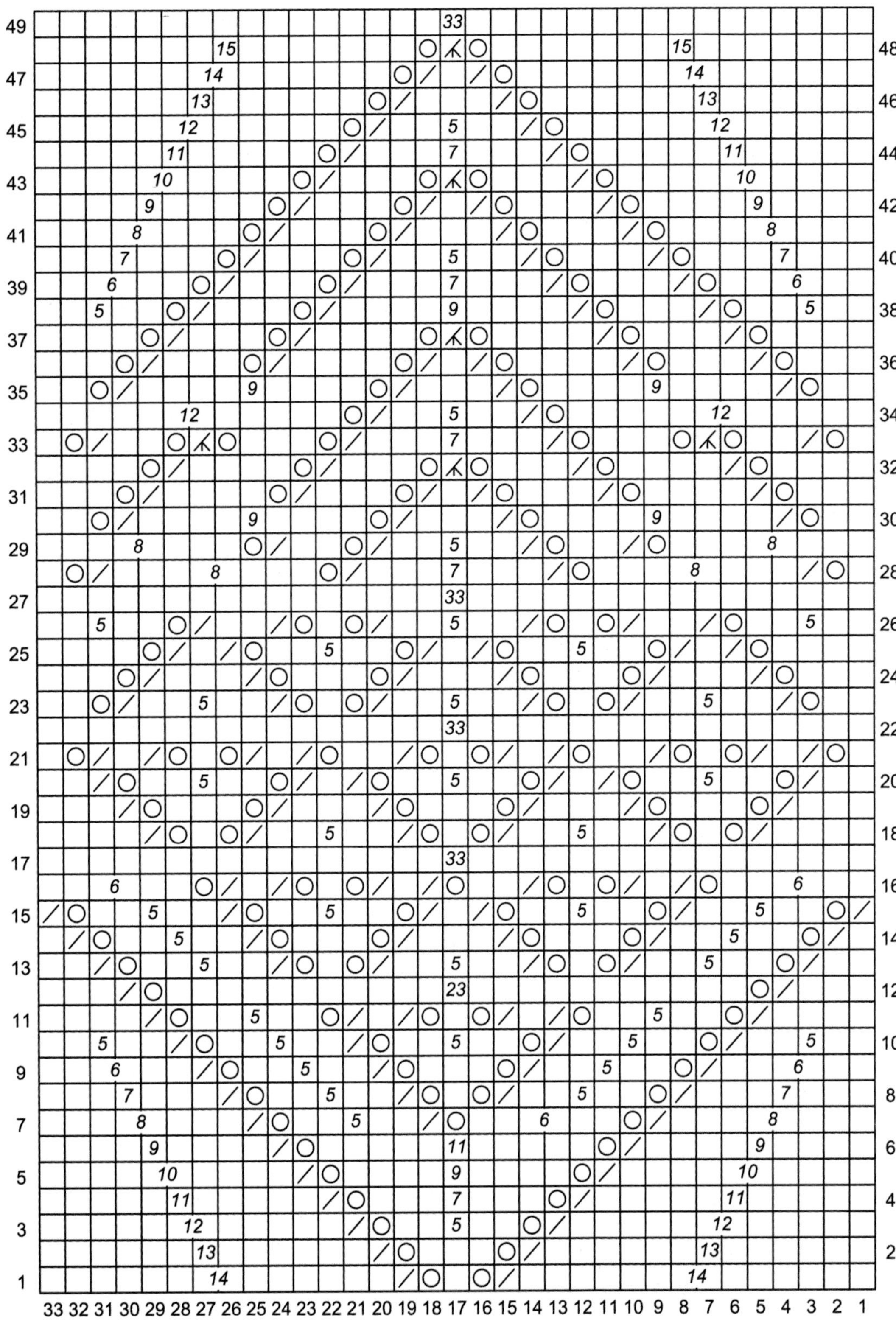

Balanced Diamond with complex centre set in broken and continuous simple Waves chart.

Row 23: K2, (yo, k2tog, k5, k2tog, yo, k1) x 2, yo, k2tog, k5, k2tog, yo, k2.
Row 24: (K3, yo, k2tog, k3, k2tog, yo) x 3, k3.
Row 25: K4, (yo, k2tog, k1, k2tog, yo, k5) x 2, yo, k2tog, k1, k2tog, yo, k4.
Row 26: K5, yo, k2tog, k2, k2tog, yo, k1, yo, k2tog, k5, k2tog, yo, k1, yo, k2tog, k2, k2tog, yo, k5.
Row 27: Knit.
Row 28: K1, yo, k2tog, k8, yo, k2tog, k7, k2tog, yo, k8, k2tog, yo, k1.
Row 29: K8, yo, k2tog, k2, yo, k2tog, k5, k2tog, yo, k2, k2tog, yo, k8.
Row 30: K2, yo, k2tog, k9, yo, k2tog, k3, k2tog, yo, k9, k2tog, yo, k2.
Row 31: K3, yo, k2tog, k4, yo, k2tog, k3, yo, k2tog, k1, k2tog, yo, k3, k2tog, yo, k4, k2tog, yo, k3.
Row 32: (K4, yo, k2tog) x 2, k3, yo, k3tog, yo, k3, (k2tog, yo, k4) x 2.
Row 33: K1, yo, k2tog, k2, yo, p3tog, yo, k3, yo, k2tog, k7, k2tog, yo, k3, yo, p3tog, yo, k2, k2tog, yo, k1.
Row 34: K12, yo, k2tog, k5, k2tog, yo, k12.
Row 35: Repeat row 30.
Row 36: (K3, yo, k2tog) x 2, k4, yo, k2tog, k1, k2tog, yo, k4, (k2tog, yo, k3) x 2.
Row 37: K4, yo, k2tog, k3, yo, k2tog, k4, yo, p3tog, yo, k4, k2tog, yo, k3, k2tog, yo, k4.
Row 38: K5, yo, k2tog, k3, yo, k2tog, k9, k2tog, yo, k3, k2tog, yo, k5.
Row 39: K6, yo, k2tog, k3, yo, k2tog, k7, k2tog, yo, k3, k2tog, yo, k6.
Row 40: K7, yo, k2tog, k3, yo, k2tog, k5, k2tog, yo, k3, k2tog, yo, k7.
Row 41: K8, (yo, k2tog, k3) x 2, k2tog, yo, k3, k2tog, yo, k8.
Row 42: K9, yo, k2tog, k3, yo, k2tog, k1, k2tog, yo, k3, k2tog, yo, k9.
Row 43: K10, yo, k2tog, k3, yo, p3tog, yo, k3, k2tog, yo, k10.
Row 44: K11, yo, k2tog, k7, k2tog, yo, k11.
Row 45: Repeat row 34.
Row 46: K13, yo, k2tog, k3, k2tog, yo, k13.
Row 47: K14, yo, k2tog, k1, k2tog, yo, k14.
Row 48: K15, yo, k3tog, yo, k15.
Row 49: Knit.

TREES AND FLOWERS

Trees and Flowers figure prominently in Shetland lace design. Trees are found large and small, in centres and in borders. They may have stems that are simple and all the same, or a range of simple and decorative stems. Trees may be very small, with only a few branching stems, or exceptionally tall, with multiple stems. Small, simple tree shapes with the same type of stems are called Branches in Unst, even when they appear upside-down. Upside-down forms with different types of stems are called Ferns or Madeiras in other parts of Shetland. See the section on Ferns for information and patterns.

There are patterns with names of flowers found in published pattern books but we found no specific flower names in the Shetland corpus. Flowers are mainly confined to the Basket o' Flooers design, which is nearly always placed along the bottom of a border. It appears like a flower or bud with 'leaves' below in a variety of stitches. The lower portion on its own has been referred to in Unst as the Cup and appears without flowers in a very old stole. This may indicate the development of the Basket o' Flooers design. It has many variations and remained popular well into the twentieth century.

Sea pinks at the shore.

4.29

Basket o' Flooers, variation 1

TEX 2019.34 Stole

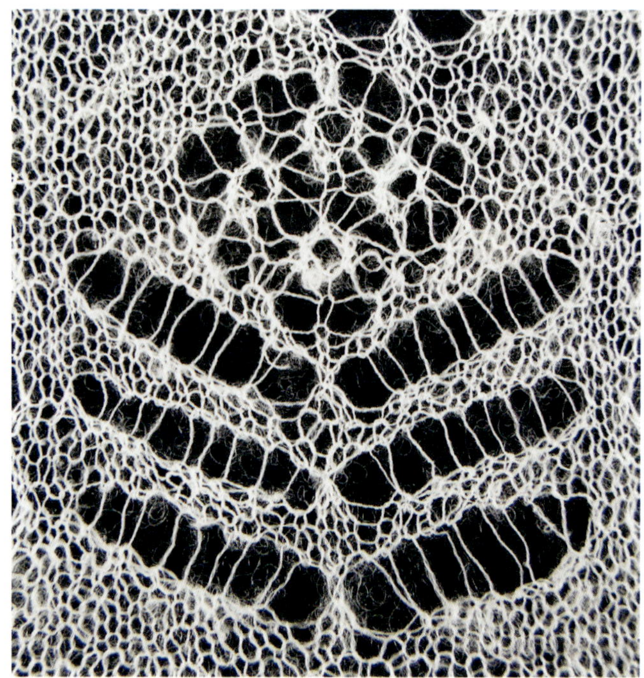

Basket o' Flooers, variation 1 original pattern.

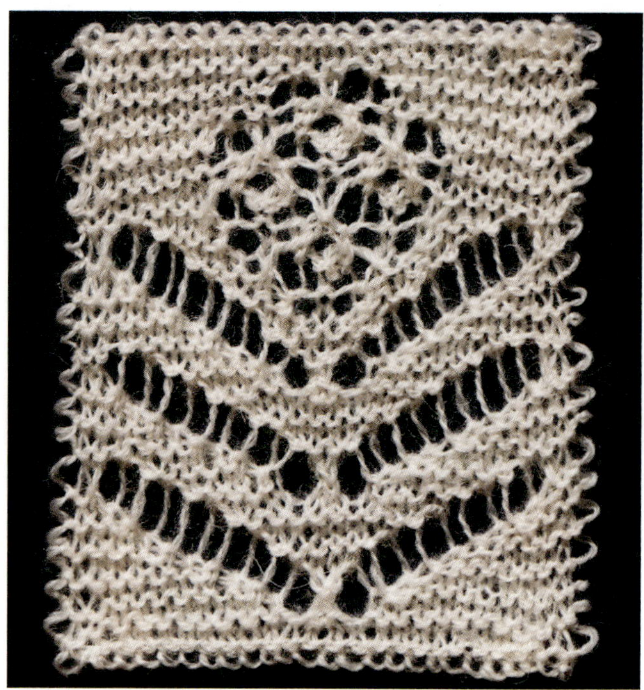

Basket o' Flooers, variation 1 original knitted sample.

A very simple form of Basket o' Flooers with well-spaced basket outline of leaves and a group of four Eyelids to form the flowers.

Row 1 (RS): K10, yo, k3tog, yo, k10. (23 sts)
Row 2 (WS): K8, k2tog, yo, k3, yo, k2tog, k8.
Row 3: K7, k2tog, yo, k5, yo, k2tog, k7.
Row 4: K6, k2tog, yo, k7, yo, k2tog, k6.
Row 5: K5, k2tog, yo, k9, yo, k2tog, k5.
Row 6: K4, k2tog, yo, k11, yo, k2tog, k4.
Row 7: K3, k2tog, yo, k13, yo, k2tog, k3.
Row 8: K2, k2tog, yo, k6, yo, p3tog, yo, k6, yo, k2tog, k2.
Row 9: K1, k2tog, yo, k5, k2tog, yo, k3, yo, k2tog, k5, yo, k2tog, k1.
Row 10: (K2tog, yo, k5) x 2, yo, k2tog, k5, yo, k2tog.
Row 11: Repeat row 4.
Row 12: Repeat row 5.
Row 13: Repeat row 6.
Row 14: Repeat row 7.
Row 15: K2, k2tog, yo, k6, yo, k3tog, yo, k6, yo, k2tog, k2.
Row 16: Repeat row 9.
Row 17: Repeat row 10.
Row 18: Repeat row 4.
Row 19: Repeat row 5.
Row 20: K4, k2tog, yo, k3, k2tog, yo, k1, yo, k2tog, k3, yo, k2tog, k4.
Row 21: K3, k2tog, yo, k4, k2tog, yo, k1, yo, k2tog, k4, yo, k2tog, k3.
Row 22: K2, k2tog, yo, k4, k2tog, yo, k3, yo, k2tog, k4, yo, k2tog, k2.
Row 23: K1, k2tog, yo, k17, yo, k2tog, k1.
Row 24: K2tog, yo, k4, k2tog, yo, k1, yo, p3tog, yo, k2tog, yo, k1, yo, k2tog, k4, yo, k2tog.
Row 25: K6, k2tog, yo, k1, yo, k2tog, k1, k2tog, yo, k1, yo, k2tog, k6.
Row 26: K5, k2tog, yo, k3, yo, p3tog, yo, k3, yo, k2tog, k5.
Row 27: Knit.
Row 28: K6, yo, p3tog, yo, k2tog, yo, k1, yo, p3tog, yo, k2tog, yo, k6.
Row 29: K6, yo, k2tog, k1, k2tog, yo, k1, yo, k2tog, k1, k2tog, yo, k6.
Row 30: K7, yo, p3tog, yo, k3, yo, p3tog, yo, k7.
Row 31: Knit.
Row 32: K9, yo, p3tog, yo, k2tog, yo, k9.
Row 33: K9, yo, k2tog, k1, k2tog, yo, k9.
Row 34: K10, yo, p3tog, yo, k10.

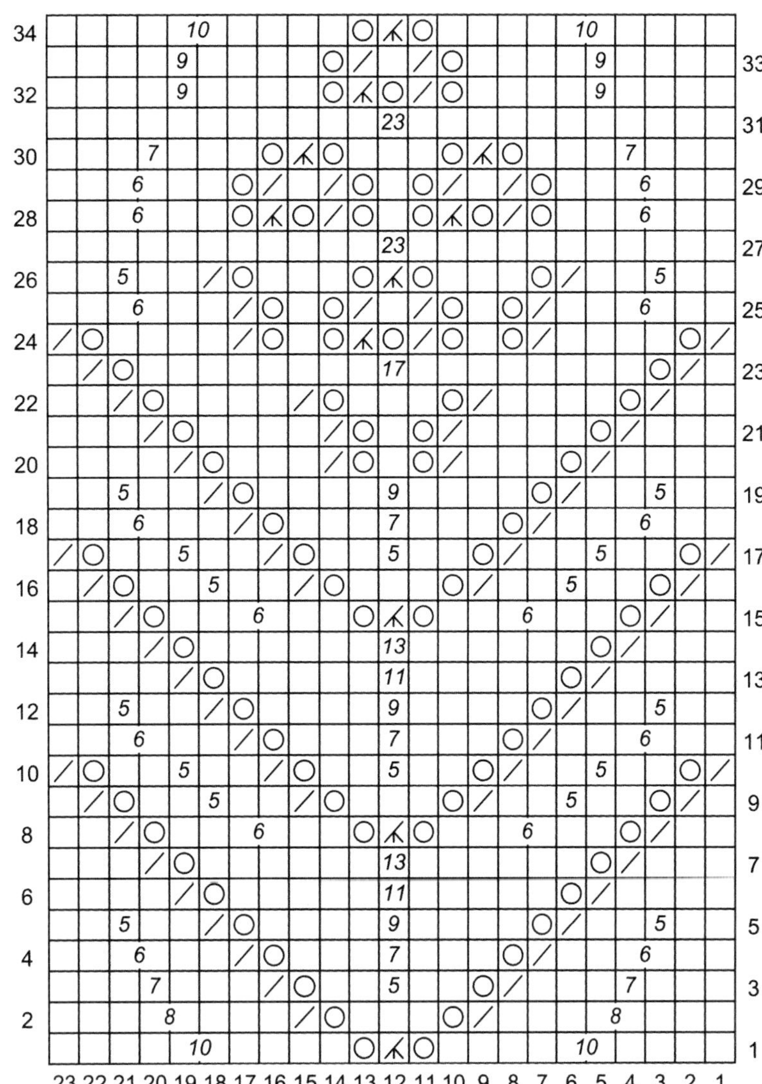

Basket o' Flooers, variation 1 original chart.

4.30

Basket o' Flooers, variation 2

TEX 1997.84 Shawl

This is the most common form of Basket o' Flooers. It has three layers of simple openwork 'V' shapes at the bottom, followed by a 'V' of Lace Holes and the flowers made of four Eyelids. Knitters have used their discretion to design a Basket o' Flooers balanced against their overall border design and gauge.

Row 1 (RS): K10, yo, k3tog, yo, k10. (23 sts)
Row 2 (WS): K8, k2tog, yo, k3, yo, k2tog, k8.
Row 3: K7, k2tog, yo, k5, yo, k2tog, k7.
Row 4: K6, k2tog, yo, k7, yo, k2tog, k6.
Row 5: K5, k2tog, yo, k9, yo, k2tog, k5.
Row 6: K4, k2tog, yo, k11, yo, k2tog, k4.
Row 7: K3, k2tog, yo, k13, yo, k2tog, k3.
Row 8: K2, k2tog, yo, k6, yo, k3tog, yo, k6, yo, k2tog, k2.
Row 9: K1, k2tog, yo, k5, k2tog, yo, k3, yo, k2tog, k5, yo, k2tog, k1.
Row 10: (K2tog, yo, k5) x 2, yo, k2tog, k5, yo, k2tog.
Rows 11–17: Repeat rows 4–10.
Row 18: Repeat row 4.
Row 19: Repeat row 5.
Row 20: K4, k2tog, yo, k5, yo twice, k2tog, k4, yo, k2tog, k4. (24 sts)

Basket o' Flooers, variation 2 original pattern.

Basket o' Flooers, variation 2 knitted sample.

Row 21: K3, k2tog, yo, k6, knit, purl into yarnovers, k6, yo, k2tog, k3.
Row 22: K2, k2tog, yo, k4, k2tog, yo x 2, k2tog twice, yo x 2, k2tog, k4, yo, k2tog, k2.
Row 23: K1, k2tog, yo, k7, p1, knit 2, k1, p1, k6, yo, k2tog, k1.
Row 24: K2tog, yo, k4, k2tog, yo x 2, k2tog x 2, yo twice, k2tog x 2, yo x 2, k2tog, k4, yo, k2tog.
Row 25: K8, p1, k2, knit, purl into yarnovers, k3, p1, k7.
Row 26: K4, k2tog, yo x 2, k2tog x 2, yo x 2, k2tog twice, yo x 2, k2tog x 2, yo x 2, k2tog, k4.
Row 27: K6, p1, k3, p1, knit 2, k1, p1, k3, p1, k5.
Row 28: K2, k2tog, (yo x 2, k2tog x 2) x 2, yo twice, (k2tog x 2, yo x 2) x 2, k2tog, k2.
Row 29: K4, p1, k3, p1, k2, knit, purl into yarnovers, (k3, p1) x 2, k3.
Row 30: Repeat row 26.
Row 31: K6, p1, k3, p1, k2tog, k1, p1, k3, p1, k5. (23 sts)
Row 32: K2, k2tog, yo x 2, k2tog x 2, yo x 2, k2tog, k3, k2tog, yo x 2, k2tog x 2, yo x 2, k2tog, k2.
Row 33: K4, p1, k3, p1, k6, (p1, k3) x 2.
Row 34: K4, k2tog, yo x 2, k2tog, k1, k2tog, yo, k1, yo, k2tog, k1, k2tog, yo x 2, k2tog, k4.
Row 35: K6, p1, k2, k2tog, yo, k1, yo, k2tog, k3, p1, k5.
Row 36: K2, k2tog, yo x 2, k2tog, k2, k2tog, yo, k3, yo, k2tog, k2, k2tog, yo x 2, k2tog, k2.
Row 37: K4, p1, k14, p1, k3.
Row 38: K6, k2tog, yo, k1, yo, k3tog, yo, k2tog, yo, k1, yo, k2tog, k6.
Row 39: K6, k2tog, yo, k1, yo, k2tog, k1, k2tog, yo, k1, yo, k2tog, k6.
Row 40: K5, k2tog, yo, k3, yo, k3tog, yo, k3, yo, k2tog, k5.
Row 41: Knit.
Row 42: K6, yo, k3tog, yo, k2tog, yo, k1, yo, k3tog, yo, k2tog, yo, k6.
Row 43: K6, yo, k2tog, k1, k2tog, yo, k1, yo, k2tog, k1, k2tog, yo, k6.
Row 44: K7, yo, k3tog, yo, k3, yo, k3tog, yo, k7.
Row 45: Knit.
Row 46: K9, yo, k3tog, yo, k2tog, yo, k9.
Row 47: K9, yo, k2tog, k1, k2tog, yo, k9.
Row 48: Repeat row 1.

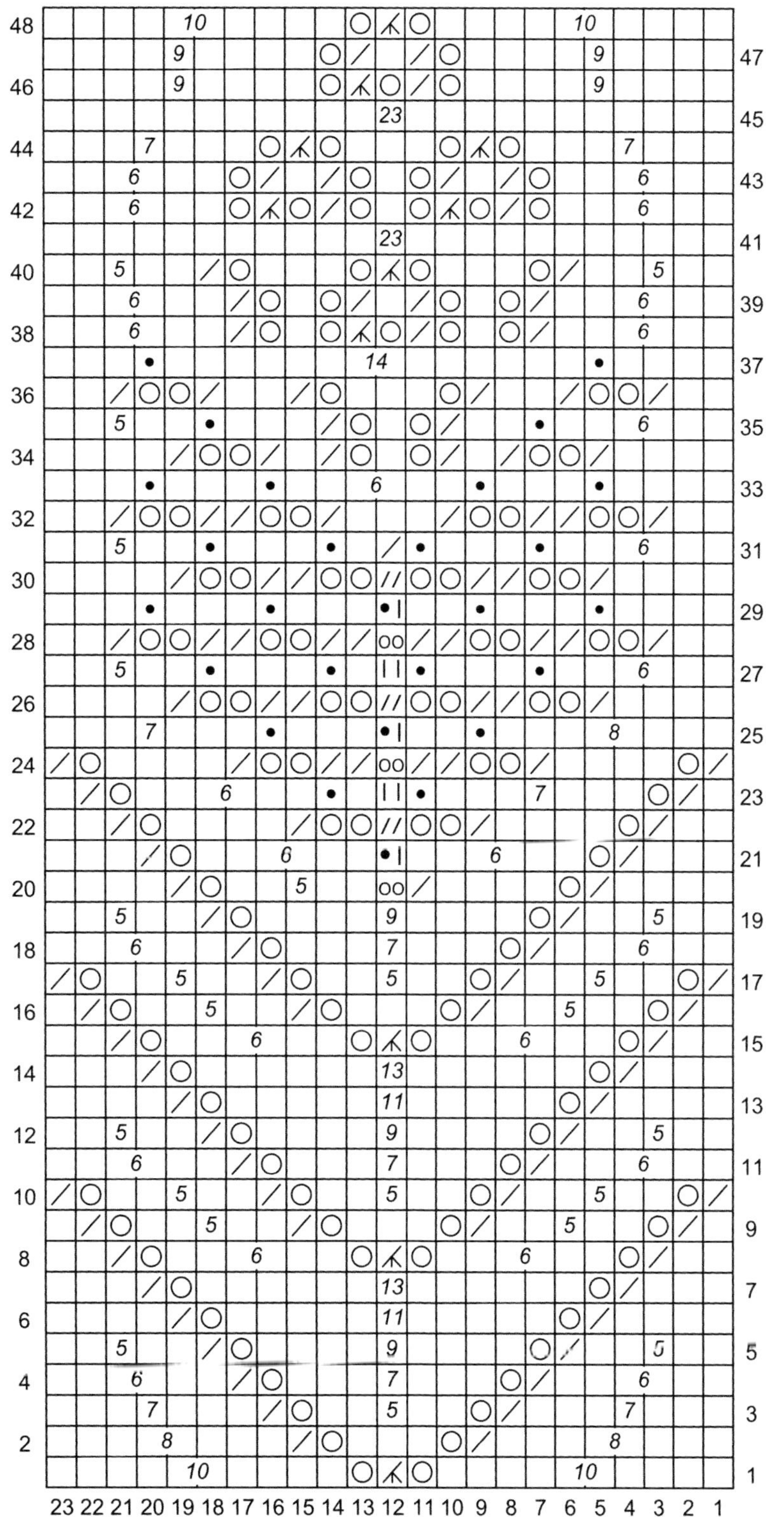

Basket o' Flooers, variation 2 chart.

4.31

Basket o' Flooers, variation 3
TEX 8933 Scarf

Basket o' Flooers, variation 3 original pattern.

In this variation the knitter chose to elongate the motif with layers of V-shapes and only a single 'bud' on top. A similar form of 'bud' is used to top Trees.

Row 1 (RS): K12, yo, k3tog, yo, k12. (27 sts)
Row 2 (WS): K10, k2tog, yo, k3, yo, k2tog, k10.
Row 3: K9, k2tog, yo, k5, yo, k2tog, k9.
Row 4: K8, k2tog, yo, k7, yo, k2tog, k8.

Basket o' Flooers, variation 3 knitted sample.

Row 5: K7, k2tog, yo, k3, yo, k3tog, yo, k3, yo, k2tog, k7.
Row 6: K6, k2tog, yo, k2, k2tog, yo, k3, yo, k2tog, k2, yo, k2tog, k6.
Row 7: K5, k2tog, yo, k2, k2tog, yo, k5, yo, k2tog, k2, yo, k2tog, k5.
Row 8: K4, k2tog, yo, k2, k2tog, yo, k7, yo, k2tog, k2, yo, k2tog, k4.
Row 9: K3, k2tog, yo, k2, k2tog, yo, k9, yo, k2tog, k2, yo, k2tog, k3.
Row 10: (K2, k2tog, yo) x 2, k11, (yo, k2tog, k2) x 2.
Row 11: K1, k2tog, yo, k2, k2tog, yo, k4, k2tog, yo, k1, yo, k2tog, k4, yo, k2tog, k2, yo, k2tog, k1.
Row 12: K2tog, yo, k2, k2tog, yo, k15, yo, k2tog, k2, yo, k2tog.
Row 13: K3, k2tog, yo, k4, k2tog, yo, k1, yo, k3tog, yo, k1, yo, k2tog, k4, yo, k2tog, k3.
Row 14: K2, k2tog, yo, k19, yo, k2tog, k2.
Row 15: K1, k2tog, yo, k4, k2tog, (yo, k1, yo, k3tog) x 2, yo, k1, yo, k2tog, k4, yo, k2tog, k1.
Row 16: K2tog, yo, k23, yo, k2tog.
Row 17: K5, k2tog, yo, k1, yo, k3tog, yo, k5, yo, k3tog, yo, k1, yo, k2tog, k5.

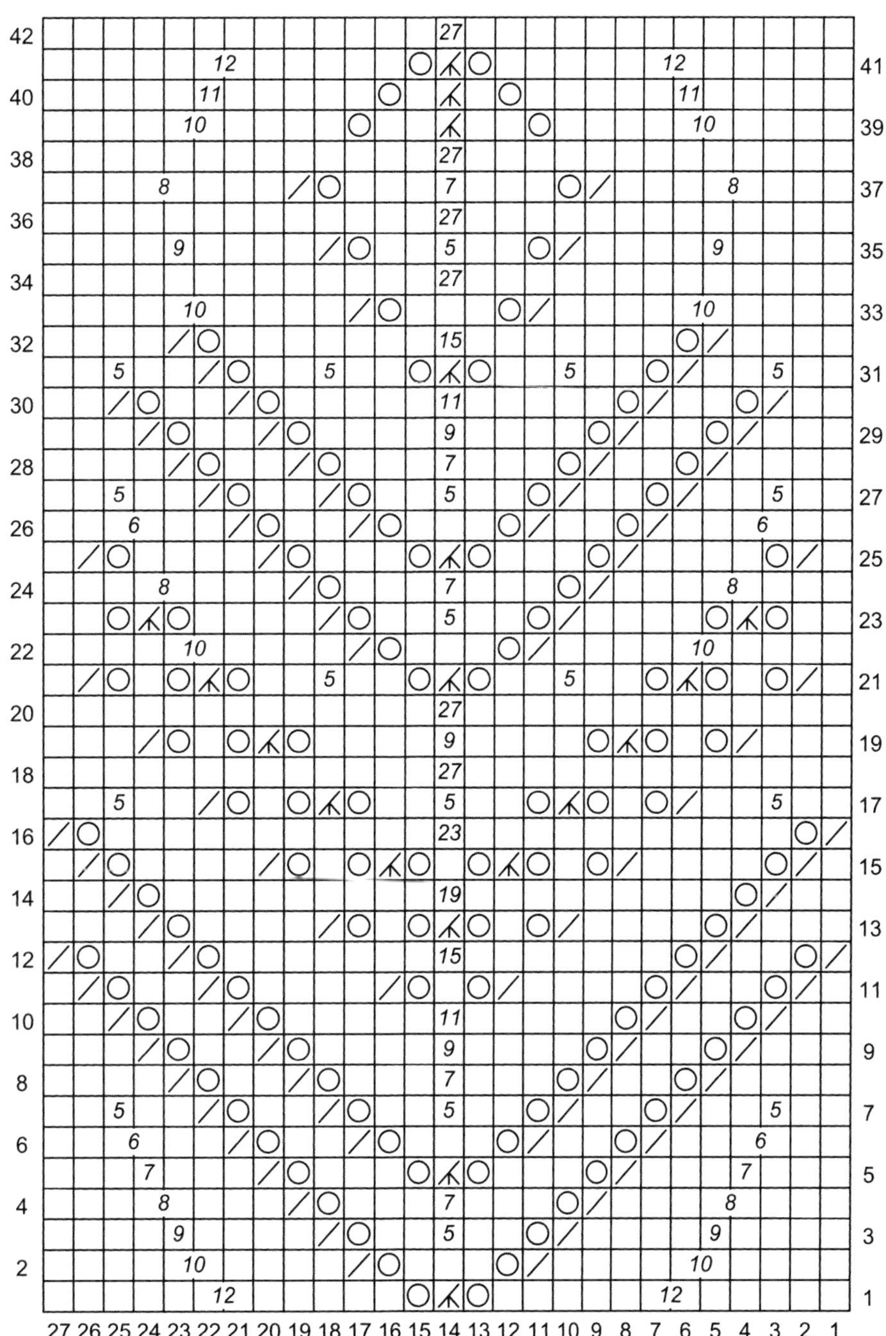

Basket o' Flooers, variation 3 chart.

Row 18: Knit.

Row 19: K3, k2tog, yo, k1, yo, k3tog, yo, k9, yo, k3tog, yo, k1, yo, k2tog, k3.

Row 20: Knit.

Row 21: K1, k2tog, yo, k1, (yo, k3tog, yo, k5) x 2, yo, k3tog, yo, k1, yo, k2tog, k1.

Row 22: Repeat row 2.

Row 23: K2, yo, k3tog, yo, k4, k2tog, yo, k5, yo, k2tog, k4, yo, k3tog, yo, k2.

Row 24: Repeat row 4.

Row 25: K1, k2tog, yo, k4, k2tog, yo, k3, yo, k3tog, yo, k3, yo, k2tog, k4, yo, k2tog, k1.

Row 26: Repeat row 6.

Row 27: Repeat row 7.

Row 28: Repeat row 8.
Row 29: Repeat row 9.
Row 30: Repeat row 10.
Row 31: K5, k2tog, yo, k5, yo, k3tog, yo, k5, yo, k2tog, k5.
Row 32: K4, k2tog, yo, k15, yo, k2tog, k4.
Row 33: Repeat row 2.
Row 34: Knit.
Row 35: Repeat row 3.
Row 36: Knit.
Row 37: Repeat row 4.
Row 38: Knit.
Row 39: K10, yo, k2, k3tog, k2, yo, k10.
Row 40: K11, yo, k1, p3tog, k1, yo, k11.
Row 41: Repeat row 1.
Row 42: Knit.

4.32

Tree, variation 1
TEX 8933 Scarf

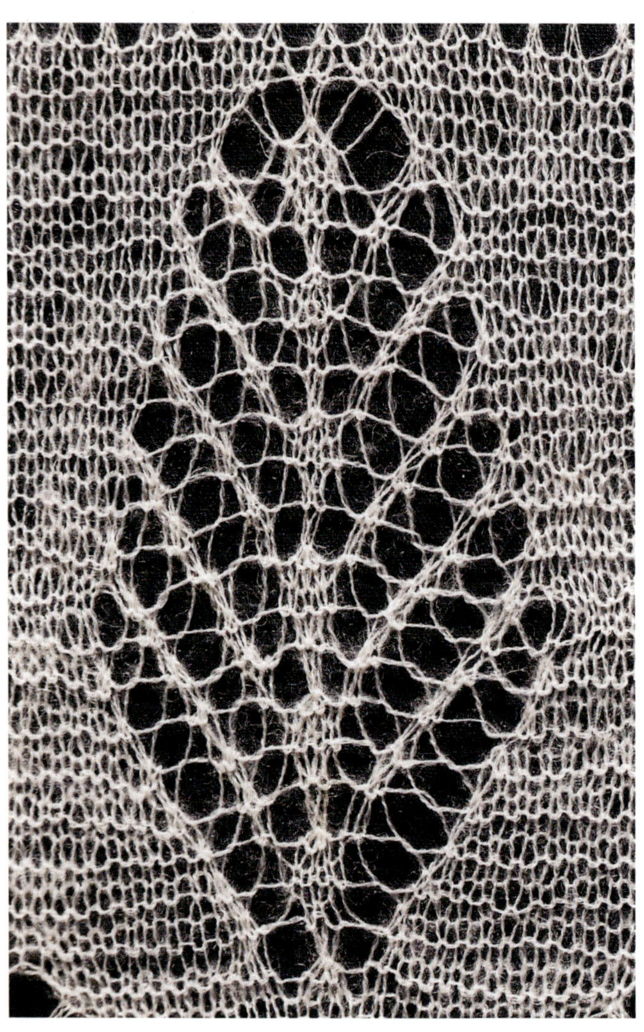

Tree, variation 1 original pattern.

Tree, variation 1 knitted sample.

This is a very simple Tree design, with a rounded top. It is a good form for narrow insertions.

Row 1 (RS): K8, yo, k3tog, yo, k8. (19 sts)
Row 2 (WS): Knit.
Row 3: K6, k2tog, yo, k3, yo, k2tog, k6.
Row 4: Knit.
Row 5: K5, k2tog, yo, k5, yo, k2tog, k5.
Row 6: Knit.
Row 7: K4, k2tog, yo, k2, yo, k3tog, yo, k2, yo, k2tog, k4.

Row 8: Knit.
Row 9: K3, k2tog, yo, k1, k2tog, yo, k3, yo, k2tog, k1, yo, k2tog, k3.
Row 10: Knit.
Row 11: K2, k2tog, yo, k1, k2tog, yo, k5, yo, k2tog, k1, yo, k2tog, k2.
Row 12: Knit.
Row 13: (K1, k2tog, yo) x 2, k2, yo, k3tog, yo, k2, (yo, k2tog, k1) x 2.
Row 14: Knit.
Row 15: (K2tog, yo, k1) x 2, k2tog, yo, k3, (yo, k2tog, k1) x 2, yo, k2tog.
Row 16: Knit.
Row 17: Repeat row 11.
Row 18: Knit.
Row 19: Repeat row 13.
Row 20: Knit.
Row 21: Repeat row 9.
Row 22: Knit.
Row 23: Repeat row 11.
Row 24: Knit.
Row 25: Repeat row 7.
Row 26: Knit.
Row 27: Repeat row 9.
Row 28: Knit.
Row 29: Repeat row 5.
Row 30: Knit.
Row 31: Repeat row 7.
Row 32: Knit.
Row 33: Repeat row 3.
Row 34: Knit.
Row 35: Repeat row 5.
Row 36: Knit.
Row 37: K7, yo, k2tog, k1, k2tog, yo, k7.
Row 38: K8, yo, p3tog, yo, k8.

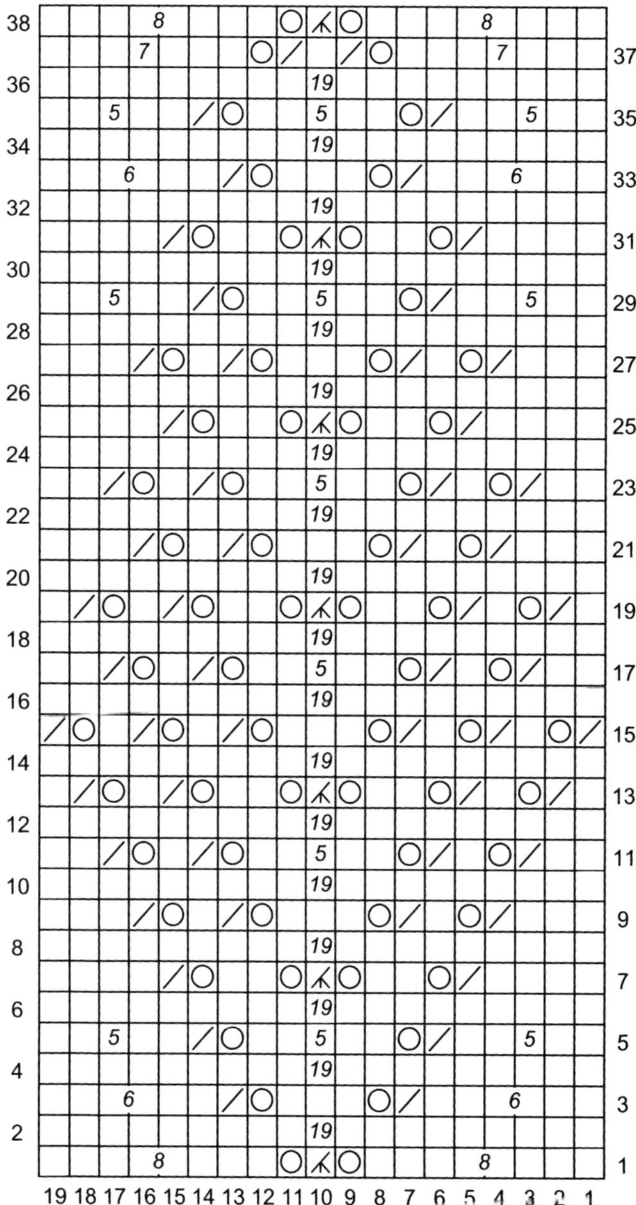

Tree, variation 1 chart.

4.33

Tree, variation 2
TEX 2004.273 Stole

This Tree design alternates plain stems with those worked in Lace Holes. The top of the Tree is inset with a plain Diamond.

Row 1 (RS): K13, k2tog, (k1, yo) x 2, k1, k2tog, k13. (33 sts)
Row 2 (WS): K12, k2tog, k1, yo, k3, yo, k1, k2tog, k12.
Row 3: K11, k2tog, k1, yo, k5, yo, k1, k2tog, k11.
Row 4: K10, k2tog, k1, yo, k7, yo, k1, k2tog, k10.
Row 5: K9, k2tog, k1, yo, k1, k2tog, yo x 2, k3tog, yo x 2, k2tog, k1, yo, k1, k2tog, k9.
Row 6: K8, k2tog, k1, yo, k3, p1, k2, p1, k4, yo, k1, k2tog, k8.
Row 7: K7, k2tog, k1, yo, k1, k2tog, yo x 2, k2tog, k3, k2tog, yo x 2, k2tog, k1, yo, k1, k2tog, k7.
Row 8: K6, k2tog, k1, yo, k3, p1, k6, p1, k4, yo, k1, k2tog, k6.

Tree, variation 2 original pattern.

Tree, variation 2 knitted sample.

Row 9: K5, k2tog, k1, yo, k1, k2tog, yo x 2, k2tog x 2, (k1, yo) x 2, k1, k2tog x 2, yo x 2, k2tog, k1, yo, k1, k2tog, k5.
Row 10: K4, k2tog, k1, yo, k3, p1, k1, k2tog, k1, yo, k3, yo, k1, k2tog, p1, k4, yo, k1, k2tog, k4.
Row 11: K3, k2tog, k1, yo, k1, k2tog, yo x 2, k2tog x 2, k1, yo, k5, yo, k1, k2tog x 2, yo x 2, k2tog, k1, yo, k1, k2tog, k3.
Row 12: K2, k2tog, k1, yo, k3, p1, k1, k2tog, k1, yo, k7, yo, k1, k2tog, p1, k4, yo, k1, k2tog, k2.
Row 13: K1, k2tog, k1, yo, k1, k2tog, yo x 2, k2tog x 2, k1, yo, k1, k2tog, yo x 2, k3tog, yo x 2, k2tog, k1, yo, k1, k2tog x 2, yo x 2, k2tog, k1, yo, k1, k2tog, k1.
Row 14: K2tog, k1, yo, k3, p1, k1, k2tog, k1, yo, k3, p1, k2, (p1, k4, yo, k1, k2tog) x 2.
Row 15: K2tog, yo, k1, k2tog, yo x 2, k2tog x 2, k1, yo, k1, k2tog, yo x 2, k2tog, k3, k2tog, yo x 2, k2tog, k1, yo, k1, k2tog x 2, yo x 2, k2tog, k1, yo, k2tog.
Row 16: K4, p1, k1, k2tog, k1, yo, k3, p1, k6, p1, k4, yo, k1, k2tog, p1, k5.
Row 17: (K1, k2tog, yo x 2, k2tog x 2, k1, yo) x 2, (k1, yo, k1, k2tog x 2, yo x 2, k2tog) x 2, k1.
Row 18: K2, (p1, k1, k2tog, k1, yo, k3) x 2, yo, k1, k2tog, p1, k4, yo, k1, k2tog, p1, k3.
Row 19: Repeat row 11.
Row 20: Repeat row 12.
Row 21: K2, k2tog, yo, k1, k2tog, yo x 2, k2tog x 2, k1, yo, k1, k2tog, yo x 2, k3tog, yo x 2, k2tog, k1, yo, k1, k2tog x 2, yo x 2, k2tog, k1, yo, k2tog, k2.
Row 22: K6, p1, k1, k2tog, k1, yo, k3, p1, k2, p1, k4, yo, k1, k2tog, p1, k7.
Row 23: K3, k2tog, yo x 2, k2tog x 2, k1, yo, k1, k2tog, yo x 2, k2tog, k3, k2tog, yo x 2, k2tog, k1, yo, k1, k2tog x 2, yo x 2, k2tog, k3.
Row 24: Repeat row 16.
Row 25: Repeat row 9.
Row 26: Repeat row 10.
Row 27: K4, k2tog, yo, k1, k2tog, yo x 2, k2tog x 2, k1, yo, k5, yo, k1, k2tog x 2, yo x 2, k2tog, k1, yo, k2tog, k4.
Row 28: K8, p1, k1, k2tog, k1, yo, k7, yo, k1, k2tog, p1, k9.
Row 29: K5, k2tog, yo x 2, k2tog x 2, k1, yo, k1, k2tog, yo x 2, k3tog, yo x 2, k2tog, k1, yo, k1, k2tog x 2, yo x 2, k2tog, k5.
Row 30: Repeat row 22.
Row 31: Repeat row 7.
Row 32: Repeat row 8.
Row 33: K6, k2tog, yo, k1, k2tog, yo x 2, k2tog x 2, (k1, yo) x 2, k1, k2tog x 2, yo x 2, k2tog, k1, yo, k2tog, k6.
Row 34: K10, p1, k1, k2tog, k1, yo, k3, yo, k1, k2tog, p1, k11.

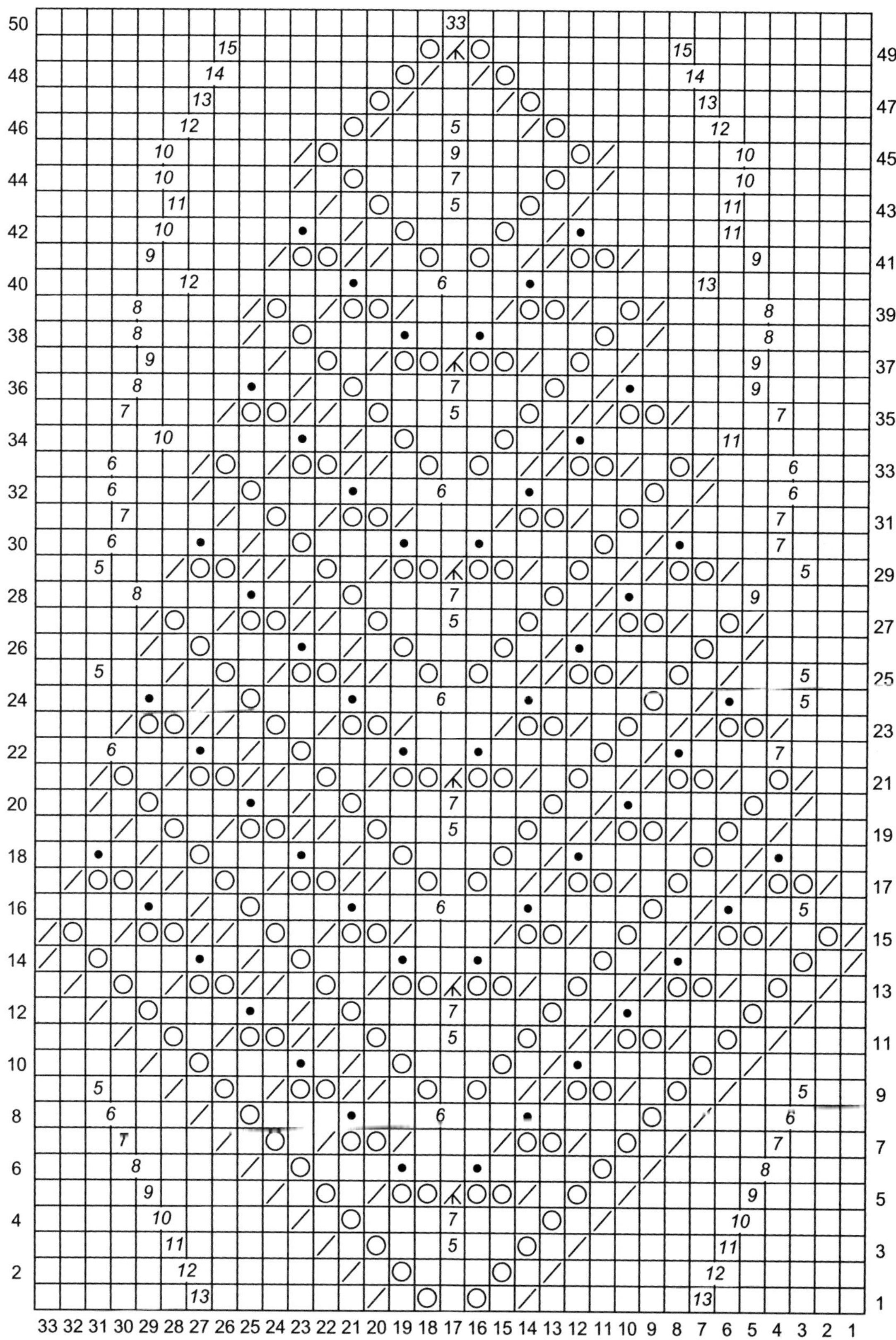

Tree, variation 2 chart.

Row 35: K7, k2tog, yo x 2, k2tog x 2, k1, yo, k5, yo, k1, k2tog x 2, yo x 2, k2tog, k7.
Row 36: Repeat row 28.
Row 37: Repeat row 5.
Row 38: Repeat row 6.
Row 39: K8, k2tog, yo, k1, k2tog, yo x 2, k2tog, k3, k2tog, yo x 2, k2tog, k1, yo, k2tog, k8.
Row 40: K12, p1, k6, p1, k13.
Row 41: K9, k2tog, yo x 2, k2tog x 2, (k1, yo) x 2, k1, k2tog x 2, yo x 2, k2tog, k9.
Row 42: Repeat row 34.
Row 43: Repeat row 3.
Row 44: Repeat row 4.
Row 45: K10, k2tog, yo, k9, yo, k2tog, k10.
Row 46: K12, yo, k2tog, k5, k2tog, yo, k12.
Row 47: K13, yo, k2tog, k3, k2tog, yo, k13.
Row 48: K14, yo, k2tog, k1, k2tog, yo, k14.
Row 49: K15, yo, k3tog, yo, k15.
Row 50: Knit.

4.34

Tree, variation 3
TEX 2019.33 Stole

Tree, variation 3 original pattern.

Tree, variation 3 knitted sample.

The beautiful design of this complex Tree has it all: a well-proportioned shape, various patterns creating different types of stems, and a pretty top. It is no wonder it was used to make the stunning centrepiece of a stole border.

Row 1 (RS): K35, yo, k3tog, yo, k35. (73 sts)
Row 2 (WS): K32, k2tog, k1, yo, k3, yo, k1, k2tog, k32.
Row 3: K31, k2tog, k1, yo, k5, yo, k1, k2tog, k31.
Row 4: K30, k2tog, k1, yo, k7, yo, k1, k2tog, k30.
Row 5: K29, k2tog, k1, yo, k3, yo, k3tog, yo, k3, yo, k1, k2tog, k29.
Row 6: K28, k2tog, k1, yo, k2, k2tog, yo, k3, yo, k2tog, k2, yo, k1, k2tog, k28.
Row 7: K27, k2tog, k1, yo, k2, k2tog, yo, k5, yo, k2tog, k2, yo, k1, k2tog, k27.
Row 8: K26, k2tog, k1, yo, k2, k2tog, yo, k7, yo, k2tog, k2, yo, k1, k2tog, k26.
Row 9: K25, k2tog, k1, yo, k2, k2tog, yo, k9, yo, k2tog, k2, yo, k1, k2tog, k25.
Row 10: K24, k2tog, k1, yo, k2, k2tog, yo, k11, yo, k2tog, k2, yo, k1, k2tog, k24.
Row 11: K23, k2tog, k1, yo, k2, k2tog, yo, k6, yo, k2tog, k5, yo, k2tog, k2, yo, k1, k2tog, k23.
Row 12: K22, k2tog, k1, yo, k2, k2tog, yo, k5, k2tog, yo, k1, yo, k2tog, k5, yo, k2tog, k2, yo, k1, k2tog, k22.
Row 13: K21, k2tog, k1, yo, k2, k2tog, yo, k17, yo, k2tog, k2, yo, k1, k2tog, k21.
Row 14: K20, k2tog, k1, yo, k2, k2tog, yo, k6, yo, k2tog, k3, k2tog, yo, k6, yo, k2tog, k2, yo, k1, k2tog, k20.

Tree, variation 3 chart.

Row 15: K19, k2tog, k1, yo, k2, k2tog, yo, k5, k2tog, yo, k1, yo, k2tog, k1, k2tog, yo, k1, yo, k2tog, k5, yo, k2tog, k2, yo, k1, k2tog, k19.
Row 16: K18, k2tog, k1, yo, k2, k2tog, yo, k23, yo, k2tog, k2, yo, k1, k2tog, k18.
Row 17: K17, k2tog, k1, yo, k2, k2tog, yo, k6, yo, k2tog, k9, k2tog, yo, k6, yo, k2tog, k2, yo, k1, k2tog, k17.
Row 18: K16, k2tog, k1, yo, k2, k2tog, yo, k5, k2tog, yo, k1, yo, k2tog, k7, k2tog, yo, k1, yo, k2tog, k5, yo, k2tog, k2, yo, k1, k2tog, k16.
Row 19: K15, k2tog, k1, yo, k2, k2tog, yo, k29, yo, k2tog, k2, yo, k1, k2tog, k15.
Row 20: K14, k2tog, k1, yo, k2, k2tog, yo, k6, yo, k2tog, k15, k2tog, yo, k6, yo, k2tog, k2, yo, k1, k2tog, k14.
Row 21: K13, k2tog, k1, yo, k2, k2tog, yo, k5, k2tog, yo, k1, yo, k2tog, k5, yo, k3tog, yo, k5, k2tog, yo, k1, yo, k2tog, k5, yo, k2tog, k2, yo, k1, k2tog, k13.
Row 22: K12, k2tog, k1, yo, k2, k2tog, yo, k14, k2tog, yo, k3, yo, k2tog, k14, yo, k2tog, k2, yo, k1, k2tog, k12.
Row 23: K11, k2tog, k1, yo, k2, k2tog, yo, k6, yo, k2tog, k6, k2tog, yo, k5, yo, k2tog, k6, k2tog, yo, k6, yo, k2tog, k2, yo, k1, k2tog, k11.
Row 24: K10, k2tog, k1, yo, k2, k2tog, yo, k5, k2tog, yo, k1, yo, k2tog, k4, k2tog, yo, k7, yo, k2tog, k4, k2tog, yo, k1, yo, k2tog, k5, yo, k2tog, k2, yo, k1, k2tog, k10.
Row 25: K9, k2tog, k1, yo, k2, k2tog, yo, k14, k2tog, yo, k3, yo, k3tog, yo, k3, yo, k2tog, k14, yo, k2tog, k2, yo, k1, k2tog, k9.
Row 26: K8, k2tog, k1, yo, k2, k2tog, yo, k6, yo, k2tog, k6, k2tog, yo, k2, k2tog, yo, k3, yo, k2tog, k2, yo, k2tog, k6, k2tog, yo, k6, yo, k2tog, k2, yo, k1, k2tog, k8.
Row 27: K7, k2tog, k1, yo, k2, k2tog, yo, k5, k2tog, yo, k1, yo, k2tog, k4, k2tog, yo, k2, k2tog, yo, k5, yo, k2tog, k2, yo, k2tog, k4, k2tog, yo, k1, yo, k2tog, k5, yo, k2tog, k2, yo, k1, k2tog, k7.
Row 28: K6, k2tog, k1, yo, k2, k2tog, yo, k14, k2tog, yo, k2, k2tog, yo, k7, yo, k2tog, k2, yo, k2tog, k14, yo, k2tog, k2, yo, k1, k2tog, k6.
Row 29: K5, k2tog, k1, yo, k2, k2tog, yo, k6, yo, k2tog, k6, k2tog, yo, k2, k2tog, yo, k9, yo, k2tog, k2, yo, k2tog, k6, k2tog, yo, k6, yo, k2tog, k2, yo, k1, k2tog, k5.
Row 30: K4, k2tog, k1, yo, k2, k2tog, yo, k5, k2tog, yo, k1, yo, k2tog, k4, k2tog, yo, k2, k2tog, yo, k11, yo, k2tog, k2, yo, k2tog, k4, k2tog, yo, k1, yo, k2tog, k5, yo, k2tog, k2, yo, k1, k2tog, k4.
Row 31: K3, k2tog, k1, yo, k2, k2tog, yo, k14, k2tog, yo, k2, k2tog, yo, k5, k2tog, yo x 2, k6, yo, k2tog, k2, yo, k2tog, k14, yo, k2tog, k2, yo, k1, k2tog, k3. (74 sts)
Row 32: K2, k2tog, k1, yo, k2, k2tog, yo, k6, yo, k2tog, k6, k2tog, yo, k2, k2tog, yo, k7, knit, purl into yarnovers, k7, yo, k2tog, k2, yo, k2tog, k6, k2tog, yo, k6, yo, k2tog, k2, yo, k1, k2tog, k2.
Row 33: K1, k2tog, k1, yo, k2, k2tog, yo, k5, k2tog, yo, k1, yo, k2tog, k4, k2tog, yo, k2, k2tog, yo, k5, k2tog, yo x 2, k2tog x 2, yo x 2, k2tog, k5, yo, k2tog, k2, yo, k2tog, k4, k2tog, yo, k1, yo, k2tog, k5, yo, k2tog, k2, yo, k1, k2tog, k1.
Row 34: K2tog, k1, yo, k2, k2tog, yo, k14, k2tog, yo, k2, k2tog, yo, k8, p1, knit 2, p1, k8, yo, k2tog, k2, yo, k2tog, k14, yo, k2tog, k2, yo, k1, k2tog.
Row 35: K4, k2tog, yo, k6, yo, k2tog, k6, k2tog, yo, k2, k2tog, yo, k5, k2tog, yo x 2, (k2tog, k1) x 2, k2tog, yo x 2, k2tog, k5, yo, k2tog, k2, yo, k2tog, k6, k2tog, yo, k6, yo, k2tog, k4. (73 sts)
Row 36: K3, k2tog, yo, k5, k2tog, yo, k1, yo, k2tog, k4, k2tog, yo, k2, k2tog, yo, k8, p1, k5, p1, k8, yo, k2tog, k2, yo, k2tog, k4, k2tog, yo, k1, yo, k2tog, k5, yo, k2tog, k3.
Row 37: K2, yo, k2tog, k14, k2tog, yo, k2, k2tog, yo, k5, k2tog, yo x 2, k2tog, k7, k2tog, yo x 2, k2tog, k5, yo, k2tog, k2, yo, k2tog, k14, k2tog, yo, k2.
Row 38: K9, yo, k2tog, k6, k2tog, yo, k2, k2tog, yo, k8, p1, k9, p1, k8, yo, k2tog, k2, yo, k2tog, k6, k2tog, yo, k9.
Row 39: K3, yo, k2tog, k2, k2tog, yo, k1, yo, k2tog, k4, k2tog, yo, k2, k2tog, yo, k5, k2tog, yo x 2, k2tog, k4, yo, k3tog, yo, k4, k2tog, yo x 2, k2tog, k5, yo, k2tog, k2, yo, k2tog, k4, k2tog, yo, k1, yo, k2tog, k2, k2tog, yo, k3.
Row 40: K15, k2tog, yo, k2, k2tog, yo, k8, p1, k3, k2tog, yo, k3, yo, k2tog, k3, p1, k8, yo, k2tog, k2, yo, k2tog, k15.
Row 41: K4, yo, k2tog, k8, k2tog, yo, k2, k2tog, yo, k5, k2tog, yo x 2, k2tog, k3, k2tog, yo, k5, yo, k2tog, k3, k2tog, yo x 2, k2tog, k5, yo, k2tog, k2, yo, k2tog, k8, k2tog, yo, k4.
Row 42: K13, k2tog, yo, k2, k2tog, yo, k8, p1, k3, k2tog, yo, k7, yo, k2tog, k3, p1, k8, yo, k2tog, k2, yo, k2tog, k13.
Row 43: K5, yo, k2tog, k5, k2tog, yo, k2, k2tog, yo, k5, k2tog, yo x 2, k2tog, k3, k2tog, yo, k3, yo, k3tog, yo, k3, yo, k2tog, k3, k2tog, yo x 2, k2tog, k5, yo, k2tog, k2, yo, k2tog, k5, k2tog, yo, k5.
Row 44: K11, k2tog, yo, k2, k2tog, yo, k8, p1, k3, k2tog, yo, k2, k2tog, yo, k3, yo, k2tog, k2, yo, k2tog, k3, p1, k8, yo, k2tog, k2, yo, k2tog, k11.

Row 45: K6, yo, k2tog, (k2, k2tog, yo) x 2, k5, k2tog, yo x 2, k2tog, k3, k2tog, yo, k2, k2tog, yo, k5, yo, k2tog, k2, yo, k2tog, k3, k2tog, yo x 2, k2tog, k5, (yo, k2tog, k2) x 2, k2tog, yo, k6.
Row 46: K9, k2tog, yo, k2, k2tog, yo, k8, p1, k3, k2tog, yo, k2, k2tog, yo, k7, yo, k2tog, k2, yo, k2tog, k3, p1, k8, yo, k2tog, k2, yo, k2tog, k9.
Row 47: K7, yo, k2tog, k3, k2tog, yo, k5, k2tog, yo x 2, k2tog, k3, k2tog, yo, k2, k2tog, yo, k9, yo, k2tog, k2, yo, k2tog, k3, k2tog, yo x 2, k2tog, k5, yo, k2tog, k3, k2tog, yo, k7.
Row 48: K11, k2tog, yo, k8, p1, k3, k2tog, yo, k2, k2tog, yo, k11, yo, k2tog, k2, yo, k2tog, k3, p1, k8, yo, k2tog, k11.
Row 49: K8, yo, k2tog x 2, yo, k5, k2tog, yo x 2, k2tog, k3, k2tog, yo, k2, k2tog, yo, k6, yo, k2tog, k5, yo, k2tog, k2, yo, k2tog, k3, k2tog, yo x 2, k2tog, k5, yo, k2tog x 2, yo, k8.
Row 50: K19, p1, k3, k2tog, yo, k2, k2tog, yo, k5, k2tog, yo, k1, yo, k2tog, k5, yo, k2tog, k2, yo, k2tog, k3, p1, k19.
Row 51: K9, yo, k2tog, k4, k2tog, yo x 2, k2tog, k3, k2tog, yo, k2, k2tog, yo, k17, yo, k2tog, k2, yo, k2tog, k3, k2tog, yo x 2, k2tog, k4, k2tog, yo, k9.
Row 52: K17, p1, k3, k2tog, yo, k2, k2tog, yo, k6, yo, k2tog, k3, k2tog, yo, k6, yo, k2tog, k2, yo, k2tog, k3, p1, k17.
Row 53: K10, yo, k2tog, k1, k2tog, yo x 2, k2tog, k3, k2tog, yo, k2, k2tog, yo, k5, k2tog, yo, k1, yo, k2tog, k1, k2tog, yo, k1, yo, k2tog, k5, yo, k2tog, k2, yo, k2tog, k3, k2tog, yo x 2, k2tog, k1, k2tog, yo, k10.
Row 54: K15, p1, k3, k2tog, yo, k2, k2tog, yo, k23, yo, k2tog, k2, yo, k2tog, k3, p1, k15.
Row 55: K11, yo, k2tog, k5, k2tog, yo, k2, k2tog, yo, k6, yo, k2tog, k9, k2tog, yo, k6, yo, k2tog, k2, yo, k2tog, k5, k2tog, yo, k11.
Row 56: K17, k2tog, yo, k2, k2tog, yo, k5, k2tog, yo, k1, yo, k2tog, k7, k2tog, yo, k1, yo, k2tog, k5, yo, k2tog, k2, yo, k2tog, k17.
Row 57: K12, yo, k2tog, (k2, k2tog, yo) x 2, k29, (yo, k2tog, k2) x 2, k2tog, yo, k12.
Row 58: K15, k2tog, yo, k2, k2tog, yo, k6, yo, k2tog, k15, k2tog, yo, k6, yo, k2tog, k2, yo, k2tog, k15.
Row 59: K13, yo, k2tog, k3, k2tog, yo, k5, k2tog, yo, k1, yo, k2tog, k5, yo, k3tog, yo, k5, k2tog, yo, k1, yo, k2tog, k5, yo, k2tog, k3, k2tog, yo, k13.
Row 60: K17, k2tog, yo, k14, k2tog, yo, k3, yo, k2tog, k14, yo, k2tog, k17.
Row 61: K14, yo, k2tog x 2, yo, k6, yo, k2tog, k6, k2tog, yo, k5, yo, k2tog, k6, k2tog, yo, k6, yo, k2tog x 2, yo, k14.
Row 62: K22, k2tog, yo, k1, yo, k2tog, k4, k2tog, yo, k7, yo, k2tog, k4, k2tog, yo, k1, yo, k2tog, k22.
Row 63: K15, yo, k2tog, k13, k2tog, yo, k3, yo, k3tog, yo, k3, yo, k2tog, k13, k2tog, yo, k15.
Row 64: K21, yo, k2tog, k6, k2tog, yo, k2, k2tog, yo, k3, yo, k2tog, k2, yo, k2tog, k6, k2tog, yo, k21.
Row 65: K16, yo, k2tog, k1, k2tog, yo, k1, yo, k2tog, k4, k2tog, yo, k2, k2tog, yo, k5, yo, k2tog, k2, yo, k2tog, k4, k2tog, yo, k1, yo, k2tog, k1, k2tog, yo, k16.
Row 66: K27, k2tog, yo, k2, k2tog, yo, k7, yo, k2tog, k2, yo, k2tog, k27.
Row 67: K17, yo, k2tog, k7, k2tog, yo, k2, k2tog, yo, k9, yo, k2tog, k2, yo, k2tog, k7, k2tog, yo, k17.
Row 68: K25, k2tog, yo, k2, k2tog, yo, k11, yo, k2tog, k2, yo, k2tog, k25.
Row 69: K18, yo, k2tog, k4, k2tog, yo, k2, k2tog, yo, k5, k2tog, yo x 2, k6, yo, k2tog, k2, yo, k2tog, k4, k2tog, yo, k18. (74 sts)
Row 70: K23, k2tog, yo, k2, k2tog, yo, k7, knit, purl into yarnovers, k7, yo, k2tog, k2, yo, k2tog, k23.
Row 71: K19, yo, k2tog, k1, k2tog, yo, k2, k2tog, yo, k5, k2tog, yo x 2, k2tog x 2, yo x 2, k2tog, k5, yo, k2tog, k2, yo, k2tog, k1, k2tog, yo, k19.
Row 72: K25, k2tog, yo, k8, p1, knit 2, p1, k8, yo, k2tog, k25.
Row 73: K20, yo, k2tog, k2, k2tog, yo, k5, k2tog, yo x 2, (k2tog, k1) x 2, k2tog, yo x 2, k2tog, k5, yo, k2tog, k2, k2tog, yo, k20. (73 sts)
Row 74: K23, k2tog, yo, k8, p1, k5, p1, k8, yo, k2tog, k23.
Row 75: K21, yo, k2tog, k6, k2tog, yo x 2, k2tog, k7, k2tog, yo x 2, k2tog, k6, k2tog, yo, k21.
Row 76: K31, p1, k9, p1, k31.
Row 77: K22, yo, k2tog, k3, k2tog, yo x 2, k2tog, k4, yo, k3tog, yo, k4, k2tog, yo x 2, k2tog, k3, k2tog, yo, k22.
Row 78: K29, p1, k3, k2tog, yo, k3, yo, k2tog, k3, p1, k29.
Row 79: K23, yo, k2tog x 2, yo x 2, k2tog, k3, k2tog, yo, k5, yo, k2tog, k3, k2tog, yo x 2, k2tog x 2, yo, k23.
Row 80: K27, p1, k3, k2tog, yo, k7, yo, k2tog, k3, p1, k27.
Row 81: K24, yo, k2tog, k4, k2tog, yo, k3, yo, k3tog, yo, k3, yo, k2tog, k4, k2tog, yo, k24.
Row 82: K29, k2tog, yo, k2, k2tog, yo, k3, yo, k2tog, k2, yo, k2tog, k29.
Row 83: K25, yo, k2tog, k1, k2tog, yo, k2, k2tog, yo, k5, yo, k2tog, k2, yo, k2tog, k1, k2tog, yo, k25.
Row 84: K31, k2tog, yo, k7, yo, k2tog, k31.
Row 85: K26, yo, k2tog, k5, yo, k2tog, k3, k2tog, yo, k5, k2tog, yo, k26.
Row 86: K34, yo, k2tog, k1, k2tog, yo, k34.
Row 87: K27, yo, k2tog, k6, yo, k3tog, yo, k6, k2tog, yo, k27.
Row 88: Knit.

Row 89: K28, yo, k2tog, k13, k2tog, yo, k28.
Row 90: Knit.
Row 91: K29, yo, k2tog, k11, k2tog, yo, k29.
Row 92: Knit.
Row 93: K30, yo, k2tog, k9, k2tog, yo, k30.
Row 94: Knit.
Row 95: K31, yo, k2tog, k7, k2tog, yo, k31.
Row 96: Knit.
Row 97: K32, yo, k2tog, k5, k2tog, yo, k32.
Row 98: Knit.
Row 99: K33, yo, k2tog, k3, k2tog, yo, k33.
Row 100: Knit.
Row 101: Repeat row 86.
Row 102: Knit.
Row 103: Repeat row 1.
Row 104: Knit.

TRIANGLES, BELLS AND COLUMNS

There remain some unusual or overlooked patterns in the Shetland lace corpus which deserve to be investigated. These patterns are seldom seen in other publications. Some may have developed in the early stages of the craft and went out of favour. They usually have a specific function to fill in spaces or link other patterns together. For that reason they may not have been sufficiently obvious in the overall design of the garment to receive widespread use. They are a minor but interesting contribution to the Shetland fine lace tradition.

Triangles

Triangle shapes are formed by grouping repeats of a small pattern together to function as an inset pattern in a triangular space. In this way they add laciness to an otherwise plain knitted section. They are found at the top or bottom of a border, with their wide flat edge forming the base or upper edge of the border. Baabie's Fancy and the Strawberry are used repeatedly in Shetland lace knitting, the former at the beginning of a border, the latter at the top of the border. They have the appearance of suspended droplets or strings of garland and add a decorative touch to a border.

Shed and corn-drying kiln.

4.35

Baabie's Fancy

TEX 1997.84 Shawl

This small pattern is named after an Unst woman named Barbara, although her exact identity is uncertain. It is found in a number of pieces in the Museum's collection and so it must have been copied by many knitters. It resembles tendrils of varying length and is always found at the bottom of a border, usually between Diamonds or inserted under the lowest Wave. It is a very simple pattern but adds complexity and a delicate touch to a space that is otherwise difficult to fill with lace. The tendrils can be made to any length to suit the space and are distributed evenly across the triangle width.

Row 1 (RS): K1, yo, k2tog, k6, (yo, k2tog, k3) x 4, yo, k2tog, k5, k2tog, yo, k1. (39 sts)

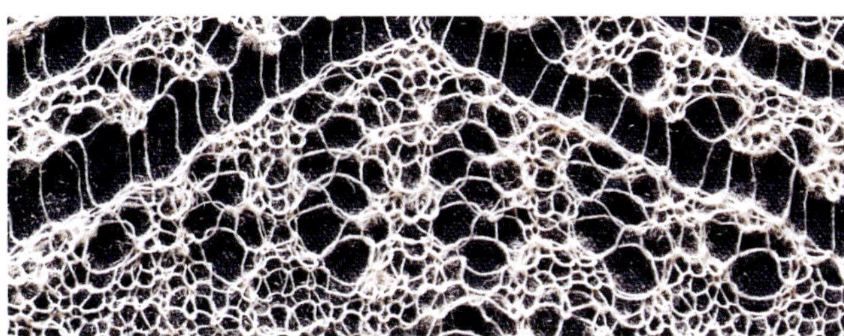

Baabie's Fancy original pattern.

Row 2 (WS): K2, yo, k2tog, k31, k2tog, yo, k2.
Row 3: K3, yo, k2tog, k2, k2tog, (yo, k1, yo, k2tog x 2) x 4, yo, k1, yo, k2tog, k2, k2tog, yo, k3.
Row 4: K4, yo, k2tog, k27, k2tog, yo, k4.
Row 5: K5, yo, k2tog, k2, (yo, k2tog, k3) x 4, yo, k2tog, k1, k2tog, yo, k5.
Row 6: K6, yo, k2tog, k23, k2tog, yo, k6.
Row 7: K7, yo, k2tog, (k1, yo, k2tog x 2, yo) x 4, k1, k2tog, yo, k7.
Row 8: K8, yo, k2tog, k19, k2tog, yo, k8.
Row 9: K9, (yo, k2tog, k3) x 3, yo, k2tog, k2, k2tog, yo, k9.
Row 10: K10, yo, k2tog, k15, k2tog, yo, k10.

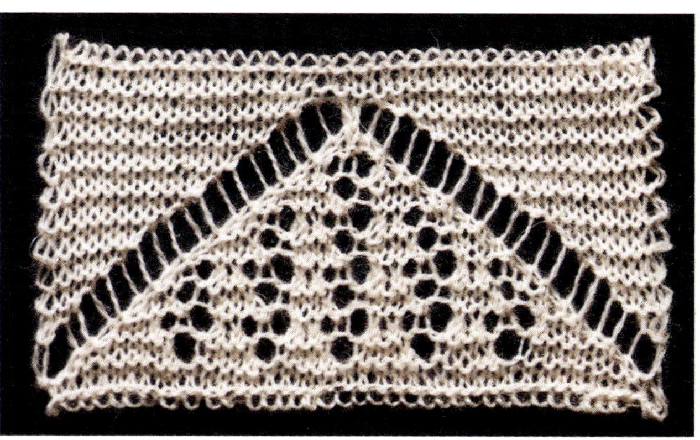

Baabie's Fancy knitted sample.

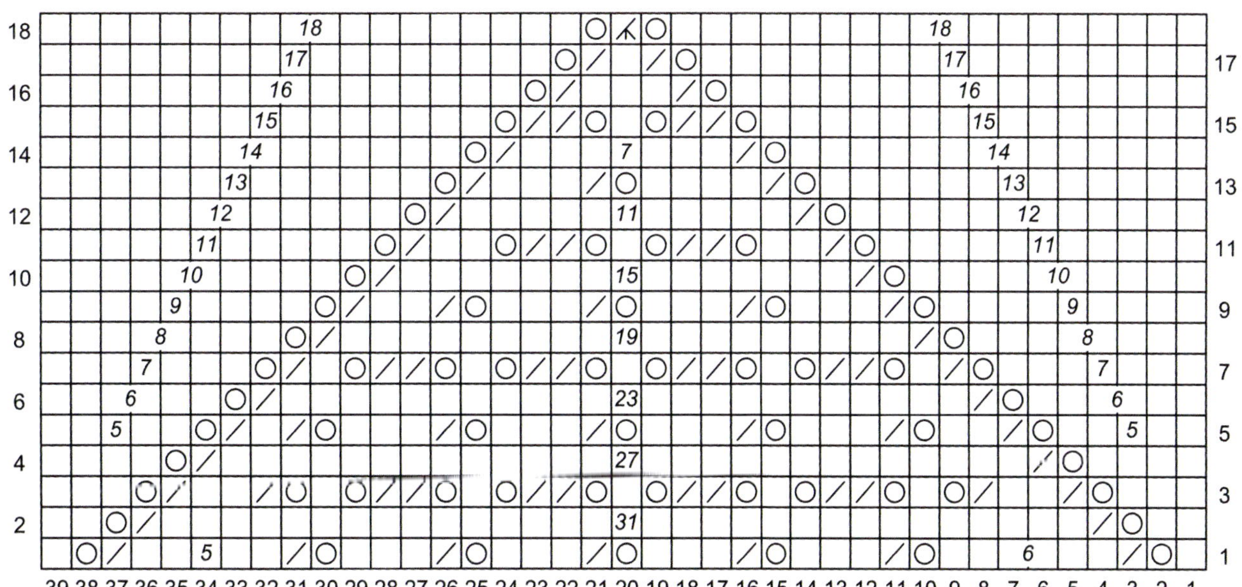

Baabie's Fancy chart.

Row 11: K11, yo, k2tog, k2, yo, k2tog x 2, yo, k1, yo, k2tog x 2, yo, k2, k2tog, yo, k11.
Row 12: K12, yo, k2tog, k11, k2tog, yo, k12.
Row 13: K13, yo, k2tog, k4, yo, k2tog, k3, k2tog, yo, k13.
Row 14: K14, yo, k2tog, k7, k2tog, yo, k14.
Row 15: K15, yo, k2tog x 2, yo, k1, yo, k2tog x 2, yo, k15.
Row 16: K16, yo, k2tog, k3, k2tog, yo, k16.
Row 17: K17, yo, k2tog, k1, k2tog, yo, k17.
Row 18: K18, yo, k3tog, yo, k18.

4.36

The Strawberry
TEX 2012.428a Stole

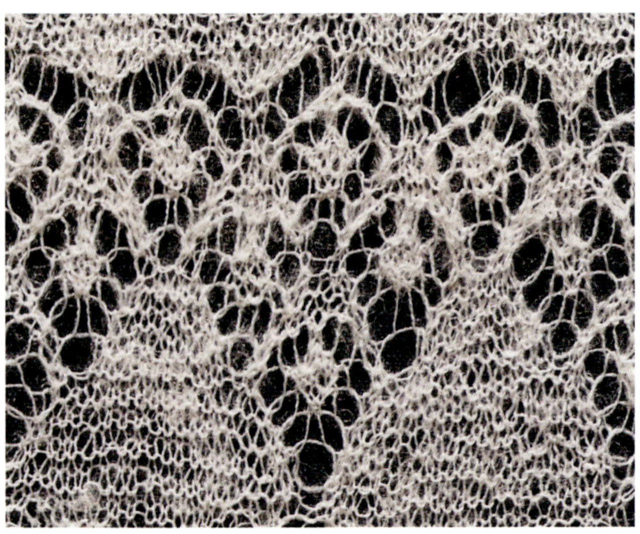

The Strawberry original pattern.

The Strawberry knitted sample.

The Strawberry pattern is commonly found and the name is recognised across Shetland. It is always placed at the top of a border because it is one of the few patterns with a straight line top edge. It is a very pretty pattern, giving the appearance of delicate swags or clusters descending into the border.

Row 1 (RS): K14, k2tog, yo, k15. (31 sts)
Row 2 (WS): Knit.
Row 3: K13, k2tog, yo, k1, yo, k2tog, k13.
Row 4: Knit.
Row 5: K12, k2tog, yo, k3, yo, k2tog, k12.
Row 6: Knit.
Row 7: K11, k2tog, yo, k5, yo, k2tog, k11.
Row 8: Knit.
Row 9: K9, k2tog, yo, k2, yo, k2tog, k1, k2tog, yo, k2, yo, k2tog, k9.
Row 10: K14, yo, p3tog, yo, k14.
Row 11: K8, k2tog, yo, k1, yo, k2tog, k5, k2tog, yo, k1, yo, k2tog, k8.
Row 12: Knit.
Row 13: K7, k2tog, yo, k3, yo, k2tog, k3, k2tog, yo, k3, yo, k2tog, k7.
Row 14: Knit.
Row 15: K6, k2tog, yo, k5, yo, k2tog, k1, k2tog, yo, k5, yo, k2tog, k6.
Row 16: Knit.
Row 17: K4, k2tog, yo, k2, yo, k2tog, k1, k2tog, yo, (k1, k2tog, yo, k2, yo, k2tog) x 2, k4.
Row 18: K9, yo, p3tog, yo, k7, yo, p3tog, yo, k9.
Row 19: K3, (k2tog, yo, k1, yo, k2tog, k5) x 2, k2tog, yo, k1, yo, k2tog, k3.
Row 20: Knit.
Row 21: K2, (k2tog, yo, k3, yo, k2tog, k3) x 2, k2tog, yo, k3, yo, k2tog, k2.

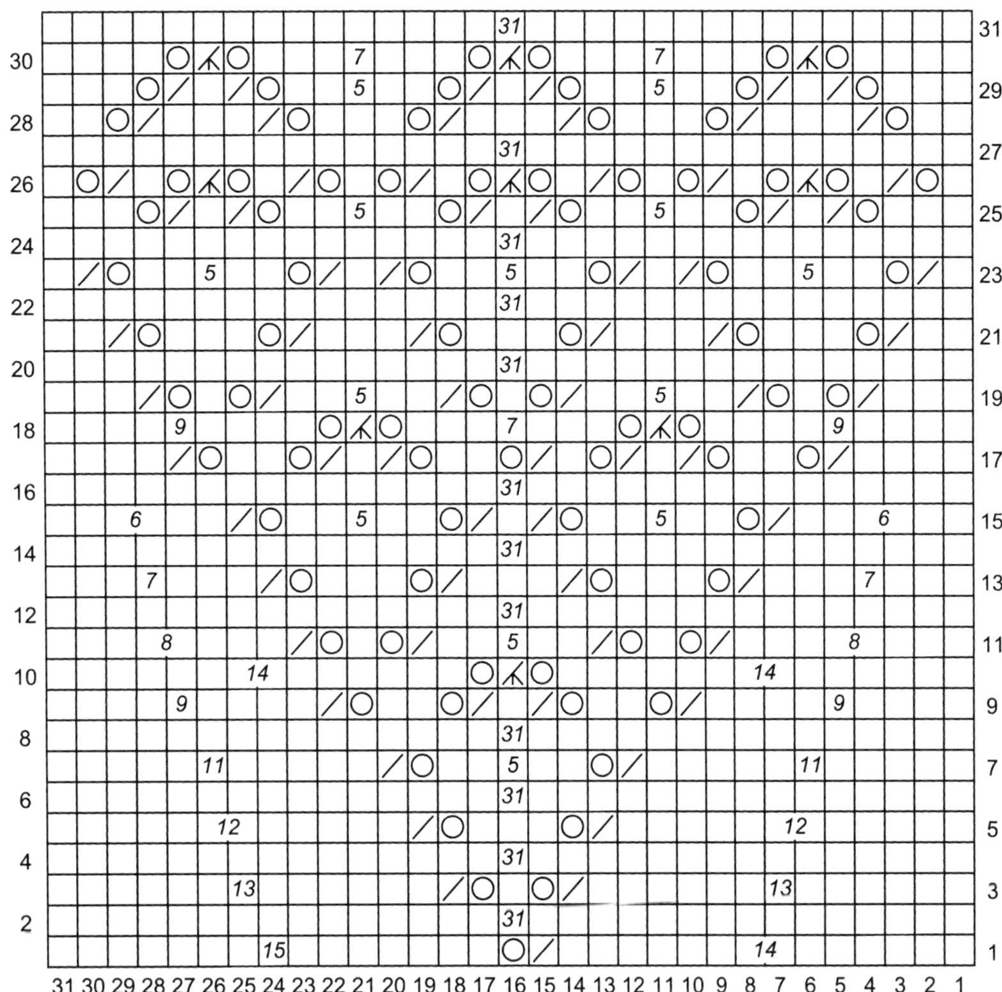

The Strawberry chart.

Row 22: Knit.
Row 23: (K1, k2tog, yo, k5, yo, k2tog) x 3, k1.
Row 24: Knit.
Row 25: K3, (yo, k2tog, k1, k2tog, yo, k5) x 2, yo, k2tog, k1, k2tog, yo, k3.
Row 26: (K1, yo, k2tog, k1, yo, p3tog, yo, k1, k2tog, yo) x 3, k1.
Row 27: Knit.
Row 28: K2, (yo, k2tog, k3, k2tog, yo, k3) x 2, yo, k2tog, k3, k2tog, yo, k2.
Row 29: Repeat row 25.
Row 30: K4, (yo, p3tog, yo, k7) x 2, yo, p3tog, yo, k4.
Rows 31: Knit.

4.37

Triangle of Peerie Fleas

TEX 81467 Scarf

Groupings of Peerie Fleas can take many forms; here they are made into a sharply defined triangle to give this artificial silk scarf a cascade effect near the top of the border. They could be recreated without the outer edge to give a more delicate appearance.

Row 1 (RS): K17, k2tog, yo, k1, yo, k2tog, k17. (39 sts)
Row 2 (WS): Knit.
Row 3: K16, k2tog, yo, k3, yo, k2tog, k16.
Row 4: Knit.
Row 5: K15, k2tog, yo, k5, yo, k2tog, k15.
Row 6: Knit.
Row 7: K14, k2tog, yo, k7, yo, k2tog, k14.
Row 8: Knit.
Row 9: K13, k2tog, yo, k9, yo, k2tog, k13.
Row 10: Knit.
Row 11: K12, k2tog, yo, k3, k2tog, yo, k1, yo, k2tog, k3, yo, k2tog, k12.
Row 12: Repeat row 3.
Row 13: K11, k2tog, yo, k5, yo, k3tog, yo, k5, yo, k2tog, k11.

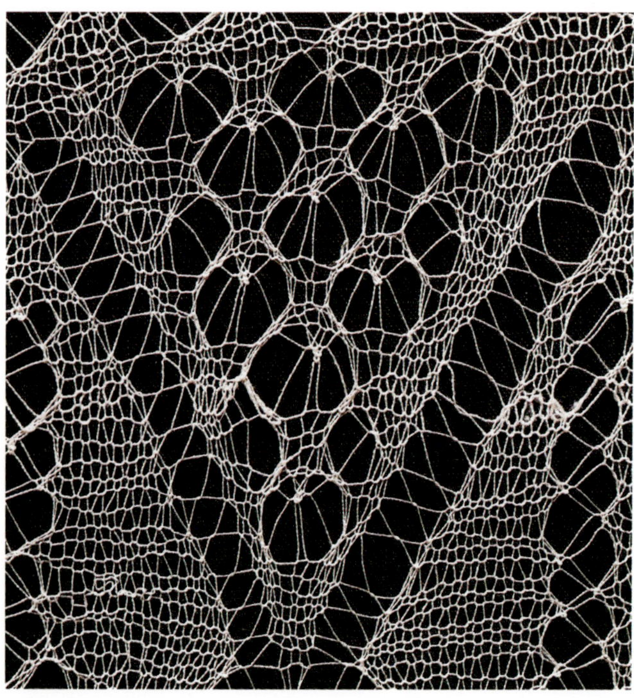

Triangle of Peerie Fleas original pattern.

Row 14: Knit.
Row 15: K10, k2tog, yo, k4, yo, k2tog, k3, k2tog, yo, k4, yo, k2tog, k10.
Row 16: K17, yo, k2tog, k1, k2tog, yo, k17.
Row 17: K9, k2tog, yo, k4, k2tog, yo, k5, yo, k2tog, k4, yo, k2tog, k9.
Row 18: Knit.
Row 19: K8, k2tog, yo, k7, k2tog, yo, k1, yo, k2tog, k7, yo, k2tog, k8.
Row 20: Repeat row 3.
Row 21: K7, k2tog, yo, k9, yo, k3tog, yo, k9, yo, k2tog, k7.
Row 22: Knit.
Row 23: K6, k2tog, yo, k5, k2tog, yo, k1, yo, k2tog, k3, k2tog, yo, k1, yo, k2tog, k5, yo, k2tog, k6.
Row 24: K12, k2tog, yo, k3, yo, k2tog, k1, k2tog, yo, k3, yo, k2tog, k12.
Row 25: K5, k2tog, yo, k7, yo, k3tog, yo, k5, yo, k3tog, yo, k7, yo, k2tog, k5.
Row 26: Knit.
Row 27: K4, k2tog, yo, k6, yo, k2tog, k3, k2tog, yo, k1, yo, k2tog, k3, k2tog, yo, k6, yo, k2tog, k4.
Row 28: K13, yo, k2tog, k1, k2tog, yo, k3, yo, k2tog, k1, k2tog, yo, k13.
Row 29: K3, k2tog, yo, k6, k2tog, yo, k5, yo, k3tog, yo, k5, yo, k2tog, k6, yo, k2tog, k3.
Row 30: Knit.

Triangle of Peerie Fleas knitted sample.

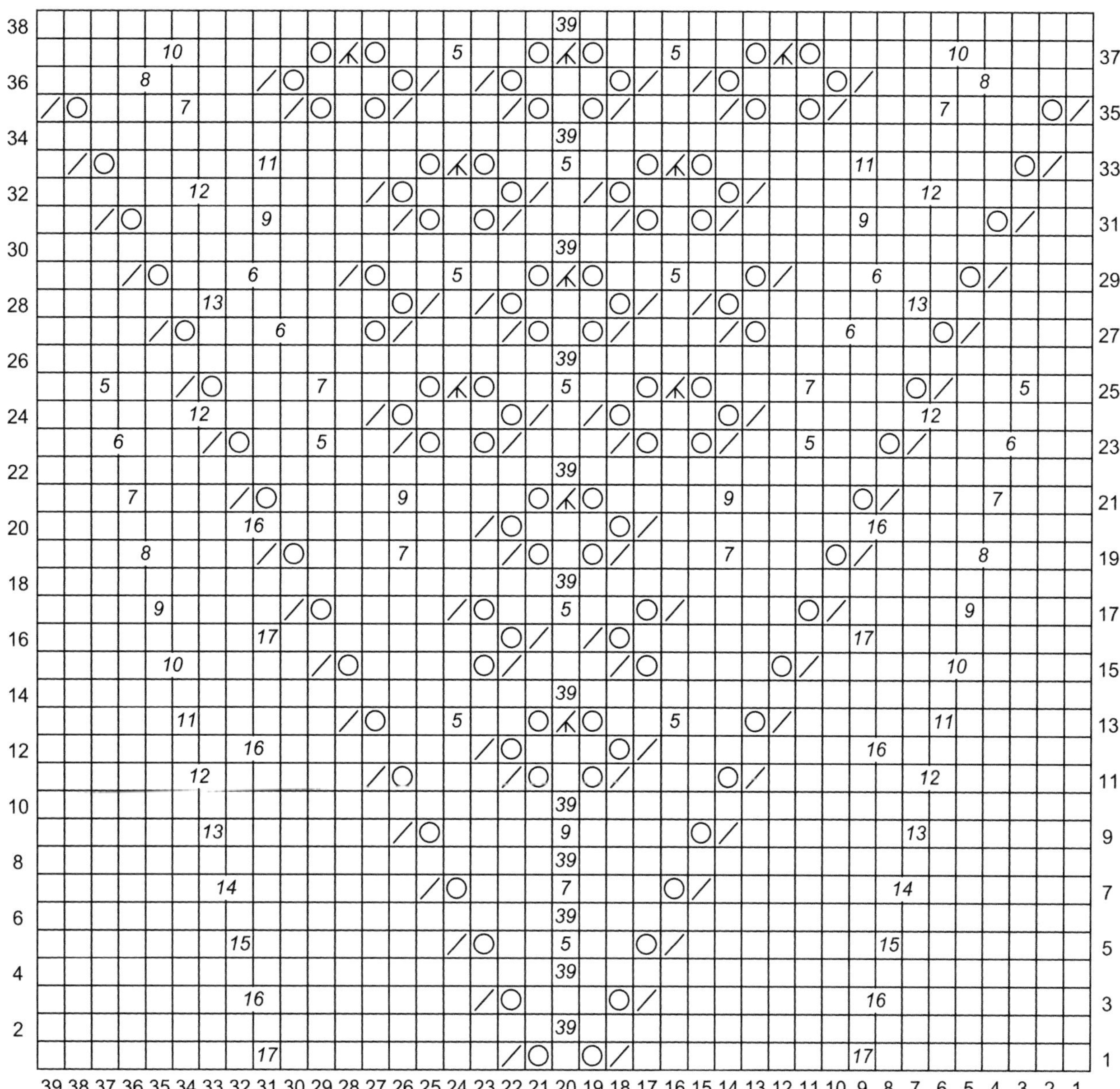

Triangle of Peerie Fleas chart.

Row 31: K2, k2tog, yo, k9, k2tog, yo, k1, yo, k2tog, k3, k2tog, yo, k1, yo, k2tog, k9, yo, k2tog, k2.

Row 32: Repeat row 24.

Row 33: K1, k2tog, yo, k11, yo, k3tog, yo, k5, yo, k3tog, yo, k11, yo, k2tog, k1.

Row 34: Knit.

Row 35: K2tog, yo, k7, (k2tog, yo, k1, yo, k2tog, k3) x 2, k2tog, yo, k1, yo, k2tog, k7, yo, k2tog.

Row 36: K8, (k2tog, yo, k3, yo, k2tog, k1) x 2, k2tog, yo, k3, yo, k2tog, k8.

Row 37: K10, (yo, k3tog, yo, k5) x 2, yo, k3tog, yo, k10.

Row 38: Knit.

Bells

The Bell shape pattern appears to be very old and seems to have faded from general use by the late nineteenth century. It is not known from contemporary lace knitting. It is found in the border of a christening shawl made for a child born in 1856 or 1858 to a minister and his wife (see Pattern 7.4). In this context it may have had references to a church bell. It was not used frequently and has been recorded in borders and centres.

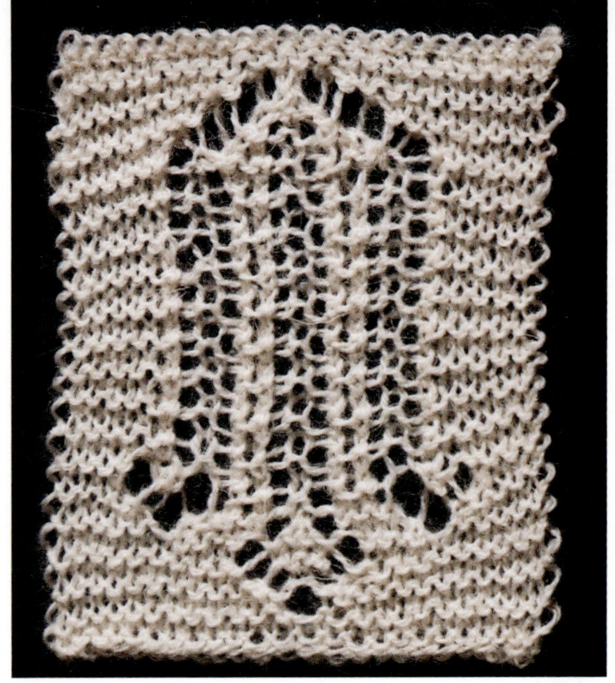

Bell with Clapper knitted sample.

4.38

Bell with Clapper

TEX 7754 Shawl

This Bell was used as a pattern in the centre of a shawl, where the patterns were arranged horizontally in distinct rows. It is similar to the Bell with Clapper, as shown in Chapter 7.

Row 1 (RS): K9, yo, k2tog, k8. (19 sts)
Row 2 (WS): Knit.
Row 3: K7, k2tog, yo, k1, yo, k2tog, k7.
Row 4: K6, k2tog, yo, k3, yo, k2tog, k6.
Row 5: K7, yo, k2tog, k1, k2tog, yo, k7.
Row 6: Knit.
Row 7: K3, yo, k2tog, k3, yo, k3tog, yo, k3, k2tog, yo, k3.
Row 8: K1, k2tog, yo, k1, yo, k2tog, k7, k2tog, yo, k1, yo, k2tog, k1.
Row 9: K2tog, yo, k2tog, (yo, k1, yo, k2tog x 2) x 2, yo, k1, (yo, k2tog) x 2.
Rows 10–26: K2, k2tog, (yo, k1, yo, k2tog x 2) x 2, yo, k1, yo, k2tog, k2.

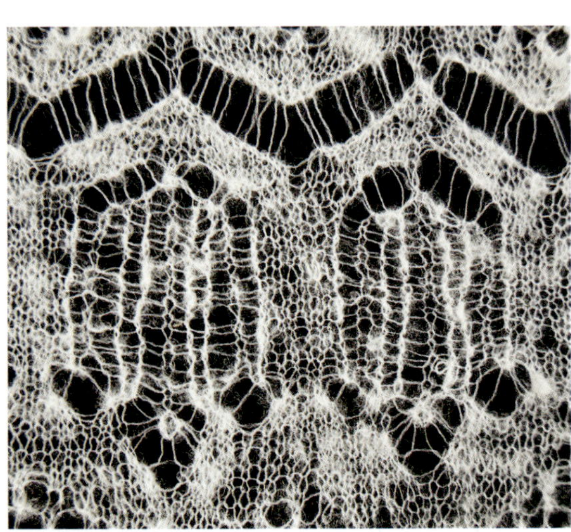

Bell with Clapper original pattern.

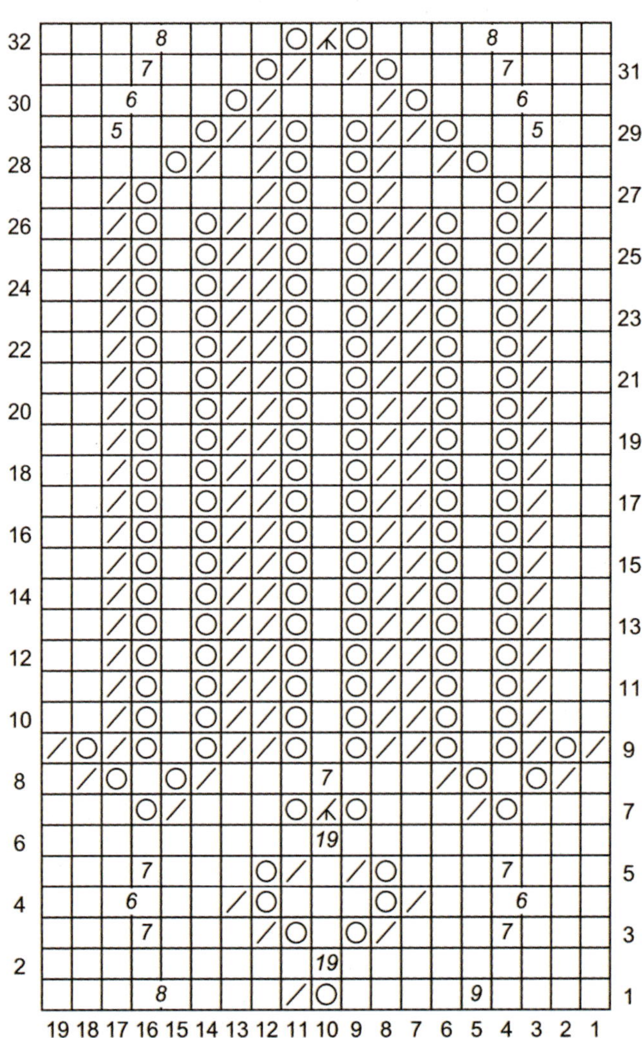

Row 27: K2, k2tog, yo, k3, k2tog, yo, k1, yo, k2tog, k3, yo, k2tog, k2.
Row 28: K4, yo, k2tog, k1, k2tog, yo, k1, yo, k2tog, k1, k2tog, yo, k4.
Row 29: K5, yo, k2tog x 2, yo, k1, yo, k2tog x 2, yo, k5.
Row 30: K6, yo, k2tog, k3, k2tog, yo, k6.
Row 31: Repeat row 5.
Row 32: K8, yo, p3tog, yo, k8.

4.39

Bell with Steek, Diamond with Steek inset, and Lace Hole Hexagon
TEX 2012.428b Stole

Bell with Steek, Diamond with Steek inset, and Lace Hole hexagon original pattern.

Bell with Steek, Diamond with Steek inset, and Lace Hole hexagon knitted sample.

Here the Bell forms the centre of a bold border design. A Steek is attached to the top of the Bell and a Diamond with Steek is placed on top. Hexagons of Lace Holes have been placed above the Bells, between the Steeks.

Row 1 (RS): Knit. (43 sts)
Row 2 (WS): K9, k2tog, yo, k1, yo, k2tog, k15, k2tog, yo, k1, yo, k2tog, k9.
Row 3: K8, k2tog, yo, k3, yo, k2tog, k13, k2tog, yo, k3, yo, k2tog, k8.
Row 4: K10, yo, p3tog, yo, k17, yo, p3tog, yo, k10.
Row 5: Repeat row 2.
Row 6: (K3, yo, k2tog, k4, k2tog, yo, k1, yo, k2tog, k4, k2tog, yo) x 2, k3.

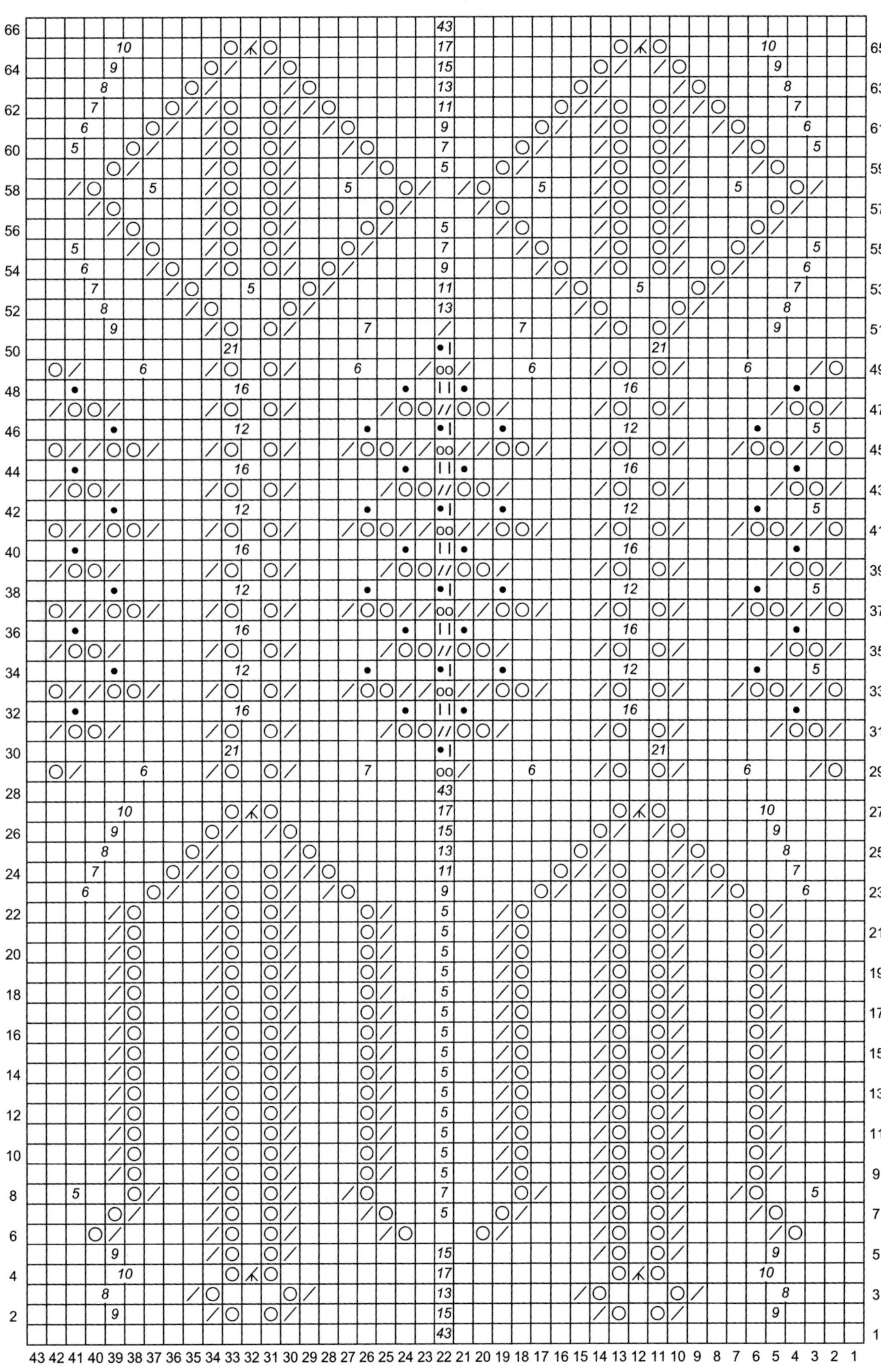

Bell with Steek, Diamond with Steek inset, and Lace Hole hexagon chart.

Row 7: K4, yo, k2tog, k3, k2tog, yo, k1, yo, k2tog, k3, k2tog, yo, k5, yo, k2tog, k3, k2tog, yo, k1, yo, k2tog, k3, k2tog, yo, k4.
Row 8: K5, yo, k2tog, k2, k2tog, yo, k1, yo, k2tog, k2, k2tog, yo, k7, yo, k2tog, k2, k2tog, yo, k1, yo, k2tog, k2, k2tog, yo, k5.
Rows 9-22: K4, k2tog, yo, k3, k2tog, yo, k1, yo, k2tog, k3, yo, k2tog, k5, k2tog, yo, k3, k2tog, yo, k1, yo, k2tog, k3, yo, k2tog, k4.
Row 23: K6, yo, k2tog, k1, k2tog, yo, k1, yo, k2tog, k1, k2tog, yo, k9, yo, k2tog, k1, k2tog, yo, k1, yo, k2tog, k1, k2tog, yo, k6.
Row 24: K7, yo, k2tog x 2, yo, k1, yo, k2tog x 2, yo, k11, yo, k2tog x 2, yo, k1, yo, k2tog x 2, yo, k7.
Row 25: K8, yo, k2tog, k3, k2tog, yo, k13, yo, k2tog, k3, k2tog, yo, k8.
Row 26: K9, yo, k2tog, k1, k2tog, yo, k15, yo, k2tog, k1, k2tog, yo, k9.
Row 27: K10, yo, k3tog, yo, k17, yo, k3tog, yo, k10.
Row 28: Knit.
Row 29: K1, yo, k2tog, k6, k2tog, yo, k1, yo, k2tog, k6, k2tog, yo twice, k7, k2tog, yo, k1, yo, k2tog, k6, k2tog, yo, k1. (44 sts)
Row 30: K21, knit, purl into yarnovers, k21.
Row 31: K1, k2tog, yo x 2, k2tog, k4, k2tog, yo, k1, yo, k2tog, k4, k2tog, yo x 2, k2tog twice, yo x 2, k2tog, k4, k2tog, yo, k1, yo, k2tog, k4, k2tog, yo x 2, k2tog, k1.
Row 32: K2, p1, k16, p1, k1, knit 2, p1, k16, p1, k3.
Row 33: K1, yo, k2tog x 2, yo x 2, k2tog, k2, k2tog, yo, k1, yo, k2tog, k2, k2tog, yo x 2, k2tog x 2, yo twice, k2tog x 2, yo x 2, k2tog, k2, k2tog, yo, k1, yo, k2tog, k2, k2tog, yo x 2, k2tog x 2, yo, k1.
Row 34: K4, p1, k12, p1, k3, knit, purl into yarnovers, k2, p1, k12, p1, k5.
Row 35: Repeat row 31.
Rows 36–47: Repeat rows 32–35.
Row 48: Repeat row 32.
Row 49: K1, yo, k2tog, k6, k2tog, yo, k1, yo, k2tog, k6, k2tog, yo twice, k2tog, k6, k2tog, yo, k1, yo, k2tog, k6, k2tog, yo, k1.
Row 50: Repeat row 30.
Row 51: K9, k2tog, yo, k1, yo, (k2tog, k7) x 2, k2tog, yo, k1, yo, k2tog, k9. (43 sts)
Row 52: Repeat row 3.
Row 53: K7, k2tog, yo, k5, yo, k2tog, k11, k2tog, yo, k5, yo, k2tog, k7.
Row 54: K6, (k2tog, yo, k1) x 2, yo, k2tog, k1, yo, k2tog, k9, (k2tog, yo, k1) x 2, yo, k2tog, k1, yo, k2tog, k6.
Row 55: K5, k2tog, yo, k2, k2tog, yo, k1, yo, k2tog, k2, yo, k2tog, k7, k2tog, yo, k2, k2tog, yo, k1, yo, k2tog, k2, yo, k2tog, k5.
Row 56: Repeat row 9.
Row 57: (K3, k2tog, yo, k4, k2tog, yo, k1, yo, k2tog, k4, yo, k2tog) x 2, k3.
Row 58: K2, k2tog, yo, k5, k2tog, yo, k1, yo, k2tog, k5, yo, k2tog, k1, k2tog, yo, k5, k2tog, yo, k1, yo, k2tog, k5, yo, k2tog, k2.
Row 59: Repeat row 7.
Row 60: Repeat row 8.
Row 61: Repeat row 23.
Row 62: Repeat row 24.
Row 63: Repeat row 25.
Row 64: Repeat row 26.
Row 65: Repeat row 27.
Row 66: Knit.

Steek columns

Steeks are used in many ways, here as columns connecting adjacent patterns. In two of the patterns they become one with the patterns they alternate with, forming a new, complex pattern. All three patterns were used at the top of borders, as a straight edge to define the end of the border before the centre pattern began.

Standing stone at Clivocast, south Unst.

4.40

Steek column with Diamonds between two Ferns
TEX 2004.364 Shawl

A long, simple Steek with Diamonds at both ends lies between two Ferns. Its position at the top of the border gives it a cascade effect when paired with the Ferns.

Row 1 (RS): K21, k2tog, yo, k1, yo, k2tog, k21. (47 sts)
Row 2 (WS): K20, k2tog, yo, k3, yo, k2tog, k20.
Row 3: K19, k2tog, yo, k5, yo, k2tog, k19.
Row 4: K18, k2tog, yo, k7, yo, k2tog, k18.
Rows 5–6: K19, yo, k2tog, k5, k2tog, yo, k19.
Row 7: K20, yo, k2tog, k3, k2tog, yo, k20.
Row 8: K21, yo, k2tog, k1, k2tog, yo, k21.
Row 9: K22, yo, k3tog, yo, k22.
Rows 10–17: K21, k2tog, yo, k1, yo, k2tog, k21.
Row 18: K9, yo, k2tog, k10, k2tog, yo, k1, yo, k2tog, k11, yo, k2tog, k8.
Row 19: Repeat row 1.
Row 20: K7, (k2tog, yo, k1, yo, k2tog, k9) x 2, k2tog, yo, k1, yo, k2tog, k7.
Row 21: K6, k2tog, yo, k3, yo, k2tog, k8, k2tog, yo, k1, yo, k2tog, k8, k2tog, yo, k3, yo, k2tog, k6.
Row 22: Repeat row 1.

Steek column with Diamonds between two Ferns original pattern.

Steek column with Diamonds between two Ferns knitted sample.

Row 23: K8, yo, k3tog, yo, k10, k2tog, yo, k1, yo, k2tog, k10, yo, k3tog, yo, k8.

Row 24: K6, yo, k2tog, k3, k2tog, yo, k8, k2tog, yo, k1, yo, k2tog, k8, yo, k2tog, k3, k2tog, yo, k6.

Row 25: Repeat row 1.

Row 26: K4, k2tog, yo, k1, yo, k2tog, k1, (k2tog, yo, k1, yo, k2tog, k6) x 2, k2tog, yo, k1, yo, k2tog, k1, k2tog, yo, k1, yo, k2tog, k4.

Row 27: K3, k2tog, yo, k3, yo, k3tog, yo, k3, yo, k2tog, k5, k2tog, yo, k1, yo, k2tog, k5, k2tog, yo, k3, yo, k3tog, yo, k3, yo, k2tog, k3.

Row 28: Repeat row 1.

Row 29: K5, yo, k3tog, yo, k3, yo, k3tog, yo, k7, k2tog, yo, k1, yo, k2tog, k7, yo, k3tog, yo, k3, yo, k3tog, yo, k5.

Row 30: K3, yo, k2tog, k9, k2tog, yo, k5, k2tog, yo, k1, yo, k2tog, k5, yo, k2tog, k9, k2tog, yo, k3.

Row 31: K4, yo, k2tog, k7, k2tog, yo, k6, k2tog, yo, k1, yo, k2tog, k6, yo, k2tog, k7, k2tog, yo, k4.

Row 32: K1, yo, k2tog, k2, yo, k2tog, k5, k2tog, yo, k2, k2tog, yo, k3, k2tog, yo, k1, yo, k2tog, k3, yo, k2tog, k2, yo, k2tog, k5, k2tog, yo, k2, k2tog, yo, k1.

Row 33: (K2, yo, k2tog) x 2, k3, k2tog, yo, k2, (k2tog, yo, k3) x 2, yo, k2tog, k3, yo, k2tog, k2, yo, k2tog, k3, (k2tog, yo, k2) x 2.

Row 34: K3, yo, k2tog, k2, yo, k2tog, k1, k2tog, yo, k2, k2tog, yo, k3, k2tog, yo, k5, yo, k2tog, k3, yo, k2tog, k2, yo, k2tog, k1, k2tog, yo, k2, k2tog, yo, k3.

Row 35: K4, yo, k2tog, k2, yo, k3tog, yo, k2, k2tog, yo, k3, k2tog, yo, k7, yo, k2tog, k3, yo, k2tog, k2, yo, k3tog, yo, k2, k2tog, yo, k4.

Row 36: (K5, yo, k2tog, k5, k2tog, yo) x 3, k5.

Row 37: K6, yo, k2tog, k3, k2tog, yo, k6, yo, k2tog, k5, k2tog, yo, k6, yo, k2tog, k3, k2tog, yo, k6.

Row 38: K7, yo, k2tog, k1, k2tog, yo, k8, yo, k2tog, k3, k2tog, yo, k8, yo, k2tog, k1, k2tog, yo, k7.

Row 39: K8, yo, k3tog, yo, k10, yo, k2tog, k1, k2tog, yo, k10, yo, k3tog, yo, k8.

Row 40: Repeat row 9.

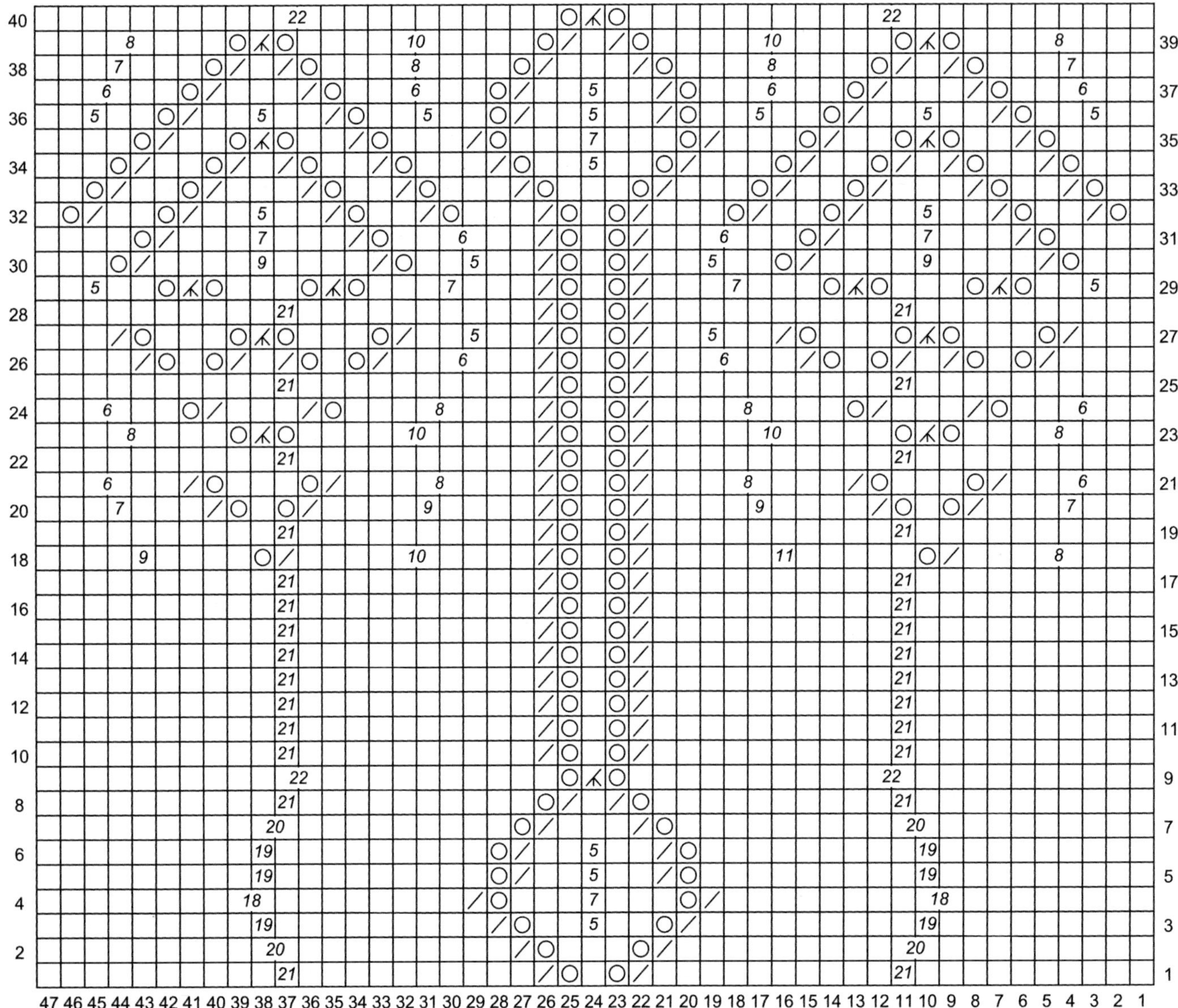

Steek column with Diamonds between two Ferns chart.

4.41

Steek columns topped by Beads

TEX 2012.428b Stole

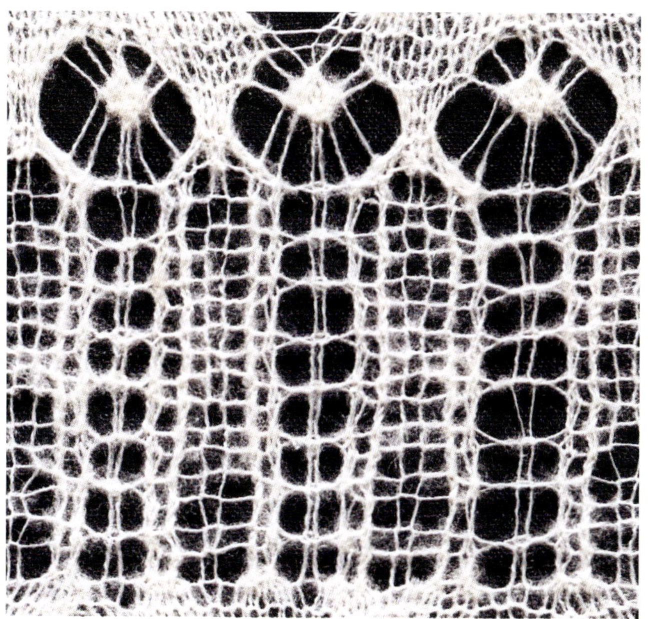

Steek columns topped by Beads original pattern.

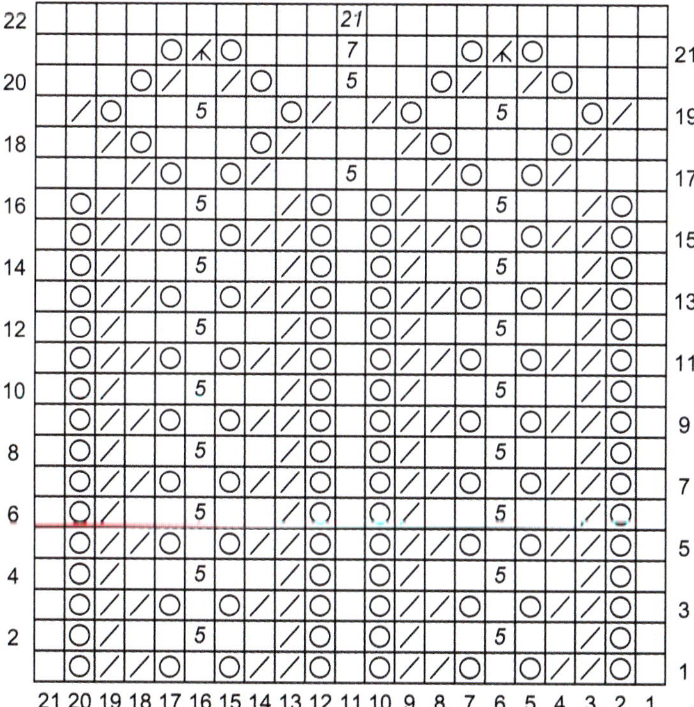

Steek columns topped by Beads chart.

Steek columns topped by Beads knitted sample.

Columns of Steeks with distinct edges are lined up, seemingly at attention, and Beads are placed on top of each one. This is the only known example of this pattern. It has a simplicity of form and British Art Nouveau look about it, but its date is unknown.

Row 1 (RS): (K1, yo, k2tog x 2, yo) x 4, k1. (21 sts)
Row 2 (WS): (K1, yo, k2tog, k5, k2tog, yo) x 2, k1.
Rows 3–16: Repeat rows 1–2.
Row 17: K3, k2tog, yo, k1, yo, k2tog, k5, k2tog, yo, k1, yo, k2tog, k3.
Row 18: K2, k2tog, yo, k3, yo, k2tog, k3, k2tog, yo, k3, yo, k2tog, k2.
Row 19: (K1, k2tog, yo, k5, yo, k2tog) x 2, k1.
Row 20: K3, yo, k2tog, k1, k2tog, yo, k5, yo, k2tog, k1, k2tog, yo, k3.
Row 21: K4, yo, k3tog, yo, k7, yo, k3tog, yo, k4.
Row 22: Knit.

4.42

Steeks with Diamonds between Hexagons inset with Beads
TEX 2004.372 Stole

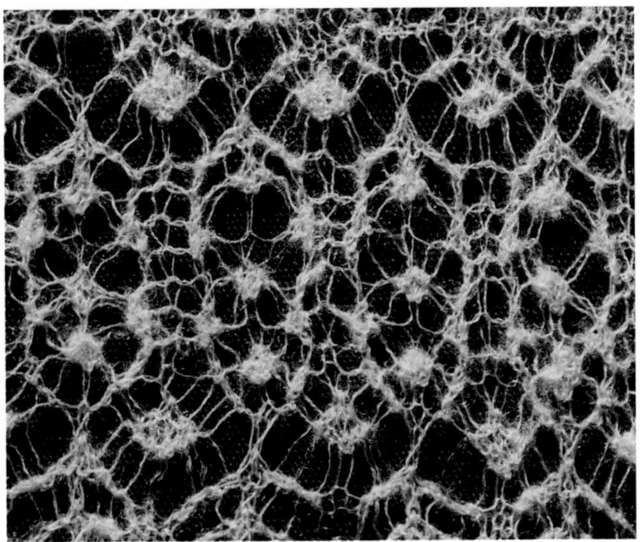

Steeks with Diamonds between Hexagons inset with Beads original pattern.

Steeks with Diamonds between Hexagons inset with Beads knitted sample.

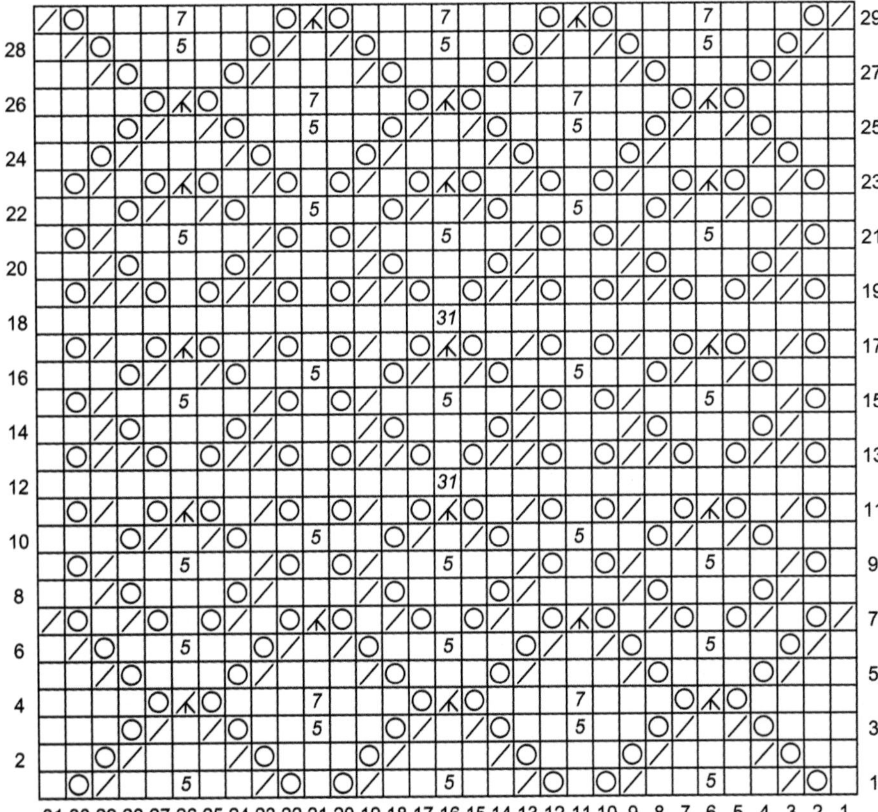

Steeks with Diamonds between Hexagons inset with Beads chart.

The stole is quite worn and damaged but this interesting little pattern is worth noting. It is made of Steeks with plain Diamonds on top and bottom, alternating with long Hexagons each with three Beads in a column. The uneven and worn nature of the hand-spun yarn in the original makes it difficult to appreciate at first but the design is interesting and pretty.

Row 1 (RS): (K1, yo, k2tog, k5, k2tog, yo) x 3, k1. (31 sts)
Row 2 (WS): K2, (yo, k2tog, k3, k2tog, yo, k3) x 2, yo, k2tog, k3, k2tog, yo, k2.
Row 3: K3, (yo, k2tog, k1, k2tog, yo, k5) x 2, yo, k2tog, k1, k2tog, yo, k3.
Row 4: K4, (yo, p3tog, yo, k7) x 2, yo, p3tog, yo, k4.
Row 5: K2, (k2tog, yo, k3, yo, k2tog, k3) x 2, k2tog, yo, k3, yo, k2tog, k2.
Row 6: (K1, k2tog, yo, k5, yo, k2tog) x 3, k1.
Row 7: K2tog, (yo, k1, k2tog, yo, k1, yo, k2tog, k1, yo, k3tog) x 2, yo, k1, k2tog, yo, (k1, yo, k2tog) x 2.
Row 8: Repeat row 5.
Row 9: Repeat row 1.
Row 10: Repeat row 3.
Row 11: (K1, yo, k2tog, k1, yo, k3tog, yo, k1, k2tog, yo) x 3, k1.
Row 12: Knit.
Row 13: (K1, yo, k2tog x 2, yo) x 6, k1.
Rows 14–19: Repeat rows 8–13.
Row 20: Repeat row 5.
Row 21: Repeat row 1.
Row 22: Repeat row 3.
Row 23: Repeat row 11.
Row 24: Repeat row 2.
Row 25: Repeat row 3.
Row 26: Repeat row 4.
Row 27: Repeat row 5.
Row 28: Repeat row 6.
Row 29: K2tog, (yo, k7, yo, k3tog) x 2, yo, k7, yo, k2tog.

CHAPTER 5

CROWNS AND A CROSS

The tradition of gifting Shetland knitting to royalty goes as far back as 1788, when King George III was given a pair of stockings (Chapman, p.50). The softness of the wool, the fine hand-spun yarn, delicate stitches and exquisite technique meant Shetland lace was considered a luxury item fit for royalty. Queen Victoria also was given stockings at the age of eighteen in 1837, the first year of her reign. She continued to purchase (and was gifted) Shetland knitted lace throughout her long reign.

When important gifts such as those for royalty were planned, a test piece was made to ensure correct spacing, layout and style of patterns. From surviving test pieces and early photographs of lace gifted to royalty, we know that crowns and other royal symbols were worked into the design. A number of pieces in the collection contain crown motifs. They likely were originally designed for fine shawls and stoles made for royalty but have been used occasionally for non-royal pieces. Shetland Museum's collection includes the test piece for the stole sent to Queen Victoria on the occasion of her eightieth birthday in 1899, two years before her death. It is decorated with crowns and crosses *pattées*. The designs may have been in reference to the Small Diamond Crown she began to wear atop her widow's veil in 1870, which has five crosses *pattées*.

A series of stoles were made to mark later royal occasions and they are recorded in early photographs by their makers. These include one made for George V and Queen Mary for their silver jubilee in 1935, and another made for George VI and Queen Elizabeth for their coronation in 1937.

Portrait photograph of Queen Victoria by Alexander Bassano. The small crown she wears here is similar to the ones that were featured in her eightieth birthday stole

Queen Victoria in her State Robes by George Park Harrison (copy after Franz Xavier Winterhalter, ART 1991.76).

The Crown of St Edward, the British crown of coronation.

Queen Victoria's eightieth birthday stole test piece, 1899.

5.1

Crown 1

TEX 2004.372 Stole

The stole includes motifs and design forms which suggest it is very old, perhaps mid-nineteenth century in origin. The large central diamond shape in the centre of the crown may be in reference to the large red spinel in the middle of the Imperial State Crown, worn by the monarch following the coronation. A portrait of the young Queen Victoria wearing the crown shows fleur-de-lis and crosses *pattées* in the actual crown rim, which have a design resemblance to the flanges radiating from the Crown in the knitted design.

Row 1 (RS): K11, (yo, k2tog) x 9, k10. (39 sts)
Row 2 (WS): Knit.
Rows 3–6: Repeat rows 1–2.
Row 7: K9, (k2tog, yo) x 2, k13, (yo, k2tog) x 2, k9.
Row 8: Knit.
Row 9: K8, (k2tog, yo) x 2, k15, (yo, k2tog) x 2, k8.
Row 10: K19, yo, k2tog, k18.
Row 11: K7, (k2tog, yo) x 2, k6, k2tog, yo, k1, yo, k2tog, k6, (yo, k2tog) x 2, k7.
Row 12: K16, k2tog, yo, k3, yo, k2tog, k16.
Row 13: K6, k2tog, yo, (k2tog, yo, k5) x 2, yo, k2tog, k5, (yo, k2tog) x 2, k6.
Row 14: K14, k2tog, yo, k7, yo, k2tog, k14.
Row 15: K5, (k2tog, yo) x 2, k4, k2tog, yo, k9, yo, k2tog, k4, (yo, k2tog) x 2, k5.
Row 16: K15, yo, k2tog, k5, k2tog, yo, k15.
Row 17: K4, (k2tog, yo) x 2, k8, yo, k2tog, k3, k2tog, yo, k8, (yo, k2tog) x 2, k4.
Row 18: K11, yo, k1, k2tog, k3, yo, k2tog, k1, k2tog, yo, k3, k2tog, k1, yo, k11.

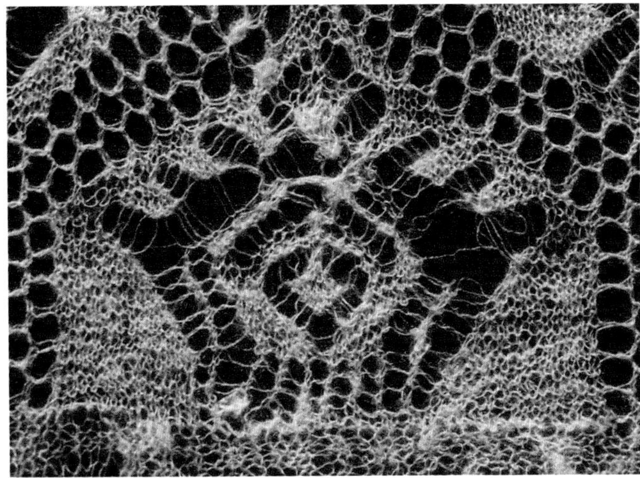

Crown 1 original pattern.

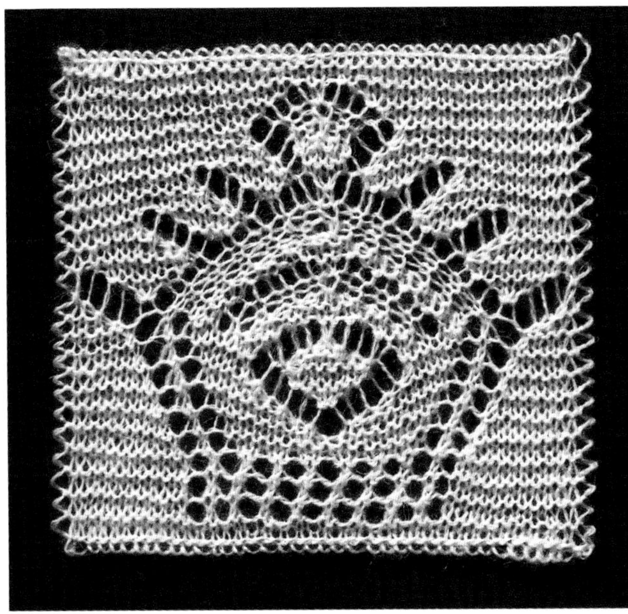

Crown 1 knitted sample.

Row 19: K3, k2tog, yo, k1, yo, k2, k2tog, k2, yo, k1, k2tog, k3, yo, k3tog, yo, k3, k2tog, k1, yo, k2, k2tog, k2, yo, k1, yo, k2tog, k3.
Row 20: K2, k2tog, yo, k3, yo, k2, k2tog, k2, yo, k1, k2tog, k7, k2tog, k1, yo, k2, k2tog, k2, yo, k3, yo, k2tog, k2.
Row 21: K1, k2tog, yo, k5, yo, k2, k2tog, k2, yo, k1, k2tog, k5, k2tog, k1, yo, k2, k2tog, k2, yo, k5, yo, k2tog, k1.
Row 22: K2tog, yo, k7, yo, k2, k2tog, k2, yo, k1, k2tog, k3, k2tog, k1, yo, k2, k2tog, k2, yo, k7, yo, k2tog.
Row 23: K10, yo, k2, k2tog, k2, yo, (k1, k2tog) x 2, k1, yo, k2, k2tog, k2, yo, k10.
Row 24: K8, k2tog, yo, k1, yo, k2, k2tog, k2, yo, k1, k3tog, k1, yo, k2, k2tog, k2, yo, k1, yo, k2tog, k8.
Row 25: K7, k2tog, yo, k3, yo, k2, k2tog, k2, yo, k3tog, yo, k2, k2tog, k2, yo, k3, yo, k2tog, k7.
Row 26: K6, k2tog, yo, k5, yo, k2, k2tog, k5, k2tog, k2, yo, k5, yo, k2tog, k6.
Row 27: K5, k2tog, yo, k7, yo, k2, k2tog, k3, k2tog, k2, yo, k7, yo, k2tog, k5.
Row 28: K12, k2tog, yo, k1, yo, k2, k2tog, k1, k2tog, k2, yo, k1, yo, k2tog, k12.
Row 29: K11, k2tog, yo, k3, yo, k2, k3tog, k2, yo, k3, yo, k2tog, k11.
Row 30: K10, k2tog, yo, k5, yo, k1, k3tog, k1, yo, k5, yo, k2tog, k10.
Row 31: K9, k2tog, yo, k7, yo, k3tog, yo, k7, yo, k2tog, k9.
Row 32: Repeat row 12.
Row 33: K15, k2tog, yo, k5, yo, k2tog, k15.
Row 34: Repeat row 14.
Row 35: K13, k2tog, yo, k9, yo, k2tog, k13.
Row 36: K15, yo, k2, k2tog, k1, k2tog, k2, yo, k15.
Row 37: K16, yo, k2, k3tog, k2, yo, k16.
Row 38: K17, yo, k1, k3tog, k1, yo, k17.
Row 39: K18, yo, k3tog, yo, k18.
Row 40: Knit.

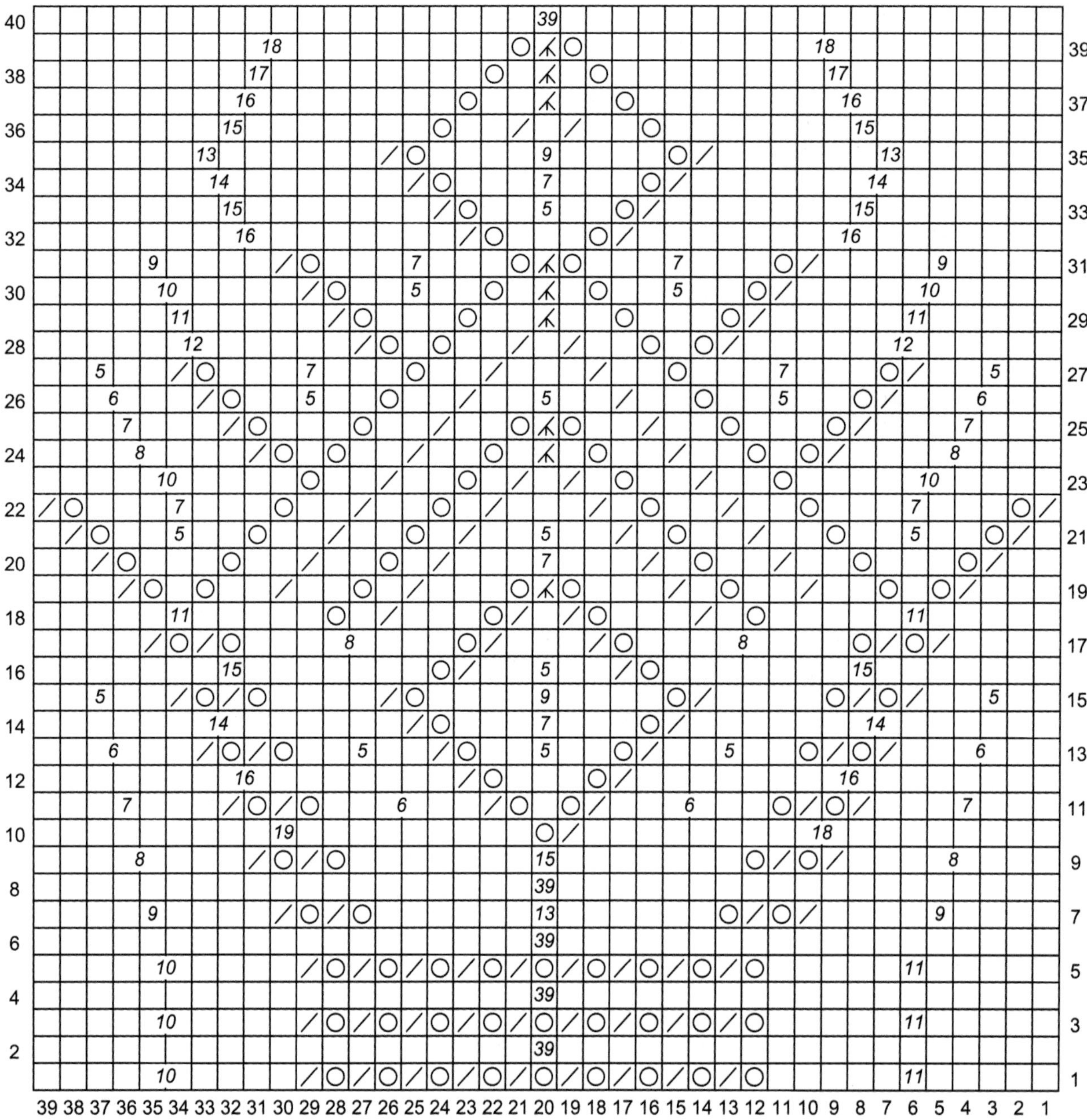

Crown 1 chart.

5.2

Crown 2

TEX 2019.33 Stole

This Crown is found as one of two main motifs in a border, surrounded by Fancy Net stitch. The other motif is a very decorative tree shape and the crown sits atop the tree. The stole was part of a private collection of knitwear from the Shetland firm of Tulloch's. It is not known if the design was intended for a special occasion.

Crown 2 original pattern.

Crown 2 knitted sample.

Row 1 (RS): K8, k2tog, (yo x 2, k2tog x 2) x 6, yo x 2, k2tog, k7. (43 sts)
Row 2 (WS): K8, (p1, k3) x 6, p1, k10.
Row 3: K10, k2tog, (yo x 2, k2tog x 2) x 5, yo x 2, k2tog, k9.
Row 4: K10, (p1, k3) x 5, p1, k12.
Row 5: K7, k2tog, yo, k25, yo, k2tog, k7.
Row 6: K15, yo, k1, k2tog, k7, k2tog, k1, yo, k15.
Row 7: K13, (yo, k1, k2tog) x 2, k5, (k2tog, k1, yo) x 2, k13.
Row 8: K6, k2tog, yo, k6, (yo, k1, k2tog) x 2, k3, (k2tog, k1, yo) x 2, k6, yo, k2tog, k6.
Row 9: K15, (yo, k1, k2tog) x 2, k1, (k2tog, k1, yo) x 2, k15.
Row 10: K10, k2tog, yo, k4, yo, k1, k2tog, yo, k1, p3tog, k1, yo, k2tog, k1, yo, k4, yo, k2tog, k10.
Row 11: K5, k2tog, yo, k10, yo, k1, k2tog, yo, k3tog, yo, k2tog, k1, yo, k10, yo, k2tog, k5.
Row 12: K9, k2tog, yo, k1, yo, k2tog, k4, yo, (k1, k2tog) x 2, k1, yo, k4, k2tog, yo, k1, yo, k2tog, k9.
Row 13: K19, yo, k1, k3tog, k1, yo, k19.
Row 14: K4, k2tog, yo, k2, k2tog, yo, k3, yo, k2tog, k5, yo, p3tog, yo, k5, k2tog, yo, k3, yo, k2tog, k2, yo, k2tog, k4.
Row 15: K17, k2tog, k1, yo, k3, yo, k1, k2tog, k17.
Row 16: K10, yo, p3tog, yo, k3, k2tog, k1, yo, k5, yo, k1, k2tog, k3, yo, p3tog, yo, k10.
Row 17: K3, k2tog, yo, k10, k2tog, k1, yo, k2, yo, k3tog, yo, k2, yo, k1, k2tog, k10, yo, k2tog, k3.
Row 18: K14, (k2tog, k1, yo) x 2, k3, (yo, k1, k2tog) x 2, k14.
Row 19: K13, (k2tog, k1, yo) x 2, k5, (yo, k1, k2tog) x 2, k13.
Row 20: K2, k2tog, yo, k8, (k2tog, k1, yo) x 2, k7, (yo, k1, k2tog) x 2, k8, yo, k2tog, k2.
Row 21: K11, (k2tog, k1, yo) x 2, k9, (yo, k1, k2tog) x 2, k11.
Row 22: K10, (k2tog, k1, yo) x 2, k11, (yo, k1, k2tog) x 2, k10.
Row 23: K1, k2tog, yo, k6, (k2tog, k1, yo) x 2, k13, (yo, k1, k2tog) x 2, k6, yo, k2tog, k1.
Row 24: K8, (k2tog, k1, yo) x 2, k15, (yo, k1, k2tog) x 2, k8.
Row 25: K7, (k2tog, k1, yo) x 2, k17, (yo, k1, k2tog) x 2, k7.
Row 26: K6, (k2tog, k1, yo) x 2, k19, (yo, k1, k2tog) x 2, k6.
Row 27: K2, yo, k1, k2tog x 2, k1, yo, k2tog, k1, yo, k9, k2tog, yo, k10, yo, k1, k2tog, yo, k1, k2tog x 2, k1, yo, k2.
Row 28: K3, yo, (k1, k2tog) x 2, k1, yo, k23, yo, (k1, k2tog) x 2, k1, yo, k3.
Row 29: K4, yo, k1, k2tog, k12, k2tog, yo, k1, yo, k2tog, k12, k2tog, k1, yo, k4.

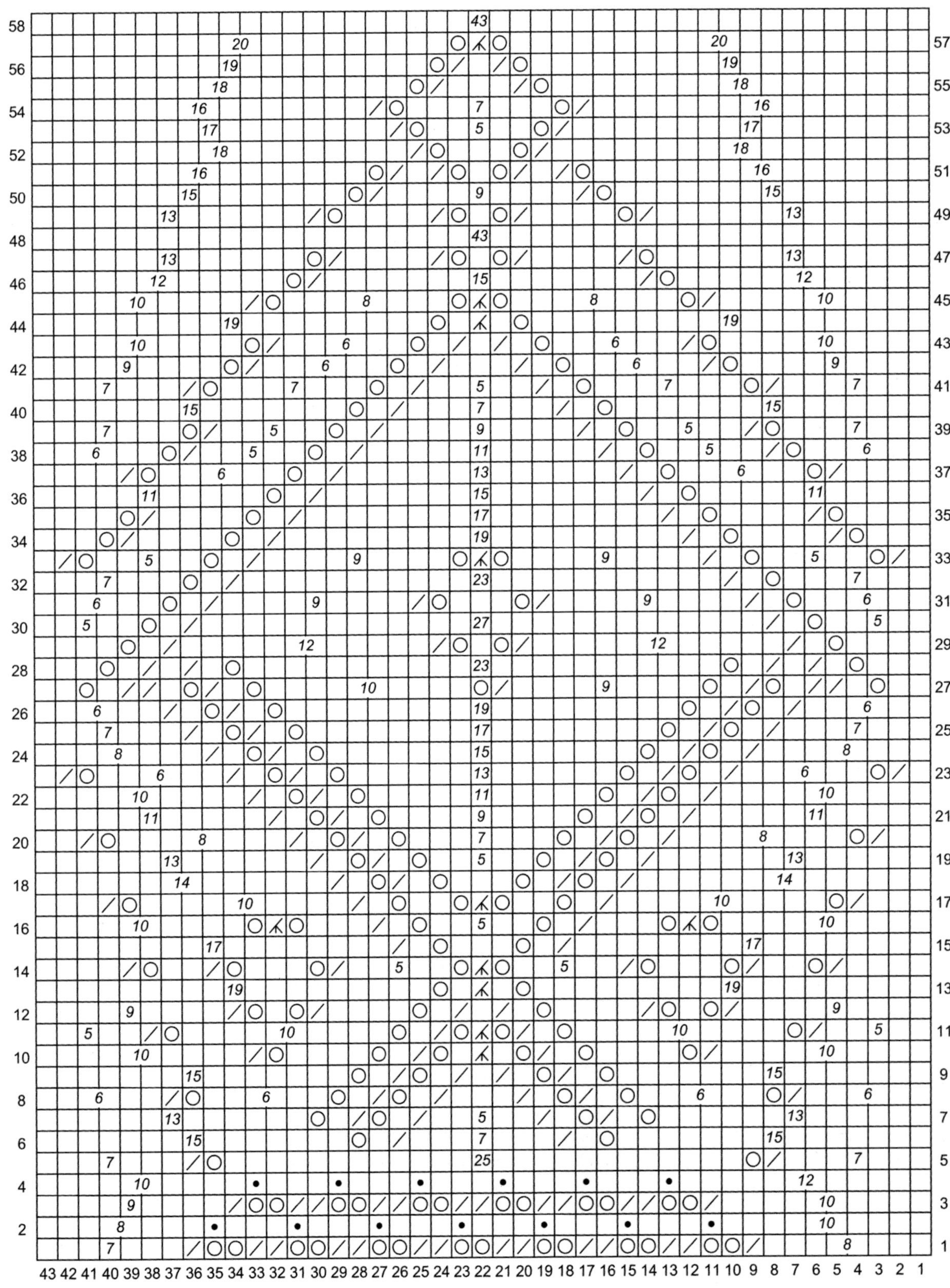

Crown 2 chart.

Row 30: K5, yo, k1, k2tog, k27, k2tog, k1, yo, k5.
Row 31: K6, yo, k1, k2tog, k9, k2tog, yo, k3, yo, k2tog, k9, k2tog, k1, yo, k6.
Row 32: K7, yo, k1, k2tog, k23, k2tog, k1, yo, k7.
Row 33: K1, k2tog, yo, k5, yo, k1, k2tog, k9, yo, k3tog, yo, k9, k2tog, k1, yo, k5, yo, k2tog, k1.
Row 34: K3, yo, k2tog, k4, yo, k1, k2tog, k19, k2tog, k1, yo, k4, k2tog, yo, k3.
Row 35: K4, yo, k2tog, k4, yo, k1, k2tog, k17, k2tog, k1, yo, k4, k2tog, yo, k4.
Row 36: K11, yo, k1, k2tog, k15, k2tog, k1, yo, k11.
Row 37: K4, k2tog, yo, k6, yo, k1, k2tog, k13, k2tog, k1, yo, k6, yo, k2tog, k4.
Row 38: K6, yo, k2tog, k5, yo, k1, k2tog, k11, k2tog, k1, yo, k5, k2tog, yo, k6.
Row 39: K7, yo, k2tog, k5, yo, k1, k2tog, k9, k2tog, k1, yo, k5, k2tog, yo, k7.
Row 40: Repeat row 6.
Row 41: K7, k2tog, yo, k7, yo, k1, k2tog, k5, k2tog, k1, yo, k7, yo, k2tog, k7.
Row 42: K9, yo, k2tog, k6, yo, k1, k2tog, k3, k2tog, k1, yo, k6, k2tog, yo, k9.
Row 43: K10, yo, k2tog, k6, yo, (k1, k2tog) x 2, k1, yo, k6, k2tog, yo, k10.
Row 44: K19, yo, k1, p3tog, k1, yo, k19.
Row 45: K10, k2tog, yo, k8, yo, k3tog, yo, k8, yo, k2tog, k10.
Row 46: K12, yo, k2tog, k15, k2tog, yo, k12.
Row 47: K13, yo, k2tog, k4, k2tog, yo, k1, yo, k2tog, k4, k2tog, yo, k13.
Row 48: Knit.
Row 49: K13, k2tog, yo, k4, k2tog, yo, k1, yo, k2tog, k4, yo, k2tog, k13.
Row 50: K15, yo, k2tog, k9, k2tog, yo, k15.
Row 51: K16, yo, k2tog, k1, k2tog, yo, k1, yo, k2tog, k1, k2tog, yo, k16.
Row 52: K18, k2tog, yo, k3, yo, k2tog, k18.
Row 53: K17, k2tog, yo, k5, yo, k2tog, k17.
Row 54: K16, k2tog, yo, k7, yo, k2tog, k16.
Row 55: K18, yo, k2tog, k3, k2tog, yo, k18.
Row 56: K19, yo, k2tog, k1, k2tog, yo, k19.
Row 57: K20, yo, k3tog, yo, k20.
Row 58: Knit.

5.3

St. Edward's Crown

TEX 2020.2 Bed jacket

This design is in the shape of St. Edward's Crown, the current crown used in the British royal coronation ceremony. It is surrounded by a pretty and feminine border in Eyelid stitch. There is little known about the provenance of the bed jacket but it was a very popular type of garment made in Shetland lace in the 1920s and 1930s. The Crown design is nearly the same as that used in a stole made for the coronation of George VI and Elizabeth in 1937.

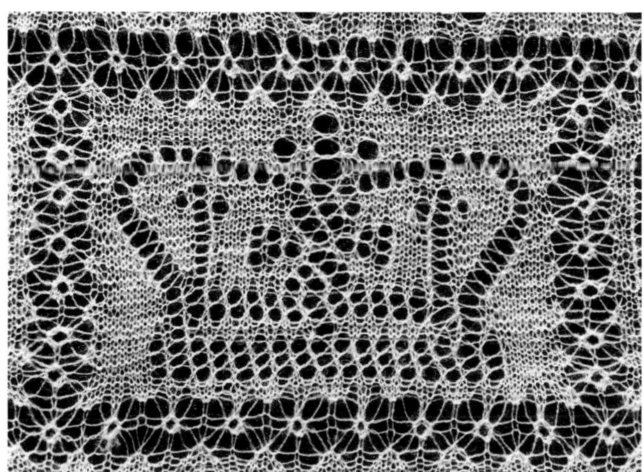

St Edward's Crown original pattern.

Rows 1–2: (K1, k2tog, yo, k1, yo, k2tog) x 10, k1. (61 sts)
Row 3: K2tog, (yo, k3, yo, k3tog) x 9, yo, k3, yo, k2tog.
Row 4: Knit.
Row 5: (K1, yo, k2tog, yo, k3tog, yo) x 10, k1.
Row 6: Knit.
Row 7: K2, (yo, k3tog, yo, k3) x 9, yo, k3tog, yo, k2.
Row 8: Knit.
Rows 9–10: K1, k2tog, yo, k1, yo, k2tog, k49, k2tog, yo, k1, yo, k2tog, k1.
Row 11: K2tog, yo, k3, yo, k2tog, k47, k2tog, yo, k3, yo, k2tog.
Row 12: Knit.
Row 13: K1, yo, k2tog, yo, k3tog, yo, k8, (yo, k2tog) x 17, k7, yo, k2tog, yo, k3tog, yo, k1.
Row 14: Knit.
Row 15: K2, yo, k3tog, yo, k9, (yo, k2tog) x 17, k8, yo, k3tog, yo, k2.
Row 16: Repeat row 9.

Stole made for the Coronation of George VI and Queen Elizabeth in 1937.

St Edward's Crown knitted sample.

Row 17: K1, k2tog, yo, k1, yo, k2tog, k8, (yo, k2tog) x 17, k7, k2tog, yo, k1, yo, k2tog, k1.

Row 18: Repeat row 11.

Row 19: Knit.

Row 20: K1, yo, p3tog, yo, k2tog, yo, k49, yo, p3tog, yo, k2tog, yo, k1.

Row 21: Knit.

Row 22: K2, yo, p3tog, yo, k51, yo, p3tog, yo, k2.

Row 23: K16, (yo, k2tog) x 13, yo, k3tog, yo, k16.

Row 24: Repeat row 9.

Row 25: K1, k2tog, yo, k1, yo, k2tog, k10, (yo, k2tog) x 13, yo, k3tog, yo, k10, k2tog, yo, k1, yo, k2tog, k1.

Row 26: Repeat row 11.

Row 27: K14, k2tog, yo, k2, yo, k2tog, k21, k2tog, yo, k2, yo, k2tog, k14.

Row 28: K1, yo, p3tog, yo, k2tog, yo, k22, (yo, k2tog) x 3, k21, yo, p3tog, yo, k2tog, yo, k1.

Row 29: K13, k2tog, yo, k3, yo, k2tog, k21, k2tog, yo, k3, yo, k2tog, k13.

Row 30: K2, yo, p3tog, yo, k24, (yo, k2tog) x 2, k23, yo, p3tog, yo, k2.

Row 31: K1, k2tog, yo, k1, yo, k2tog, k6, k2tog, yo, k4, yo, k2tog, k21, k2tog, yo, k4, yo, k2tog, k6, k2tog, yo, k1, yo, k2tog, k1.

Row 32: K1, k2tog, yo, k1, yo, k2tog, k17, k2tog, yo, k5, yo, k2tog, k4, yo, k2tog, k17, k2tog, yo, k1, yo, k2tog, k1.

Row 33: K2tog, yo, k3, yo, k2tog, k4, k2tog, yo, k5, yo, k2tog, k6, yo, k2tog, k5, k2tog, yo, k6, k2tog, yo, k5, yo, k2tog, k4, k2tog, yo, k3, yo, k2tog.

Row 34: K23, k2tog, yo, k3, yo, k2tog, k1, k2tog, yo, k3, yo, k2tog, k23.

Row 35: K1, yo, k2tog, yo, k3tog, yo, k4, k2tog, yo, (k6, yo, k2tog) x 2, k5, (k2tog, yo, k6) x 2, yo, k2tog, k4, yo, k2tog, yo, k3tog, yo, k1.

Row 36: K23, k2tog, yo, k5, yo, k2tog, k4, yo, k2tog, k23.

Row 37: K2, yo, k3tog, yo, k4, k2tog, yo, k7, yo, k2tog, k21, k2tog, yo, k7, yo, k2tog, k4, yo, k3tog, yo, k2.

Row 38: K29, (yo, k2tog) x 2, k28.

Row 39: K1, k2tog, yo, k1, yo, k2tog, k2, k2tog, yo, k8, yo, k2tog, k21, k2tog, yo, k8, yo, k2tog, k2, k2tog, yo, k1, yo, k2tog, k1.

Row 40: K1, k2tog, yo, k1, yo, k2tog, k22, (yo, k2tog) x 3, k21, k2tog, yo, k1, yo, k2tog, k1.

Row 41: K2tog, yo, k3, yo, k2tog, k2, yo, k2tog, k5, (yo, k2tog) x 3, k17, (k2tog, yo) x 3, k5, k2tog, yo, k2, k2tog, yo, k3, yo, k2tog.

Row 42: Knit.

Row 43: K1, yo, k2tog, yo, k3tog, yo, k3, yo, k2tog, k7, yo, k2tog, k21, k2tog, yo, k7, k2tog, yo, k3, yo, k2tog, yo, k3tog, yo, k1.

Row 44: K27, (k2tog, yo) x 3, k28.

Row 45: K2, yo, k3tog, yo, k5, yo, k2tog, k13, k2tog, yo, k7, yo, k2tog, k13, k2tog, yo, k5, yo, k3tog, yo, k2.

Row 46: K1, k2tog, yo, k1, yo, k2tog, k17, k2tog, yo, k11, yo, k2tog, k17, k2tog, yo, k1, yo, k2tog, k1.

Row 47: K1, k2tog, yo, k1, yo, k2tog, k5, yo, k2tog, k8, k2tog, yo, k6, k2tog, yo x 2, k2tog, k5, yo, k2tog, k8, k2tog, yo, k5, k2tog, yo, k1, yo, k2tog, k1.

Row 48: K2tog, yo, k3, yo, k2tog, k12, k2tog, yo, k8, p1, k10, yo, k2tog, k12, k2tog, yo, k3, yo, k2tog.

Row 49: K12, yo, k2tog, k3, k2tog, yo, k23, yo, k2tog, k3, k2tog, yo, k12.

Row 50: K1, yo, p3tog, yo, k2tog, yo, k7, (k2tog, yo) x 2, k27, (yo, k2tog) x 2, k7, yo, p3tog, yo, k2tog, yo, k1.

Row 51: K25, k2tog, (yo x 2, k2tog x 2) x 2, yo x 2, k2tog, k24.

Row 52: K2, yo, p3tog, yo, k20, (p1, k3) x 2, p1, k22, yo, p3tog, yo, k2.

Row 53: Knit.

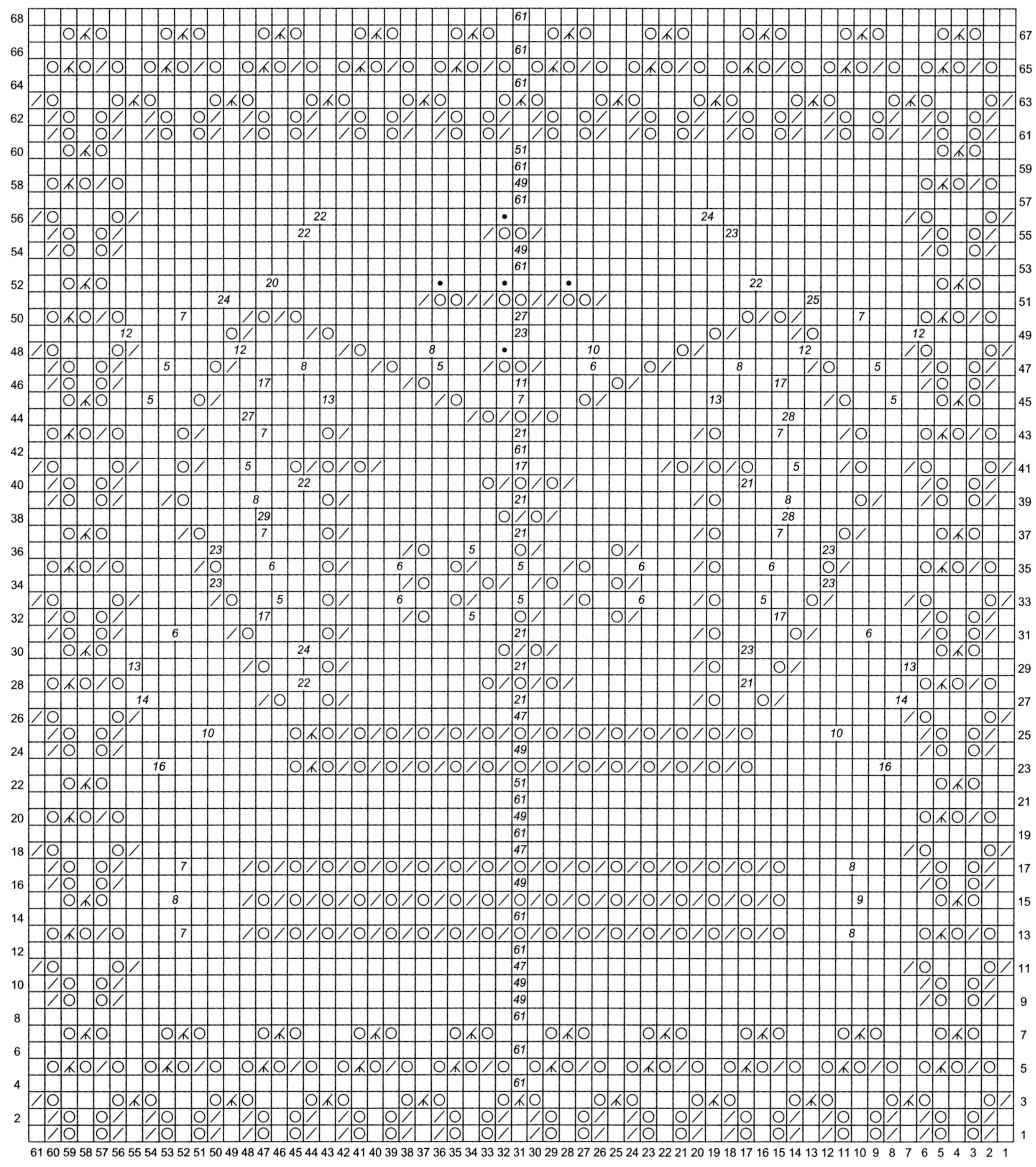

St Edward's Crown chart.

Row 54: Repeat row 9.
Row 55: K1, k2tog, yo, k1, yo, k2tog, k23, k2tog, yo x 2, k2tog, k22, k2tog, yo, k1, yo, k2tog, k1.
Row 56: K2tog, yo, k3, yo, k2tog, k22, p1, k24, k2tog, yo, k3, yo, k2tog.
Row 57: Knit.
Row 58: Repeat row 20.
Row 59: Knit.
Row 60: Repeat row 22.
Rows 61–62: (K1, k2tog, yo, k1, yo, k2tog) x 10, k1.
Row 63: Repeat row 3.
Row 64: Knit.
Row 65: Repeat row 5.
Row 66: Knit.
Row 67: Repeat row 7.
Row 68: Knit.

5.4

Cross pattée

TEX 2020.2 Bed jacket

The cross *pattée* was used increasingly with the crown as a symbol of royalty. Eyelid stitch in the arms of the Cross and decorative stitches in the centre suggest it is modelled after the cross *pattée* decorating St Edward's Crown. The design was used with the Cross to make a border for a bed jacket, and may not have been associated with a royal gift. It is an example of designs borrowed or influenced by patterns seen elsewhere, but in this application it would not be seen publicly. Like the Crown in the same garment, it is surrounded by a border in Eyelid stitch to add a feminine touch to this intimate garment.

Rows 1–2: (K1, k2tog, yo, k1, yo, k2tog) x 10, k1. (61 sts)
Row 3: K2tog, (yo, k3, yo, k3tog) x 9, yo, k3, yo, k2tog.
Row 4: Knit.
Row 5: (K1, yo, k2tog, yo, k3tog, yo) x 10, k1.
Row 6: Knit.

Cross pattée original pattern.

Row 7: K2, (yo, k3tog, yo, k3) x 9, yo, k3tog, yo, k2.
Row 8: Knit.
Rows 9–10: K1, k2tog, yo, k1, yo, k2tog, k49, k2tog, yo, k1, yo, k2tog, k1.
Row 11: K2tog, yo, k3, yo, k2tog, k47, k2tog, yo, k3, yo, k2tog.
Row 12: Knit.
Row 13: K1, yo, k2tog, yo, k3tog, yo, k8, (yo, k2tog) x 17, k7, yo, k2tog, yo, k3tog, yo, k1.
Row 14: Knit.
Row 15: K2, yo, k3tog, yo, k11, yo, k2tog, k25, k2tog, yo, k11, yo, k3tog, yo, k2.
Row 16: K1, (k2tog, yo, k1, yo, k2tog, k22) x 2, k2tog, yo, k1, yo, k2tog, k1.
Row 17: K1, k2tog, yo, k1, yo, k2tog, k12, yo, k2tog, k8, k2tog, yo, k1, yo, k2tog, k8, k2tog, yo, k12, k2tog, yo, k1, yo, k2tog, k1.
Row 18: K2tog, yo, k3, yo, k2tog, k1, k2tog, yo, k17, k2tog, yo, k3, yo, k2tog, k17, yo, k2tog, k1, k2tog, yo, k3, yo, k2tog.

Cross pattée knitted sample.

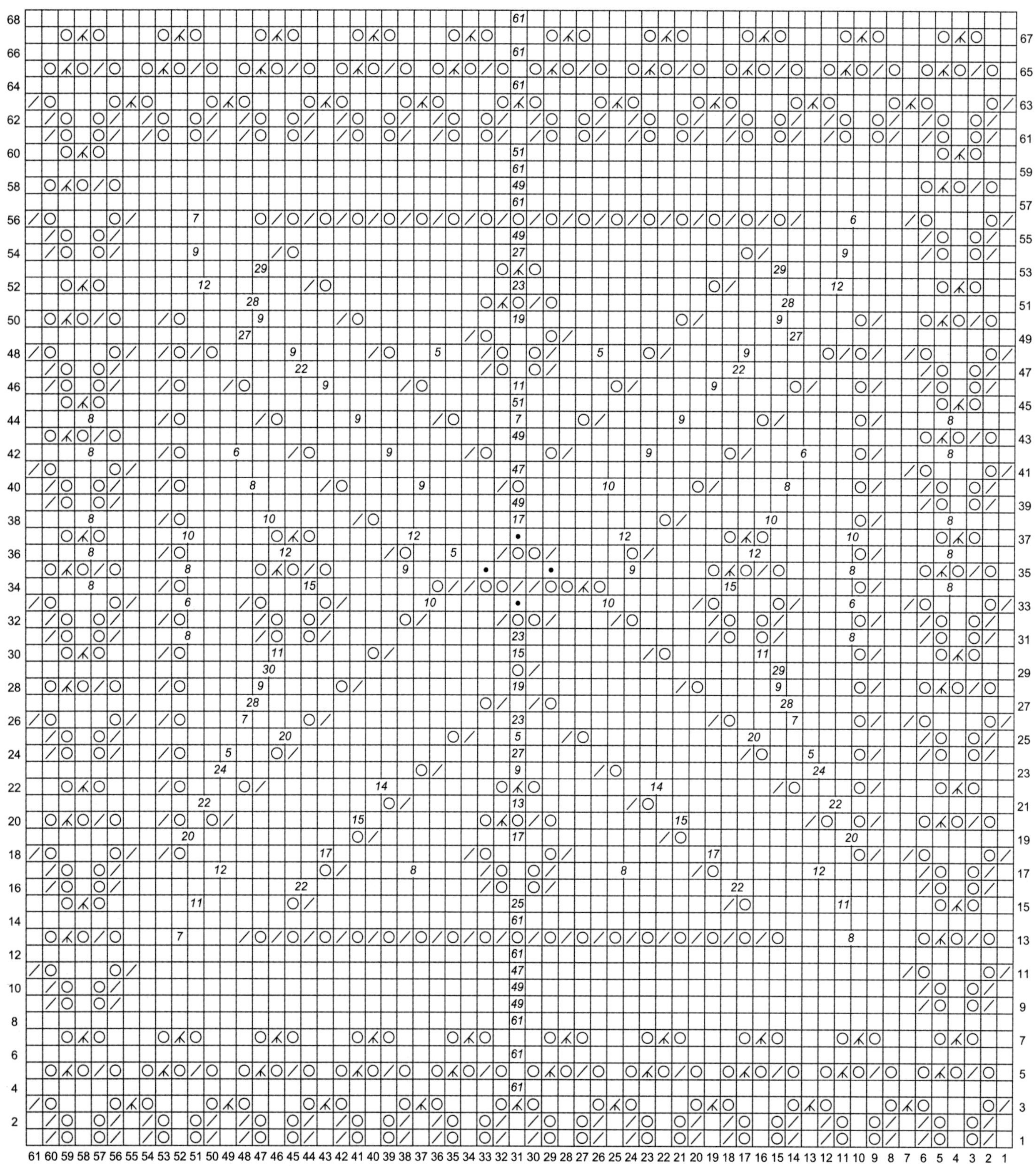

Cross pattée chart.

Row 19: K20, yo, k2tog, k17, k2tog, yo, k20.
Row 20: K1, yo, p3tog, yo, k2tog, yo, k2, k2tog, yo, k1, yo, k2tog, k15, yo, p3tog, yo, k2tog, yo, k15, k2tog, yo, k1, yo, k2tog, k2, yo, p3tog, yo, k2tog, yo, k1.
Row 21: K22, yo, k2tog, k13, k2tog, yo, k22.
Row 22: K2, yo, p3tog, yo, k3, k2tog, yo, k3, yo, k2tog, k14, yo, p3tog, yo, k14, k2tog, yo, k3, yo, k2tog, k3, yo, p3tog yo, k2.
Row 23: K24, yo, k2tog, k9, k2tog, yo, k24.
Row 24: K1, k2tog, yo, k1, yo, k2tog, k2, k2tog, yo, k5, yo, k2tog, k27, k2tog, yo, k5, yo, k2tog, k2, k2tog, yo, k1, yo, k2tog, k1.
Row 25: K1, k2tog, yo, k1, yo, k2tog, k20, yo, k2tog, k5, k2tog, yo, k20, k2tog, yo, k1, yo, k2tog, k1.
Row 26: K2tog, yo, k3, yo, k2tog, k1, k2tog, yo, k7, yo, k2tog, k23, k2tog, yo, k7, yo, k2tog, k1, k2tog, yo, k3, yo, k2tog.
Row 27: K28, yo, k2tog, k1, k2tog, yo, k28.
Row 28: K1, yo, p3tog, yo, k2tog, yo, k2, k2tog, yo, k9, yo, k2tog, k19, k2tog, yo, k9, yo, k2tog, k2, yo, p3tog, yo, k2tog, yo, k1.
Row 29: K29, k2tog, yo, k30.
Row 30: K2, yo, p3tog, yo, k3, k2tog, yo, k11, yo, k2tog, k15, k2tog, yo, k11, yo, k2tog, k3, yo, p3tog, yo, k2.
Row 31: K1, k2tog, yo, k1, yo, k2tog, k8, k2tog, yo, k1, yo, k2tog, k23, k2tog, yo, k1, yo, k2tog, k8, k2tog, yo, k1, yo, k2tog, k1.
Row 32: K1, k2tog, yo, k1, yo, k2tog, k2, k2tog, yo, k4, k2tog, yo, k1, (yo, k2tog, k4) x 2, k2tog, yo x 2, k2tog, k3, k2tog, yo, k4, k2tog, yo, k1, yo, k2tog, k4, yo, k2tog, k2, k2tog, yo, k1, yo, k2tog, k1.
Row 33: K2tog, yo, k3, yo, k2tog, k6, k2tog, yo, k3, yo, k2tog, k10, p1, k10, k2tog, yo, k3, yo, k2tog, k6, k2tog, yo, k3, yo, k2tog.
Row 34: K8, k2tog, yo, k15, yo, (k2tog x 2, yo x 2) x 2, p3tog, yo, k15, yo, k2tog, k8.
Row 35: K1, yo, k2tog, yo, k3tog, yo, k8, yo, k2tog, yo, k3tog, yo, k9, p1, k3, p1, k9, yo, k2tog, yo, k3tog, yo, k8, yo, k2tog, yo, k3tog, yo, k1.
Row 36: K8, k2tog, yo, k12, k2tog, yo, k5, k2tog, yo x 2, k2tog, k4, yo, k2tog, k12, yo, k2tog, k8.
Row 37: K2, yo, k3tog, yo, k10, yo, k3tog, yo, k12, p1, k12, yo, k3tog, yo, k10, yo, k3tog, yo, k2.
Row 38: K8, k2tog, yo, k10, k2tog, yo, k17, yo, k2tog, k10, yo, k2tog, k8.
Row 39: Repeat row 9.
Row 40: K1, k2tog, yo, k1, yo, k2tog, k2, k2tog, yo, k8, k2tog, yo, k9, k2tog, yo, k10, yo, k2tog, k8, yo, k2tog, k2, k2tog, yo, k1, yo, k2tog, k1.
Row 41: Repeat row 11.
Row 42: K8, k2tog, yo, k6, k2tog, yo, k9, k2tog, yo, k3, yo, k2tog, k9, yo, k2tog, k6, yo, k2tog, k8.
Row 43: K1, yo, k2tog, yo, k3tog, yo, k49, yo, k2tog, yo, k3tog, yo, k1.
Row 44: K8, k2tog, yo, k4, k2tog, yo, k9, k2tog, yo, k7, yo, k2tog, k9, yo, k2tog, k4, yo, k2tog, k8.
Row 45: K2, yo, k3tog, yo, k51, yo, k3tog, yo, k2.
Row 46: K1, k2tog, yo, k1, yo, k2tog, (k2, k2tog, yo) x 2, k9, k2tog, yo, k11, yo, k2tog, k9, (yo, k2tog, k2) x 2, k2tog, yo, k1, yo, k2tog, k1.
Row 47: Repeat row 16.
Row 48: K2tog, yo, k3, yo, k2tog, k1, (k2tog, yo) x 2, k9, k2tog, yo, k5, k2tog, yo, k1, yo, k2tog, k5, yo, k2tog, k9, (yo, k2tog) x 2, k1, k2tog, yo, k3, yo, k2tog.
Row 49: K27, k2tog, yo, k3, yo, k2tog, k27.
Row 50: K1, yo, p3tog, yo, k2tog, yo, k2, k2tog, yo, k9, k2tog, yo, k19, yo, k2tog, k9, yo, k2tog, k2, yo, p3tog, yo, k2tog, yo, k1.
Row 51: K28, yo, k2tog, yo, k3tog, yo, k28.
Row 52: K2, yo, p3tog, yo, k12, k2tog, yo, k23, yo, k2tog, k12, yo, p3tog, yo, k2.
Row 53: K29, yo, k3tog, yo, k29.
Row 54: K1, k2tog, yo, k1, yo, k2tog, k9, k2tog, yo, k27, yo, k2tog, k9, k2tog, yo, k1, yo, k2tog, k1.
Row 55: Repeat row 9.
Row 56: K2tog, yo, k3, yo, k2tog, k7, (yo, k2tog) x 17, k6, k2tog, yo, k3, yo, k2tog.
Row 57: Knit.
Row 58: K1, yo, p3tog, yo, k2tog, yo, k49, yo, p3tog, yo, k2tog, yo, k1.
Row 59: Knit.
Row 60: K2, yo, p3tog, yo, k51, yo, p3tog, yo, k2.
Rows 61–62: (K1, k2tog, yo, k1, yo, k2tog) x 10, k1.
Row 63: Repeat row 3.
Row 64: Knit.
Row 65: Repeat row 5.
Row 66: Knit.
Row 67: Repeat row 7.
Row 68: Knit.

CHAPTER 6

LACE EDGES, INNER LACE EDGES, AND AN INNER BORDER

The most common Shetland lace garments – stoles, scarves and shawls – have three main components: a centre, two or four borders, and a lace edge. As a separate but important part of lace design and construction, the lace edge helped to define Shetland lace and set it apart from attempted copies of the craft. Many early knitting patterns, and the later machine-knitted lace made to mimic hand-made Shetland lace, did not include a separately worked lace edge. All Shetland lace garments, including blouses, mitts, veils, and stockings, generally have a lace edge. The choice of lace edge pattern or combined patterns usually complements the size of the piece, its complexity of design, and sometimes it mirrors specific patterns found elsewhere in the design. The lace edge enhances the pretty laciness of the piece and finishes its edges in a decorative way.

Some garments have one or more additional bands knitted alongside the lace edge. We have referred to these elements as 'inner lace edges' because of their location and relationship with the lace edge. In some later blouses they became important parts of the main body design.

Some shawls also have what we have termed an 'inner border'. These are one or more bands worked around the top of the border, usually a continuous horizontal pattern or very small motifs worked in a horizontal line. They appear set apart from the main border design and visually frame the centre but constructively are not part of it.

LACE EDGES

A lace edge's main function is to give the garment a defined edge. It may be a simple single pattern or be very elaborate, incorporating two or more patterns. The lace edge is typically scalloped, some low and rounded, others having defined points with sharp peaks. The choice of a lace edge may incorporate patterns from the border or centre, providing design correlation and cohesion among parts of the garment. The lace edge's 'weight', where a significant amount of plain knitting gives it more weight and the use of open patterns less weight, often compares favourably with the overall size, yarn weight, knitting gauge and design of the whole garment. In the finest pieces, where very decorative lace edges are often used, it adds to the ethereal nature and prettiness of the design. The lace edge is knitted as a long, narrow strip, the stitches lying perpendicular to the border fabric.

The lace edge and two inner lace edges of an exquisite late-1920s blouse. (TEX 2020.5)

6.1

Lace edge of Lace Holes, variation 1

TEX 1997.84 Shawl

Lace Holes in a single Zigzag form the middle of this lace edge, while each peak is made of nine Lace Holes.

Row 1 (WS): Yo, k3, yo, k2tog, k1, p1, k3, yo, k2tog, k8. (21 sts)
Row 2 (RS): K7, k2tog, yo, k1, k2tog, yo x 2, k2tog x 2, yo, k5.
Row 3: Yo, k6, yo, k2tog, k1, p1, k3, yo, k2tog, k6. (22 sts)
Row 4: K5, k2tog, yo, k1, k2tog, yo x 2, k2tog x 2, yo, k1, k2tog, yo x 2, k2tog, k3.
Row 5: Yo, k5, p1, k3, yo, k2tog, k1, p1, k3, yo, k2tog, k4. (23 sts)
Row 6: K3, k2tog, (yo, k1, k2tog, yo x 2, k2tog x 2) x 2, yo x 2, k2tog, k2.
Row 7: Yo, k4, (p1, k3) x 2, yo, k2tog, k1, p1, k3, yo, k2tog, k2. (24 sts)

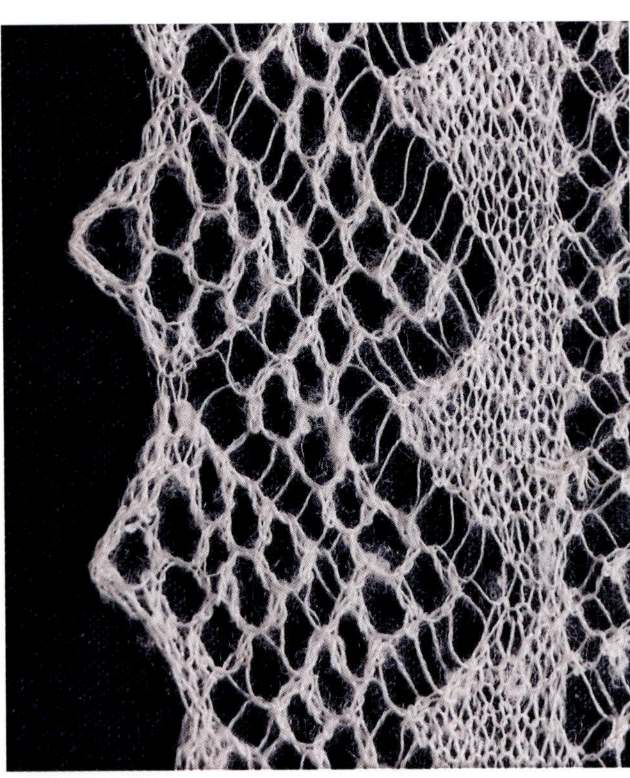

Lace edge of Lace Holes, variation 1 original pattern.

Lace edge of Lace Holes, variation 1 knitted sample.

Row 8: K1, k2tog, (yo, k1, k2tog, yo x 2, k2tog x 2) x 2, yo x 2, k2tog x 2, yo x 2, k2tog, k1.
Row 9: Yo, k2tog, k1, (p1, k3) x 2, p1, k2tog, yo, k4, p1, k2tog, yo, k3.
Row 10: K4, yo, k2tog x 2, yo x 2, k2tog, k1, yo, (k2tog x 2, yo x 2) x 2, k2tog, k1, k2tog. (23 sts)
Row 11: Yo, k2tog, k2, p1, k3, p1, k2tog, yo, k4, p1, k2tog, yo, k5.
Row 12: K6, yo, k2tog x 2, yo x 2, k2tog, k1, yo, k2tog x 2, yo x 2, k2tog, k2, k2tog. (22 sts)
Row 13: Yo, k2tog, k3, p1, k2tog, yo, k4, p1, k2tog, yo, k7.
Row 14: K8, yo, k2tog x 2, yo x 2, k2tog, k1, yo, k2tog, k3, k2tog. (21 sts)
Row 15: Yo, k2tog, k1, k2tog, yo, k4, p1, k2tog, yo, k9.
Row 16: K10, yo, k2tog x 2, yo x 2, k2tog, k1, yo, k2tog x 2. (20 sts)

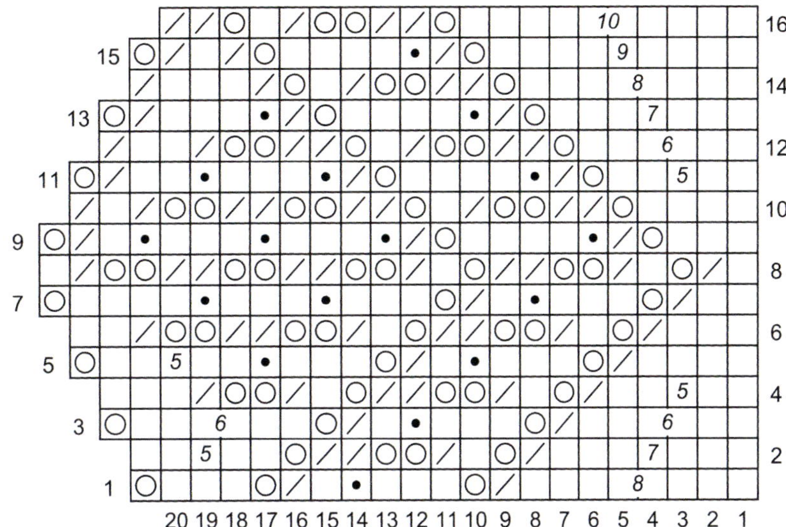

Lace edge of Lace Holes, variation 1 chart.

6.2

Lace edge of Lace Holes, variation 2

TEX 2004.171 Stole

This lace edge is nearly the reverse design of Pattern 6.1. Here the Zigzag of Lace Holes is placed at the outer edge, while a triangle of twenty Lace Holes forms the edge on the inside.

Lace edge of Lace Holes, variation 2 original pattern.

Row 1 (WS): K3, yo, k4, p1, (k2tog, yo) x 2, k4, p1, k2. (20 sts)
Row 2 (RS): K3, k2tog, yo x 2, k2tog, k1, yo, k2tog, yo, k2tog x 2, yo x 2, k2tog, k1, yo, k3. (21 sts)
Row 3: K3, yo, k4, p1, (k2tog, yo) x 2, k4, p1, k4. (22 sts)
Row 4: K1, k2tog, yo x 2, k2tog x 2, yo x 2, k2tog, k1, yo, k2tog, yo, k2tog x 2, yo x 2, k2tog, k1, yo, k3. (23 sts)
Row 5: K3, yo, k4, p1, (k2tog, yo) x 2, k4, p1, k3, p1, k2. (24 sts)

Lace edge of Lace Holes, variation 2 knitted sample.

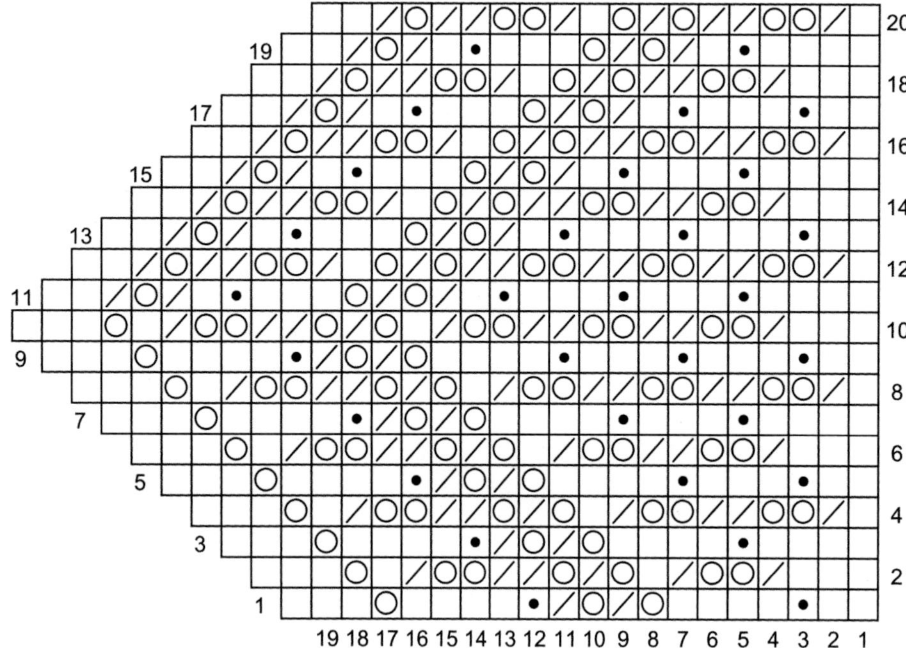

Lace edge of Lace Holes, variation 2 chart.

Row 6: K3, k2tog, yo x 2, k2tog x 2, yo x 2, k2tog, k1, yo, k2tog, yo, k2tog x 2, yo x 2, k2tog, k1, yo, k3. (25 sts)
Row 7: K3, yo, k4, p1, (k2tog, yo) x 2, k4, p1, k3, p1, k4. (26 sts)
Row 8: K1, k2tog, (yo x 2, k2tog x 2) x 2, yo x 2, k2tog, k1, yo, k2tog, yo, k2tog x 2, yo x 2, k2tog, k1, yo, k3. (27 sts)
Row 9: K3, yo, k4, p1, (k2tog, yo) x 2, k4, (p1, k3) x 2, p1, k2. (28 sts)
Row 10: K3, k2tog, (yo x 2, k2tog x 2) x 2, yo x 2, k2tog, k1, yo, k2tog, yo, k2tog x 2, yo x 2, k2tog, k1, yo, k3. (29 sts)
Row 11: K2, k2tog, yo, k2tog, k1, p1, k3, (yo, k2tog) x 2, k1, (p1, k3) x 2, p1, k4. (28 sts)
Row 12: K1, k2tog, (yo x 2, k2tog x 2) x 2, yo x 2, k2tog x 2, yo, k2tog, yo, k1, k2tog, yo x 2, k2tog x 2, yo, k2tog, k2. (27 sts)
Row 13: K2, k2tog, yo, k2tog, k1, p1, k3, (yo, k2tog) x 2, k1, (p1, k3) x 2, p1, k2. (26 sts)
Row 14: K3, k2tog, (yo x 2, k2tog x 2) x 2, yo, k2tog, yo, k1, k2tog, yo x 2, k2tog x 2, yo, k2tog, k2. (25 sts)
Row 15: K2, k2tog, yo, k2tog, k1, p1, k3, (yo, k2tog) x 2, k1, p1, k3, p1, k4. (24 sts)
Row 16: K1, k2tog, (yo x 2, k2tog x 2) x 2, yo, k2tog, yo, k1, k2tog, yo x 2, k2tog x 2, yo, k2tog, k2. (23 sts)
Row 17: K2, k2tog, yo, k2tog, k1, p1, k3, (yo, k2tog) x 2, k1, p1, k3, p1, k2. (22 sts)
Row 18: K3, k2tog, yo x 2, k2tog x 2, yo, k2tog, yo, k1, k2tog, yo x 2, k2tog x 2, yo, k2tog, k2. (21 sts)
Row 19: K2, k2tog, yo, k2tog, k1, p1, k3, (yo, k2tog) x 2, k1, p1, k4. (20 sts)
Row 20: K1, k2tog, yo x 2, k2tog x 2, yo, k2tog, yo, k1, k2tog, yo x 2, k2tog x 2, yo, k2tog, k2. (19 sts)

Diamond lace edges

A common design form of lace edge uses Diamonds as the main element, with plain or Lace Hole Zigzags framing the outer edge. Diamonds may be single or in sets of three. They are usually plain knit, but in some cases they have yarn over centres, creating a more complex effect. Although these patterns are very similar, they show how different weights of yarn and gauge affect the look of the pattern.

6.3

Lace edge with single plain Diamond

TEX 2020.3 Blouse

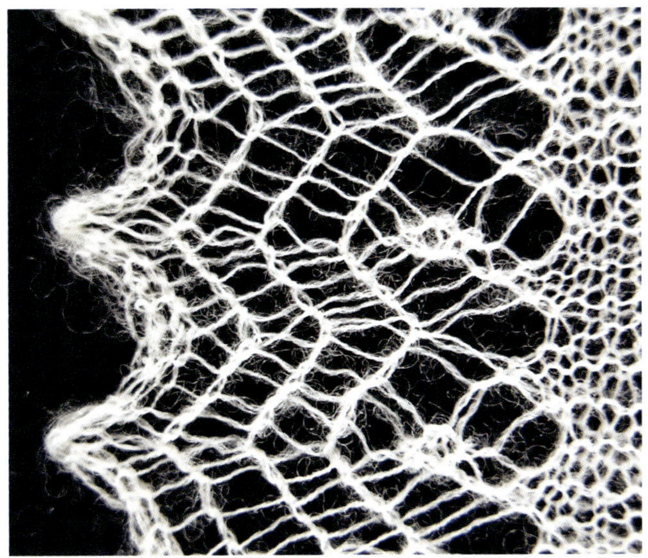

Lace edge with single plain Diamond original pattern.

A single, plain knit Diamond is made very lacy by additional Zigzags. This extends the width of the lace edge without making it excessively weighty in appearance, a bonus for very fine, delicate garments.

Row 1 (RS): K3, (yo, k2tog) x 3, yo, k3. (13 sts)
Row 2 (WS): Yo, k2tog, k1, (yo, k2tog) x 3, yo, k4. (14 sts)
Row 3: K5, (yo, k2tog) x 3, yo, k3. (15 sts)
Row 4: Yo, k2tog, k1, (yo, k2tog) x 3, yo, k1, yo, k2tog, k3. (16 sts)
Row 5: K2, k2tog, yo, k3, (yo, k2tog) x 2, yo, k2tog, yo, k3. (17 sts)
Row 6: Yo, k2tog, k1, (yo, k2tog) x 3, yo, k5, yo, k2tog, k1. (18 sts)
Row 7: K3, yo, k2tog, k1, (k2tog, yo) x 4, k2tog, k2. (17 sts)
Row 8: Yo, k2tog x 2, (yo, k2tog) x 3, yo, p3tog, yo, k4. (16 sts)
Row 9: K4, (k2tog, yo) x 4, k2tog, k2. (15 sts)
Row 10: Yo, k2tog x 2, (yo, k2tog) x 4, k3. (14 sts)
Row 11: K2, (k2tog, yo) x 4, k2tog, k2. (13 sts)
Row 12: Yo, k2tog x 2, (yo, k2tog) x 4, k1. (12 sts)

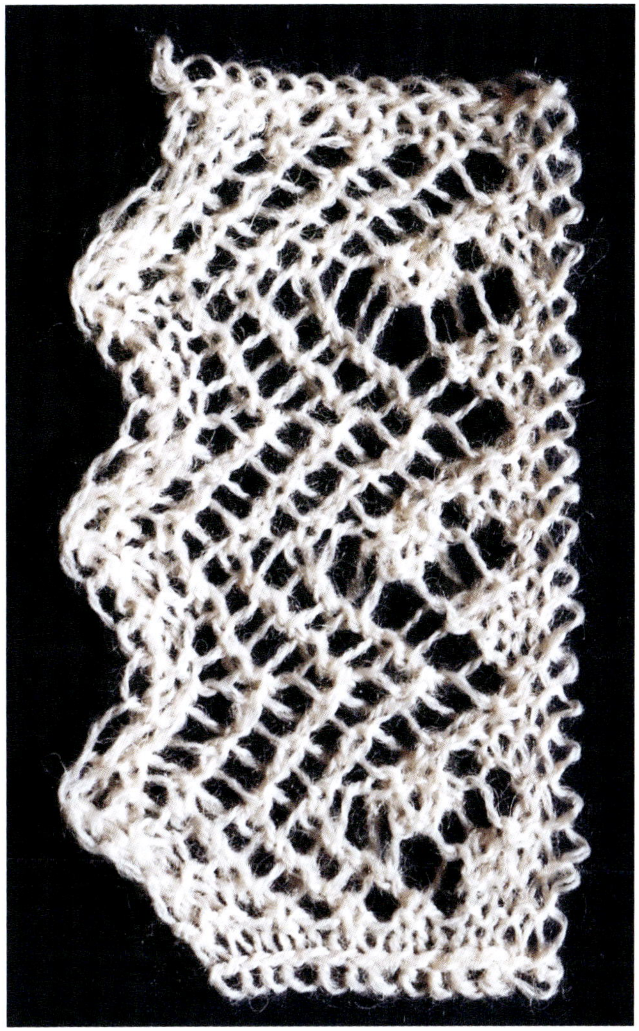

Lace edge with single plain Diamond knitted sample.

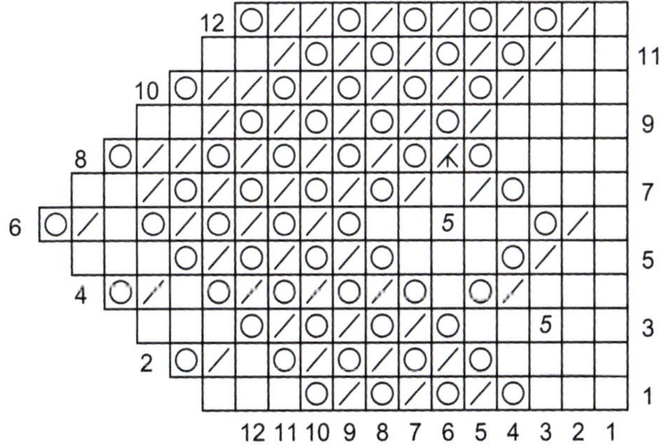

Lace edge with single plain Diamond chart.

6.4

Lace edge with three plain Diamonds

TEX 2014.25 Shawl

This basic pattern for a very open lace edge uses a Zigzag of Lace Holes and three plain Diamonds in the repeat. The Diamond repeats are spaced close together, giving this edge a different appearance than the lace edge in Pattern 6.5.

Row 1 (WS): K3, yo, k2tog, yo, k4, p1, k2tog, yo, k1, yo, k2tog, k3. (19 sts)

Row 2 (RS): K2, k2tog, yo, k3, yo, k2tog x 2, yo x 2, k2tog, k1, yo, k2tog, yo, k3. (20 sts)

Row 3: K3, yo, k2tog, yo, k4, p1, k2tog, yo, k5, yo, k2tog, k1. (21 sts)

Row 4: K2tog, yo, k7, yo, k2tog x 2, yo x 2, k2tog, k1, yo, k2tog, yo, k3. (22 sts)

Row 5: K3, yo, k2tog, yo, k4, p1, k2tog, yo, k1, yo, k2tog, k3, k2tog, yo, k2. (23 sts)

Row 6: K3, yo, k2tog, k1, k2tog, yo, k3, yo, k2tog x 2, yo x 2, k2tog, k1, yo, k2tog, yo, k3. (24 sts)

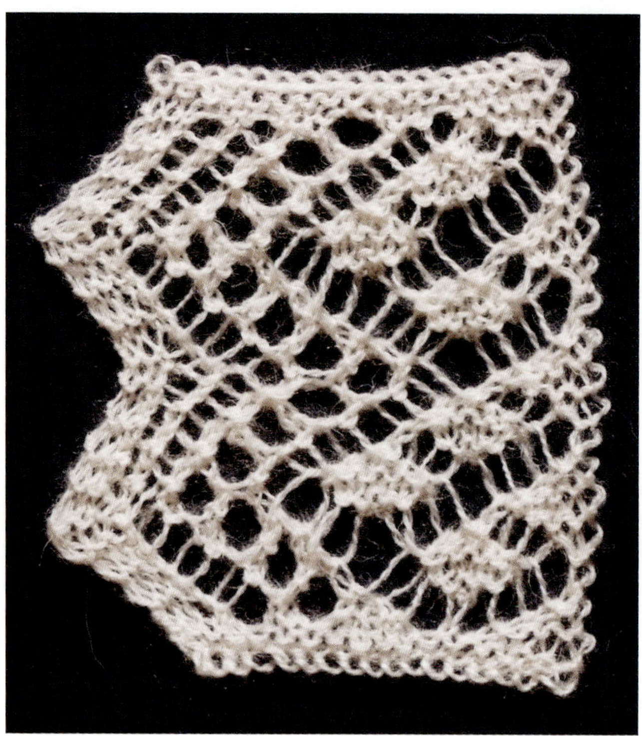

Lace edge with three plain Diamonds knitted sample.

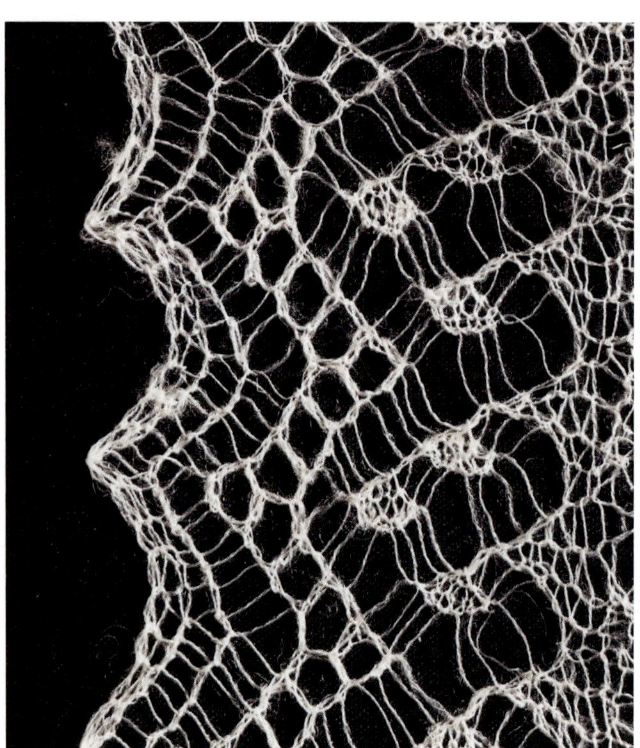

Lace edge with three plain Diamonds original pattern.

Row 7: K3, yo, k2tog, yo, k4, p1, k2tog, yo, k5, yo, k3tog, yo, k4. (25 sts)

Row 8: K4, k2tog, yo, k7, yo, k2tog x 2, yo x 2, k2tog, k1, yo, k2tog, yo, k3. (26 sts)

Row 9: K2, (k2tog, yo) x 2, k2tog, k1, p1, k3, yo, k2tog, k3, k2tog, yo, k1, yo, k2tog, k3. (25 sts)

Row 10: K2, k2tog, yo, k3, yo, k2tog, k1, k2tog, yo, k1, k2tog, yo x 2, k2tog x 2, (yo, k2tog) x 2, k2. (24 sts)

Row 11: K2, (k2tog, yo) x 2, k2tog, k1, p1, k3, yo, k3tog, yo, k5, yo, k2tog, k1. (23 sts)

Row 12: K2tog, yo, k6, k2tog, yo, k1, k2tog, yo x 2, k2tog x 2, (yo, k2tog) x 2, k2. (22 sts)

Row 13: K2, (k2tog, yo) x 2, k2tog, k1, p1, k3, yo, k2tog, k3, k2tog, yo, k2. (21 sts)

Row 14: K3, yo, k2tog, k1, k2tog, yo, k1, k2tog, yo x 2, k2tog x 2, (yo, k2tog) x 2, k2. (20 sts)

Row 15: K2, (k2tog, yo) x 2, k2tog, k1, p1, k3, yo, k3tog, yo, k4. (19 sts)

Row 16: K4, k2tog, yo, k1, k2tog, yo x 2, k2tog x 2, (yo, k2tog) x 2, k2. (18 sts)

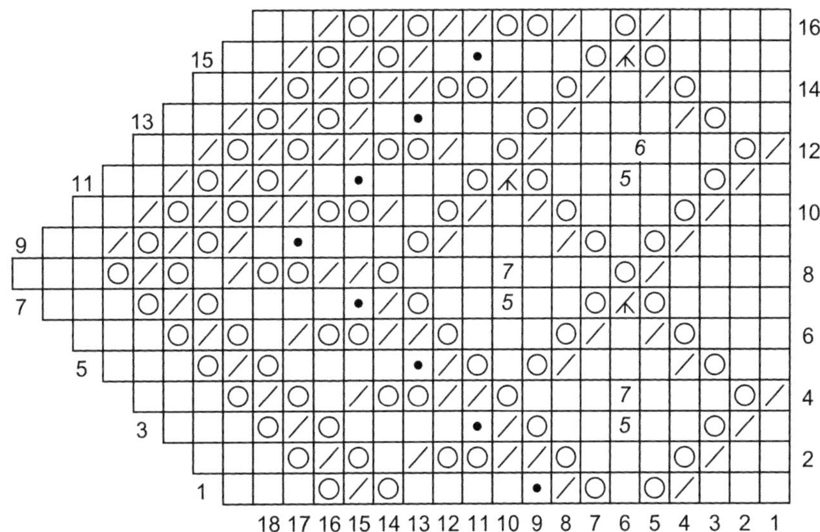

Lace edge with three plain Diamonds chart.

6.5

Lace edge with three Diamonds forming a Heart

TEX 2004.372 Stole

This stole has broken and fuzzy threads due to wear but it has a beautiful and unusual lace edge worth recording. The inner component is a series of three Diamonds placed together to form a sideways heart shape. It is very similar to 6.4 in its construction but the further spacing of the Diamonds away from the Lace Hole Zigzag and in a vertical direction means they are more noticeable.

Row 1 (RS): K1, k2tog, (yo x 2, k2tog x 2) x 2, (yo, k2tog) x 3, k1. (17 sts)
Row 2 (WS): K2, (yo, k2tog) x 2, yo, k4, p1, k3, p1, k2. (18 sts)
Row 3: K3, k2tog, yo x 2, k2tog x 2, yo x 2, k2tog, k1, (yo, k2tog) x 2, yo, k2. (19 sts)
Row 4: K2, (yo, k2tog) x 2, yo, k4, p1, k3, p1, k4. (20 sts)
Row 5: K5, k2tog, yo x 2, k2tog x 2, yo x 2, k2tog, k1, (yo, k2tog) x 2, yo, k2. (21 sts)
Row 6: K2, (yo, k2tog) x 2, yo, k4, p1, k3, p1, k6. (22 sts)
Row 7: K7, k2tog, yo x 2, k2tog x 2, yo x 2, k2tog, k1, (yo, k2tog) x 2, yo, k2. (23 sts)
Row 8: K2, (yo, k2tog) x 2, yo, k4, p1, k3, p1, k8. (24 sts)

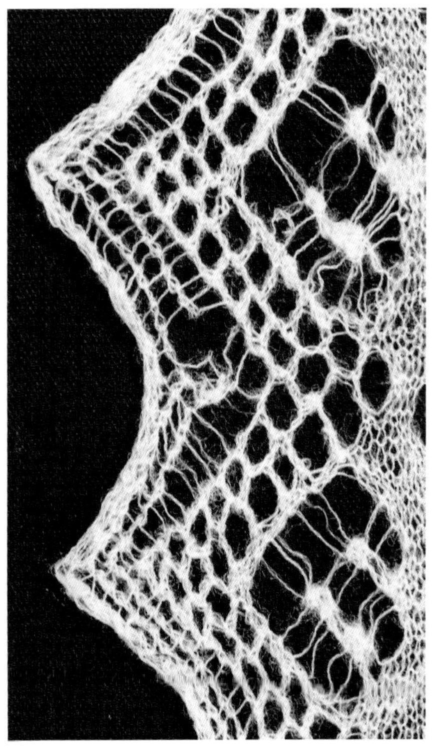

Lace edge with three Diamonds forming a heart original pattern.

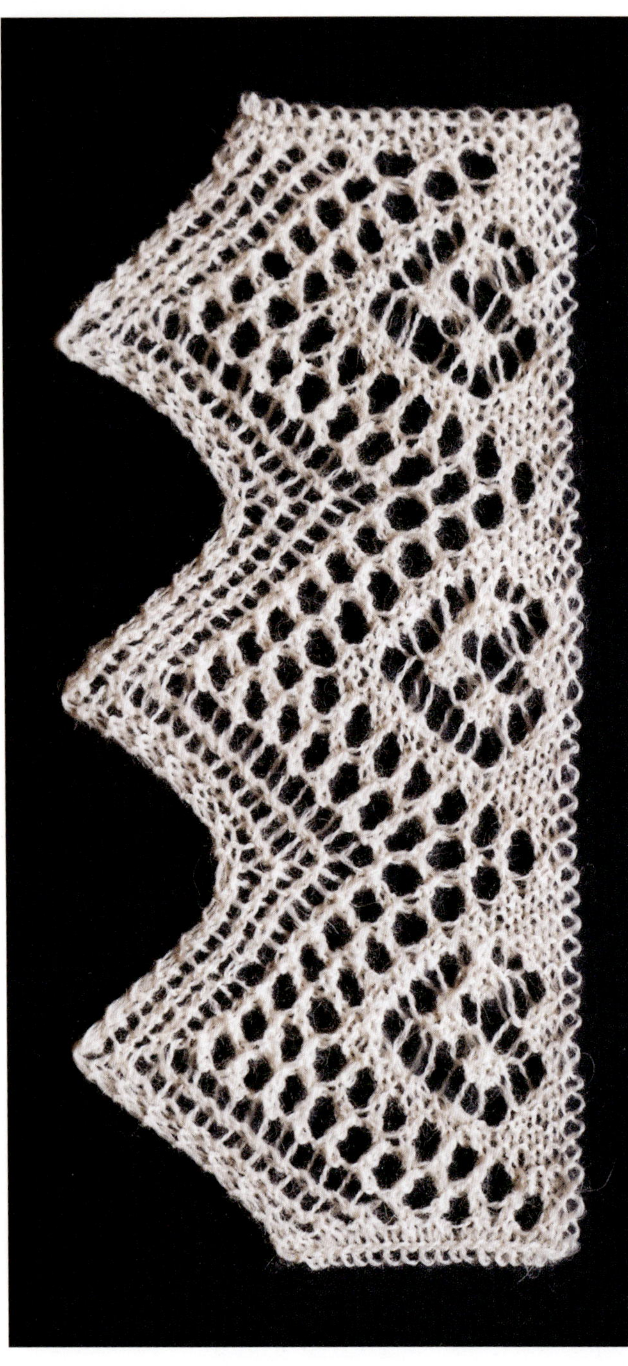

Lace edge with three Diamonds forming a heart knitted sample.

Row 9: K5, yo, k2tog, k2, k2tog, yo x 2, k2tog x 2, yo x 2, k2tog, k1, (yo, k2tog) x 2, yo, k2. (25 sts)
Row 10: K2, (yo, k2tog) x 2, yo, k4, p1, k3, p1, k2, k2tog, yo, k1, yo, k2tog, k3. (26 sts)
Row 11: K2, k2tog, yo, k3, yo, k2tog, k2, k2tog, yo x 2, k2tog x 2, yo x 2, k2tog, k1, (yo, k2tog) x 2, yo, k2. (27 sts)
Row 12: K2, (yo, k2tog) x 2, yo, k4, p1, k3, p1, k2, k2tog, yo, k5, yo, k2tog, k1. (28 sts)
Row 13: K3, yo, k2tog, k1, k2tog, yo, k1, yo, k2tog, k2, k2tog, yo x 2, k2tog x 2, yo x 2, k2tog, k1, (yo, k2tog) x 2, yo, k2. (29 sts)
Row 14: K2, (yo, k2tog) x 2, yo, k4, p1, k3, p1, k2, k2tog, yo, k3, yo, p3tog, yo, k4. (30 sts)
Row 15: K5, yo, k2tog, k4, yo, k2tog, k2, k2tog, yo x 2, k2tog x 2, yo x 2, k2tog, k1, (yo, k2tog) x 2, yo, k2. (31 sts)
Row 16: K1, (k2tog, yo) x 2, k2tog, yo, k2tog, k1, p1, k3, p1, k5, yo, k2tog, k1, k2tog, yo, k1, yo, k2tog, k3. (30 sts)
Row 17: K2, k2tog, yo, k3, yo, k3tog, yo, k3, k2tog, (yo x 2, k2tog x 2) x 2, (yo, k2tog) x 3, k1. (29 sts)
Row 18: K1, (k2tog, yo) x 2, k2tog, yo, k2tog, k1, p1, k3, p1, k5, yo, k2tog, k4, yo, k2tog, k1. (28 sts)
Row 19: K3, yo, k2tog, k1, k2tog, yo, k3, k2tog, (yo x 2, k2tog x 2) x 2, (yo, k2tog) x 2, yo, k2tog, k1. (27 sts)
Row 20: K1, (k2tog, yo) x 3, k2tog, k1, p1, k3, p1, k5, yo, p3tog, yo, k4. (26 sts)
Row 21: K9, k2tog, (yo x 2, k2tog x 2) x 2, (yo, k2tog) x 3, k1. (25 sts)
Row 22: K1, (k2tog, yo) x 3, k2tog, k1, p1, k3, p1, k10. (24 sts)
Row 23: K7, k2tog, (yo x 2, k2tog x 2) x 2, (yo, k2tog) x 3, k1. (23 sts)
Row 24: K1, (k2tog, yo) x 3, k2tog, k1, p1, k3, p1, k8. (22 sts)
Row 25: K5, k2tog, (yo x 2, k2tog x 2) x 2, (yo, k2tog) x 3, k1. (21 sts)
Row 26: K1, (k2tog, yo) x 3, k2tog, k1, p1, k3, p1, k6. (20 sts)
Row 27: K3, k2tog, (yo x 2, k2tog x 2) x 2, (yo, k2tog) x 3, k1. (19 sts)
Row 28: K1, (k2tog, yo) x 3, k2tog, k1, p1, k3, p1, k4. (18 sts)

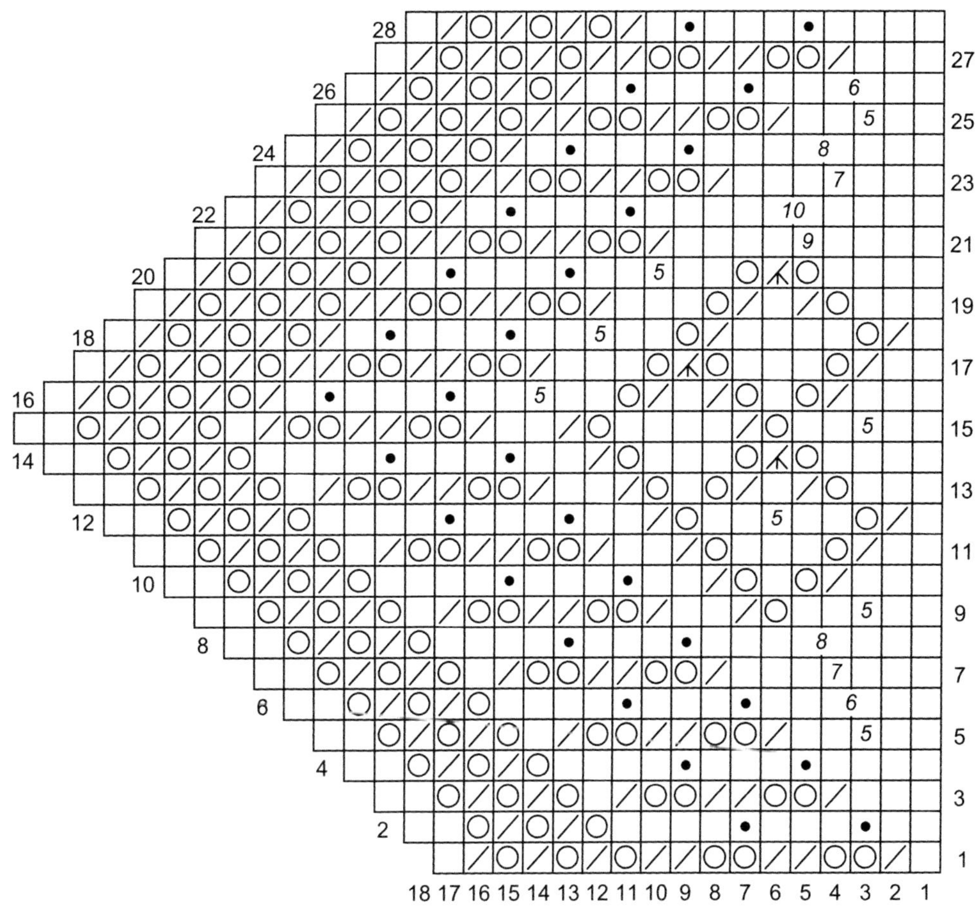

Lace edge with three Diamonds forming a heart chart.

6.6

Lace edge with three openwork Diamonds

TEX 2004.364 Shawl

This lace edge is similar to Pattern 6.4 but here the Diamonds are made open with two yarn overs in each.

Row 1 (WS): K3, yo, k2tog, yo, k4, p1, k2tog, yo, k1, yo, k2tog, k4. (20 sts)

Row 2 (RS): K3, k2tog, yo, k3, yo, k2tog x 2, yo x 2, k2tog, k1, yo, k2tog, yo, k3. (21 sts)

Row 3: K3, yo, k2tog, yo, k4, p1, k2tog, yo, k5, yo, k2tog, k2. (22 sts)

Row 4: (K1, k2tog, yo) x 2, k1, yo, k2tog, k1, yo, k2tog x 2, yo x 2, k2tog, k1, yo, k2tog, yo, k3. (23 sts)

Row 5: K3, yo, k2tog, yo, k4, p1, k2tog, yo, k1, yo, k2tog, k3, k2tog, yo, k3. (24 sts)

Row 6: K4, yo, k2tog, k1, k2tog, yo, k3, yo, k2tog x 2, yo x 2, k2tog, k1, yo, k2tog, yo, k3. (25 sts)

Row 7: K3, yo, k2tog, yo, k4, p1, k2tog, yo, k5, yo, p3tog, yo, k5. (26 sts)

Row 8: K5, (k2tog, yo, k1) x 2, yo, k2tog, k1, yo, k2tog x 2, yo x 2, k2tog, k1, yo, k2tog, yo, k3. (27 sts)

Row 9: K2, (k2tog, yo) x 2, k2tog, k1, p1, k3, yo, k2tog, k3, k2tog, yo, k1, yo, k2tog, k4. (26 sts)

Row 10: K3, k2tog, yo, k3, yo, k2tog, k1, k2tog, yo, k1, k2tog, yo x 2, k2tog x 2, (yo, k2tog) x 2, k2. (25 sts)

Row 11: K2, (k2tog, yo) x 2, k2tog, k1, p1, k3, yo, p3tog, yo, k5, yo, k2tog, k2. (24 sts)

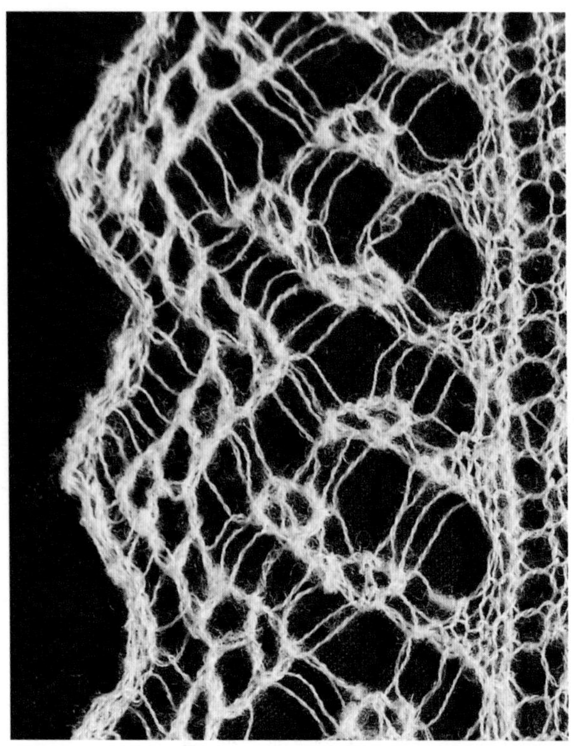

Lace edge with three openwork Diamonds original pattern.

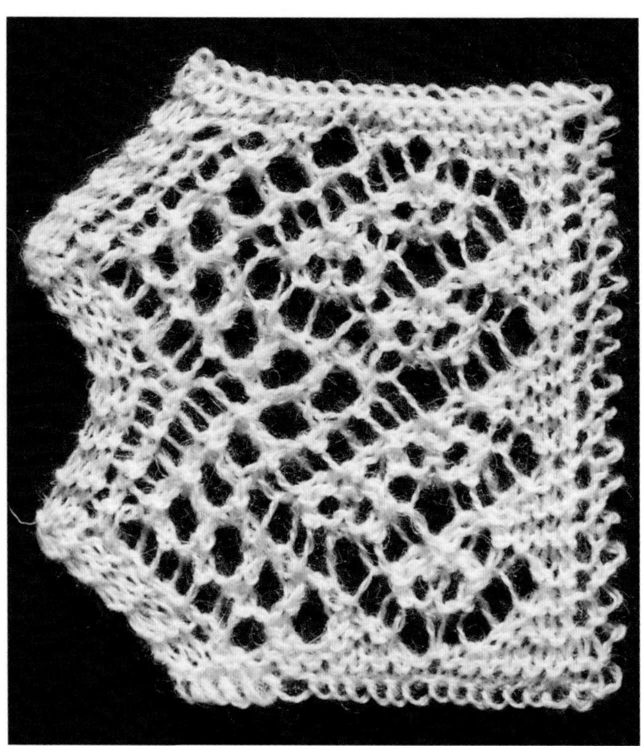

Lace edge with three openwork Diamonds knitted sample.

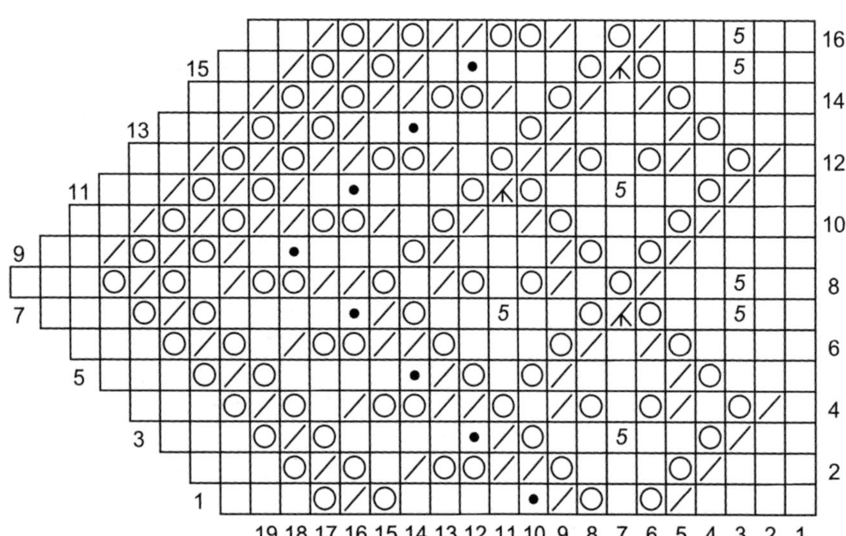

Lace edge with three openwork Diamonds chart.

Row 12: (K1, k2tog, yo) x 2, k1, yo, k2tog x 2, yo, k1, k2tog, yo x 2, k2tog x 2, (yo, k2tog) x 2, k2. (23 sts)
Row 13: K2, (k2tog, yo) x 2, k2tog, k1, p1, k3, yo, k2tog, k3, k2tog, yo, k3. (22 sts)
Row 14: K4, yo, k2tog, k1, k2tog, yo, k1, k2tog, yo x 2, k2tog x 2, (yo, k2tog) x 2, k2. (21 sts)
Row 15: K2, (k2tog, yo) x 2, k2tog, k1, p1, k3, yo, p3tog, yo, k5. (20 sts)
Row 16: K5, k2tog, yo, k1, k2tog, yo x 2, k2tog x 2, (yo, k2tog) x 2, k2. (19 sts)

Lace edges with Circles

Another, more unusual lace edge design uses Circles as the main feature. The centres of the Circles are small Diamond shapes that appear encircled by a ring of stitches. Their single, plain knit row in the middle extends their height and anchors them within the openwork. The Circle lace edge is not very common but appears in a shawl, a veil, and later blouses, the latter created by members of the Sutherland family. The Circle lace edges used in these garments all have slightly varying centres as well as scale, appropriate to the garment they were intended for.

Wild angelica.

6.7

Lace edge with Circle centre, version 1

TEX 2004.303 Shawl

A plain Diamond shape is surrounded by openwork forming a Circle. The very fine gauge of the yarn makes the Diamond

Lace edge with Circle centre, variation 1 original pattern.

Lace edge with Circle centre, variation 1 knitted sample.

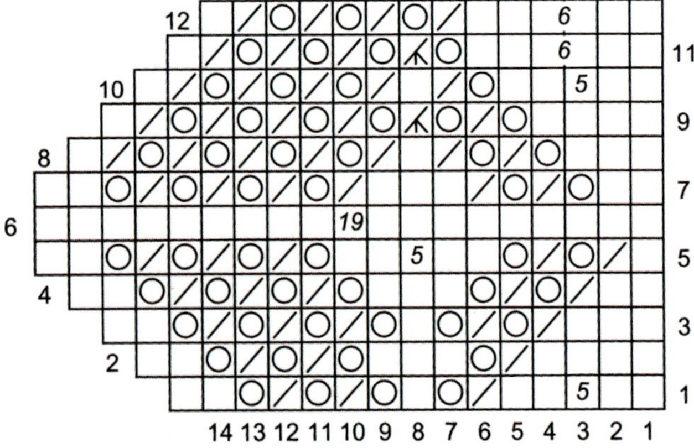

Lace edge with Circle centre, variation 1 chart.

appear suspended. The lace edge is extended outward by the depth of the peaked edge for a shawl.

Row 1 (RS): K5, k2tog, yo, k1, (yo, k2tog) x 2, yo, k2. (15 sts)
Row 2 (WS): K2, (yo, k2tog) x 2, yo, k3, yo, k2tog, k4. (16 sts)
Row 3: K3, (k2tog, yo) x 2, k1, (yo, k2tog) x 3, yo, k2. (17 sts)
Row 4: K2, (yo, k2tog) x 3, yo, k3, (yo, k2tog) x 2, k2. (18 sts)
Row 5: K1, (k2tog, yo) x 2, k5, (yo, k2tog) x 3, yo, k2. (19 sts)
Row 6: Knit.
Row 7: K2, (yo, k2tog) x 2, k3, (k2tog, yo) x 4, k2.
Row 8: K1, (k2tog, yo) x 4, k2tog, k1, (k2tog, yo) x 2, k3. (18 sts)
Row 9: K4, yo, k2tog, yo, k3tog, (yo, k2tog) x 4, k1. (17 sts)
Row 10: K1, (k2tog, yo) x 3, k2tog, k1, k2tog, yo, k5. (16 sts)
Row 11: K6, yo, k3tog, (yo, k2tog) x 3, k1. (15 sts)
Row 12: K1, (k2tog, yo) x 3, k2tog, k6. (14 sts)

6.8

Lace edge with Circle centre, version 2
TEX 2012.492 Veil

The centre of this Circle has a resemblance to Bead stitch and creates a very small spot within the decorative lace edge. The scale of this version fits well with the small rectangular woman's hat veil or baby face veil it was intended for.

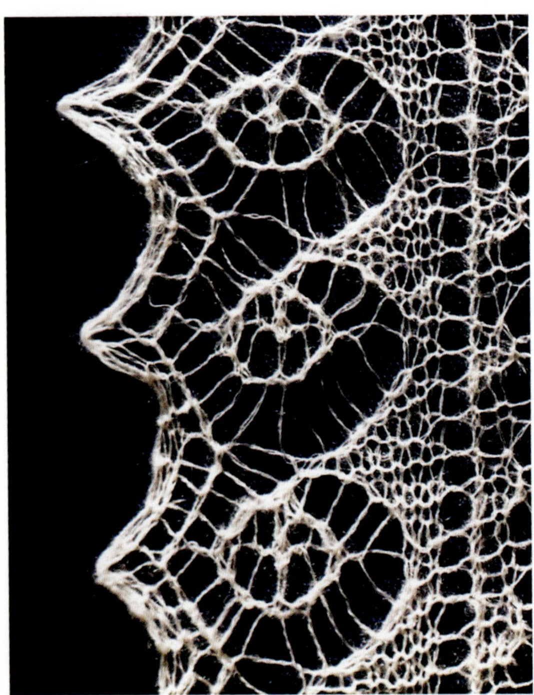

Lace edge with Circle centre, variation 2 original pattern.

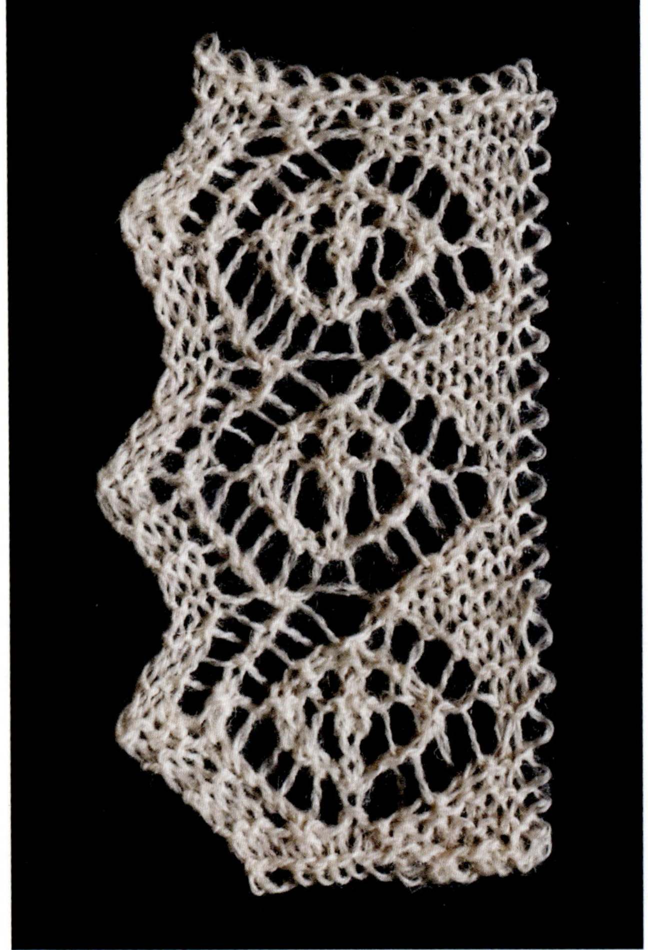

Lace edge with Circle centre, variation 2 knitted sample.

Row 1 (RS): K5, k2tog, yo, k1, yo, k2tog, yo, k3. (14 sts)
Row 2 (WS): K3, yo, k2tog, yo, k3, yo, k2tog, k4. (15 sts)
Row 3: K3, k2tog, yo, k5, yo, k2tog, yo, k3. (16 sts)
Row 4: K3, yo, (k2tog, yo, k1) x 2, yo, k2tog, k1, yo, k2tog, k2. (17 sts)
Row 5: (K1, k2tog, yo) x 2, k3, yo, k2tog, k1, yo, k2tog, yo, k3. (18 sts)
Row 6: Knit.
Row 7: K3, yo, k2tog, k1, yo, k3tog, yo, k1, (k2tog, yo) x 2, k2tog, k2. (17 sts)
Row 8: K2, (k2tog, yo) x 2, k2tog, k3, k2tog, yo, k4. (16 sts)
Row 9: K5, yo, k2tog, k1, (k2tog, yo) x 2, k2tog, k2. (15 sts)
Row 10: K2, (k2tog, yo) x 2, p3tog, yo, k6. (14 sts)
Row 11: K6, (k2tog, yo) x 2, k2tog, k2. (13 sts).

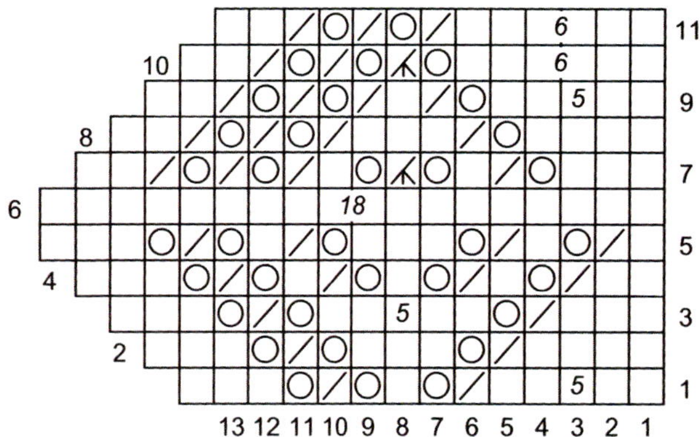

Lace edge with Circle centre, variation 2 chart.

INNER LACE EDGES

In most Shetland lace garments the perimeter is formed by a single lace edge. Occasionally knitters included one or more additional patterned bands between the lace edge and the border. We have called these insertions 'inner lace edges' because they are knitted as an extension of the lace edge and are always placed at its inner side. Most inner lace edges are

Sea and stone, Lerwick.

narrow with simple elements but a few are exceptionally wide. In design they are separate from the lace edge, as they are different patterns or pattern groupings from those used in the lace edge and add additional complexity to the overall design of the piece. Functionally they extend the outer limits of the garment. This feature is especially marked when used in blouses, where inner lace edges may serve as additional horizontal bands between the lace edge and the main garment pattern. Wide inner lace edges have also been used with lace edges to form entire short sleeves in blouses (see Patterns 7.10 and 7.11).

6.9

Inner lace edge 1
TEX 2020.5 Blouse

A very simple but lacy form of inner lace edge used in shawls and other garments.

Row 1 (RS): K3, yo, k2tog, k2. (7 sts)
Row 2 (WS): K1, k2tog, yo, k4.
Row 3: K2, k2tog, yo, k3.
Row 4: K4, yo, k2tog, k1.
Rows 5–12: Repeat rows 1–4.

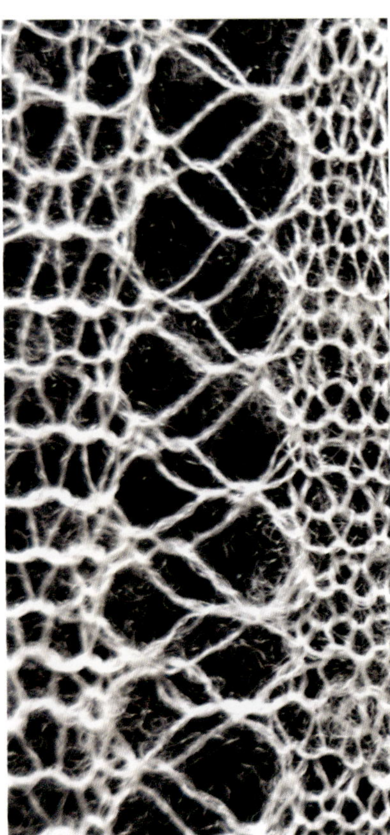

Inner lace edge 1 original pattern.

Inner lace edge 1 knitted sample.

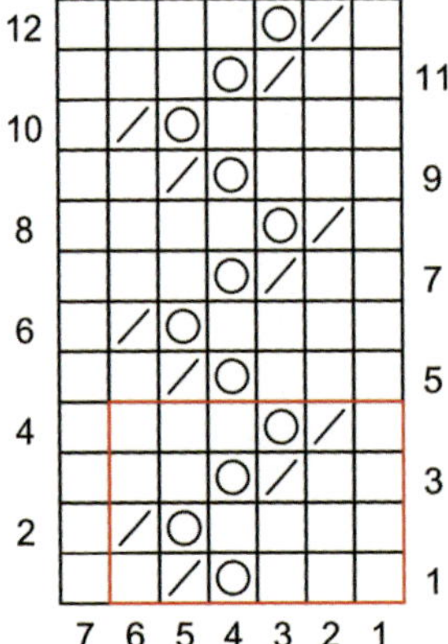

Inner lace edge 1 chart.

6.10

Inner lace edge 2

TEX 81467 Scarf

This inner lace edge appears rather simple and similar to Pattern 6.9, but is more complex to make. The historical garment was knitted in rayon, giving an open and defined appearance to the pattern.

Row 1 (RS): K3, yo, k2tog x 2, yo, k3. (10 sts)
Row 2 (WS): K1, p2tog, yo, k1, 1/1 RC, k1, yo, p2tog, k1.
Row 3: K2tog, yo, k1, k2tog, yo x 2, k2tog, k1, yo, k2tog.
Row 4: K2, yo, p2tog, k2, p2tog, yo, k2.
Row 5: Repeat row 1.
Rows 6–9: Repeat rows 2–5.

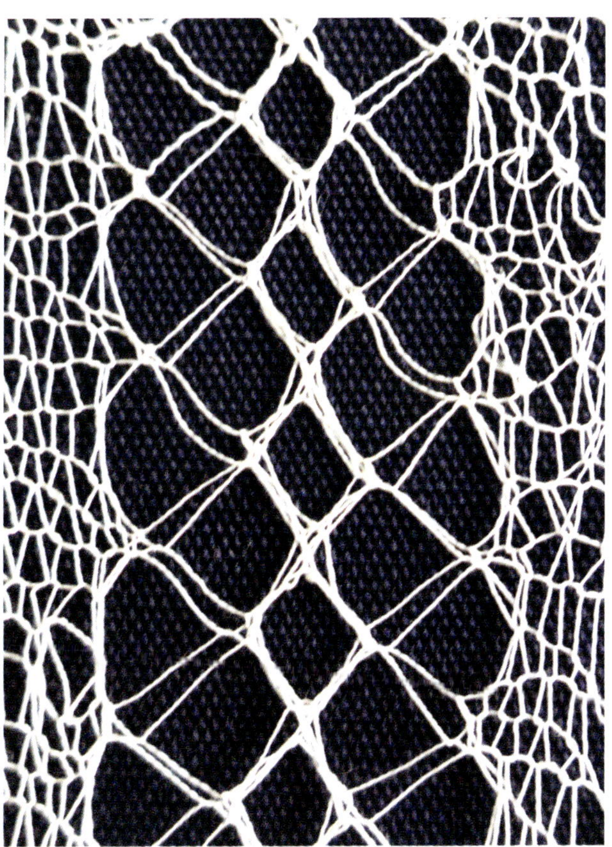

Inner lace edge 2 original pattern.

Inner lace edge 2 knitted sample.

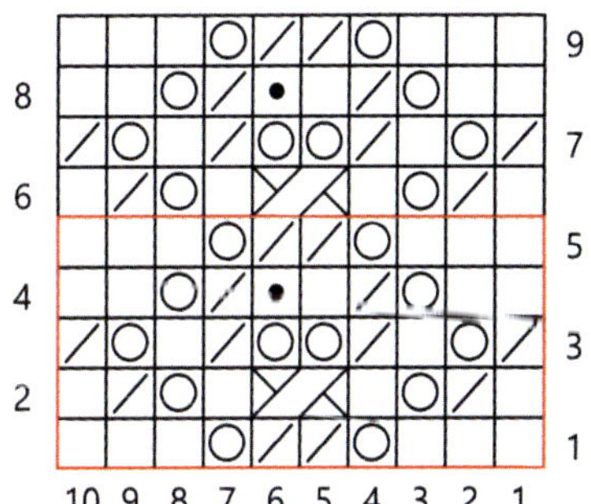

Inner lace edge 2 chart.

6.11

Inner lace edge 3

TEX 2004.303 Shawl

Another interesting inner lace edge that extends horizontally and resembles birds in flight.

Row 1 (RS): K3, yo, k2tog, k3, k2tog, yo, k3. (13 sts)
Row 2 (WS): (K1, k2tog, yo, k1, yo, k2tog) x 2, k1.
Row 3: K2, yo, k2tog, k1, yo, k3tog, yo, k1, k2tog, yo, k2.
Row 4: Knit.
Rows 5–12: Repeat rows 1–4.

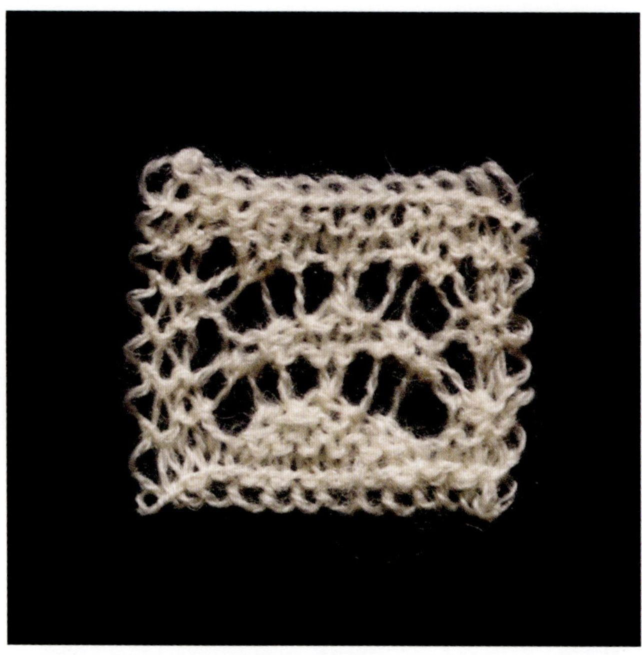

Inner lace edge 3 knitted sample.

Inner lace edge 3 original pattern.

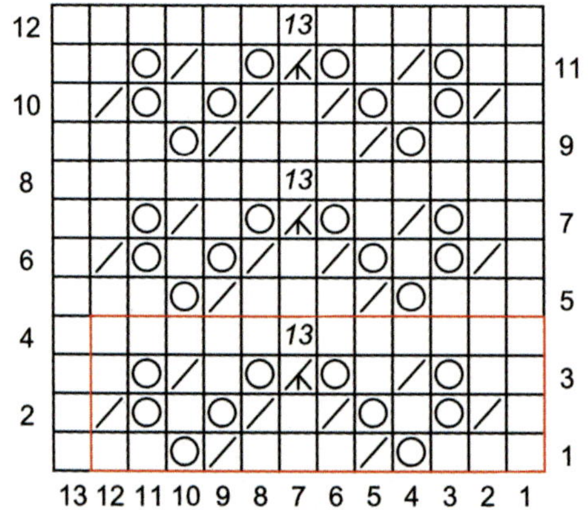

Inner lace edge 3 chart.

6.12

Inner lace edge 4

TEX 2020.3 Blouse

This is a very simple design of a Steek and a partial Eyelid stitch variation, repeated end to end. The Eyelid variation is expanded below with two yarn overs and then contracted again two rows further, which gives it a pronounced rounded appearance between the Steeks.

Rows 1–12: K2, k2tog, yo, k1, yo, k2tog, k2. (9 sts)
Row 13: K2, yo, k3, yo, k2.
Row 14: Knit.
Row 15: K1, k2tog, yo, k3tog, (yo, k2tog) x 2, k1.
Row 16: K2, yo, k2tog, k1, k2tog, yo, k2.
Row 17: K3, yo, k3tog, yo, k3.

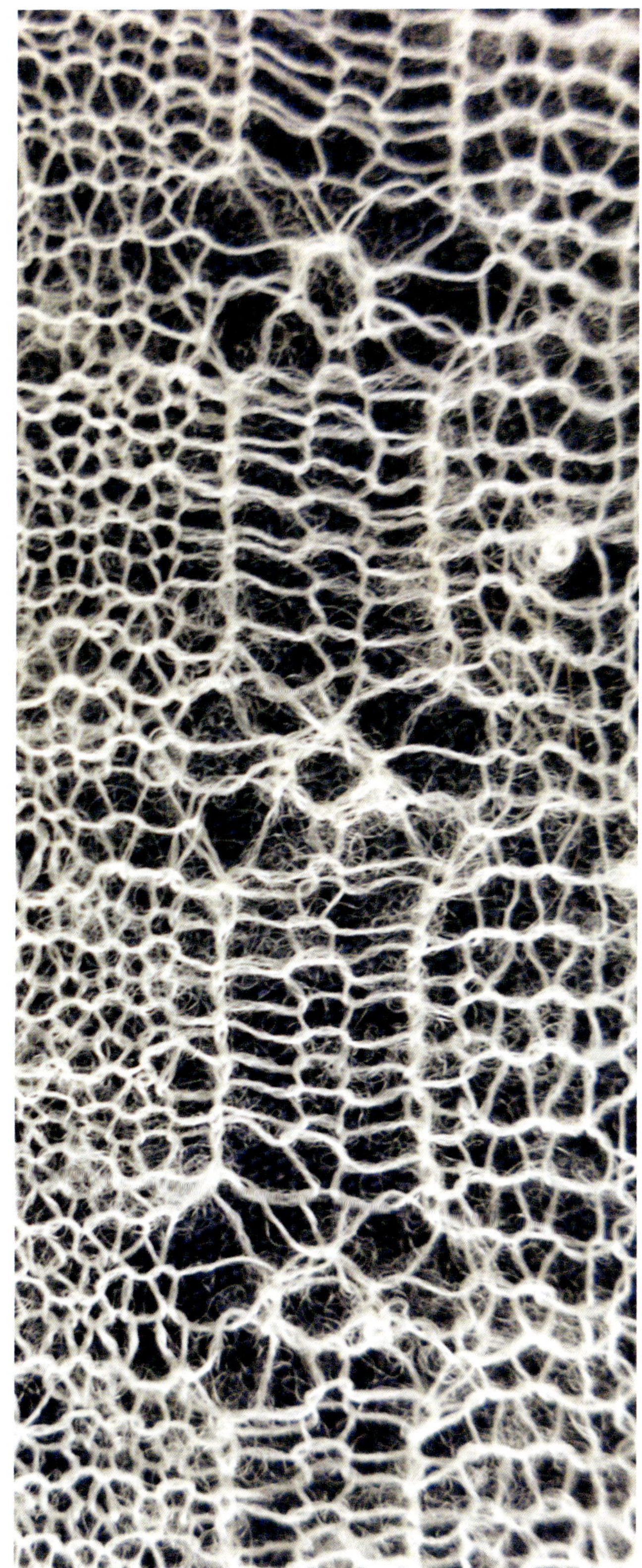

Inner lace edge 4 original pattern.

Inner lace edge 4 knitted sample.

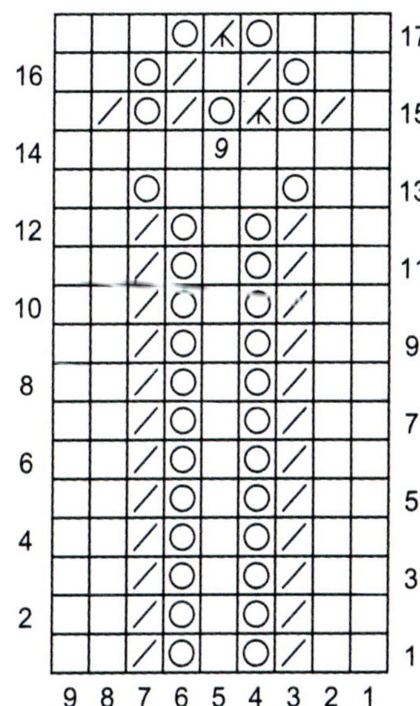

Inner lace edge 4 chart.

6.13

Inner lace edge 5

TEX 2004.372

A very old and worn stole contains an unusual inner lace edge that merits recording. It forms a delicately curving frond made of two yarn overs every other row. They require a k3tog at one side to keep the stitch numbers accurate. The k3tog stitches form an abrupt edge, which is somewhat odd and may be why this pattern is not recorded elsewhere. Fronds have been used in lace edges, where there is usually a k2tog between the fronds and at one of the outer edges, thereby avoiding an abrupt edge.

Row 1 (RS): Knit. (12 sts)
Row 2 and all WS rows: Knit.

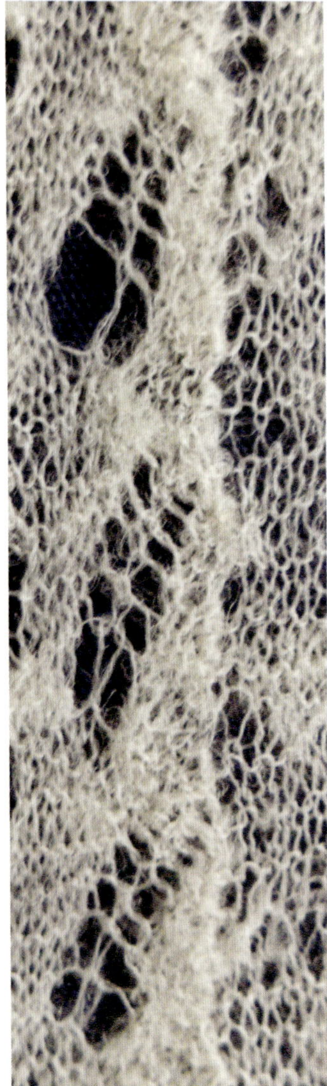

Inner lace edge 5 original pattern.

Row 3: K1, k3tog, k6, (yo, k1) x 2.
Row 5: K1, k3tog, k5, yo, k1, yo, k2.
Row 7: K1, k3tog, k4, yo, k1, yo, k3.
Row 9: K1, k3tog, k3, yo, k1, yo, k4.
Row 11: K1, k3tog, k2, yo, k1, yo, k5.
Row 13: K1, k3tog, (k1, yo) x 2, k6.

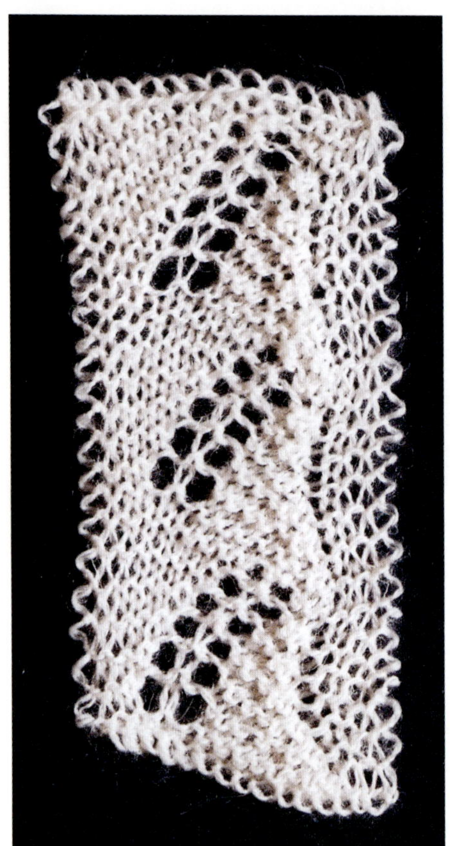

Inner lace edge 5 knitted sample.

	12	11	10	9	8	7	6	5	4	3	2	1	
14						12							
			6				O		O		⋏		13
12						12							
			5			O		O			⋏		11
10						12							
					O		O				⋏		9
8						12							
				O		O					⋏		7
6						12							
			O		O			5			⋏		5
4						12							
		O		O			6				⋏		3
2						12							
						12							1

Inner lace edge 5 chart.

6.14

Inner lace edge 6

TEX 2020.5 Blouse

A bold Zigzag line dotted on either side with large Eyelid stitches makes a dramatic inner lace edge for a blouse hem. This garment was made with three inner lace edges (see Patterns 6.9 and 6.15).

Row 1 (RS): K1, yo, k2tog, yo, k3tog, yo, k13. (19 sts)
Row 2 (WS): K3, yo, k2tog, k1, yo, k2tog, k5, yo, k2tog, k1, k2tog, yo, k1.
Row 3: K2, yo, k3tog, yo, k5, k2tog, yo, k1, k2tog, yo, k4.
Row 4: K5, yo, k2tog, k1, yo, k2tog, k9.
Row 5: K8, k2tog, yo, k1, k2tog, yo, k6.
Row 6: K7, yo, k2tog, k1, yo, k2tog, k7.
Row 7: K6, k2tog, yo, k1, k2tog, yo, k8.
Row 8: K9, yo, k2tog, k1, yo, k2tog, k5.

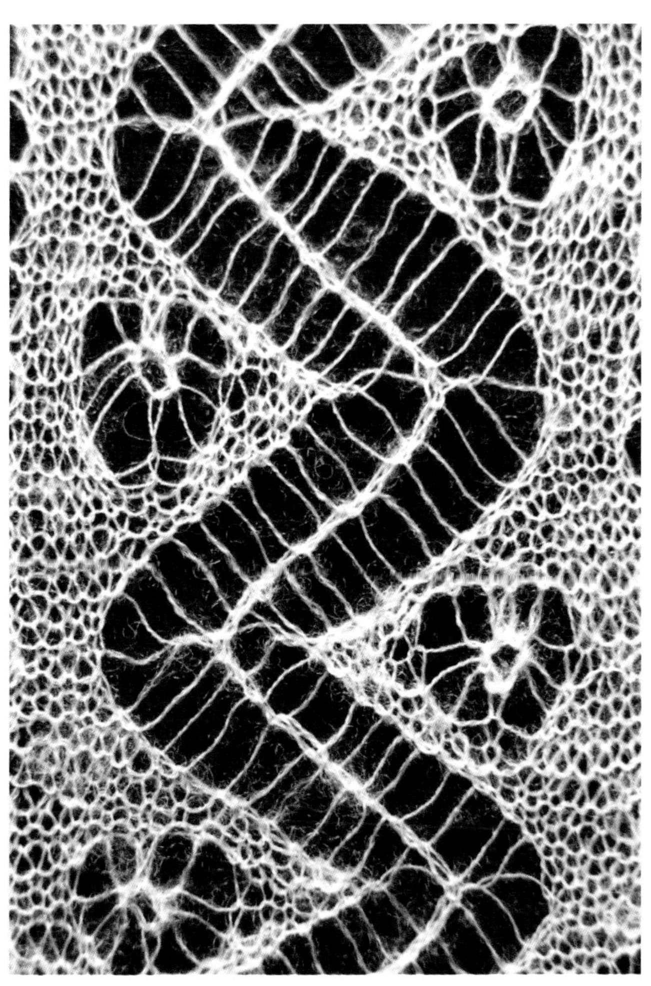

Inner lace edge 6 original pattern.

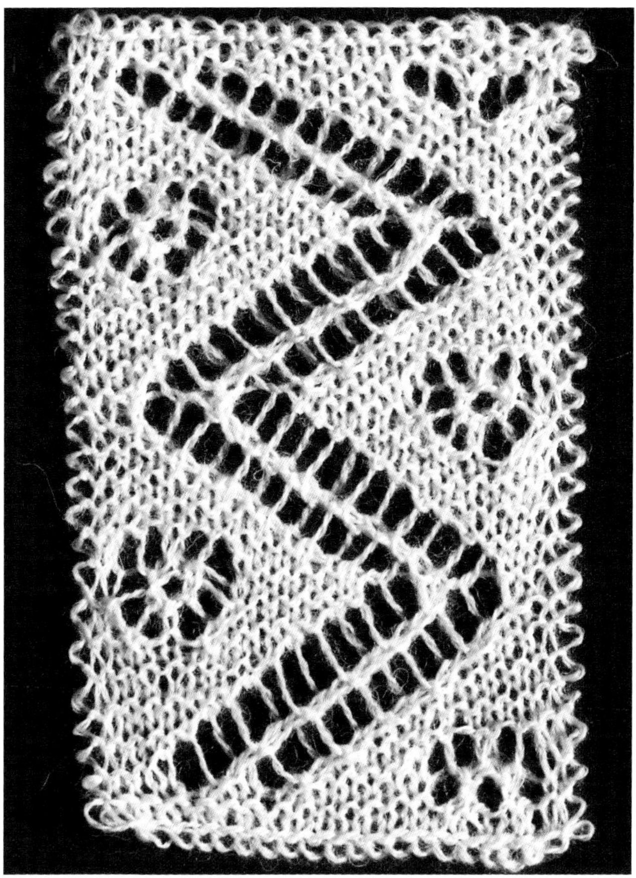

Inner lace edge 6 knitted sample.

Row 9: K4, k2tog, yo, k1, k2tog, yo, k10.
Row 10: K11, yo, k2tog, k1, yo, k2tog, k3.
Row 11: K2, k2tog, yo, k1, k2tog, yo, k6, k2tog, yo, k1, yo, k2tog, k1.
Row 12: K2tog, yo, k3, yo, k2tog, k6, (yo, k2tog, k1) x 2.
Row 13: K13, yo, k2tog, yo, k3tog, yo, k1.
Row 14: K1, yo, k2tog, k1, k2tog, yo, k5, k2tog, yo, k1, k2tog, yo, k3.
Row 15: K4, yo, k2tog, k1, yo, k2tog, k5, yo, k3tog, yo, k2.
Row 16: K9, k2tog, yo, k1, k2tog, yo, k5.
Row 17: K6, yo, k2tog, k1, yo, k2tog, k8.
Row 18: K7, k2tog, yo, k1, k2tog, yo, k7.
Row 19: K8, yo, k2tog, k1, yo, k2tog, k6.
Row 20: K5, k2tog, yo, k1, k2tog, yo, k9.
Row 21: K10, yo, k2tog, k1, yo, k2tog, k4.
Row 22: K3, k2tog, yo, k1, k2tog, yo, k11.
Row 23: K1, k2tog, yo, k1, yo, k2tog, k6, yo, k2tog, k1, yo, k2tog, k2.
Row 24: (K1, k2tog, yo) x 2, k6, k2tog, yo, k3, yo, k2tog.
Rows 25–48: Repeat rows 1–24.

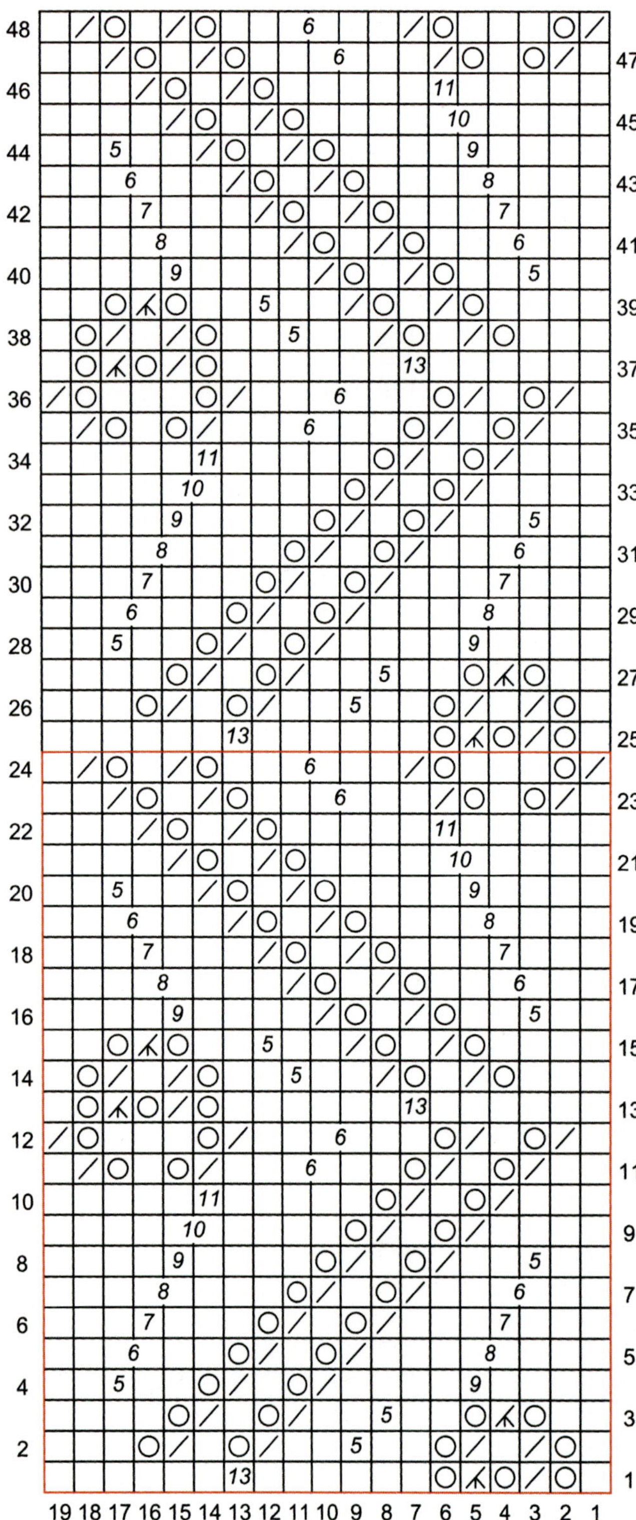

Inner lace edge 6 chart.

6.15

Inner lace edge 7

TEX 2020.5 Blouse

The third inner lace edge for a beautiful and delicate blouse is made of simple stitches but placed in succession on a diagonal. They form a dramatic lower band.

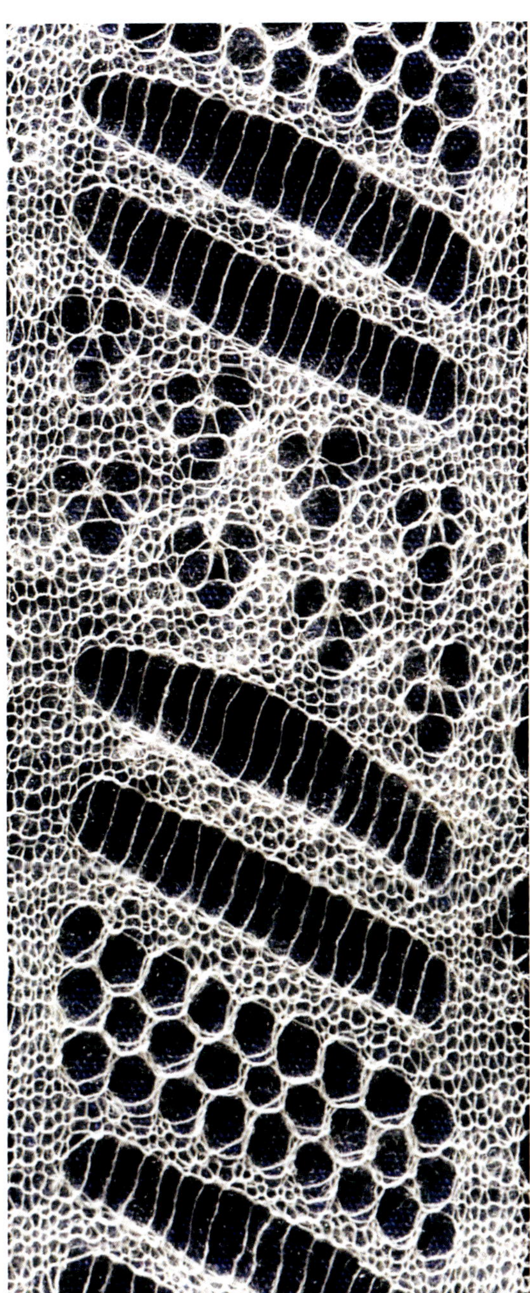

Inner lace edge 7 original pattern.

Row 1 (RS): K1, k2tog, yo x 2, k2tog, k6, yo, k2tog, k8. (21 sts)
Row 2 (WS): K7, k2tog, yo, k8, p1, k3.
Row 3: K3, k2tog, yo x 2, k2tog, k6, yo, k2tog, k6.
Row 4: K5, k2tog, yo, k8, p1, k5.
Row 5: K1, k2tog, yo x 2, k2tog x 2, yo x 2, k2tog, k6, yo, k2tog, k4.
Row 6: K3, k2tog, yo, k8, (p1, k3) x 2.
Row 7: K3, k2tog, yo x 2, k2tog x 2, yo x 2, k2tog, k6, yo, k2tog, k2.

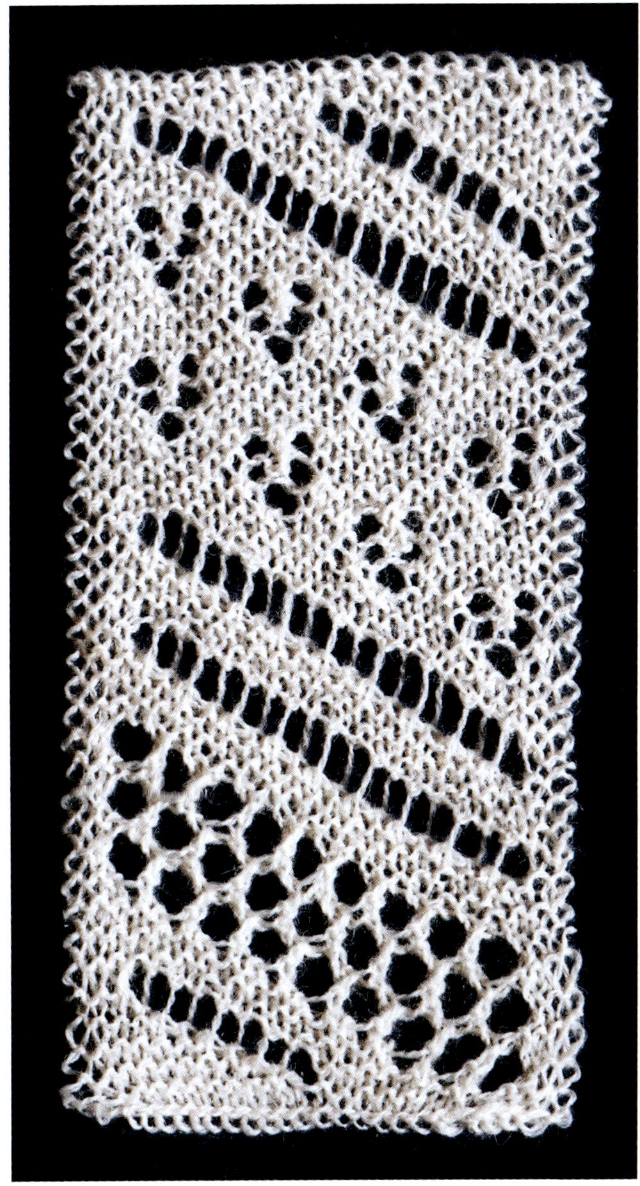

Inner lace edge 7 knitted sample.

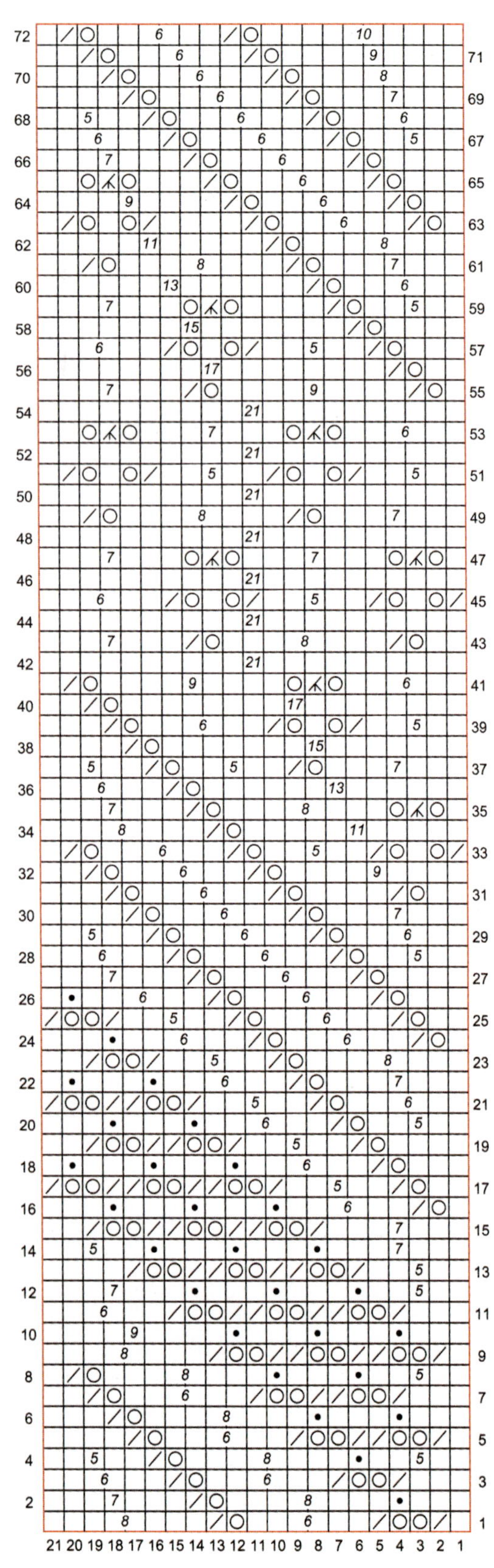

Inner lace edge 7 chart.

Row 8: K1, k2tog, yo, k8, p1, k3, p1, k5.
Row 9: K1, k2tog, (yo x 2, k2tog x 2) x 2, yo x 2, k2tog, k8.
Row 10: K9, (p1, k3) x 3.
Row 11: K3, k2tog, (yo x 2, k2tog x 2) x 2, yo x 2, k2tog, k6.
Row 12: K7, (p1, k3) x 2, p1, k5.
Row 13: K5, k2tog, (yo x 2, k2tog x 2) x 2, yo x 2, k2tog, k4.
Row 14: K5, (p1, k3) x 2, p1, k7.
Row 15: K7, k2tog, (yo x 2, k2tog x 2) x 2, yo x 2, k2tog, k2.
Row 16: (K3, p1) x 3, k6, k2tog, yo, k1.
Row 17: K2, yo, k2tog, k5, k2tog, (yo x 2, k2tog x 2) x 2, yo x 2, k2tog.
Row 18: K1, (p1, k3) x 2, p1, k6, k2tog, yo, k3.
Row 19: K4, yo, k2tog, k5, k2tog, yo x 2, k2tog x 2, yo x 2, k2tog, k2.
Row 20: (K3, p1) x 2, k6, k2tog, yo, k5.
Row 21: K6, yo, k2tog, k5, k2tog, yo x 2, k2tog x 2, yo x 2, k2tog.
Row 22: K1, p1, k3, p1, k6, k2tog, yo, k7.
Row 23: K8, yo, k2tog, k5, k2tog, yo x 2, k2tog, k2.
Row 24: K3, p1, (k6, k2tog, yo) x 2, k1.
Row 25: K2, yo, k2tog, k6, yo, k2tog, k5, k2tog, yo x 2, k2tog.
Row 26: K1, p1, (k6, k2tog, yo) x 2, k3.
Row 27: K4, yo, k2tog, k6, yo, k2tog, k7.
Row 28: (K6, k2tog, yo) x 2, k5.
Row 29: (K6, yo, k2tog) x 2, k5.
Row 30: K4, k2tog, yo, k6, k2tog, yo, k7.
Row 31: K2, yo, k2tog, k4, yo, k2tog, k6, yo, k2tog, k3.
Row 32: K2, k2tog, yo, k6, k2tog, yo, k9.
Row 33: K2tog, yo, k1, yo, k2tog, k5, yo, k2tog, k6, yo, k2tog, k1.
Row 34: K8, k2tog, yo, k11.
Row 35: K1, yo, k3tog, yo, k8, yo, k2tog, k7.
Row 36: K6, k2tog, yo, k13.
Row 37: K7, (yo, k2tog, k5) x 2.
Row 38: K4, k2tog, yo, k15.
Row 39: K5, k2tog, yo, k1, yo, k2tog, k6, yo, k2tog, k3.
Row 40: K2, k2tog, yo, k17.
Row 41: K6, yo, k3tog, yo, k9, yo, k2tog, k1.
Row 42: Knit.
Row 43: K2, yo, k2tog, k8, yo, k2tog, k7.
Row 44: Knit.
Row 45: K2tog, yo, k1, yo, k2tog, k5, k2tog, yo, k1, yo, k2tog, k6.
Row 46: Knit.
Row 47: K1, (yo, k3tog, yo, k7) x 2.
Row 48: Knit.

Row 49: K7, yo, k2tog, k8, yo, k2tog, k2.
Row 50: Knit.
Row 51: (K5, k2tog, yo, k1, yo, k2tog) x 2, k1.
Row 52: Knit.
Row 53: K6, yo, k3tog, yo, k7, yo, k3tog, yo, k2.
Row 54: Knit.
Row 55: K1, yo, k2tog, k9, yo, k2tog, k7.
Row 56: K17, k2tog, yo, k2.
Row 57: K3, yo, k2tog, k5, k2tog, yo, k1, yo, k2tog, k6.
Row 58: K15, k2tog, yo, k4.
Row 59: K5, yo, k2tog, k4, yo, k3tog, yo, k7.
Row 60: K13, k2tog, yo, k6.
Row 61: Repeat row 49.
Row 62: K11, k2tog, yo, k8.
Row 63: K1, yo, k2tog, k6, yo, k2tog, k4, k2tog, yo, k1, yo, k2tog, k1.
Row 64: K9, k2tog, yo, k6, k2tog, yo, k2.
Row 65: K3, yo, k2tog, k6, yo, k2tog, k3, yo, k3tog, yo, k2.
Row 66: K7, k2tog, yo, k6, k2tog, yo, k4.
Row 67: K5, (yo, k2tog, k6) x 2.
Row 68: K5, (k2tog, yo, k6) x 2.
Row 69: K7, yo, k2tog, k6, yo, k2tog, k4.
Row 70: K3, k2tog, yo, k6, k2tog, yo, k8.
Row 71: K9, yo, k2tog, k6, yo, k2tog, k2.
Row 72: K1, k2tog, yo, k6, k2tog, yo, k10.

6.16

Inner lace edge 8

TEX 2020.4 Blouse

A very dramatic pattern, swirling on the diagonal, forms a wide inner lace edge for the lower bodice of a blouse.

Row 1 (RS): K9, k2tog, yo, k3, k2tog, yo, k10. (26 sts)
Row 2 (WS): (K3, k2tog, yo) x 2, k1, yo, k2tog, k3, yo, k2tog, k8.
Row 3: K7, (k2tog, yo, k3) x 2, yo, k2tog, k3, yo, k2tog, k2.
Row 4: K1, k2tog, yo, k3, k2tog, yo, k5, yo, k2tog, k3, yo, k2tog, k6.
Row 5: K5, k2tog, yo, k3, k2tog, yo, k7, yo, k2tog, k3, yo, k2tog.
Row 6: K2, yo, k2tog, k3, yo, k2tog, k1, (yo, k2tog, k3) x 2, yo, k2tog, k4.
Row 7: (K3, k2tog, yo) x 2, k6, (k2tog, yo, k3) x 2.
Row 8: K4, yo, k2tog, k3, yo, k2tog, k1, (yo, k2tog, k3) x 2, yo, k2tog, k2.

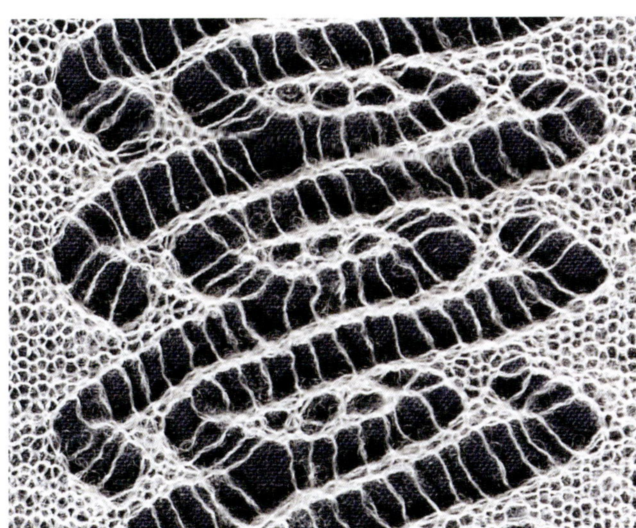

Inner lace edge 8 original pattern.

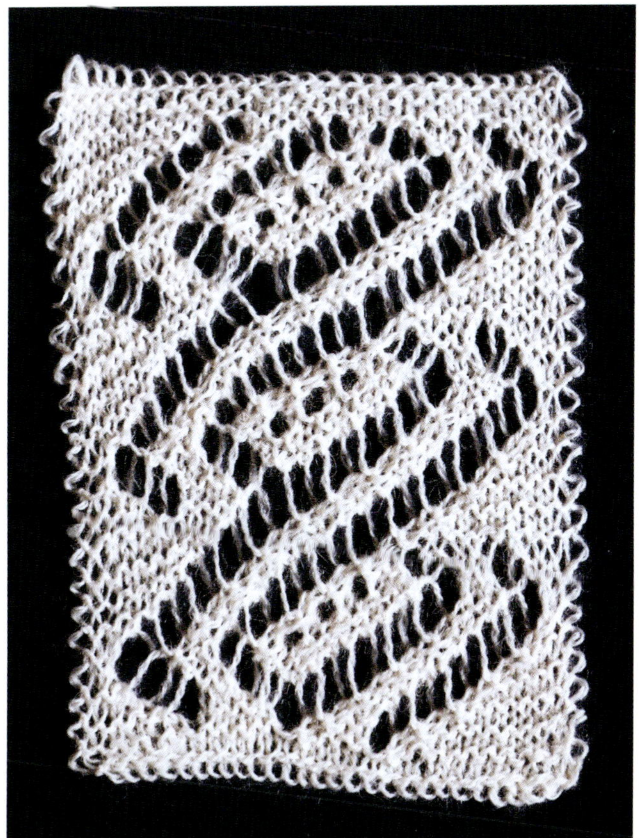

Inner lace edge 8 knitted sample.

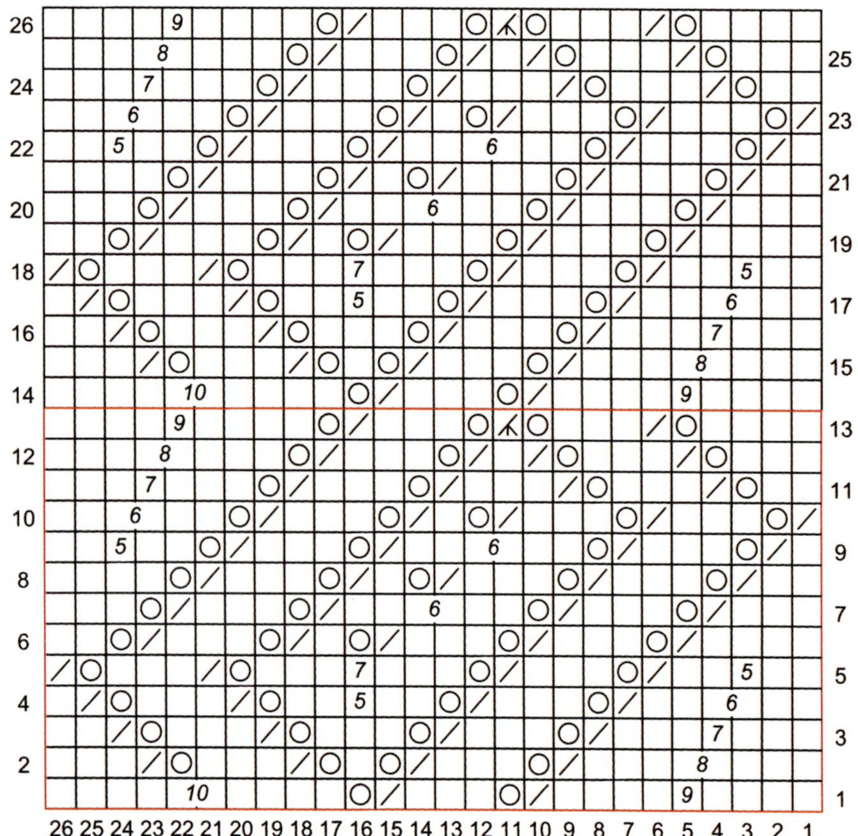

Inner lace edge 8 chart.

Row 9: K1, k2tog, yo, k3, k2tog, yo, k6, k2tog, yo, k3, k2tog, yo, k5.

Row 10: K6, yo, k2tog, k3, yo, k2tog, k1, (yo, k2tog, k3) x 2, yo, k2tog.

Row 11: K2, (yo, k2tog, k3) x 2, k2tog, yo, k3, k2tog, yo, k7.

Row 12: K8, yo, k2tog, k3, yo, k2tog, k1, (k2tog, yo, k3) x 2.

Row 13: K4, yo, k2tog, k3, yo, k3tog, yo, k3, k2tog, yo, k9.

Row 14: K10, yo, k2tog, k3, yo, k2tog, k9.

Row 15: K8, k2tog, yo, k3, k2tog, yo, k1, (yo, k2tog, k3) x 2.

Row 16: K2, (k2tog, yo, k3) x 2, yo, k2tog, k3, yo, k2tog, k7.

Row 17: K6, k2tog, yo, k3, k2tog, yo, k5, yo, k2tog, k3, yo, k2tog, k1.

Row 18: K2tog, yo, k3, k2tog, yo, k7, yo, k2tog, k3, yo, k2tog, k5.

Row 19: K4, (k2tog, yo, k3) x 2, k2tog, yo, k1, k2tog, yo, k3, k2tog, yo, k2.

Row 20: (K3, yo, k2tog) x 2, k6, (yo, k2tog, k3) x 2.

Row 21: K2, (k2tog, yo, k3) x 2, k2tog, yo, k1, k2tog, yo, k3, k2tog, yo, k4.

Row 22: K5, yo, k2tog, k3, yo, k2tog, k6, yo, k2tog, k3, yo, k2tog, k1.

Row 23: (K2tog, yo, k3) x 2, k2tog, yo, k1, k2tog, yo, k3, k2tog, yo, k6.

Row 24: K7, (yo, k2tog, k3) x 2, k2tog, yo, k3, k2tog, yo, k2.

Row 25: (K3, yo, k2tog) x 2, k1, k2tog, yo, k3, k2tog, yo, k8.

Row 26: K9, yo, k2tog, k3, yo, p3tog, yo, k3, k2tog, yo, k4.

INNER BORDER

Occasionally lace knitters placed a horizontal pattern at the top of the shawl border, which, when finished, appears to encircle the centre square of the shawl. We have termed this structure an 'inner border', since it is placed at the top, or innermost side of the border, rather than worked as the outermost edge of the centre. Inner borders are less common than inner lace edges and their purpose is unclear. They have no obvious function except to extend the border and make the whole shawl design appear more complex. Their patterns run horizontally and may be seen to visually interrupt the flow from border to centre.

6.17.

Inner border 1
TEX 81300

This pretty pattern is found as an inner border in several shawls but with variations in size. Here we have presented the largest form found in one shawl, but smaller and more delicate shawls show the pattern shorter in stature by having fewer rows on either side of the centre.

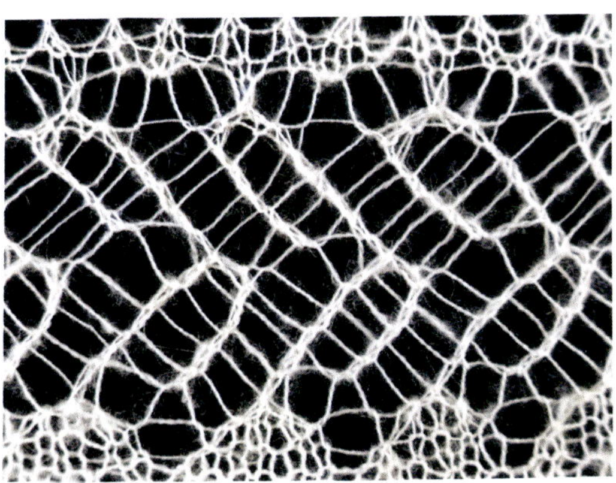

Inner border 1 original pattern.

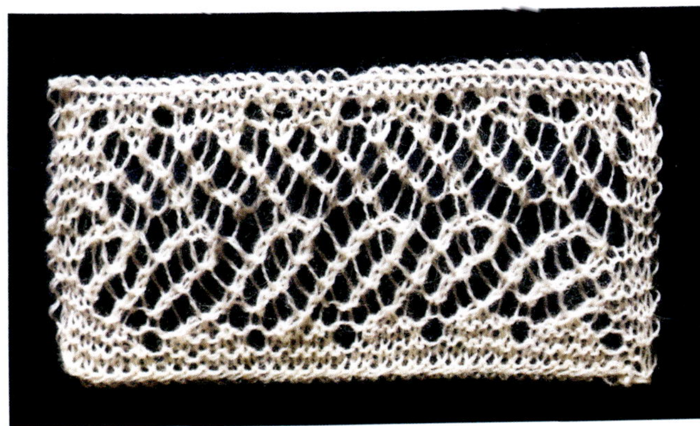

Inner border 1 knitted sample.

Row 1 (RS): K1, (yo, k2tog, k4) x 3. (19 sts)
Row 2 (WS): Knit.
Row 3: K2, (yo, k2tog, k1, k2tog, yo, k1) x 2, yo, k2tog, k3.
Row 4: K2, k2tog, (yo, k3, yo, p3tog) x 2, yo, k3.
Row 5: K3, (k2tog, yo, k1) x 4, k2tog, yo, k2.
Row 6: K3, (yo, k2tog, k1) x 4, yo, k2tog, k2.
Row 7: (K1, k2tog, yo) x 6, k1.
Row 8: K2, (yo, k2tog, k1) x 4, yo, k2tog, k3.
Row 9: K2, (k2tog, yo, k1) x 4, k2tog, yo, k3.
Row 10: (K1, yo, k2tog, k1, k2tog, yo) x 3, k1.
Row 11: K2, (yo, k3tog, yo, k3) x 2, yo, k3tog, yo, k2.
Row 12: Repeat row 9.
Row 13: (K1, yo, k2tog) x 6, k1.
Row 14: Repeat row 5.
Row 15: Repeat row 6.
Row 16: Repeat row 7.
Row 17: Knit.
Row 18: Repeat row 10.
Row 19: Repeat row 11.
Row 20: Knit.

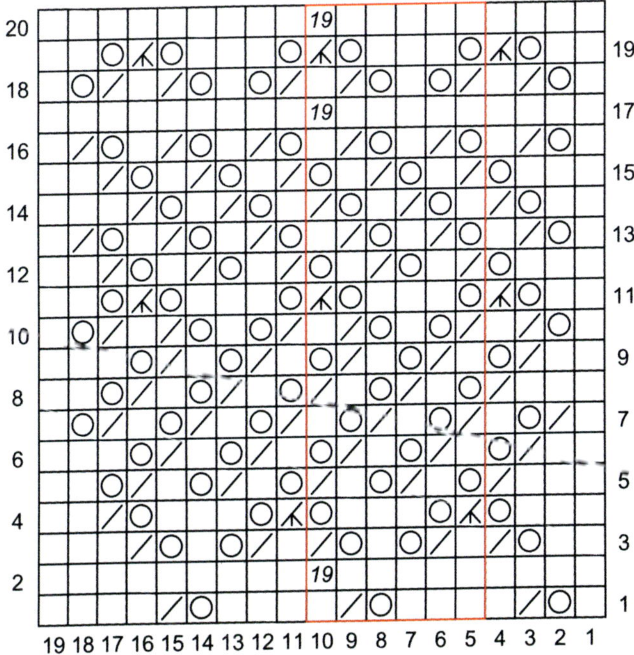

Inner border 1 chart.

CHAPTER 7

SHETLAND LACE IN CONTEXT

Each lace pattern or motif is a small but elemental part of a large landscape of lace fabric. Their individual descriptions in this study have necessitated a detailed, focused approach to understanding their specific design elements. Examining the patterns in such detail makes it difficult to understand what part they played in the larger design of the garment. Most of the patterns are from shawls, scarves and stoles. Such flat pieces made for trade, especially by the 1890s, generally followed a formulaic method using a large but still limited range of patterns for lace edges, borders and centres. When knitting for production, many lace knitters used a repertoire of patterns they were comfortable working with and made substitutions in border motifs or a different centre or lace edge for the same border. It is not possible to know whether this was simply to have a change from knitting the same design or part of design innovation in a knitter's body of work. Both motivations may have been at work, since a lace knitter may have practised her craft for eighty years or more.

Three-dimensional garments such as blouses were more prescriptive in design. Pattern repeats were required to fit a desired garment shape and a certain body size. Elements such as neck edges and sleeves required specific pattern placement. By the time blouses became popular in the 1920s, not all lace knitters had embraced the change from flat to three-dimensional work. Shetland Museum has several excellent examples of blouses using the finest hand-spun Shetland wool of all lace pieces in the collection. The blouses are also some of the most creative and innovative design examples in Shetland lace knitting. They were made by members of the Sutherland family, who had decades of success with designing and making many exquisite examples of shawls and stoles in the Shetland lace tradition.

We have selected a few of the most represented garments in the preceding chapters to highlight the way Shetland lace was designed, and to show the context within the larger garment of individual patterns chosen by the knitter. This provides information on the spacing and repetition of patterns and how they were juxtaposed and combined to create a complex lace fabric. In some cases, individual patterns slightly changed shape due to the gauge or tension of patterns they were adjacent to. Skilled knitters took this into consideration when choosing patterns and their placement.

An important function of the Museum's collection is to gather and hold as much of the story of individual lace pieces as possible. This places the piece in its historical context and its significance to users. Through this process we also hope to identify the maker(s), to enable us to compare designs with other surviving work and build a picture of an individual's style of design and workmanship.

A shawl showing extreme density and complexity of Shetland lace design. The patterns include Crown, various Ferns, Baabie's Fancy, different Waves, Paisley motif (see Pattern 4.9) facing in two directions, Trees, Branches, and Bell with Clapper (see Pattern 4.38). (TEX 7754)

We also have presented here the histories of two shawls that were lovingly saved and generously shared by the families who owned them following donation into the collection. These rare examples of Shetland lace histories explain the significance of shawls to families and the circumstances of some shawl makers. Like most Shetland women, the majority of shawl makers were poor, hard-working, and committed to numerous jobs and chores, in addition to lace spinning or knitting, to make ends meet.

Shawl

TEX 1997.84

This well-designed shawl uses a wide Wave around Diamonds inset with Branches in the centre of the border, framed by Knotty Waves. This is balanced with the decorative and pretty elements, Basket o' Flooers (see Pattern 4.30), Baabie's Fancy (see Pattern 4.35) at the bottom of the border and Strawberry (similar to Pattern 4.36) to finish the border top. It has a Puzzle version centre and a lace edge heavily endowed with Lace Holes (see Pattern 6.1), which also provide balance with the wide, bold border.

TEX 1997.84 Shawl.

The shawl was associated with The Shetland Shop in Bridge of Allan, Scotland, which sold knitwear from Shetland, *c.*1930–1970. The shawl belonged to a British woman living in Kitale, Kenya, who presumably bought it from her friend, the shop owner.

Shawl

TEX 2004.172

Most Shetland shawls were made square but some were made as triangles and the Museum's collection has several. This construction is unusual for a triangular shawl because here it is made similar to a square shawl, beginning at the lower border and working up, rather than beginning at the lower point of the triangular centre. The centre

TEX 2004.172 Shawl.

pattern therefore hung on the diagonal when worn, although this may not have detracted from the visual intricacy of the design.

We have focused on the two top patterns in the border: the pretty Fern with Steek (see Pattern 4.17) and the Fern inset with three Plain Diamonds and Branch (see Pattern 4.22). Both patterns have stitches that also appear in the centre pattern to provide design continuity. These two Ferns are also smaller and more delicate than the two Ferns used below them in the border, so that visually they gradually 'lighten' the weight of the border as it nears the centre. The single border join is well designed and executed, as this was the visual focal point at the wearer's lower back, from which the triangular shawl fanned outwards towards the shoulders.

The shawl was made in the early 1930s by a woman aged eighty at the time. It was purchased at William Jardine & Sons, Edinburgh for £3.3s by a man for his future wife. She wore it for evening wear at professional and social occasions into the 1960s. Their daughter later donated it and provided its historical background.

Shawl

TEX 2004.364

This is one of the most complex shawls in the Museum's collection. Unfortunately we do not know anything of its history. Its large, wide centre (see Pattern 3.2) is a relatively small pattern repeat of Diamond shapes, including a Branch. The border is a series of Waves and mainly Diamond shapes, comprising several Ferns and an unusual motif of combined elements in the middle of the border. This pattern is not separated from a series of four Ferns with another Wave, as it would have been difficult to do so without further spacing of patterns. Note how some Waves form sharp peaks, while others are more rounded, caused by the pattern tensions they are moving within and around.

We have focused on the set of patterns at the top of the border (see Pattern 4.4), as they form an unusual and clever pattern combination to fill the deep 'troughs' formed by the uppermost Wave. Together they form a swag effect, with a straight upper line against the centre pattern and alternating lengths of pattern hanging below. The spacing of the combination pattern repeats was made very accurately, as the two Ferns on either side of the Steek tuck in nicely within the V-shapes formed by the Wave.

TEX 2004.364 Shawl.

The lace edge (6.6) is a wide example within the Shetland lace tradition and complements the size of this large shawl. Its openwork Diamonds and Lace Hole Zigzag combination form a complex edge, befitting this beautiful piece.

The Sutherland Christening Shawl

One of the oldest, most unusual and best documented shawls in the collection is the Sutherland Christening Shawl. Its history sheds some light on the making of bespoke, special shawls for specific customers and reflects the importance of christening shawls in family life through the generations.

The shawl is believed to have been made by Elizabeth Mouat, who lived at Eshaness in Northmavine. Elizabeth worked as a domestic servant in the role of nurse to Amelia 'Amy' Duthie Sutherland, born in 1858 to the Reverend James Sutherland and his wife Catherine (*née* Walker). He was the Church of Scotland minister for Northmavine Parish from 1848 to 1888, and the family lived at the Manse in Hillswick, close by the kirk.

Early christening shawls were often made in a triangular shape because of their purpose to wrap a small infant and allow the excess fabric to drape below the child while held at the baptismal font. The top of the shawl is usually the longest edge and some christening shawls have a rounded peak at the centre of this edge to form a head covering for the baby. The Sutherland shawl has a hood rather than a peak, which is knitted in the same pattern as the main body and sewn on. A woollen drawstring is threaded around the hood and at the neck, ensuring this is a functioning hood. It is the only known Shetland christening shawl with such a construction.

The shawl's design is complex. It has a V-shaped centre and a wide border, with a striking pattern of squares with holes around the centre and part of its construction. The border has a set of unusual motifs that may be seen to be representative of the family it was intended for. The first pattern in the border is the Bell, in this variation with Clapper. A set of unusual Waves in Lace Holes surround a series of patterns that, seen from a distance, may combine to resemble a face with beard and moustache. Above this is a combination of motifs that may represent a stringed musical instrument. It is not clear whether these patterns do indeed have any significance for the family of a minister. We have charted the complex centre (see Pattern 3.4), which is also used in the hood. The Bell with Clapper motif in the lower border is found in another, undated shawl (see Pattern 4.38) but its appearance here confirms this pattern developed within the first two decades of Shetland lace design.

Amelia, aged six with her mother Catherine, 1864.

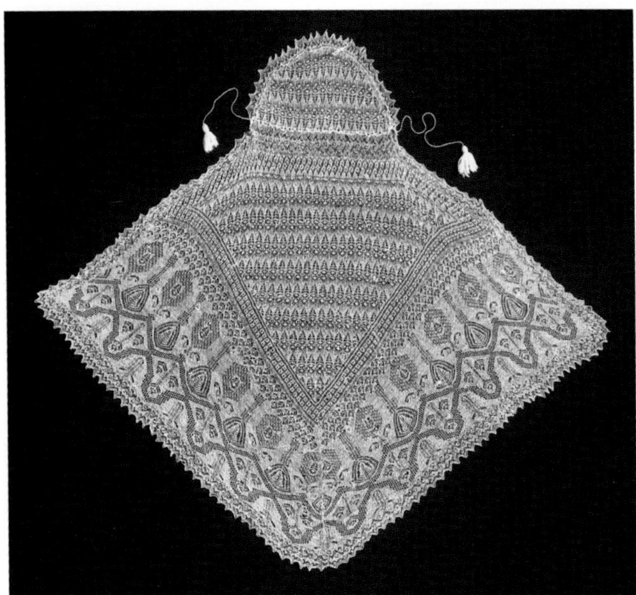

The Sutherland Christening Shawl.

The shawl was thought to have been made in 1857, the year before Amy's birth on 4 January 1858. But recent research has revealed that a first child was born to Catherine in early 1856, and died before or soon after birth in April 1856. The shawl may have been made for this child, its gender and name unknown.

Family records indicate the shawl has been used at the christenings of many infants through the family line, with Amelia being the first. She was followed by a sister, Margaret Rose,

Amelia's great-great-grandson in the christening shawl, 1945.

in 1859. Amelia later married a minister and had ten children. She died in 1901, a week after her tenth child was born. All of her children were christened in the shawl. Amelia's fifth child and eldest surviving daughter inherited the shawl and christened her two children in it. Her daughter, Amelia's granddaughter, donated the shawl to Shetland Museum in 1986. In 2018 one of Amelia's great-granddaughters visited Shetland and enquired about the shawl. We are grateful to the family for providing further information about the shawl's history and continued use down the generations. The last child to be christened in it, the fourth generation after Amelia, was born in 1945.

Scarf

TEX 8933

Not all Shetland lace pieces are complicated or crowded with patterns. Some, like this scarf, are rather simple. It has a centre (see Pattern 2.1) using the most basic of lace knitting stitches – knit, yarn over, k2 tog – which accentuates the long line and narrowness of this garment. The border is a playful mix of Flowers and Trees combined with angular Waves and a Diamond. The centre Waves are intentionally placed to form open, diamond-shaped areas within which a single Branch (see Pattern 4.24) has been placed. The Basket o' Flooers (see Pattern 4.31) has a top 'bud' that resembles the top of the uppermost Tree (see Pattern 4.32). This is not a densely populated border, which makes each motif visibly stand on its own. The maker or makers of this fine scarf are unknown.

TEX 8933 Scarf.

Stole

TEX 2012.428b

The age and history of this stole is unknown but the unconventional design, including the pointed nature of the part Print o' Da Wave stitch in the centre, would indicate early in the craft, perhaps mid-nineteenth century. The border starts with plain and Lace Hole 'broken' Waves but these designs individually also were called the Cup and formed the bottom or 'basket' element of the lovely Basket o' Flooers pattern

TEX 2012.428b Stole.

Anna Swanwick (1813–1899), author, suffragist and philanthropist, is believed to have worn shawl TEX 2014.25.

variations. Included in the border is a Bell with Clapper motif, connected to a Diamond by a Steek (see Pattern 4.39). At the top of the border is a column of Steeks topped with plain Diamonds (see Pattern 4.41), which form a straight edge before the beginning of the centre.

The unusual centre is flanked by Zigzags, within which a series of Diamonds with four varying centres are placed in a column (see Pattern 2.15.a). See Chapter 4 for further information on the row repeat problems between these two patterns. Framing a pretty diamond lattice column of Peerie Fleas in the centre are two narrow Zigzags with small 'thorns', each effectively forming one half of a Print o' Da Wave (see Pattern 2.15.b). This is pattern experimentation at its best, where the knitter played with conventional elements in unusual ways to form a very striking and unique garment.

Shawl

TEX 2014.25

This striking shawl was made in the second half of the nineteenth century and was worn by Anna Swanwick (1813–1899), author, translator, feminist, and philanthropist. Swanwick was a close associate to some of the most learned members of British society in the late nineteenth century. In 1866 she signed John Stuart Mill's petition to Parliament for the enfranchisement of women, more than fifty years before women won the right to vote. In the 1880s she was Vice-President of the Browning Society and the shawl is reputed to have been placed on her shoulders by the poet Robert Browning (1812–1889).

The shawl's centre (see Pattern 3.3) is combination of Lace Hole, Plain and Bead Diamonds, and a Tree; four rather small motifs that together make a delicate lace fabric. The shawl would have been folded in half to form a triangle, with the borders being the showiest part of the garment. Here the knitter has designed a varied but complementary set of patterns. The majority are different Diamonds set among various Waves. We selected the diamond shape made of four Ferns set in a Wave of Eyelids (see Pattern 4.26), which lies below a Balanced Diamond made of Beads (see Pattern 4.13). The top of the border changes to a more varied scene, with a Fern similar to but larger than the Diamond of four Ferns below. Above this is a rare Elongated Diamond with a Fancy centre stitch flanked by Zigzags (see Pattern 4.7). A Tree and other small patterns fill the spaces between the Elongated Diamonds but much plain knit fabric is left, which creates a

TEX 2014.25 Shawl.

white opaque look to the lace fabric here, again drawing the eye to this part of the garment.

The shawl is beautifully finished with a delicate lace edge of Lace Hole Zigzag and three plain Diamonds in combination. The border joins are excellently done in this shawl, where the patterns flow evenly across the seams. This feature, and the unusual and varied pattern choices are what make this one of the better designed and executed large shawls in the Shetland lace tradition.

Stole

TEX 2012.428a

The exact date of this stole is unknown, but it likely originated between the 1890s and the First World War period.

TEX 2012.428a Stole.

It is a good example of what became a classic type of well-designed stole for sale. The design is well-balanced, with a pretty Puzzle centre (see Pattern 3.7) and a prominent bank of varied Waves in the middle of the border, offset above and below by the more delicate Balanced Diamond of Eyelid inset with Branch (see Pattern 4.16), Strawberry (see Pattern 4.36), and Basket o' Flooers patterns (see Pattern 4.30 for similar). To fill in spaces between these prominent motifs are a Tree and Branch placed point-to-point and Baabie's Fancy (see Pattern 4.35 for similar). Many stoles and shawls used variations of these beautiful patterns in this period.

Jeannie's Wedding Ring Shawl

TEX 2013.39

Despite having hundreds of pieces of fine knitted lace in the collection, we rarely know who made them. Knitters did not label their work. The maker or makers were anonymised once the piece was on the merchant's shelves and the shop ledger was marked with their payment or credit.

Occasionally lace garments are donated in which we are provided information about when it was made and the maker's story. Such information provides precious insight

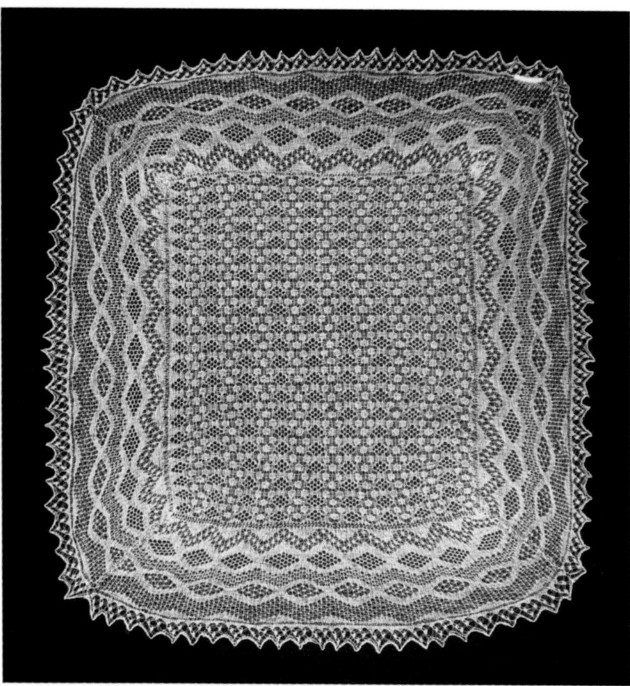

Jeannie's Wedding Ring Shawl.

into the conditions within which this incredibly skilled craft was practised in homes across Shetland. There is a common misconception that Shetland's lace knitters were middle or upper class ladies of society, spending afternoons 'at the needle' in their parlour. This was rarely the case. Most professional lace spinners and knitters lived on crofts and had responsibilities in caring for families and animals or taking on various crofting chores throughout the year. Some supplemented their income with other work such as seasonal fish gutting. Most knitted non-lace, everyday garments such as socks and spencers for trade when they were not focusing on lace.

For the large shawl, TEX 2013.39, we have been given information about the knitter and a tentative identity of the spinner. Their story is more typical of the circumstances of shawl makers, spinners and knitters throughout Shetland before the 1970s.

The shawl was knitted in about 1904 by Miss Jane 'Jeannie' Halcrow (1886–1980) of Hoswick, Sandwick. She was the eldest of three and only daughter of a family whose father was a fisherman. Girls learned to knit at an early age and in the 1901 census Jeannie self-identifies as a professional knitter working from home, then aged fourteen. She knitted Fair Isle garments, lace christening shawls and this shawl she referred to as a 'wedding ring' shawl. Her mother Catherine (*née* Johnston) probably spun the yarn for the shawl, which is very fine and even.

Jeannie selected two common patterns for the centre, a Diamond of Lace Holes and a plain Hexagon, but she arranged them in atypical fashion, creating a geometric pattern (see Pattern 3.1). The central pattern is so unusual that when the shawl was brought to Lerwick in the late 1970s to be cleaned and dressed by the main shawl dresser at the time, 'Wirsity' Willie, he commented that he had not seen the design before. The border is a series of Waves and Diamonds, all incorporating common small patterns. An old woman in the community taught Jeannie the lace edge, known as the Queen's Lace.

A knitter's work was her own, and although she may have borrowed ideas from others, most shawl designs are unique. Knitters typically did not have formal design training. They saw other knitting in the homes of friends and family or were taught patterns as Jeannie was. From there they began to build their own range of designs.

At the age of 24 Jeannie followed the herring fleets down the east coast of Britain, working as a fish gutter. This was

Jeannie, seated far right, with fellow gutters. Her fingers are wrapped with cloth strips to protect them from sharp knives, fish scales and salt.

Jeannie (standing), her grandmother and mother, c.1905.

seasonal work, usually done outdoors, and it wreaked havoc on the gutter's hands. Cuts from sharp knives and fish scales were aggravated by packing salt, which also was drying to the skin. Gutters wrapped their fingers in cloth strips to ease the discomfort and protect them. The income was welcomed by women with few work opportunities and there was a sense of camaraderie among the crews of women.

In 1931, then 45 years old, Jeannie married widower Robert Mann, father of two, and they had twenty years together before he died in 1951. Occasionally she gutted fish when a big catch was landed. She continued to live in Lerwick until her death in 1980, aged 93. She kept her 'wedding ring' shawl and it passed to her granddaughter, who kindly donated it to Shetland Museum.

THE RISE OF THE FINE LACE BLOUSE

In the 1920s, women's dress styles changed dramatically. For most women skirts were no longer ankle length, corsets were abandoned and a greater range of sport and leisure wear was available. Fewer women were wearing large shawls, the mainstay garment of the Shetland lace industry since its inception in the late 1830s. Some lace knitters moved with the times and began to make tunic- and waist-length blouses using very fine wool or cotton yarns. They worked creatively with traditional patterns, applying them to the three-dimensional garments with stunning results.

Both of the blouses below were donated by a woman whose husband had Shetland family connections. The couple lived in England and appear to have been very sociable. It is likely the donor wore the blouses to various events.

Blouse

TEX 2020.3

This very delicate, short blouse was made by one or more members of the Sutherland family in the late 1920s or early 1930s. The motifs in the lower torso were previously used in the stole presented to Queen Victoria in 1899 (see page 154).

The blouse has an upper bodice in Eyelid stitch, below which is a wide Wave of Fancy Net flanked by Knotty Waves. The lower torso has elaborate Ferns and two alternating designs of Eyelid Diamond and an unusual Fern-like motif. It is finished with a Zigzag and Knotty Wave pairing at the V-neck, and a wide, peaked Zigzag lace edge with plain Diamonds (see Pattern 6.3) mirroring the neck band. An inner lace edge has been added to lengthen the blouse (see Pattern 6.12). The sleeves are simply made from the Eyelid pattern and finished with the inner lace

TEX 2020.3 Blouse.

edge and lace edge patterns. The blouse design beautifully complements the female form in the setting of the Waves and the shaping from bust to lower edge. The lower part of the blouse has 'weight' and modesty with the wide spacing of the motifs, while making the upper part of the blouse more feminine and transparent. There is design continuity throughout with the choice and repetition of patterns.

Blouse with jabot

TEX 2020.5

A second blouse, also made by the Sutherland family in the same period, is styled slightly differently. The body and sleeves are slightly longer, due to two stunning inner lace edges (see Patterns 6.14 and 6.15) above the decorative lace edge. We have also included the narrow band of meandering stitches (see Pattern 6.9) at the top of this very wide hem formed by these unusual elements. The inner lace edges may be unique to this garment – their design has not been recorded before – yet they are made simply from known and long-used elements, such as Zigzag, Lace Holes, and Eyelid. They are striking and modern, fitting designs for a blouse that is seductive in its transparency and femininity.

A jabot made with the same lace edge and torso patterns of Fancy Net and Diamonds of Lace Holes is sewn to the lower V-neck. An unusual tall, vertical motif resembling a stylised tree with a lower section resembling Knotty Wave and topped by an openwork Diamond finishes this superb blouse.

TEX 2020.5 Blouse with jabot.

CHAPTER 8

CONCLUSION

Shetland knitted lace, from the beginning of the craft, has been defined by its attention to detail in all aspects of its creation. The finest and most even wool fibres from the native breed of sheep were selected, and the wool was carefully handled and processed before spinning commenced. Some pieces were made with single yarns; others were knitted from two-ply yarns. In both cases the yarns were spun as smoothly and evenly as possible to ensure that the intricate patterns would be visually defined. The yarns were reduced to the narrowest diameter possible, giving Shetland knitted lace its delicate, gossamer quality. The inherent strength of the native wool fibres made these fine textiles robust, while their softness retained the wool's thermal qualities.

The lace pieces also are noted for their pattern variety and complexity within a set construction formula. The flat garments of stoles, scarves and shawls were made with a large central pattern or patterns, two borders (or four in the case of shawls), and a lace edge around the perimeter of the whole. Within these three components, knitters were able to create endless combinations of lace fabric designs with often-used patterns or their variations. Some patterns lost favour or were changed considerably through variations to create new versions unrecognisable from earlier forms. In other cases, knitters created wholly new designs, which became inspiration for others over a period of nearly 200 years.

The majority of Shetland knitted lace was made in this way but there were exceptions. The craft quickly became fashionable early in Queen Victoria's reign. As a result, Shetland knitters kept abreast of fashion styles, helped in part by special orders for specific garment types and the Victorian woman's fondness for a wide variety of accessories. Merchants' records and surviving garments show that Shetland knitted lace was used to make a large range of pieces in different fibres such as silk, mohair and cotton. The surviving pieces include both public and intimate garments. Others were soft furnishings for the home or for personal use, such as lingerie bags. The customer base was rarely local and quickly became international.

Throughout, the lace knitter was free to create her own designs within the parameters of the piece's intended use. Some motifs, like Crosses, were designed for specific recipients and occasions. The freedom to design and create encouraged design innovation and continuous cycles of new pattern development and their variations. The eighty-five patterns recorded here are only a fraction of the many patterns found in Shetland lace knitting surviving in collections. They form a solid base with which Shetland's lace knitters of the past can teach us about their craft and inspire its continuation.

'Lucky Minnie's Oo', floss in bloom, Fair Isle.

REFERENCES

Carter, W., *The Royal Victoria Knitting Book*, vol. 2 (W. Carter, 1849).

Chapman, R., *The history of the fine lace knitting industry in nineteenth and early twentieth century Shetland*, PhD thesis, https://theses.gla.ac.uk/6763/ (University of Glasgow, 2015).

Gaugain, Mrs, *The Lady's Assistant in Knitting, Netting and Crochet Work*, vol. 2 (I.J. Gaugain, 1842).

Miller, S., *Heirloom Knitting* (Shetland Times Ltd, 2002).

INDEX